MURDERED
IN CENTRAL AMERICA

MURDERED
IN CENTRAL AMERICA

The Stories of Eleven U.S. Missionaries

Donna Whitson Brett
Edward T. Brett

ORBIS BOOKS

Maryknoll, New York 10545

The Catholic Foreign Mission Society of America (Maryknoll) recruits and trains people for overseas missionary service. Through Orbis Books Maryknoll aims to foster the international dialogue that is essential to mission. The books published, however, reflect the opinions of their authors and are not meant to represent the official position of the society.

Permissions

Anthony Lewis, "Showing His Colors," copyright © 1981 by The New York Times Company. Reprinted by permission; Frank Hammer, "Not Really Big Deal Killing in Salvador," copyright © 1984 by The New York Times Company. Reprinted by permission; James Carney, *To Be a Revolutionary: An Autobiography* (Harper and Row, Publishers, Inc.), © 1985 by Padre J. Guadalupe Carney Fund, Communication Center #1, used by permission; Ana Carrigan, *Salvador Witness: The Life and Calling of Jean Donovan* (Simon & Schuster), © 1984 by Ana Carrigan, used by permission; Judith M. Noone, *The Same Fate as the Poor* (Maryknoll Sisters Publication), © 1984 by the Maryknoll Sisters of St. Dominic, Inc., used by permission; Robert L. Koenig, "Faith Led 'Padre Guadalupe' to Honduras," © 1983 by *St. Louis Post-Dispatch,* used by permission; Bob Adams, " 'Father Guadalupe'—Reluctant Rebel," © 1983 by *St. Louis Post-Dispatch,* used by permission; Rev. David Monahan, ed., *The Shepherd Cannot Run: Letters of Stanley Rother* (Archdiocese of Oklahoma City, 1984), used by permission; Juanita Klapheke, "For Casimir on the Anniversary of His Death," unpublished poem (1976), used by permission; Betty Campbell and Peter Hinde, *Following the Star: The Liberation Process of the People,* ed. Gary MacEoin (Religious Task Force, Washington, D.C.), used by permission; Gary Miller's recollections of events concerning the death of John David Troyer are used by permission; Francis Xavier Holdenried, "Terror in Guatemala" (*America,* July 17, 1982), used by permission.

LIBRARY OF CONGRESS
Library of Congress Cataloging-in-Publication Data

Brett, Donna Whitson.
    Murdered in Central America : the stories of eleven U.S.
missionaries / Donna Whitson Brett and Edward T. Brett.
      p. cm.
    Bibliography: p.
    Includes index.
    ISBN 0-88344-624-3 (pbk.)
    1. Missionaries—Central America—Biography. 2. Missionaries—
United States—Biography. 3. Christian martyrs—Central America—
Biography. 4. Catholic Church—Missions—Central America.
5. Central America—Church history—20th century. I. Brett, Edward
Tracy, 1944- . II. Title.
BV2842.B73 1988
266'.023'730728—dc19
[B]   87-37216
                                               CIP

**TO THOSE WHO HAVE DIED VIOLENTLY
WHILE STRUGGLING FOR JUSTICE IN CENTRAL AMERICA
AND WHOSE BIOGRAPHIES WILL NEVER BE WRITTEN**

Contents

PART IV
POSTSCRIPT

Foreword

Murdered in Central America is an engrossing, inspirational, and disturbing book. The book takes us into the lives and work of eleven U.S. missionaries killed in Central America since 1975. It tells us who these men and women were, what work they were doing, and why they were doing it. Taken alone as a recounting of their lives and work, the book could be a modern day supplement to Butler's *Lives of the Saints.*

The book also has a darker, very disturbing aspect. Taken as a record of the actions and reactions of the U.S. government in relation to the deaths of these men and women of God, the book tells a troublesome, if not shameful story. The families of U.S. missionaries murdered in Central America have been shocked to see their government try to excuse or justify the missionaries' murders, smear the memories of murdered missionaries, lie about the circumstances of the murders to protect the murderers, and acquiesce in cover-ups after the murders. Families of these murder victims have had to sue the U.S. government to get even snippets of information about their deaths. This book vividly sets forth the contrast between the work of the murdered missionaries and the actions of our government after their murders; that contrast should shake even the cynical reader.

The personal experience of my family, after the death of my sister Ita, is only a short chapter of that terrible story. The Ford family has heard our sister described by Jeane Kirkpatrick as a guerrilla activist and described by Alexander Haig as a roadblock runner who exchanged gunfire with Salvadoran soldiers; all to justify or minimize the circumstances of her death. We were assured by Secretary of State Muskie that our sister's murder was being vigorously investigated by the Salvadoran government, and then were told by U.S. Ambassador to El Salvador Robert White that the investigation was a hoax, designed to justify the continuation of U.S. military aid to the government whose soldiers had murdered the women.

After long months of stalling and misrepresentations by U.S. government agencies about the circumstances of the churchwomen's deaths, the families of the four women murdered in El Salvador were forced to sue our government for that information, under the Freedom of Information Act. For our pain, we were rewarded with boxes of blacked-out documents. The Orwellian justification given to the court for stonewalling the families' pleas for information was that it would jeopardize the security interests of the U.S. government to reveal to the families what it knew about the circumstances of the deaths of their daughters and sisters.

But the stories of the missionaries, as told in this book, are important not only for the information about the missionaries themselves, but also for the information about the people among whom and for whom they lived, worked, and died. Tens, if not hundreds, of thousands of people have been murdered in Central America in the past decade. Most of those who have been murdered have been poor and unknown to us in North America. We have seen many people try to put labels, such as leftist, guerrilla, or communist, on these anonymous murder victims. If the murdered missionaries are described by Central American or U.S. government representatives with the same labels as those given to many of the poor and unknown murder victims, what does that tell us about those murder victims, and those who would label them?

The justice systems of most Central American countries are not prepared or disposed to investigate and bring to trial the murderers of missionaries or other unarmed civilians. In El Salvador alone, no officer or official has been tried for any of the tens of thousands of murders that have been committed in that country in the past decade. Tragically, the recent Arias peace plan proposal has been used by the government of El Salvador as a smoke screen to justify a broad, unwarranted amnesty for the murderers of the tens of thousands of unarmed civilians in El Salvador. As this foreword is written, the Salvadoran judicial system has turned loose the two trigger men who murdered the American land reform workers, and is considering an application by the murderers of the churchwomen for amnesty. More importantly, the murderers of tens of thousands of people in that tortured country will not be investigated or punished, and a well-oiled murder machine, equipped with the latest in U.S. weaponry, remains in place.

This book, however, should not be put down without any sense of hope. Central America has drawn and is drawing committed, faith-filled people to work for peace with justice. That work is fragile and needs our support. What better memorial to the men and women described in this book than for all of us to work for and pray for the cause of peace with justice in Central America?

WILLIAM P. FORD
January 1988

Preface

We can trace our interest in Central America to a morning in February 1982 when we heard over the radio that James Miller, a Christian Brother from Wisconsin, had been gunned down at a mission school in Huehuetenango, Guatemala. Ed was then teaching at the College of Santa Fe, an institution run by the Christian Brothers in Santa Fe, New Mexico, and several members of the faculty there had known Jim quite well. At a memorial mass, Greg Robertson read a long letter he and his wife, Maura, had recently received from Jim, describing his work with the Mayan Indians, "the forgotten ones of Guatemala," as he called them, and his strong desire to remain there in spite of increasing risk to his personal safety. Later, no one we asked could explain why Miller had been killed, apparently by a right-wing death squad, when his political views could hardly have been considered radical or even leftist.

Moved by Jim's testimony, we researched Guatemala's recent history for an article on him (later published in *America*). What we found was disturbing: Not only Miller, but many other churchpeople—a few North Americans, but mostly Indian catechists—had been killed, many after enduring torture. They were targeted not because they advocated revolution or violence, but because, in one sense, they *were* subversive, for they were laboring against the status quo—a long-entrenched system of injustice that kept a majority of Guatemalans poor and powerless to change their fate.

Our research did not end with Jim Miller, but led to this volume of biographies. These eleven men and women were chosen because, to our knowledge, they are the only North American missionaries who have been killed—or who died under mysterious circumstances—in Central America. The reason we chose only North Americans, who actually represent but a tiny fraction of churchworkers murdered in that troubled region, is that we believe North Americans can more easily comprehend the reality of Central America if they witness the suffering and turmoil there through the eyes of men and women very much like themselves.

Without the help of many of the missioners' friends, co-workers, and relatives, this book would not have been possible, and we would like to extend special thanks to all those who contributed in any way. For the chapter on Casimir Cypher, we are grateful to Sister Mary García, Bishop Nicholas D'Antonio, Michael Gable, Michael Briseño, Janet Melvin, and Fathers Ronald Olson, Anselm Romb, and Loren Koziol. We thank Virginia Carney Smith, John Patrick Carney, Drs. Eileen and Joseph Connolly, and Leyda

Barbieri for their help and observations on Guadalupe Carney. For their contributions to the chapter on William Woods, we thank Bishop John Mc-Carthy, Mrs. William H. Woods, Phillip Berryman, and Fathers Rafael Dávila, Alfred Smith, Ronald Hennessey, and Delbert Robinson. We are indebted to Mrs. Frankie Williams, Franz and Gertrude Rother, Sister Marita Rother, and Fathers Marvin Leven and David Monahan for their insights on Stanley Rother. For the chapter on John David Troyer, we are grateful for the testimony of Gary Miller, who very kindly gave us permission to use it, and for the comments of Alvin and Luellen Troyer, Harry Hertzler, Harold Wenger, Delton Franz, and Rich Sider. The chapter on James Miller was enhanced by the observations of Don Geng, Gregory and Maura Robertson, and Brothers Nicholas Geimer, Stephen Markham, Gerard Pihaly, and H. Lewis Twohig. For the chapter on Frank Holdenried, we are grateful to Richard Smith, Reverends David Leeper Moss and Gerry Phelps, Sister Betty Campbell, Father James Curtin, and Congressman Stephen Solarz. And, finally, for the sections on Dorothy Kazel, Jean Donovan, Ita Ford, and Maura Clarke, we thank William Ford II, Sister Martha Owen, Joseph and Malvina Kazel, Raymond and Patricia Donovan, Fathers Paul Schindler, Lawrence McMahon and James Brockman, Sisters Kay Kelly, Sheila Tobbe, Christine Rody and Barbara Sever, Josie and Frank Cuda, Rita Mikolajczyk, Mary Frances Eklinger, Barbara Murock, and Melanie and Arthur McDonald. In regard to Ita and Maura, we are particularly grateful to Sister Judy Noone and the Maryknoll Sisters for granting us permission to quote from her fine work, *The Same Fate as the Poor.*

We also thank our editors, Eve Drogin, Hank Schlau, and John Eagleson, for their advice, and LaRoche College for a grant to defray part of the cost of our work.

The encouragement and enthusiasm of our friends, Darryl Birkenfeld and Richard and Lucille Wark, and all those in the Pittsburgh Religious Task Force on Central America are hereby gratefully acknowledged, as well as the support of our extended families, especially Marion Brett for her careful typing, Edward C. Brett for his proofreading, and every patient relative who cared for our children at critical times. And finally, we thank our daughters, Tracy and Erin, for their cheerful willingness to cooperate in our endeavor.

MURDERED
IN CENTRAL AMERICA

Introduction

In Latin America and elsewhere, Catholic priests, nuns, brothers, and bishops, Protestant pastors, and layworkers from several Christian faiths have been tortured and murdered by the thousands in recent years. Some believe that their untimely deaths have occurred because the church has wandered from its true spiritual mission, maliciously involving itself, instead, in politics; judgments or insinuations are often made that these religious workers were "subversives" or "communists." Unfortunately, such indictments are made not only by Latin American oligarchs and military officers, but also by some political officials in the United States. Even some churchpeople—both Catholic and Protestant, in the United States as well as elsewhere—echo these charges.

It is therefore important to remember that such accusations are not peculiar to the twentieth century. According to the Gospel of Luke, Christ, himself, was a victim of them:

> They began their accusation by saying, "We found this man inciting our people to revolt, opposing payment of the tribute to Caesar, and claiming to be Christ, a king." Pilate then said to the chief priests and the crowd, "I find no case against this man." But they persisted, "He is inflaming the people with his teaching all over Judaea; it has come all the way from Galilee, where he started, down to here " [Luke 23:2–6].

We likewise hear people referring to those Christians of today who are committed to social justice as members of the "new church," as if the "old church" had never championed the cause of the poor and defenseless. The fact is that throughout history there have always been Christians who made a "preferential option for the poor and oppressed." Unfortunately, too often these Christians have been a minority. Perhaps this is changing, especially in Latin America, and perhaps this is why churchpeople are dying today in such large numbers. This book is the story of a mere handful of these people—U.S. missionaries who were martyred in Central America because of their Christian commitment to the poor. Their kind exist worldwide, however, in South America, the Philippines, Haiti, South Africa, the Soviet Union, Poland, and everywhere else—including the United States. Their worldwide presence does not signal the birth of a new church, but the extension of a church that has always existed side by side and sometimes on the periphery with "Christians" who have lost their vision while pursuing power, prestige, and wealth.

Indeed, the story of the Latin American church today—with its champions of the oppressed on the one hand, and its oligarchy, military, and "conformist"

1

churchpeople on the other—merely parallels the church that first came to the New World with the Spanish conquistadors in the sixteenth century. A few examples will illustrate the point.

When Christopher Columbus first landed in America he knelt on the ground, gave a prayer of thanks to God, and named the island he had discovered San Salvador (Holy Savior). Upon encountering the natives, he was somewhat disappointed for they were not the sophisticated "Indians" he had expected to find. Nevertheless, he again gave thanks to God; historian Samuel Eliot Morison explains why:

> He observed "how easy it would be to convert these people—and to make them work for us." In other words, enslave them but save their souls. Indeed, it seems to have been from the sailors who returned from this voyage that every Spaniard got the idea that no white man need do a hand's turn of work in the New World—God had provided docile natives to labor for the lords of creation![1]

Columbus's vision was shared by countless conquistadors and Spanish colonists, but also by a large number of the Spanish clergy. These "conformist" clergymen became rich and powerful in the New World by giving their religious sanction to the violence perpetrated by their countrymen, while denouncing any "nonconformist" priest who had the courage to speak out for justice. The actions of the "conformist" clergy are typified by Padre Vicente de Valverde and the part he played in Francisco Pizarro's conquest of the Incas:

> When Atahualpa [emperor of the Incas] and his escort appeared for the rendezvous [with Pizarro] in the square of Cajamarca, he found it deserted, for Pizarro had concealed his men in some large buildings opening on the square. Then the priest Vicente de Valverde came forward, accompanied by an interpreter, to harangue the bewildered Inca concerning his obligations to the Christian God and the Spanish king until the angry emperor threw down a Bible, which Valverde had handed him. At a signal from Pizarro, his soldiers, supported by cavalry and artillery, rushed forward to kill hundreds of the terrified Indians.[2]

As soon as the Spaniards established their first settlement in America on the island of Hispaniola, they began a labor system called the *encomienda,* whereby the Indians were forced into slavery. They encountered unexpected opposition, however, in a group of Dominicans, especially Padre Antonio de Montesinos. When he was chosen as preacher for the Sunday masses of Advent in 1511, he took this opportunity to castigate the colonists for their brutality towards the native population:

> Tell me by what right and under what law do you hold these Indians in such cruel and horrible servitude? By what authority do you make such

detestable war against these people who were dwelling gently and peacefully in their lands, and visit death and destruction on so many of them? Why do you oppress and weaken them by denying them medicine when they are sick so that they die from the excessive work that you demand? In other words, you kill them every day to gain wealth! Are you concerned to see that someone teaches them about their God and Creator? Do you attend to having them baptized, hear Mass, observe feast days and Sundays? Are they not men? Do they not have souls? Are you not commanded to love them as yourselves? Don't you understand this? Why are you so sunk in lethargy, so fast asleep?[3]

The settlers were incensed at Montesinos' words, especially when he added that he could no longer grant them absolution: "You are all living in mortal sin, and you will live and die in sin because of the cruelty and tyranny with which you abuse these innocent people."[4] The colonists wrote the King demanding that Montesinos be expelled from Hispaniola. The King, in turn, reprimanded the troublemaker, informing him that he would be recalled if he continued to speak "such dangerous opinions."[5]

Occasionally the actions of the "nonconformist" clergy led to a change of heart in their "conformist" counterparts. Such was the case with Padre Bartolomé de Las Casas. He had come from Spain to America in 1502. He became a priest as well as an *encomendero,* with Indians forced to work for him. His conversion, influenced by the earlier sermons of Montesinos, took place around 1514, when he gave up his life of comfort, devoting himself instead to the defenseless Indians. In 1515 he sailed to Spain in an attempt to convince the Crown to outlaw the system of *encomienda.* He was named "Universal Protector of the Indians" by Archbishop Jiménez de Cisneros of Toledo and in December 1519 was chosen to defend the Indians before the Emperor Charles V at the royal court at Barcelona. Arguing against him was the "conformist" Franciscan bishop of Tierra Firme (Panama), Juan de Quevedo, who claimed the Indians were slaves by nature. After working with Indians in Venezuela and Guatemala, Las Casas became bishop of Chiapas in 1544. By this time he had written several tracts against the mistreatment of the native population and more than anyone else was responsible for the New Laws of the Indies, proclaimed in 1542, which regulated Indian tribute, freed Indian slaves, and prohibited their forced labor. Seeing that the New Laws were enforced in his diocese was no easy task, especially since many secular and regular clergy did all they could to undermine the bishop. Only the Dominicans backed Las Casas and that was not enough. They and the bishop were forced to leave Chiapas when the Spanish colonists refused to give them financial support. Las Casas went to Guatemala where he met with Bishop Marroquín of that diocese and Bishop Valdivieso of Nicaragua in an attempt to devise a policy whereby the New Laws might be enforced. The Spanish colonists of Guatemala so hated Las Casas that they tried to seize him before he returned to Chiapas. They failed, but after only a few months in his diocese he was expelled by his Spanish congregation. He was forced to sail to Spain where he spent the remaining years of his life continuing to struggle for justice for the Indian.[6]

Whereas Las Casas had placed his own life in jeopardy as a result of his commitment to justice, his friend Antonio de Valdivieso was actually murdered because he chose to defend the Indians. Appointed bishop of Nicaragua in 1544, he immediately began championing their cause. He wrote letters to the King in Spain and to his officials describing how Governor Rodrigo de Contreras and his family brutalized the Indians, refusing to abide by the New Laws:

> He sought to inform the King of the injustices which were being commit-ted and of the danger which he felt for his own life. The president of the court (*Audiencia*) reported that the Nicaraguan bishop "feared each day that he would be killed." Valdivieso wrote that he suspected that the letters which he was sending to the court were being intercepted and destroyed, and that he feared that there would soon be persecution against him as well as against the Indians. "I write these letters hurriedly in order that Your Majesty might be aware . . . of the great need that exists in these parts for justice." And although Valdivieso labored contin-ually for the welfare of the Indians, he reported that each day they were more oppressed. He also noted that the situation was growing more critical each day as the climate of opinion turned steadily against him.[7]

Governor Contreras became so incensed with the bishop that he concluded he must be killed. He hired some of Pizarro's ex-soldiers, who had come to Nicaragua from Peru, to eliminate Valdivieso. One of them, Juan Bermejo, led a "death squad" to the bishop's house in León, where they stabbed him to death on February 26, 1550.

Montesinos, Las Casas, and Valdivieso are only three of hundreds of clergy-men who took risks on behalf of the oppressed. Another was Padre Cristóbal de Pedraza, whom the Crown appointed as the first "Protector and Defender of the Indians" for Honduras in 1537. Arriving at his new post in 1538, he was full of idealistic plans to convert the Indians through preaching, kindness, and good example. As Protector and later as the province's first bishop, Pedraza spoke out often against violations in the *encomienda* system and the unlawful seizure and sale of Indian slaves.

Pedraza was appalled by the havoc wrought by the conquistadors and earlier governors of Honduras; he wrote to the Crown that the provincial governor López de Salcedo had sold Indians into slavery to pay his debts:

> And he seized so many Indians from the land that he totally destroyed it. . . . It was not only the misfortune of those he seized, but upon seeing their parents, spouses, children, brothers, sisters and relatives carried off, bound with rope and in chains, and put into ships to be sold, the few who remained fled for the hills and abandoned their pueblos. And

because in the hills they did not have supplies . . . they died of hunger in such numbers that in a pueblo of one or two thousand households not one person was left . . . not a man or woman, adult or child.[8]

In another letter to Spain he complained: "Is it not a disgraceful injustice that these indigenous peoples should be forced against their will to serve the Spaniards who in turn kick them, beat them, tie them to trees and posts as if they were slaves, and even kill them?"[9] Pedraza was denounced most for his decrees forbidding illegal employment of free Indians in the mines, and in spite of the fact that royal treasury officials condemned these decrees to the King, Pedraza was able to win support on this matter from the Crown.[10]

Still another defender of the Indians was Bishop Pablo de Torres of Panama (1547–1554), who excommunicated the Spanish *encomenderos* for their mistreatment of the Indians, only to be condemned himself by "conformist" archbishop Jerónimo de Loaysa and forced to return to Spain, where he was accused of treason and forbidden ever again to enter Panama.[11]

Unfortunately, the idealistic efforts of the early colonial churchmen did not survive as a widespread movement on behalf of the subjugated peoples in the New World. A reason can perhaps be offered in explanation. Whereas the Spanish monarch Charles V (1516–1556) was, on the whole, sympathetic with the causes of the "nonconformist" clergy, his son Philip II (1556–1598) was more concerned with the religious wars in Europe. When financial pressures increased on the Spanish monarchy because of these costly wars, concern for Indian welfare dwindled. If oppression of the Indians produced more gold and silver to be used to destroy Protestant heretics, so be it. Stanley and Barbara Stein describe the result of the new religious atmosphere:

Gone were the earlier days of evangelistic experimentation with Amerindian culture to forge a society without oppression and misery, a society of Christian communitarians molded in the spirit of More's *Utopia*. Gone were the pioneer and exhilarating days of experiments in education for the sons of the Amerindian nobility. The demands of both metropolitan and colonial society and economy required the church to abandon its crusading and reformist zeal.[12]

Nevertheless, throughout the following centuries, the voices of a few clerical champions of the powerless were heard. In the seventeenth century, for instance, Padre Vázquez de Espinosa eloquently condemned the mistreatment of Indians in a way that is reminiscent of Las Casas. Indians were often tricked into entering the *obrajes* (workshops) by offers of liquor or a small amount of money, he reports in his *Compendium and Description of the West Indies*. Once inside they were enslaved and never permitted to leave:

In this way they have gathered in and duped many married Indians with families, who have passed into oblivion here for twenty years, or longer, or their whole lives, without their wives or children knowing anything about them; for even if they want to get out, they cannot, thanks to the great watchfulness with which the doormen guard the exits.[13]

He further describes how Incas in Peru were sometimes forced to stay deep within the mines all week without seeing the light of day except on Sundays when they were allowed to attend mass and how they were given no food but that which their wives brought to the mines for them.[14]

In the eighteenth century the Mexican Jesuit theologian Francisco Javier Alegre conjured up memories of the earlier "nonconformist" missionaries when he denounced the black slave trade, while Pedro José Márquez, also a Mexican Jesuit, argued that the concepts of racial superiority and inferiority were philosophically absurd. In the nineteenth century, bold actions of some clergymen continued: In 1821, thirteen Guatemalan priests signed a declaration of independence from Spain, while one of them, Simón Cañas, insisted that blacks be given full rights as citizens under the new constitution.[15] This took place in spite of royalist archbishop Ramón Casaus y Torres of Guatemala, who condemned the rebels with such harsh words as the following:

> Their black hearts conspire against the sovereign majesty of the Nation that has given them existence, religion, and honor, against the most beloved King, a man most worthy of being loved. . . . The God of the armies and the God of vengeance clearly directs us . . . to confound on every arrogant front the intent to throw off the gentle yoke of His divine law and that of Spanish dominion. . . . For however much the wolves may howl, they will never advance their cause.[16]

Perhaps most similar to the sixteenth-century "nonconformist" missionaries, however, was Padre Manuel de Jesús Subirana, who was sent from Cuba to the province of Yoro in Honduras in the 1850s to convert the Hicaque Indians. Upon his arrival he found the Hicaques not only unbaptized but marginalized, physically weak, and exploited by Ladinos through forced labor, debt peonage, and by being paid ridiculously low prices for their products. Missionaries sent to convert them in the eighteenth century had counted on soldiers to force the Indians to accept baptism and had attempted to relocate this forest-dwelling tribe of hunters in agricultural *reducciones* (Indian towns formed by missionaries). The Hicaque had acquired the reputation of being resistant to conquest and conversion but, over the decades, resistance had ceased. Disease, servitude, and hard labor that went unpaid by Ladinos for weeks, all took their toll on the Hicaque's independent spirit.[17]

Padre Subirana began a series of projects to improve the lot of the Hicaques. He informed various Honduran officials of the miserable treatment of the Indians by Ladinos, accusing them not only of exploiting the Indians economically, but also of beating the men, robbing the women and boys, and raping the girls.[18] When the governor of the province, Jesús Quiroz, rounded up Hicaques to transport sarsaparilla to the coast for his personal gain in this lucrative trade, fourteen of them died from exhaustion and disease. Subirana "protested this abuse energetically and the central government placed a limit on the excessive ambition of the governor," which lasted only until the priest's death, however.[19]

Believing that the only way to convert the Indians was to relieve their suffering, Subirana arranged for their debts to be cancelled and taught the Indians that they were free and could refuse to work for unfair wages. Furthermore, he declared null and void any contracts between Indians and Ladinos that were not signed in his presence or that of another authorized by him. He also pleaded with the national government to allow the Hicaques to continue to grow tobacco after it was decreed that the crop could be cultivated only in the plains of Santa Rosa.[20] He organized them into villages to instruct them on how to pool their labor for common gain and how to obtain the same price for their produce as Ladinos. Like the *reducciones,* these villages also served the priest's purposes of gathering the Indians together to facilitate evangelization, but unlike the *reducciones* the Indians were not compelled to settle there. Subirana's most significant effort was his work in obtaining land and titles of ownership for the Hicaques in 1864.[21] The twentieth-century missionary James "Guadalupe" Carney would later term this pioneering work the "first effective agrarian reform in Honduras."[22] Because of his efforts to alleviate their misery, Subirana was able to baptize thousands of Hicaques, but unfortunately, after his death, his projects were taken over by priests who collaborated with the governor. By the late nineteenth century, the Hicaques had lost their best land to Ladinos. Thus the fifteen years or so of Subirana's work proved to be little more than an interlude. The destruction of the Hicaque culture was renewed and many of the Indians fled to more inaccessible mountain regions.

Priests like Vásquez de Espinosa, Alegre, Márquez, Cañas, and Subirana were rare, however, in post-sixteenth-century Latin America. Many clergymen in the seventeenth and eighteenth centuries served as apologists for the power structure and those who did not tended to remain silent in the face of unjust political institutions. In the anti-clerical Liberal period of the nineteenth and twentieth centuries—at least prior to 1960—the church, faced with serious problems of its own, concerned itself hardly at all with ameliorating the condition of the poor classes. At best, some churchmen displayed what might be termed a "benevolent" approach to missionary work. Typical of this group was the Franciscan Fray Fernando Espino, who worked in *reducciones* in eastern Honduras from 1668 to 1681. In his memoirs he describes his experiences: He was asked by a rancher to preach to the Indians in the Olancho area of Honduras because Spanish settlers were being "victimized" by these people and "were powerless to defend themselves."[23] The rancher had taken two recently converted Indians with him to help persuade Espino to accept the Honduran assignment. At first, perhaps fearing for his personal safety, the friar was reluctant, but then one of the Indians rebuked him: "Padre, don't you say that those who are not baptized are going to hell, a place of fire and demons? Well, if you do not send our parents and relatives to Heaven . . . then God will punish you if they die without baptism."[24] A few days later, both of the Indians died of an illness, and Father Fernando was so inspired by their faith and resignation to the will of God that he decided to undertake the Honduran venture.

Fray Fernando not only labored for the Indians' spiritual welfare but also assisted them with their physical needs: "There I catechized and baptized them, instructing them in the Catholic faith; I made little houses for them and *milpas* (fields) of corn."[25] While Espino was certainly not an outspoken critic of Spanish institutional injustice as had been Montesinos, Las Casas, Valdivieso, and so many other sixteenth-century churchmen, he was nevertheless a "benevolent" priest and seems to have been a gentle and compassionate man.

Perhaps the most famous churchman to take the "benevolent" approach was the Jesuit, Pedro Claver, who came to the Caribbean port of Cartagena from Spain in 1610. Cartagena was the major slave market in Spanish America; about a thousand black slaves were shipped there each month. Claver would board every ship upon its arrival. Since about one slave in three died on the sea journey, the ships arrived with large numbers of slaves who were near death. Claver would first baptize the dying. Next he would hand out food, brandy, and tobacco to those who had survived the voyage. Claver trained blacks who spoke the various African dialects as catechists, and it is said that in his forty-four year ministry he baptized more than 300,000 slaves. Yet, in all those years, Padre Pedro never once spoke against the institution of slavery. As the authors of *The Saints: A Concise Biographical Dictionary* note:

> Claver accepted slavery as an inevitable though regrettable element in the social system. It was with the slaves as victims of the social system rather than with the system itself that he was concerned. His life was dedicated to reforming the individual rather than to reforming the system. His heroic predecessor at Cartagena, Father [Alonso de] Sandoval, combined Claver's love for the individual slave with the [nineteenth-century English Protestant abolitionist, William] Wilberforce's hatred of slavery. He collected all the relevant facts about the slave trade and wrote a book which is one of the most effective attacks on this infamous traffic and is still an invaluable source book for historians of slavery.[26]

While Claver remained mute when confronted with the immoral institution of slavery, Padre Sandoval, although not as outspoken as the earlier "nonconformist" clergy, nevertheless writes occasionally with a flash of insight reminiscent of Montesinos or Las Casas:

> [The slaves] arrive looking like skeletons; they are led ashore, completely naked, and are shut up in a large court or enclosure . . . and it is a great pity to see so many sick and needy people denied all care or assistance, for

as a rule they are left to lie on the ground, naked and without shelter. . . . I recall that I once saw two of them, already dead, lying on the ground on their backs like animals, their mouths open and full of flies, their arms crossed as if making the sign of the cross . . . and I was astounded to see them dead as a result of such great inhumanity.[27]

It is interesting to note that whereas Pedro Claver was canonized in 1888, Alonso de Sandoval not only is not canonized but is all but forgotten except to a few historians.

In summary, throughout its history the Latin American church has always consisted of a large percentage of "conformist" clergy, a substantial number of "benevolent" priests and religious, and a small group of "nonconformist" clerics. This last division was strongest in the sixteenth century; from the seventeenth through the mid-twentieth century, "nonconformist" clergy and religious existed but were extremely rare. The post-sixteenth-century Latin American church primarily labored for the salvation of the soul of the individual. It did this through a parish structure which placed primary emphasis on dispensing the sacraments. Its clergy preached homilies against personal sins such as drunkenness and fornication; little was ever said, however, against political, social, and economic institutional structures which robbed the masses of their human dignity. At its best, the church ignored the injustices emanating from these structures; at its worst, it indirectly supported them by encouraging the oppressed to accept their lot with humility and passivity. Resignation to the miseries of this life, the masses were told, would merit them a high place in heaven. In short, it was God's will that they suffer.

Such ecclesiastical attitudes finally began to change as a result of Pope John XXIII's *aggiornamento*, his call for the renewal and modernization of the Catholic church culminating in Vatican II (1962–1965). Now it was realized that championing human development and social justice went hand in hand with saving souls. The scriptures stressed not only the hereafter, but justice and dignity in this world as well.[28] Strong emphasis was placed on the social encyclicals of Popes Leo XIII and Pius XI as well as on the social teachings of Pius XII. John XXIII issued two encyclicals himself, *Mater et Magistra* and *Pacem in Terris*, which further extended the views of his predecessors. As Edward Cleary comments:

John spoke about just wages and strikes as did previous popes. But he also discussed economic aid, the use of farm surpluses at the international level, and in a forceful statement asked the well fed to look after the undernourished "without imperialistic aggrandizement." He called for the state to take a more active role, and even talked about state ownership. Many of the things he said sounded like favorable comments on distinctive features in some socialist countries. . . . Catholics and socialists, both striving for social justice, would meet and cooperate.

Persons in the Third World and in non-Catholic churches noted the change of tone in *Pacem in Terris*. The encyclical goes beyond the Catholic world; it addresses all Christians and all persons of good will. . . .

John also opened a new topic: he warned against colonialism and new forms of imperialism.[29]

At a time when desperate poverty and oppression were escalating throughout the Third World, the conciliar fathers issued *Gaudium et Spes*. Perhaps the most important document of Vatican II, it condemned the hoarding of wealth and power for the benefit of a small segment of society. It further noted that the right to private property is not an unlimited right. It must be weighed against the benefits to society accrued from public ownership. But more importantly, it stipulated that all persons are entitled to the basic earthly necessities of life and therefore when individuals or their families are in extreme need, they are morally justified in taking from the excessive wealth of others.[30]

Perhaps as important as its contents, *Gaudium et Spes* introduced a radically new methodology to Catholic theological study.

The methodology used in the document turns traditional theology on its head. Instead of proceeding in the time-honored fashion, discussing theological or biblical principles and then applying them to a present-day situation, *Gaudium et Spes* reverses the process: it begins with a careful analysis of the de facto situation, then turns to sacred scripture and theology for reflection on that situation, and finally, as a third step, makes pastoral applications. Theological reflection thus becomes the second, not the first, step.[31]

Gaudium et Spes likewise went beyond the traditional philosophical and theological approach, employing the social and behavioral sciences.[32]

The Latin American hierarchy did not play a major part in the proceedings of Vatican II. It did learn much from them, however, and it agreed to hold a general conference of Latin American bishops at Medellín, Colombia, in order to apply the principles of Vatican II to the Latin American situation. After two years of preparation, the conference was held in 1968. Its importance cannot be overestimated; using the methodology of *Gaudium et Spes*, it changed the direction of the Latin American church from one aligned, at least indirectly, with the power structure to one that sided with the poor and oppressed. As Cleary states:

The final document would say, in brief, that the church is a sinful church in a sinful (unjust) society, one marked by structured inequalities. Latin America, it went on, is a region suffering from two massive evils: external dominance and internal colonialism. Change was obviously called for and the church wished to take part in the change. The church chose the side of the poor. It must reach out to them, and to the whole continent.

This would be accomplished through evangelization and lay participation (*pastoral de conjunto*) from which grassroots communities (*comunidades de base*) would emerge.[33]

Comunidades de base were the key element in the church's siding with the oppressed. Adopting and expanding the consciousness-raising techniques used by Paulo Freire in educating the poor, the church began training catechists who formed small, grassroots groups of *campesinos* (peasants) and urban poor for bible study and prayer. Biblical passages are read and the group reflects on them, rooting them in the actualities of their everyday lives. The catechist serves as coordinator rather than leader. Eventually the group members learn about themselves from a gospel-based orientation. They realize that it is not God's will that they suffer; as God's people they are not created to serve the rich, but to have human dignity. They realize that they have a right to basic physical necessities for themselves and their families and that they are not inferior to the wealthy. In studying the gospel of Luke, for instance, they learn that Jesus called the rich landowner, who hoarded his grain, a fool (12:16–21) and that he said, "It is easier for a camel to pass through the eye of a needle than for a rich man to enter the kingdom of God" (18:25); they also reflect on the parable of the rich man and Lazarus (16:19–31). In the other books of both the Old and New Testaments, they learn more about God's commitment to the poor and oppressed:

They interpret the exodus as applying to them. They read Amos about helping the widow and the orphaned. And they reflect on Jesus as the one who came to liberate them. They are quick to catch on that liberation is more than spiritual. Often their discussion centers on not having to live in the unfavorable conditions that they once thought unchangeable. Health, education and landownership become topics of reflection, replacing resignation and suffering, as in the past.[34]

Since basic Christian community members often helped organize or joined labor unions, agrarian organizations, and cooperatives and took part in nonviolent protests demanding human rights, many of the Latin American elites soon concluded that the Medellín-based church was responsible for this new peasant aggressiveness. Thus, in several countries, the military and security forces were turned against the clergy. Priests began to be tortured and killed and the more conservative "conformist" clergy attempted to return the Latin American church to its former state of "political noninvolvement." It seemed that the conservatives might prove successful when they gained control of the agenda of the Latin American bishops' conference held at Puebla, Mexico, in 1979. The progressives, however, aided by the writings of the theologians of liberation, not only reaffirmed the commitments of Medellín but actually expanded them:

There would be no turning back. Indeed, the bishops at Puebla went further. They more clearly and fully committed the church to the service of the poor and spoke of its preferential option for the poor and oppressed. They also took a more explicit and stronger stand for human rights. The experience of the years since the Medellín conference had taught the church new political and moral lessons. . . .

The church of promise at Medellín was becoming the church of fulfillment at Puebla.[35]

As a result of Medellín and Puebla, as well as Vatican II, the Catholic church in Latin America shifted its priorities. Now a larger percentage of clergy and religious joined the swelling ranks of the "nonconformists"; the numbers of "benevolent" clergy also grew. Although the percentage of "conformists" declined drastically, they nevertheless remained an important factor. Just as the Catholic church committed itself to the poor, so did most mainline Protestant churches and some evangelical groups. At the same time, however, many fundamentalist and Pentecostal churches—most of them based in the United States—increased their missionary commitment in Latin America. As the Catholic church lost favor with the elite power structure in several Latin nations, many of these conservative churches moved in to fill the gap. Preaching resignation and passivity to the sufferings of this life, they received tacit support from the oligarchies and military leaders. Thus, as tensions developed between progressive Christian churches and the oligarchic-military establishments, strained relations also escalated between several Christian denominations and within some of the Christian churches themselves, especially the Catholic church.

Finally, one more outgrowth of Pope John XXIII's *aggiornamento* must be mentioned since it directly bears on the lives of most of those included in this book. In 1961, as the Catholic church was making ready for Vatican II, Pope John issued a call for the Catholic churches of the United States, Canada, and Europe to commit 10 percent of their priests and religious to mission work in Latin America.[36] As a result of this plea, hundreds of North Americans— priests, nuns, brothers, and laypeople—pledged themselves to this apostolate. Many Europeans did the same. Entering a world of poverty for the first time, they reacted in different ways. Some, fearing communist undertones in the demands of the marginalized for change, sided with the "conformist" faction. The majority, however, committed themselves to the poor in either a "nonconformist" or "benevolent" manner. Many believed a truly just society could not become a reality unless oppressive institutional structures were changed: Ita Ford, Maura Clarke, Dorothy Kazel, Jean Donovan, and James "Guadalupe" Carney could perhaps best be placed among this group, although their views were certainly not identical. Still others attempted in one way or another to follow the "benevolent," non-political approach. Included among these were Bill Woods, Casimir Cypher, and Stanley Rother. Still others defy categorization. John Troyer tried to avoid even the slightest hint of political involvement;

yet he belonged to a conservative religious group that seemed to accept, without question, the Guatemalan government's claim that it needed to take "unusual" actions to stifle the growth of communism. Frank Holdenried had a deep-seated fear of what he perceived to be Soviet-sponsored communist movements in Central America. Yet he felt that the U.S. and Central American governments' policies in the area actually fostered the growth of the Marxist-Leninist ideology they were meant to stifle. He also thought U.S. business investments could be beneficial to Latin America if they were only made in a more moral, less greedy way. James Miller, basically conservative in his political views, was considered a reactionary Somocista collaborator by the Sandinistas in Nicaragua, yet he, along with the rest of his Christian Brother community, was viewed with suspicion by the right-wing Guatemalan government because of their commitment to Indian youth.

Thus, the U.S. missionary-martyrs can certainly not be cast in the same mold. They do have one thing in common, however. They all worked with the poor, hoping to better the lives of the powerless both spiritually and physically. Unfortunately, to do this in most Latin American countries places one in conflict with the government whether or not one wishes it. To work with the marginalized is to risk the possibility of arrest, torture, and death. These eleven U.S. missionaries, along with thousands of others—from Latin America, North America, and elsewhere—were willing to take that chance. Certainly most missionaries do not seek martyrdom; the eleven who were killed in Central America, along with countless others, faced the possibility of death voluntarily. They did not want to die, but if that could be the price of bringing the gospel message to the oppressed, they were willing to accept that possibility. Although they might not meet all the requirements of martyrdom in the strict, traditional Catholic sense, they all died because they bore witness to the gospel and as a result paid the ultimate price—death. To the authors of this book, such witness merits fully the title of martyr.

Here follow, then, the stories of eleven U.S. martyrs. Thousands from other countries—priests, religious, and catechists, Catholic and Protestant—have likewise been murdered because of their gospel commitment to the poor and to justice. In all probability, many more will suffer the same fate in years to come. These martyrs are part of a long tradition going back to the days of the apostles. In Latin American history, they share the same Christian commitment initially undertaken by the sixteenth-century "nonconformist" priests, and as martyrs who have struggled with and on behalf of the poor and defenseless, they are one with Antonio de Valdivieso. It is hoped that their stories will cause us to reflect on our own commitment (or lack of commitment) to the oppressed of the world and that their example will inspire many others to become more actively involved in the creation of a just society in Central America and elsewhere.

PART I

HONDURAS

And a merchant said, Speak to us of Buying and Selling.
And he answered and said:
To you the earth yields her fruit, and you shall not want if you but know how to fill your hands.
It is in exchanging the gifts of the earth that you shall find abundance and be satisfied.
Yet unless the exchange be in love and kindly justice, it will but lead some to greed and others to hunger. . . .
And before you leave the market place, see that no one has gone his way with empty hands.
For the master spirit of the earth shall not sleep peacefully upon the wind till the needs of the least of you are satisfied.

KAHLIL GIBRAN
The Prophet

Michael "Casimir" Cypher

Michael "Casimir" Cypher

Conventual Franciscan Missionary

Michael Jerome Cypher, born on January 12, 1941, was raised on a small cattle farm near Medford, Wisconsin, growing up with his eight brothers and three sisters in an old farmhouse that had once belonged to his grandparents. Michael's parents, Elizabeth and Lawrence, reared their large family in a religious environment that was uncomplicated by the confusion and sophisticated materialism of urban existence. The Cyphers were not self-conscious about their Catholicism; the walls of the home were covered with religious pictures. Simplicity, love of the land, respect for nature, and the desire and ability to grow things were bred into Michael, and friends unanimously remember him as "down-to-earth" and "unsophisticated."

Two of the nine Cypher boys, Leonard and Michael, left the old farmhouse in Medford at the age of fourteen to attend Saint Mary's Minor Seminary in Crystal Lake, Illinois. Leonard was a senior there when Michael entered as a freshman. (Leonard, too, was to become a priest, but later left the priesthood.) Mike was "a very quiet and simple boy, very much down to earth" and "not all that fond of studies,"[1] recalls Father Ronald Olson, his religion and music teacher; nevertheless, he did well enough in school. He preferred math and science and more practical subjects; as for his writing ability, it was "an English teacher's nightmare," Father Anselm Romb claims.[2] But Michael was always anxious to help, and Olson gratefully remembers him as a senior staying up late for several nights drawing sketches and scenes for a choral program Olson was preparing. He also sang in the choir for that program and contributed his bass voice to a couple of barbershop quartet numbers.[3]

Because Michael had a rather indifferent attitude to intellectual activities and a preference for "getting his hands dirty" working on manual projects, he was often kidded by his prefect, Father John Chrysostom, who was himself fastidious and a lover of the classics, art, and literature. In spite of their diametrically opposed interests, Father John developed a deep respect for

Mike. The vice-prefect, Father Philip Wozniak, remembers him as "certainly no model student," and somewhat mischievous, but praises his utterly wholesome character.[4] This was a scenario that was to be replayed often in Cypher's life. Teachers, rectors, missionaries, a novelist he knew in California would be initially exasperated or even repelled by his straightforward, "earthy" ways, but would eventually be won over by his simplicity, his sensitivity to nature, his inability to hold a grudge.

Mike graduated from Saint Mary's Seminary in 1959 and went on to the Conventual Franciscan's novitiate in Lake Forest, Illinois. There he took as his religious name "Casimir," after the ascetic son of a fifteenth-century Polish king. He then attended Loyola University in Chicago and graduated on June 9, 1964.

After graduation, he went on for theological studies at Assumption Seminary in Chaska, Minnesota, a tiny town southwest of Minneapolis-Saint Paul. There the rural atmosphere, familiar to him from childhood, appealed to him. "He was content with the simple things in life," notes Olson. "There was nothing sophisticated about him. He was a very plain person, not known as a great speaker . . . and not seen as a great or strong leader."[5]

The years he spent in Chaska studying theology coincided with the years of post-Vatican II changes occurring throughout the Catholic church. If the laity were perhaps confused and hesitant about the demise of some of their traditions, seminarians were usually in the vanguard demanding speedier and more radical changes. They were particularly anxious to revamp seminary life. A fellow seminarian at that time, Kent Biergans, clearly remembers Cas's total lack of concern for the "burning" issues of the day:

In many ways we were idealists, in many ways radicals, in many ways immature. Cas was not a part of the seminary turmoil. I don't remember him ever being a part of the discussion to push for change or to complain about the seminary administration. He was more apt to be in a friendly card game and drinking a beer than he was to be in a hot debate. He seemed to slide through such concerns on a different level. He seemed untouched by the turbulence around him. He lived his simple life in peace and shared it with those around him.[6]

Throughout his life, Casimir would remain remarkably oblivious to political issues, both within the church and without.

Cypher was ordained on March 9, 1968, in the cathedral of Saint Paul in Saint Paul, Minnesota. His first assignment as a priest was to Saint Anthony's parish in Rockford, Illinois, where he did not distinguish himself as a well-organized shepherd of the flock, but was nonetheless well liked by the parishioners there. At Saint Anthony's Casimir began to acquire his lasting reputation as carefree and absent-minded. His superiors would have to remind him to buy a new suit or shoes or have his habit cleaned, but he would then forget or simply not bother, thinking his appearance unimportant. He was also unbothered by the petty details dictated to the rest of humanity by conventional society. Philip Wozniak, rector of the Franciscan House of Studies in Chicago, recalls the wake of exasperated confusion that followed Casimir around on the occasions when he would visit:

> He lost everything of importance, e.g., key to the house, keys to the car. He frequently violated community order by innocently forgetting to inform his superiors when and where he was going. He never had his own cigarettes. It would do no good to give him a whole package. He would have left them somewhere and ask for more. He made too many appointments for the same hour and the same day, and he frequently would not be at home when all these people arrived.[7]

Sometime during these four years or so of pastoral duties, Cypher became drawn to missionary work. But there were obstacles in his path. First of all, his province, Saint Bonaventure, did not have a mission. This problem was eventually solved when he asked to go to Honduras, where a mission had been established by another province of his order. But a second obstacle remained: Casimir could not speak Spanish.

In an effort to prepare him somewhat for life in Central America, the Franciscans sent Cypher to a Spanish-speaking parish—Our Lady of Guadalupe—in Hermosa Beach, California. He was not there long before the people dubbed him "Father Colombo," perceiving some remarkable similarities between their disheveled, forgetful associate pastor and the popular television detective. Olson, who was also in California at this time, recalls:

> The people in Hermosa Beach loved him, even though he was seen as forgetful, somewhat disorganized and carefree. He always had time for anyone, regardless of what he was doing. He may have exasperated a few. Some thought he had no priestly class. Yet his homilies and liturgies were very sincere, down to earth and to the point. I doubt if he knew any Spanish at the time . . . but he was able to touch everyone with his genuineness.[8]

Nevertheless, he did manage to antagonize at least one influential member of the parish, Leonard Wibberley, author of *The Mouse That Roared*. Wibberley reveals that his outright antipathy for Casimir eventually developed into friendly respect:

> I thought him stupid; that is, dull in his wits and incapable of adequate self-expression. . . . His face lacked expression, or, if it had a natural expression at all, it seemed to me one of truculence.
>
> Later, I came to realize I had misjudged Father Casimir. The change occurred one Christmas after a school play. He seemed genuinely to enjoy the performance and the children who participated. Afterwards I

found him standing in the semidark of the playground almost as if he didn't want to leave. When I held out my hand and wished him a Merry Christmas, he was charitable enough to take it—though I deserved to have him ignore me, for I had been a pompous ass in the way I treated him.

Thereafter I came to have more regard for him. He was short and looked as though he should have been a blacksmith rather than a clergyman. He had a direct and uncomplicated mind, and so was not bedeviled by the frustrations and indecisions of lesser mentalities. He thought deeply, I am told, but didn't say much, and this habit of deep thought got him into constant trouble.

He could be guaranteed, for instance, to lose any car in a parking lot because he was involved with some question of ethical worth rather than where he left an automobile—all this I learned from his fellow priests.

Father Casimir, I suppose, could have stayed in Hermosa Beach or some equally comfortable parish for a long time. He was a good priest, and well liked on the whole. But he got it into his head that that wasn't what he had become a priest for; his purpose, he apparently decided, was not to be comfortable but to help the poor. He knew that there were a lot of poor to be helped, and somehow or other he got himself transferred from comfortable Hermosa Beach to not-so-comfortable Honduras.[9]

In October 1973, still unskilled in speaking Spanish, Casimir left California, destined for the rugged and primitive department of Olancho in Honduras.

Although it is bordered by three countries in various stages of revolution—Nicaragua, El Salvador, and Guatemala—Honduras itself is not yet embroiled in revolt. Nevertheless, it does share with its neighbors a similar heritage of dictatorship, landowning and military elites, and a large, poverty-stricken peasantry whose unanswered demands for true land reform bring them time and again to the point of desperation.

Honduras is the second largest nation in Central America—only Nicaragua is larger; but with around four million people, it has one of the sparsest populations. Nearly all of Honduras's industry is controlled by foreign corporations (80 percent),[10] while most of the best agricultural land is owned by two U.S. fruit companies, United Fruit and Standard Fruit, and by a few plantation owners and cattlemen, whose farms and ranches produce crops and meat for export rather than for home consumption. Complicating the uneven distribution of land is the fact that only about 25 percent of the land is arable because of the country's mountainous terrain. Thus, 90 percent of the *campesino* population is forced to live on a per capita income of about $100 a year.[11] This unfortunate nation is one of the poorest in the Western Hemisphere:

Life expectancy and malnutrition are the worst in the region—in some areas as many as nine out of ten children are malnourished. Nowhere else in Central America is the lack of proper nourishment so noticeable as in the rural areas of Honduras. Children stand outside dirt homes with bloated stomachs, and the *campesinos* stare lifelessly as travelers pass through their towns.[12]

Following the long dictatorship of Tiburcio Carías Andino (1933–1949) and a contested election in 1954, a forward-looking president, Dr. Ramón Villeda Morales, was elected in 1957. Villeda Morales, after sponsoring a labor code and a social security program, turned his attention to the touchy problem of agrarian reform, and in 1962 he signed into law legislation that would tax unproductive land based on a percentage of its declared value. Villeda Morales was cautious, however, and did not limit the amount of cultivated land that could be held by an individual. Moreover, the Honduran Congress had made it very difficult to expropriate any private holdings. Nevertheless, even this moderate reform antagonized the large landholders and the United Fruit Company and helped lay the groundwork for a coup one year later, in which the military under Colonel Oswaldo López Arellano seized control of the government ten days before the scheduled presidential election.[13]

After several years of thwarting the reforms initiated by his predecessor, López Arellano assumed a more positive attitude toward land reform in the late 1960s; and when he again took over the government in 1972, he was ready to get serious. At that time, twenty thousand peasants joined in a "hunger march" and converged on the capital of Tegucigalpa demanding meaningful land reform. Hoping to stem the growing discontent of the hungry *campesinos*, in December 1972 López Arellano made them the long-awaited promise of land. The *campesinos* were able to exert pressure on López's regime because, despite their illiteracy and poverty, they have remarkably well-developed peasant unions. In northern Honduras, one reason for this was the famous sixty-nine-day strike of 1954, during which laborers for United Fruit, later joined by those of Standard Fruit, demanded an end to deplorable wages and working conditions. Although the workers did obtain union recognition, they gained only a fraction of their other demands. After the strike United Fruit mechanized its operations, dismissing almost 50 percent of its workers. This proved a boon to peasant organization, for the former banana laborers became subsistence farmers and provided the peasantry in the area with a core of experienced union activists.[14]

In southern Honduras, however, an important impetus to peasant organization was the Catholic church. In the 1960s, the church, perhaps realizing the opportunity it had lost during the strike to identify with and support the laborers, began to turn its attention to the peasants living in ignorance and hunger. Recruiting lay leaders from traditional church groups like the Caballeros de Cristo Rey and the Legion of Mary, it developed *cursos de capacitación* (courses in human promotion), consumer and farming cooperatives, and rural radio schools. With the backing of the bishops and clergy, lay leaders thus began to educate *campesinos*, help them organize, and dispel their fatalistic acceptance of existence without basic human rights. An eventual result of these efforts was the progressive National Peasants Union (UNC), which grew rapidly and was supported by the small but vigorous Christian Democratic Party.[15]

The UNC soon began to organize in Olancho. Like church leaders in southern Honduras, the bishop of Olancho, Nicholas D'Antonio, encouraged peasants to educate themselves and to unite in the struggle for land reform. He turned a vacant diocesan school building in Juticalpa, the seat of government in Olancho, into a "human promotion center" called El Centro Santa Clara. D'Antonio, a Franciscan from Rochester, New York, recalls the courses offered there:

> Our conscientization program . . . brought the *campesino* to a true sense of his human dignity as a child of God and an equal with his richer brothers. The earth, he learned, was created by God and intended for the benefit of all mankind and not only for a select few believed to be favored by destiny, heredity or politics. A poor farmer remarked, after a series of courses, "I feel like I've been reborn. It's like I've come out of the dark into the light."[16]

Many of the *campesino* leaders turned out by the Centro Santa Clara were trained by a dynamic young Colombian churchworker, Iván Betancur. A close friend, Luis Emilio Henao, describes Iván's work:

> Iván had a great capacity for turning an illiterate *campesino* into a leader. . . . His discussions on the analysis of reality were so concrete and so disturbing, as he would begin asking simply: "What do you see in your villages?" And their answers were simple: "We see trees, animals, houses, etc." And afterwards, with questions as simple as this: "And who do the trees belong to?", he would begin to penetrate the terrible reality of exploitation of fine lumber in Olancho.[17]

The local landowning elite were antagonized by the *campesinos'* growing assertiveness and by the church's efforts to educate them. D'Antonio continues:

> . . . Some would visit our Center only to look for slogans or other material and quote them out of context. Soon we were labelled Communists and foreign agitators. Threats were made against our lives, . . . and I earned two nice titles, "The Mad Communist Bishop" and "The Hangman of Olancho."[18]

Thus by the early 1970s tensions were building in Olancho. While landowners prepared to defend their privileges against growing demands for change, *campesinos*, on the other hand, were desperate and hungry. Lacking enough land of their own, they worked on the large plantations and ranches in the area, earning salaries as low as fifty cents per day, receiving no benefits, and subjected to being fired at will by their employers. Watching in frustration, they often saw huge tracts of unused land being taken over by the already wealthy landowners, often with dubious legal title.[19]

But the peasants of Olancho, newly organized into the UNC, began to place their hopes in a strategy being used elsewhere in Honduras—land recuperations. By occupying en masse unused national or *ejido* (communal) lands, the *campesinos'* goal was to force authorities to recognize their plight and to implement the 1962 Agrarian Reform Law. Because of the church's efforts on the *campesinos'* behalf, it was not long before the large landholders were accusing the bishop and churchworkers of promoting these "land invasions," as the wealthy preferred to call them. Nearly all the priests and religious in Olancho were foreigners, due to the severe shortage of clergy in Honduras, and this served to complicate the issue immensely, since churchworkers were seen as malevolent "foreign agitators" by local ranchers. In 1971, Iván Betancur, by now a parish priest in the town of Catacamas, Olancho, became the target of repeated harassment. "Get out, priest" was painted on the town walls, and his residence was even dynamited.[20]

As the land recuperations continued, perhaps a fatal clash was inevitable in this wild and isolated province. At any rate one occurred on February 18, 1972, over a piece of land called "La Talanquera." Bishop D'Antonio was an eyewitness to much of what transpired:

Honduras has a fairly good agrarian reform program, but due to the created interests of power groups, it travels at a snail's pace. The peasants observed that there is plenty of uncultivated land around serving no social purpose and, in many cases, not even legally owned or registered; so, because of dire necessity, they began to pressure the Agrarian Reform Institute and the government to accelerate the reform. If ignored, they threatened to "recuperate property" which, in justice, already belonged to them as Honduran citizens. They complained that more importance was given to a cow than to a human being.

The Director of the local office of the INA (National Agrarian Institute) in Olancho was an opportunist who attempted to please both the rich and the poor. On the 15th of February 1972, he gave the go-ahead signal to a group of organized farmers to take over a piece of property called LA TALANQUERA. Euphoric with the good news, about 40 adult men, with their wives and children, settled themselves in the area and immediately began to prepare the soil for planting in time for the rainy season. The Honduran flag and placards were set up which read "We need land to work on," "We want justice and peace," "We are Catholics," "We don't want violence," and "We want to dialogue." The "owner" of La Talanquera complained to the police. Several arrived with the hope of convincing them to leave. They agreed on condition that the owner himself come and dialogue with them. He failed to show up; instead, he prevailed upon the Director of the INA to petition soldiers from the capital to get the "invaders" off the property. The troops arrived, 95 men strong, armed with automatic weapons. On February 18, at 2:00 P.M., shots were heard; six *campesinos* were brutally murdered while their companions, wives and children scattered in panic to save their lives and lost themselves in the wooded mountains. Four others were seriously injured and two taken prisoner after a cruel beating. A sergeant received a bullet wound in the back when the order to fire and charge was given by the Captain. I confessed the dying soldier and saw the wound for myself, a gaping, bleeding hole, the size of the palm of my hand. The Doctor's diagnosis: caused by a high-powered rifle bullet. Naturally, to defend themselves, the soldiers and the enemies of the *campesinos* said that the sergeant died of a machete wound when attacked by the "invaders."

My efforts to get help were fruitless. The telegraph and telephone lines were cut off for four days. The bodies were left unattended until late at night that same day. My deacon [Luis Henao] offered to remove the corpses and take them to their families in the parish vehicle assisted by the brother of one of the dead. My deacon, now a priest, wrote a six-page description of this horror story which the nation's principal newspaper published in full. I authenticated the article with my signature.

The news of the massacre scandalized and angered every strata of society and leaked out to the world press. The communication media blared out its protest and demanded that justice be meted out. In my homily that next Sunday, I exhorted my infuriated people not to resort to vengeance. I encouraged a cooling off period and a time for reflection. I called that awful day "Good Friday Anticipated" (it was the Lenten season) and honored the brave men who died as martyrs. I encouraged dialogue on all sides and blamed what happened not on the rich, the soldiers or the *campesinos*; I blamed the massacre on the injustice rampant throughout Latin America and the world.

Calling the "invaders" martyrs angered and embarrassed the government and the military. The nationally organized Landowners and Cattlemen Association lashed out an attack in the press and radio against me personally as the "Promoter of Land Invasions" and the cause of the present strife. When things began to settle down, the government sent an investigating committee to Olancho in order to dialogue with the Campesino League [UNC], the Organized Landowners and Cattlemen and myself. I opened the session with a quote from Luke 4:16-19, but the meeting in the Town Hall was a farce. The *campesinos* were not justly represented. The majority of those present were the landowners and cattlemen and their friends. Although the meeting settled nothing, it did cool off tempers. I explained that at no time had I organized or even encouraged the *campesinos* to "invade" private property or to utilize violence of any kind. But I was sneered at and not believed. In a sense, I couldn't altogether blame the "rich," because at no time had I openly condemned the invasions. Why I didn't do so was because I was informed by the leaders of the *campesinos* and the office of the INA, that the land "recuperations" were done legally. The law was plain. If property wasn't serving a social function and the owner could not prove his legal right to it, then the peasants could take it.[21]

After the violence at La Talanquera, the harassment of churchworkers did not diminish. In March 1972 Padre Iván and Deacon Henao were denounced in front of government offices for inciting the *campesinos* and indoctrinating them in guerrilla tactics.[22] In April the bishop was arrested briefly by a drunken police chief and a month later was interrogated (and exonerated) by national authorities for possible links to communists.[23] In order to counteract the allegations that the church in Olancho had close ties with the left-of-center Christian Democrats through the *campesino* union, D'Antonio sold El Centro Santa Clara to the UNC for an insignificant sum and exhorted his pastoral workers not to use parish centers for partisan purposes. The *campesinos* renamed the building "Instituto 18 de Febrero" in memory of those who died at La Talanquera. The symbolic sale of the Center to peasants, however, further antagonized D'Antonio's enemies, who then began to look for a way to obtain the building for a school.[24]

No doubt the conflict at La Talanquera influenced a decisive political shift on the national level; for after it and the huge hunger march on Tegucigalpa mentioned earlier, López Arellano made his momentous promise to speed up land reform.

In late 1973, Father Casimir Cypher arrived in Olancho to work in the village of Gualaco. Michael Gable, a lay missioner, went out to meet him; knowing something of the recent history of animosity and bloodshed in the region, he thought the man who stood smiling in front of him was not cut out for this mentally and physically grueling mission work. But, like others before him, Mike soon realized his first impression was deceptive:

When first you met him you thought what a simple man he was. Then you came to understand his intelligence, his deep spirituality, the way he loved all things, the way he wanted most of all to serve God and to help the people and you understood that this was a most unusual man.[25]

Casimir began work in San Gerónimo parish in Gualaco as an assistant of Father Emil Cook, another Conventual Franciscan. They split up the territory, which included about sixty villages and five hundred square miles of hilly and mountainous terrain, riding horseback or on burros over rocky, unpaved paths to reach the *campesinos* who needed their ministry or help. The first few months were extremely difficult, Casimir told his family; the visits to remote villages often took days by horseback. Once he even tried walking, but found that much worse.[26]

Casimir's reputation as absent-minded and disorganized continued unchallenged in this remote parish in Olancho, just as it had in the United States. In Gualaco, where the television detective Colombo was unheard of, amused comments were passed around about the aptness of his name "Casimiro," which translates into Spanish "I almost see." Sister Mary García, a Franciscan missionary from Colorado who had worked many years in Olancho, recalls, "When we had Prelature meetings, he would always be as much as a day late and we would say 'Here comes Casi-miro.' "[27] But Father "I-almost-see" was a more than welcome addition to mission life in Gualaco. The simplicity of his life and his unpatronizing identification with the *campesinos*—farmers like himself—rapidly endeared him to them and to other missionaries.

He shared a room with Mike Gable at the mission, and the two became close friends, often staying up late at night talking, laughing, and telling stories. Casimir spent his spare time painting, whittling, or filling a notebook with poetic meditations and artistic doodles. Another diversion for him was a small garden patch that he tended in the center of the mission compound; Mike would often look up from his work and see Casimir, sloppily dressed, standing on the edge of his garden, leaning on a hoe and smoking a cigar. In a poem, "For Casimir on the Anniversary of His Death," Juanita Klapheke, another co-worker, describes this disheveled newcomer on the mission scene:

> He's not much to look at
>   this slightly balding man
>   with a bit of a paunch and baggy pants
>   dirty, dull-green t-shirt
>   three-days growth of beard on his face
>   and the stub of a cigar hanging from his mouth.
> He stands there in rapt attention to some inner voice.
>   His hands work with wood and knife
>   whittling a piece of tree
>   into some image of life.[28]

Life at the mission was not always slow-paced and serene, however. One day in particular stands out vividly from the rest. A fifteen-year-old boy had been critically wounded by a machete while chopping sugar cane in the fields; his father, after tying a dirty bandana on the arm as a tourniquet, brought the boy to Mike, who often dispensed first aid for those isolated *campesinos*. Mike stared at the mean gash that slit the boy's arm from fingers to elbow. As the blood pulsed out of the wound, Gable tried not to panic; he quickly flipped through a first aid guide he kept on hand, only to find the advice: "Call doctor immediately." But even the nearest telephone was hours away; the boy would easily bleed to death before long. The villagers were beginning to gather quietly in the doorway when Mike called for Casimir, who suggested that they kneel and pray the Our Father. Since they could offer no more physical aid, the missioner obeyed. When they finished the prayer, the bleeding had stopped. Surprised, Mike sprinkled sulfa on the wound and bound it up with gauze and tape. A little later, Mike found Casimir working in his garden; the priest looked over at him, leaned on his hoe, and said, "See, Michael, miracles still happen."

Three or four weeks after this incident, Gable saw the boy and his father down by a nearby stream. The dressing on the wound had not been changed; it was black and ugly, and Mike feared the arm was or would soon be infected. He begged the *campesino* to bring his son back to the mission to have the arm checked and cleaned, but they never did show up.[29]

Although Padre Casimiro struggled diligently with his Spanish from the moment he arrived in Honduras, he never was able to master the tongue. Sometimes his sermons seemed to evoke more amusement than inspiration. One memorable one was his homily on "Noah and the Ark." Trying to get his point across with a minimum of words, he mimicked the antics of the animals clambering up the plank to the deck of the ark. The children were soon in hysterics. And as he preached in his own incomprehensible brand of mixed Spanish and English, the *campesinos* and English-speaking missioners began to shake with laughter.[30] Casimir's "Noah and the Ark" sermon would gain enough notoriety for Klapheke also to include a reference to it in her commemorative poem:

> Casimir,
>> tell us again the story of the "Grand Barque"
>> tell us again in your broken Spanish
>> the story of a man who had to crowd all
>> those animals on his hastily built ship
> preach to us once again the homilies only you and I
>> could share because your Spanish was as bad as mine.
>> Come on, they will understand now![31]

In the spring of 1974 Casimir returned to Hermosa Beach for a visit. At that time, his friend Leonard Wibberley saw him and commented on his change in appearance:

> When he came back the first time, it was hard to recognize him. He wasn't a stocky, strong blacksmith kind of man any longer. He had lost so much weight that he looked like a rather skinny boy.
>
> "Riding a burro," he said, "it takes weight off you. I ride a burro everywhere."[32]

Ronald Olson, Cas's former instructor, who was now teaching in California, also remembers this visit:

> In 1974 he returned to California for a short rest . . . and a chance to talk up the missions. I vividly recall his visiting Bishop Montgomery High School, talking with many of the students, offering the Liturgy and sharing his simple sermons. It was powerful. He touched the students so

profoundly that a number of them wanted to join him. Some in fact did journey to Honduras that summer with Fr. Allen Ramirez and helped around the mission for about six weeks.[33]

A few months after his return to Gualaco, Casimir made a long journey by horseback to remote villages in the mountains, during which time an insect bite became seriously infected. He came back to Gualaco burning up with fever. He lost so much weight on his once stocky frame that he looked almost emaciated; he visited a clinic in Honduras, but in late 1974 it was decided that he should go back to the United States for tests and medical treatment. During the several months he spent recuperating in the United States, he visited and spent Christmas with his mother, brothers, and sisters in Medford (his father was dead), traveled to the parish he had served in Rockford, Illinois, and managed to see many of his old friends. Wozniak remembers:

> Fr. Casimir and I had long talks about his work in Honduras. He wanted to bring the love of God to these people he found so bereft of most ordinary consolations. While he saw his work as simply traveling from one small town to another, speaking and ministering to people who didn't see a priest often enough, he had a much [broader] vision of what that precise work would accomplish over several generations. . . . He was totally absorbed in making God known and loved by those to whom he went. When he had to return to the U.S. for medical tests, he was as cheerful as ever, but he worried that he might not be able to return to his people. He was very happy to find that his physical problems were not serious, and he looked forward to his return. Six months later he was dead.[34]

For Mike Gable, who by this time was living back in the United States, it was an unexpected pleasure that Casimir was now available to concelebrate his wedding in January 1975. He was also surprised, and touched, that his friend had scraped together enough money for a rather generous wedding gift. On the evening before his departure for Olancho, Cypher revealed to another friar a modest plan he hoped to put into effect upon his return to Honduras. His dream, he told Anselm, was to establish a small village made up of *campesinos* of strong faith and good will whose example of a wholesome family life would be an encouragement for other families, perhaps eventually other villages, to follow.[35]

When he arrived back in Honduras in early 1975, Casimir did not return to assist at the parish in Gualaco, but instead went alone to the tiny village of San Esteban about forty miles north. He was there only a few months when a long-awaited pickup truck was sent for his use by Catholic Relief Services. Although some mountain paths were too narrow and rocky even for the pickup, the missionaries had hoped that its arrival would make at least some of their travel easier.[36] It was indirectly because of this truck that Casimir would unwittingly play a role in the next bloody explosion over land in Olancho.

By this time, the hopes Honduran *campesinos* had once placed in López Arellano's promises of land reform were beginning to wane. An emergency measure, called Decree Number 8, had been announced on December 26, 1972, which granted peasants the use of *ejido* and national lands and forced land-owners to rent out their uncultivated holdings; this was intended as a tempo-rary measure while the government prepared a new agrarian reform law. Although the greatest percentage by far of the property affected by Decree Number 8 was national land, it had earned for López Arellano the vigorous opposition of the powerful landholders, who feared that he was indeed serious about carrying out his plan for permanent land reform.[37] Thus, in February 1973 the president of FENAGH (National Federation of Farmers and Ranch-ers) protested the decree in a letter to the Minister of Natural Resources; and in March 1974 ranchers' associations in Olancho and elsewhere joined together to issue a pronouncement against agrarian reform couched "in such angry terms that it seemed to be a declaration of war," according to Honduran historian Longino Becerra.[38] Nevertheless, López Arellano went ahead with his plan. The new Agrarian Reform Law, which was finally proclaimed in late 1974, had as its goal the distribution of 600,000 hectares of land to 120,000 *campesino* families in five years. This law was more radical than the one of 1962 since a limit of five hundred hectares was placed on most properties. However, it was fundamentally designed to encourage modern capitalistic agriculture and to put an end to the string of land occupations by peasants, and thus could hardly be called revolutionary.[39] But FENAGH did not waste any time in denouncing the law, claiming that it "attacked private property, the democratic system, liberty and individuality."[40]

It is hardly surprising that López Arellano's tenure in office would soon come to an ignominious end. In early April 1975 it was revealed in the *Wall Street Journal* that a $1.25 million bribe had been paid by United Brands (United Fruit) to a high-ranking Honduran official, who had promised in return to lower the banana tax. Although the guilty official was eventually discovered to be the Minister of Economy, López Arellano himself was forced to resign in the midst of the scandal when he refused to allow a Honduran investigating commission to examine his bank accounts. Nonetheless, some believe that the bribery scandal was merely an excuse used by the traditional power structure in Honduras and the banana monopolies to rid themselves of a regime that was bent on political, social, and economic change.[41]

With the ascension of Colonel Juan Alberto Melgar Castro to power in April 1975, there was a shift toward the right in Honduran politics. But Melgar Castro was not an ultraconservative, and the UNC felt an attempt should be made to convince the new regime of the necessity to execute López Arellano's land reform law. Poor crops and the devastating after-effects of Hurricane Fifi, which had killed 8,000 Hondurans and left 300,000 homeless in Septem-ber 1974, were contributing to the urgency of the situation. Thus, on May 18, 1975, there were again mass land occupations by hungry peasants in Olancho and elsewhere. They disbanded, however, two days later, when the military intervened and many of their leaders were arrested.[42] The UNC soon followed this up with a seizure of bridges around the country on June 13.[43] Neither of these actions produced the desired effect on Melgar Castro's regime, however. Consequently, the UNC decided to resort to a strategy that had yielded results in the past; haunted by the prospect of starvations, the union began to organize another peaceful hunger march. The plan was for thousands of peasants to converge on Tegucigalpa, as they had in 1972, in order to demand implementation of the land reform law, legal recognition for their union, and the release of *campesinos* imprisoned in the land recuperations.[44] In Juticalpa, Olancho, about eighty-five miles away from the capital, the march was scheduled to begin in the early morning hours of June 25.

While the spring of 1975 had been rather uneventful for Padre Casimiro in the remote village of San Esteban, the church in Juticalpa and Catacamas was enduring new threats and accusations. Although his ministry by this time was in marriage counseling and not in educating *campesinos*, Iván Betancur had remained outspoken when confronted by injustice. When local merchants arranged an excessive hike in the cost of basic food items, his parish in Catacamas denounced the action. The local radio station refused to transmit Iván's Sunday masses, but much more ominous were the rumors afloat that all foreign clergy would soon be expelled permanently and that the lives of the bishop and some priests were in danger.[45] Iván wrote a friend in May 1975: "The farmers and ranchers cannot bear us, especially me. . . . These days, naturally, things are more agitated and many rumors abound. There are rumors that really are impudent, rumors that are a little frightening, but we have faith that they will not be realized."[46]

Meanwhile, the day of the big march drew nearer. Bishop D'Antonio was away from Olancho; he had gone to Rome in mid-May to attend a conference on charismatic renewal in the Catholic church, and on his return had stopped off in the United States to visit his mother. Back in Olancho, Betancur was looking forward to the arrival in late June of his mother and future sister-in-law, María Elena Bolívar, from Colombia. Behind the scenes, however, sinister plans were also being formulated in Olancho, as local ranchers and military officers plotted to disrupt the *campesinos'* upcoming hunger march.[47]

By unhappy coincidence, Padre Casimiro happened to be in Juticalpa on that crucial day. He had left his parish in San Esteban the day before to bring a *campesino* in need of medical attention to San Francisco de la Paz. While driving on a rocky, unpaved road in the newly arrived pickup, he had struck a tree and damaged the truck. In order to have it repaired, he had gone on to Juticalpa and stayed over there while he waited for the pickup to be ready.

Thus, on the evening of June 24, while the *campesinos* around Olancho were busily preparing for their march the next day, Casimiro took this opportunity to pay a visit to Sister Mary García. They had coffee together and spoke briefly about the march, but, as was typical of Cypher, the complicated politics of the event did not particularly interest him, and the conversation switched to other matters. Sister Mary brought up the subject of clothes; perhaps she, like Cas's superiors in the States, was gently hinting that an improvement in his wardrobe would not make him an unworthy disciple of the original great lover of poverty, Francis of Assisi himself. Casimir laughed and said he had enough clothes to last him the rest of his life, but Sister Mary made him take some she had been saving for him anyway. The conversation, ironically enough, turned briefly to the subject of death, and then they said good-night.[48]

Around 3 o'clock the next morning, about one thousand *campesinos* left Juticalpa and began the long march to Tegucigalpa. Several who were not participating in the march stayed behind in the Centro Santa Clara. Suspecting nothing out of the ordinary, Casimir walked into town around 9:30 that morning to check on his truck and do a little shopping. But unknown to Casimir, trouble was brewing at the Center. Led by some of their teachers, schoolchildren from Juticalpa, who had been enticed by promises of candy, were holding a demonstration outside to demand that part of the *campesinos'* building be used for classroom space. A small plane was circling above; there were many soldiers present, both on foot and in vehicles. Local landowners and the school supervisor looked on from their cars. One of the teachers in the demonstration unsheathed a pistol and tried to kick down the doors and enter the building by force. While the peasants' attention was thus occupied, a group of plainclothesmen from the National Department of Investigation (DIN) swarmed in via another entrance and proceeded to surround and shoot at the *campesinos* trapped within the Center.[49]

Around this time, in all of the confusion, Casimir was detained as he passed through the Central Park. Exactly why the soldiers picked him out of the crowd and then arrested him is not known. He was wearing old work clothes, not his Franciscan habit. But he was obviously a foreigner and therefore possibly a priest; and the landholders had already made it clear that they were suspicious of foreign clergy. Some believe the troops were already on the lookout for another foreigner, a French priest named Michel Pitón, who was thought to have the keys to the Center, which at that moment was under attack. It is believed that the soldiers who detained Cypher saw his given name, "Michael," on his driver's license, and this may have convinced them that Casimir was the Padre Michel they were seeking.

Padre Casimiro, in his stumbling, heavily accented Spanish, was not able to communicate adequately. When the soldiers demanded the keys to the Center, he was confused; having lived in Gualaco and San Esteban, he was not at all familiar with *campesino* activities in Juticalpa. But no delicate distinctions were to be drawn that day anyway; "Michael" or "Casimir," activist or apolitical, it was all the same to his captors.

Inside the Center several *campesinos* and one government agent had been shot and were already either dead or dying. Several peasants were being beaten and interrogated. Others lay bleeding on the floor. Some, including a few women who were later freed, had hidden in various rooms of the building and waited in terror, expecting at any moment to be discovered and killed.[50] The captured priest was led into this nightmare.

He was questioned, and then kicked and beaten with rifles because his faltering answers were unsatisfactory. He was stripped of his clothes and insulted. According to one eyewitness, the officer in charge, Major José Enrique Chinchilla, pointed to the dead *campesinos* and told Casimir, "This is the religion that you practice and preach, a religion of hate."[51] He struck the priest in the face and cursed him. After this ordeal, he was taken, along with the *campesino* prisoners, from the Center to the jail.

In the meantime, Sister Mary García and a Honduran priest had been told of Casimir's arrest and the beatings and were trying to locate Major Chinchilla to convince him of Casimir's lack of involvement in the hunger march and to bring food to him, wherever he was being held. As they searched for the major, they saw ranchers and soldiers rushing back and forth in the streets of Juticalpa. Unable to find Chinchilla, they were eventually able to speak to another high-ranking officer, Major Díaz, when he drove by in his car. The major told them that Casimir was a prisoner because the problems in Olancho were due to the instigation of foreign religious and that all foreigners had to be arrested. He looked at Sister Mary and said, "You too, Sister." The Honduran priest pleaded for Cypher, "But Father Casimiro lives in San Esteban and it was just by accident that he was in town. He doesn't even know what it's all about." Díaz said he would see what could be done for him and drove off. Sister Mary was immediately arrested by a soldier nearby and taken off to jail.[52] Without a doubt, those in authority realized by this time that the priest they had in custody was not the Father Michel they were looking for. But Casimir could serve their purpose just as well, which was, through intimidation and fear, to suppress the church's work on behalf of the *campesinos*.

Unaware of the turbulence in Olancho, Iván Betancur was driving from Tegucigalpa to Juticalpa, chatting happily with his prospective sister-in-law, María Elena, and with Ruth García, a Honduran university student. His mother and María Elena had recently flown in from Colombia for their visit. That morning, Iván had left Mrs. Betancur in the capital to fly the next day to Juticalpa, thinking the car trip too arduous for an elderly woman. Betancur, María Elena, and Ruth had then set out by car on the long trip to Juticalpa.

Along the way, Padre Iván stopped in Campamento and was warned by nuns that Juticalpa was under military control. Nevertheless, he decided to continue in that direction. Some distance later, Iván stopped at a sawmill for gasoline, and there realized the gravity of the situation when he saw mobilized troops and some men he knew to be hostile. At this point he tried to turn back; racing along the road in his car, he was chased by two vehicles and was soon overtaken. He and the two young women were forced to return to the sawmill. There they were held till nightfall when they were conducted to an hacienda called "Los Horcones" ("The Pitchforks") owned by Manuel "Mel" Zelaya.[53]

Late that night in Juticalpa, Casimir and five *campesino* leaders were selected from the thirty-two arrested during that day's confrontation. The six men were tied up and then brought in their underwear by pickup truck to Los

Horcones. A full account of what then occurred is not known. Some say Iván's tongue was cut off and his teeth pulled out; others believe the women were raped and the two priests castrated. A few facts have come to light, however: Padre Iván was tortured in some way to obtain his confession on tape that he had engaged in "subversive activities"; later, an autopsy performed in Colombia at the request of his family revealed that he had in fact been castrated.[54] According to court records, the *campesinos* and the two women and priests were brought one at a time into a room in the hacienda to be interrogated, and in the early morning hours of June 26 all nine were executed.[55] They had probably endured torture. Their bodies were thrown into a deep well at the hacienda, which was then dynamited to hide any clues. Evidence still existed, however, for the well was only partially concealed, and Iván's car was a silent testimonial to the deeds. Therefore, a tractor was used to move earth over the well, and Betancur's car was doused with gasoline and set on fire.

On June 26, confusion and fear reigned in Olancho. Those who had set out the day before on the march had been stopped in their tracks by soldiers, fortunately without any bloodshed, and were returning to Juticalpa. But five of the *campesino* leaders arrested at the Centro Santa Clara had mysteriously disappeared from the jail the night before; their anguished families feared the worst. And where were Iván and Casimir? María Elena and Ruth? Mrs. Betancur had arrived in Juticalpa as scheduled the morning of the 26th, but her son had not met her at the airfield; she had made her way to the cathedral to wait for him, and there she sat, bewildered and frightened by the turmoil around her. Sister Mary García and other church personnel, under armed guard, were flown to San Pedro Sula, where they were questioned and placed under house arrest. Their house in Juticalpa had been raided, and money, a tape recorder, and camera had been stolen. On the afternoon of the 26th, four priests who had been held overnight in jail were driven in an open truck to the Juticalpa airport. While the priests waited to be transported to the capital for interrogation, local ranchers gathered to taunt them and call for their expulsion from the country. Meanwhile, in the United States, Bishop D'Antonio was stunned and nearly fainted when he received word of the attack on the Center and the disappearance of Iván and Casimir. He later learned that his own residence in Juticalpa had been ransacked and that wealthy landowners, finding the bishop unavailable for execution, had placed a $5,000 (10,000 *lempira*) price upon his head.[56]

And Olancho was not the only province affected. On June 25 marchers from all over the country had been stopped by soldiers and turned back. In the departments of Yoro and Choluteca, where the Catholic church had also worked closely with the peasants, foreign nuns, priests, and seminarians were rounded up, arrested, and sent to San Pedro Sula or Tegucigalpa for interrogation; several were expelled from the country. Human promotion centers and church-affiliated radio stations were also closed down.[57]

In Olancho, word was put out by the military that those who were missing had escaped from jail, that the law-abiding soldiers had been ordered not to shoot them as they fled, and that Padre Casimiro himself had been seen in various places engaged in subversive activities. In an attempt to distract public attention, alarmist reports appeared in local newspapers: "600 men flee to the mountains; an outbreak of guerrilla activity is feared. Army prepared to safeguard order."[58]

No one was convinced by these lies. Word that something terrible had occurred in Olancho circulated throughout the nation; demands for an investigation were made by students and friends of Ruth García at the University of Honduras and by the Catholic hierarchy and religious workers; and the Colombian and U.S. embassies wanted an explanation for the mysterious disappearance of their citizens. The government under Colonel Juan Melgar Castro reluctantly complied.

After five days of intense excavation at Los Horcones, the tortured and mutilated bodies—and the grim truth—finally came to light on July 18, three weeks after the murders took place. Casimir had not fled to the hills and joined a guerrilla group; what was left of him was discovered at the bottom of a 120-foot well.

Father Michael "Casimir" Cypher was buried on July 20, 1975, inside the church of Gualaco, his first parish in Olancho. On a "next of kin" form Cypher had completed a few months earlier he had written: "I intend to be working in a parish or at least living in a friary and it is my wish that I be buried in the same town in which I die. I want no more for my burial than a pauper. If you have to spend money, then have a party and thank God for my death."[59] His family respected his wishes and the body was never returned to Wisconsin. Among his few effects were found his art supplies and a notebook filled with simple meditations, stories, poems, and drawings.

Soon after his death, Casimir's mother, seventy-four years old, tried to reconcile herself to the tragedy: "I just hope that he didn't die in vain. I guess he wasn't the one they were looking for; but someone had to be the one."[60]

The day Padre Casimiro was buried in Gualaco was also planned as a day of mourning for the massacre victims by the entire Catholic church in Honduras. It so happened that on that day the wealthy ranchers and farmers were meeting in Comayagua for their annual reunion. At the conclusion of this meeting, FENAGH, the landowners' federation, issued a statement in which they tried to exonerate themselves from the recent events in Olancho:

> FENAGH deplores the events that occurred in Olancho, which have saddened Honduran families, deepening the class struggle and creating an atmosphere of anxiety and anarchy.
>
> "Love one another," Christ said. "Hate one another," preaches our clergy. The lack of Honduran priests has necessitated the importing of foreigners for the propagation of the Catholic faith but this circumstance must not justify the interference of foreign clergy in the socio-political affairs of the country, since the action of the church ought to be directed

toward a search for harmony and concord among Hondurans and not to sponsor class hatred.[61]

Juan Antonio Zambrano, the treasurer of the Olancho Cattle Farmers Association, went even further; interviewed by a reporter for the *New York Times*, he claimed the massacre was the result of "the political agitation by priests and Christian Democrats, and behind them, Communists. . . . If the Bishop [D'Antonio] and his agitators return, we won't be responsible for the consequences."[62] Thus, less than a month after the brutal incident occurred, the ranchers had made their view clear that it was the clergy themselves who were to be blamed for the tragedy.

Nevertheless, on July 23, 1975, a special Military Commission charged with investigating the events stated that FENAGH was indeed implicated. Moreover, the commission revealed that the brutal deeds were not mere impetuous reactions, but were in fact the result of a carefully planned plot involving FENAGH and elements of the business sector "to create a climate of chaos and confrontation in the department of Olancho and other parts of the nation." A cover-up had also been attempted: the commission found that Major Chinchilla, with the backing of Mel Zelaya and AGAO (Olancho Cattle Farmers Association), had attempted to bribe a journalist in order to deflect public opinion from the reality of the deeds that had occurred in Olancho. Four men were specifically named in the report as being responsible for the Olancho murders: Two were military men—Major José Enrique Chinchilla and Lieutenant Benjamín Plata—and two were wealthy landholders—José Manuel Zelaya and Carlos Bahr.[63] Although the commission was careful not to implicate the ruling regime of Colonel Melgar Castro, the fact that there had been a simultaneous nationwide round-up and interrogation of clergy and religious the day of the march and a prohibition of autopsies on the victims found in the well is a dubious claim to innocence.[64]

There was an initial outcry made by the U.S. embassy in Tegucigalpa and promises made by the State Department to the Conventual Franciscan Order and to Casimir's friends Michael and Kathy Gable that the U.S. "Embassy and Department of State will continue to follow this case very closely and to make our views known to the Government of Honduras as strongly as possible."[65] On July 22, 1975, the Colombian government withdrew its ambassador from Honduras;[66] the United States, however, protested the execution of one of its citizens merely with harsh words. Frustrated at the lack of action on the part of the United States, the head of the Franciscan province that sponsored the Olancho mission, Father Lawrence Mattingly, wrote to President Gerald Ford:

While the details of [Cypher's] death are sketchy, we are deeply disturbed by the fact that little, if any, diplomatic action has been taken by our State Department to determine what precipitated this horror. When the murder of an American citizen on foreign soil, particularly one who literally gave his life for the people he served, can be treated with such apparent indifference by his government, then the values that fashion that government become very questionable indeed. His life cannot be restored, but a firm application by you of the principles for which he gave his life—such as justice—can greatly help to insure that such a tragedy does not happen again.

We are not men of vengeance, yet our deep concern for the safety of our remaining confrere in Honduras, Father William F. (Emil) Cook, prompts us to urge you to use every peaceful means at the disposal of your Office to bring about a political and economic climate in that troubled land that will minimize the possibilities for a recurrence of such needless bloodletting. Your expressed concern for the well-being of all Americans is valid only if it is a concern for the well-being of each individual American.[67]

The pursuit of justice lapsed with the passage of time. The four men named in the Military Commission's report were imprisoned; but the two civilians, Carlos Bahr and Mel Zelaya, used their considerable economic resources to spend their days in jail enjoying every comfort from home. Moreover, Zelaya was chauffered home to Juticalpa often to spend extended weekends with his family.[68] In February 1978 the two military men, Major Chinchilla and Lieutenant Plata, were found guilty and sentenced, although at his trial Chinchilla had claimed he had only acted on orders from his superiors.[69] Mel Zelaya, at whose ranch the inhuman deeds occurred, who had been explicitly named by the commission as one of those directly responsible for the murders and as the one who had supplied the murder weapon,[70] would be a free man. But the travesty continued, for in September 1980, the perpetrators of the Horcones massacre were freed by a general amnesty promulgated by the National Constituent Assembly. Conveniently, the Supreme Court had earlier condemned them of "homicide," not "assassination," thus making them eligible for a future amnesty. Numerous organizations indignantly protested this action, but to no avail.[71] No real attempt had been made therefore to curtail the power of Honduran landowners or to end the repression of *campesinos* and churchworkers.

The Franciscan Fathers of Hartland, Wisconsin, could perhaps have predicted this outcome. On August 2, 1975, saddened by the inexplicable murder of a fellow friar, they had sent the following telegram to the Honduran ambassador in Washington:

YOUR PROTECTION AND INTEREST IN UNITED STATES CIVILIANS IN HONDURAS LEAVES MUCH TO BE DESIRED ESPECIALLY IN REGARDS TO THE MURDER OF FATHER CASIMIR CYPHER OBVIOUSLY BUSINESS INTERESTS ARE MORE IMPORTANT THAN HUMAN LIVES

–FRANCISCAN FATHERS[72]

The response by the ambassador five days later was an early indication of the indifferent path that justice would take in Honduras to punish Casimir's murderers:

Dear Fathers and Brothers in Christ:

Your message of vehement protest for the terrible murder of the late Padre Casimiro and other innocent and good people that lost their lives fighting spiritually for social justice in Honduras and particularly in Olancho, is also condemned by me, by the Government and by the people of Honduras, who represent 80-90% of Roman Catholics, as you well know. Our Lord Jesus Christ was also fighting and struggling for social justice 2000 years ago and was crucified for it. The Lord did not talk then of vengeance, but of love, when He said: "Forgive them for they do not know what they do."

You would do better following His teachings and steps. Give love and understanding rather than hatred and vengeance.

Yours sincerely in Christ,

Dr. Roberto Lazarus
Ambassador[73]

Padre Casimiro is still remembered in Juticalpa, Gualaco, and San Esteban. Years after his death, Franciscan friars visiting Olancho from the United States have found his picture in the homes of many peasants and have watched *campesinos* place flowers at his grave. A large cross was erected to the memory of all the men and women who died on June 25–26, 1975, but this memorial was destroyed by the landowners.[74] There is now a cement monument in Juticalpa bearing the names of the fourteen *Martires del Pueblo* (martyrs of the people); this number includes the nine victims of Los Horcones as well as the five *campesinos* who died when the peasants' Center was attacked. Besides María Elena, Ruth, Iván, and Casimiro, those executed were Alejandro Figueroa, Juan Benito Montoya, Oscar Ovidio Ortiz, Arnulfo Gómez, Fausto Cruz, Francisco Colindres, Lincoln Coleman, Roque R. Andrade, Máximo Aguilera, and Bernardo Rivera.

Casimir Cypher had been all but oblivious to the politcal issues at stake in Honduras; yet ironically, he would be the first of eleven North American missionaries linked by violent death to thousands of Central American victims of repression. Working in Olancho only a few months, still struggling to learn Spanish, and with his dream of founding a village of faith-filled *campesinos* untried, Casimir was murdered before his full potential as a missionary had a chance to unfold.

James "Guadalupe" Carney

2

James "Guadalupe" Carney

Jesuit Missionary

Casimir Cypher was the first North American missionary killed while working in Central America; Father James "Guadalupe" Carney was the most recent. Both died in the department of Olancho; both had worked closely with poor and isolated *campesinos*. But Carney, by the time of his death at the age of fifty-eight, had served in Central America for two decades and had become somewhat of a legend in Honduras. Whereas Cypher was an uncomplicated man who steered clear of political matters, Carney was driven to strive for justice as an ardent participant in the struggle for land reform; and this dedication would transform him into a "revolutionary" priest—a Christian Marxist.

Carney tells the story of this transformation in a six-hundred-page manuscript that he gave to his sister and brother-in-law the Thanksgiving before he was killed. He called his autobiography "The Metamorphosis of a Revolutionary," but it has since been published under the title *To Be a Revolutionary*, taken from a quotation of his: "To be a Christian is to be a revolutionary."[1] In it he describes with straightforward clarity his "metamorphosis" from a Jesuit who once believed "that for loving the poor it was enough to . . . share their life with them, be present among them as a witness of Christ, . . . without getting involved in politics, without criticizing or denouncing the injustices that they suffer,"[2] into a revolutionary, a man who would one day join a small group of Honduran guerrillas as their chaplain.

On October 28, 1924, James Francis Carney was born in Chicago, the third child and first son of Joseph Carney and Catherine Hanley Carney; the arrival of four more children eventually completed the family. The Carneys moved about the Midwest for several years, living in Dayton and Toledo, Ohio, before settling down in Saint Louis, Missouri, in 1941.

Joseph and Catherine placed a strong emphasis on their children's spiritual development. The family said the rosary every night, and the parents were willing to make nearly any sacrifice in order to have their five daughters and two sons educated in Catholic schools. In those years of strict fasting before communion, the Carneys would wrap all the faucets the night before one of the children made his or her first communion, so that no one, particularly the first communicant, would accidentally be unable to receive. The two Carney boys, Jim and Pat, were only seventeen months apart in age; both were altar boys and were often invited by the nuns to assist at the liturgies in the convent. The boys had what Pat describes as a "very moral reputation" among their classmates.[3]

As a toddler, Jim had been somewhat sickly, and his mother once told Pat that Jim had exercised ever since she could remember to build up his strength. As a result of his preoccupation with weight-lifting, bike-riding, wrestling, and football, Jim was a well-rounded, fiercely competitive athlete. Although as a senior he was one of the best players on Saint Louis University High's football team, he was unable to compete because he did not satisfy the one-year residency requirement. He did, however, earn a scholarship to play football at Saint Louis University.

Like many young men at this time, Jim's college years were interrupted by war, and he soon found himself serving in the Army Corps of Engineers rather than studying and playing football at Saint Louis University. In Marseilles, France, he worked in camps where he came into contact with Moslems who were refugees from the North African theater of war. Perhaps because of this contact, one of Jim's favorite spiritual models in later life was Charles de Foucald, a nobleman in the French army and renowned explorer of North Africa, who eventually embraced a life of extreme voluntary poverty, living in austerity among African Moslems. De Foucauld, although he lived in peace and was respected by most Moslems, died a violent death at the hands of a small band of Senusite Moslems in 1916. Carney retained a lifetime devotion to this martyr, stating that one of the three books that most influenced him in his spiritual development was de Foucald's *In the Heart of the Masses.*[4]

After the war, Jim returned home and made plans to study civil engineering at the University of Detroit. Before settling down to study, however, Jim, along with his brother Pat and a friend from Saint Louis, spent a month during the summer tamping railroad ties and doing construction work in Minnesota.[5] Always attracted to the outdoors and perhaps somewhat restless after the excitement of his wartime experiences, it was Jim's idea to make their summer a real adventure by roughing it as much as possible. They traveled all over Minnesota by hopping freight trains; in order to find out which train was going where, they simply approached a railroad yardman, who would usually be very helpful, even giving them warnings so they would not be discovered. To pass the time in the boxcars, Jim would pull out his harmonica and the others would join in singing.

But not everyone was as sympathetic as the yardmen. Jim was frequently stopped and questioned by the FBI; after a few of these inexplicable incidents, they finally asked an agent the reason for this and were told that Jim, with his crew-cut, steel-rimmed glasses, and army duffle-bag slung over his shoulder, looked suspicious. The fact that he wore his old army fatigues and usually needed a shave probably also contributed to the agents' uneasiness. Perhaps the authorities would not have been so wary if they had seen that the young men, after hopping off the freight car, would head for the nearest Catholic church to find out when morning mass was, for Jim saw to it that the threesome attended mass and communion every day.

With the money Jim and Pat earned in Minnesota, they decided to extend their summer adventure into California, where an army buddy of Jim's lived. They wired most of their Minnesota earnings to California, and set out with only about ten dollars apiece in their pockets; this would force them to continue roughing it as they made their way half-way across the country. As a result, Pat says, "We were hungry a lot . . . and waited long periods of time for a ride." They often accepted free meals from those who gave them rides or subsisted on grapes and oranges. Sometimes they were picked up by the police for sleeping in parks or hotel lobbies and were escorted to the local jail to pass the rest of the night. They arrived in California in the rumble seat of a convertible, sunburned and sick because of the 120 degree heat of the Mojave Desert but still enchanted by the magnificent scenery. Although they spent very little time visiting Jim's friend, Pat managed to lose not only all of his own money, but also his brother's, to the "one-armed bandits" in Las Vegas. They had to swallow their pride and wire home for money to take the train back to Missouri. But it had been a vagabond summer, full of camaraderie, one that led Pat to reflect after his brother's death, "wherever Jim was, there was adventure and a certain romance."[6]

That fall, Jim began his studies in engineering at the University of Detroit, a Jesuit college. There Jim remained for two years during a most crucial time in his life. Working as an unskilled laborer in a Ford assembly plant to help with college expenses, he began to worry that he could not possibly spend his life tied down to a salaried job. Moreover, even though he still went to daily mass and communion, his philosophy courses at the university were stirring up some serious doubts about the existence of God. His inner turmoil and sense of restlessness were enhanced by the fact that he had fallen in love—with Colleen, a dark-haired, green-eyed beauty, who was the product of a strict Irish-Catholic upbringing; Jim writes:

> After a few months I obtained her consent to kiss her on the lips, but that is as far as our sexual activity went. I was twenty-three years old and certainly wanted to enjoy full sexual pleasure, but especially with Colleen, who was so pure, I would not give myself the pleasure of even thinking of sinning with her. Both of us, indeed, were thinking about marriage; we were deeply in love.
>
> . . . But I did not really want to get married; I wanted to wander through the world looking for God, helping the poor. I was afraid of getting married and losing my freedom to go around the world having

new adventures. If I married, I thought, I would have to be an engineer to take care of Colleen and the twelve kids we would undoubtedly have. I did not want to be an engineer; it appeared to me now as slavery, like being in a prison, working every day for a salary. I had to go around looking for God, getting to know other parts of the world.[7]

So, with this in mind Jim resolved to become a Jesuit missionary. If he later found that his search for God was in vain, he could always leave the Jesuits and marry someone else, for he realized he would lose Colleen in the process.

Colleen responded to his plans with tears, but Jim was eventually to thank God "for the crisis that he sent me, the doubts about his existence that made me consider him, God, the most important thing in the world—which is exactly what he is."[8]

In August 1948, at the age of twenty-four, he began thirteen years of rigorous spiritual and intellectual training to prepare him for the Jesuit priesthood. The life of discipline offered by the order appealed to Jim, and he later told his brother that he would have chosen it even if it had not led to the priesthood.[9] When he began to suffer severe headaches during his first year of training, however, he sometimes blamed them on the strict demands placed on the seminarians. But, determined not to leave, he learned to cope, once in a while by bending the rules.

Jim was able to continue some aspects of his beloved outdoor life as a seminarian. He participated in all types of sports; in fact, he was frequently spoken of as the best all-around athlete among the Jesuits. He went on long walks with other seminarians, often on all-day hikes and swims if it was allowed, and sometimes when it wasn't. One misadventure, involving a swim across the dangerous Missouri River and a long walk and hitch-hike back to the seminary that caused him to be seven hours late for lunch, nearly got him thrown out of the Society of Jesus just one week before taking vows.[10]

During his years of Jesuit training, Jim managed to maneuver his way in the direction that appealed most to him—a life among the poor as a missionary. When the opportunity came for him to travel to British Honduras (now Belize) as part of his training, he asked for permission and received it. He spent the years 1955 through 1958 there teaching English and elocution at Saint John's College, and—more to his liking—working with the Ketchi Indians and poverty-stricken blacks. After his return to the United States and three years of theology at Saint Mary's College in Kansas, Jim was ordained a priest on June 15, 1961.

He went immediately to Honduras during the summer of 1961, but had to return to the United States for one more year of theology. Finally, in 1962, Jim Carney, now thirty-eight years old, began his new life in Honduras, a country that had attracted his interest for years. When Carney arrived there, he found ubiquitous poverty in a tropical land broken by mountains and hills. The country then supported a sparse population of only about 2.2 million, mostly peasants who subsisted by farming meager plots of land. Primitive agricultural methods prevailed; only one-quarter of these *campesinos* even farmed with a plow. And they often watched their babies die before the age of five, for their country had one of the highest infant mortality rates in the world. In the rural areas where priests were scarce half the couples living together had not been formally married.[11] Not surprisingly, the Honduran *campesinos*, although nominally Roman Catholic, were not particularly religious, and the most isolated ones never saw a priest regularly.[12]

But hope was in the air. On the international level, U.S. President John Kennedy and Pope John XXIII were awakening interest in the area. Kennedy's Alliance for Progress had called for extraordinary socioeconomic development in Latin America over the next decade: $100 billion—$20 billion from the United States and the rest from Latin American sources—was to be invested in the region, while the various participating countries were expected to legislate land and tax reform. Too, Pope John had stirred the Catholic church with his call for an ecumenical council, Vatican II; and the church's views on social justice were evolving from a preoccupation with paternalism to a more active identification with the poor. In the United States in 1961, the hierarchy had taken its cue from the urgent words of Pope John and had called for volunteers to become missionaries among their poor neighbors living in Central America. And in Honduras, the church was growing more aware of the peasant whose existence was a virtual enslavement to hunger, suffering, ignorance and the whims of the elite.

Unfortunately, though, the Alliance did not achieve the desired economic goals or long-range social reform. Instead, the investments served to increase the profits of the United States companies and Honduras's already wealthy landholders. These relatively few ranchers and farmers began to expand their lands to raise more cattle for foreign markets and to grow more commercial export crops. How did they acquire these new lands?

> The investment boom in commercial agriculture (especially in cattle and cotton) . . . led to an illegal expansion of large haciendas over peasant-tilled lands. The oligarchs' agents simply strung barbed wire around the area they wanted, then expelled any families found inside the barbed-wire compound. Peasants who tried to take wood from these areas to cook food were jailed on order of the new owner.[13]

The alliance thus aggravated the land problem and worsened the uneven distribution of wealth in Honduras (as well as in other countries). Another ominous development that had begun with the U.S. training programs of the 1950s and continued under the alliance was the growth of the "autonomous and virtually supreme" Honduran army, which in 1957 had been permitted by the constitution to disobey a presidential order that military leaders considered unconstitutional.[14] One year after Carney arrived in Honduras, he would be witness to the brutal consequences of the military's increasing strength, as Colonel López Arellano overthrew President Villeda Morales in October 1963 and hundreds of Villeda's Civil Guard, many of them unarmed and asleep in their barracks, were slain.[15]

Upon his arrival in Honduras, Carney went to Minas de Oro in the department of Comayagua for a few months, where he became known as "Padre Guadalupe." He chose this name because, among the Jesuits in Honduras, there were already a "Padre Santiago" and "Brother Jaime," the Spanish translations of "James," but also because of his long-standing devotion to Our Lady of Guadalupe. After a few months in Minas de Oro, Carney was transferred to the department of Yoro, where over the years, he would work in many different parishes and towns.

The enthusiastic newcomer envisioned a better future for the *campesinos* with whom he began to work: One day, through much labor and sacrifice, they would have enough food to eat, health care, schools, a bit of land. Carney later described the impoverished conditions in which rural Hondurans lived—the same conditions he had seen as a young priest and wanted so much to alleviate:

The houses of the great majority of the Honduran *campesinos* . . . [have] dirt floors, roofs of leaves, . . . walls of sticks or cane. . . . There is only one room, six meters long and five meters wide. Generally there is a little kitchen apart, or if not, the earthen stove for firewood has to fit in one of the corners of the house. Perhaps there are two or three rope beds or canvas cots in which up to maybe eight children and their parents must sleep. One teenager might sleep in a hammock. I am describing all of this for those who may not be aware of the life of the poor in Central America.

The food of the greater part of this people consists of rice, beans, corn tortillas, and coffee three times a day. They eat a tiny bit of meat in soup or a little bit of cheese. . . .

As for illiteracy, as in every branch of development, Honduras has been the worst of all Latin American countries, with the exception of Haiti which is even worse. Officially, 55% of the Hondurans in 1965 were illiterate and now, in 1981, they say that it has fallen to 45%, but [in] the mountain villages 90% of the adult *campesinos* do not know how to read or write.[16]

Carney also was astonished at the low salaries of *campesinos*. In 1965, a man earned just seventy-five cents for an eight-hour day of hard manual labor under a hot sun; and often the task was aggravated by the worker's malnutrition and anemia.[17] While he was deeply concerned with their spiritual welfare, Carney also began to work toward the physical improvement of the peasants' lives as well.

As he worked with the Honduran *campesinos* his identification with them grew. Wearing the coarse cotton shirt of the peasant, old khaki pants and worn shoes, he traveled the paths to hundreds of isolated villages on foot, or by mule, horse, motorcycle, or jeep. He existed on meager, monotonous fare, slept on dirt floors, washed in the streams, and learned to cope with snakes, scorpions, and rats, like the *campesinos* did. His memoirs testify to why a middle-class, well-educated North American priest would choose hardship, insecurity, and austerity rather than the comfortable life that would have been his had he remained in his native land:

There were some things in the Gospels that I began to understand in the novitiate: especially that Jesus was one of the poor masses of the world. The meditations on the birth of Jesus in a stable were an enlightenment of the Holy Spirit for me. God freely chose His mother; He chose a poor *campesino* girl. He wanted to be one of the poor. That I clearly saw in the Gospels. I also understood right from the novitiate that to be a disciple of Christ, one has to sell all that he has, give it to the poor, and follow the poor Jesus, becoming one of the poor also, identifying yourself with the poor, incarnating yourself in the poor.[18]

Guadalupe would not allow his religious beliefs to dissipate into a sentimental convenience:

If I love the Honduran poor, the *campesinos* especially, I have to share their life as much as possible. I do not want to eat better than they, for example. For me, to follow Christ in poverty means to be completely dependent on God's Providence, trust completely in Him to take care of us. . . . I don't want social security, or life insurance, or savings in the bank, or medical attention in the U.S.A. when I get sick, etc.[19]

His single-mindedness in attempting to live the gospel would lead one fellow missionary to comment that working with him "was like being with Jesus Christ."[20]

In 1964 he began work at a parish in El Progreso in the department of Yoro. There, in January 1965, after studying how Maryknoll priests in Peru were training village catechists to lead bible services, he and two other Jesuits introduced a new form of religious celebration for the villages that, because of Honduras's chronic shortage of priests, rarely saw a priest. They called these services "Sunday celebrations" and began to teach about fifty literate *campesinos* how to lead their communities in prayer, bible readings, and song every Sunday a priest was not present. Later that year, Canadian priests in southern Honduras developed a better system and called their apostolic leaders "Delegates of the Word of God" and their Sunday gatherings "Celebrations of the Word of God." The Jesuits in Yoro adopted the new terminology and booklets. Gradually, Delegates were trained for all the more isolated parishes of Honduras; indeed, the method seems to have spread from Honduras to the rest of Central America, Panama, and Mexico.[21]

It was also in El Progreso that Carney began to acquire his reputation as an outspoken champion of justice, as he immersed himself in an agrarian controversy and at the same time emerged in the national spotlight.

As was mentioned above, peasants, particularly after 1963, were often evicted from the lands they were cultivating by powerful landholders with dubious legal claims. In May 1966, a dispute between *campesinos* and landowners heated up in an area known as Las Guanchías. About twelve thousand peasants lived on the contested lands, which had been rented by the Tela Railroad Company (United Fruit) from the powerful Bográn family. The *campesinos* had been planting their cornfields there for years, since the Tela had abandoned the land; and the thirteen peasant villages of Las Guanchías, organized into ANACH (National Association of Honduran Peasants), had a copy of a decree by a past Honduran president granting them these lands for family farms.

When the rental contract between the Tela Railroad company and the Bográns was not renewed in 1966, the family sold about half of the land to a wealthy Colombian to use for growing bananas; they planned to use the rest of the land for raising cattle. The *campesinos* would simply have to leave the fields they had already planted with corn and beans. But without land they would starve. Carney spoke out in favor of the peasants from two of the villages involved, El 4 de Marzo and El Socorro, in a meeting called to discuss the issue. In the presence of landowner Luis Bográn Paredes, representatives of the National Agrarian Institute (INA), and armed soldiers, Carney said it was unjust to evict the *campesinos* from the land they had occupied for years and that taking the land away from peasants was no way to carry out land reform.[22] Shocked at the gringo padre's audacity, Luis Bogán told the press "that come what may [*the campesinos*] had to abandon their villages and settle on a [much smaller] piece of land, . . . and that he was going to send a telegram to the Archbishop of Tegucigalpa informing him that the parish priest of El Progreso was a communist, and that he could back up his accusation since he had the support of the Armed Forces."[23]

Carney's intervention in the matter caused such an uproar in the national press that the villagers of El 4 de Marzo and El Socorro were not evicted. Before long the newspaper *La Prensa* noted that the Bográn family was demanding "an intense investigation into the background of this upstart priest."[24] But still Carney refused to back down; and on several occasions, he bluntly confronted Luis Bográn Fortín, another member of this influential family:

> I spoke several times with him at his great cattle ranch called "El Rancho," in Guanchías, but he did not like it when I told him that he loved his cows more than his *campesino* brothers, that he was giving food to his cattle, [while] taking it from the peasants, [and] that every economist was saying that the ranch ought to be located on the mountainsides and that the good lands of the valley ought to be used for farming.[25]

But the peasants of El Socorro never forgot that Padre Guadalupe had spoken out for them. After Carney's death in 1983, Father Fernando Bandeira wrote to the family:

The idea of the people of Socorro of rebuilding [the church] seems very good to us as homage to Padre Guadalupe. There it was where he began his struggle to gain the lands for the *campesinos*. The idea is to be able to do it with the assistance of other peasants and that it may remain as the church remembrance of Padre Guadalupe. The cement blocks which they [are using] Lupe bought them ten years ago. . . . [26]

The little church would be called "Our Lady of Guadalupe."

In the midst of the controversy between Carney and the Bográns, ANACH came to his defense in a press release. Thus began a fourteen-year period of close association between Carney and this important *campesino* union. ANACH had been founded in 1962 in an attempt to draw strength from the original peasants' union, the radical FENACH (National Federation of Honduran Peasants). ANACH had the backing of the U.S. AFL-CIO's Latin American offshoot, ORIT (Inter-American Regional Organization of Labor), and AIFLD (American Institute for Free Labor Development). At first ANACH provided conservative support for the government in rural areas. However, it later inherited members from the more militant FENACH, which had been repressed by the state, and by the mid-1960s ANACH had become more aggressive in its demands for change. The 1962 Agrarian Reform Law of Villeda Morales had remained on the books, although the INA after López Arellano's coup did little to enforce it from 1963 to 1967. But in 1967, López appointed a more progressive official, Rigoberto Sandoval, to head the agrarian institute, and it was under him—partly due to pressures from ANACH—that land reform began to inch forward in the late 1960s, as the peasants' land occupations, "recuperations," increased. At this time, too, INA began to make the formation of *campesinos* into cooperatives the basis for granting land to them. In spite of these steps, though, most peasant claims continued to be turned down; moreover, the cooperatives formed in order to obtain land were organized into still another peasant organization, FECORAH, which was favored by the Honduran state in an attempt to weaken the more aggressive ANACH and UNC.[27]

Carney took on his work with ANACH in addition to his parish ministry. He spent long hours organizing agricultural and consumer cooperatives; and over the years he would help establish more than a hundred agricultural and sixty consumer co-ops. He encouraged *campesinos* to save ten cents a week, pool their resources and purchase land; he also arranged for them to meet every week to study cooperativism and often accompanied them as a witness in their effort to occupy and recuperate land.[28]

In one case, Carney went straight to the top and wrote to the general manager of the United Fruit Company in Boston concerning the plight of four *campesino* villages in a region called Guaymas. They wanted to buy 850 acres of the company's land to start a cooperative, Carney explained, but the company's general manager in Honduras had turned down their request. The executive in Boston also refused, but on second thought, consented to the plan a few months later. The reason for this about-face, Carney later learned, was that United Fruit had heard about his work with ANACH and also about the newspaper controversy surrounding his run-in with the Bográn family in Las Guanchías and feared that these four villages and many others would invade the contested lands if United Fruit proved too inflexible.[29]

In another case, Carney organized an entire village, which joined ANACH in order to demand the return of their communal lands. The landowner who had taken the land tried to scare off the *campesinos* and Padre Guadalupe with hired gunmen. Many of the villagers gave up the battle because of these threats, but in the end about thirty of the villagers did receive land, although only a fraction of what was rightfully theirs.[30]

Carney was threatened with physical harm on many an occasion by agitated landowners and was often warned by *campesinos* to stay away from certain areas where known thugs awaited him. But in the struggles for land, Carney was moved more by the suffering of the peasants than by fears for his own safety. In May 1967, the family of a local ANACH leader, a woman, was attacked while eating supper in their home. She, her husband, and one son were wounded; two of her other sons were killed. At the gravesite Guadalupe reflected on the fact that the same gunmen who had killed the two young men had also threatened him, yet he was still alive.

> Now, with this funeral, I was completely sure that I wanted to give my life for the poor *campesinos*, so that no more of them would be killed in the class struggle. I strongly felt that Christ would grant me this great grace of being a martyr for the sake of justice. I felt completely committed to identifying myself with the *campesinos* in their fight for land.[31]

Such encounters with death and even with the hardships Honduran peasants endured in their day-to-day existence made visits back to the United States difficult for Carney. On these trips, especially in the early years, Jim experienced a kind of culture shock and often found it painful to witness the relative comfort and wealth in which his family and most North Americans lived in comparison to the misery of his Honduran friends. At first he was somewhat blunt about this and unintentionally offended his family; if this was pointed out to him, though, it would trouble him deeply. As Pat puts it: "There never was any doubt about where Jim stood on things. If he had not been so genuine, he would have antagonized almost everyone."[32] But there are more fond memories of Jim's visits than otherwise. He would play the harmonica and guitar as his nieces and nephews gathered around, and he was particularly helpful in getting spiritual messages across to them during the confusing teen years. His own spirituality was evident: he often would retire to his room for hours to read and meditate, and would rise at 5 A.M. to pray before saying mass. Although he used ear plugs when he slept, the slightest noise at night could wake him, and he would thus spend this time in prayer as well. His family also grew in concern for the Central American poor through Jim and remembers the prayer he always added to the grace before meals: "Lord, have mercy on those who are hungry all over the world."[33]

By the late 1960s, Honduran *campesinos* were even worse off than in 1962 when Carney arrived. Many had lost to powerful ranchers the small plots of land they once had; unemployment had jumped 25 percent between 1961 and 1967 (and this figure did not include seasonally employed coffee workers); and labor and welfare programs begun by Villeda Morales had been put on the back burner by López Arellano.[34] In 1968, the level of hardship rose even further when the government levied a high (10 to 30 percent) tax on many consumer items. The tax hit the poor hardest. Alarmed by a strike that was called to protest the unfair tax, López Arellano jailed union leaders, announced a thirty-day state of siege to eliminate "subversion," and cracked down on newspapers and editors. Although he had just returned from visiting family in the United States and had had no role whatever in organizing the strike, Carney was arrested as a "subversive agitator" by the secret police, who deported him to Guatemala, a dangerous place for a man with Carney's views.[35] However, a sympathetic American ambassador, Joseph John Jova, protested to the Honduran government and ensured Carney's immediate return. After the Jesuit superior in Tegucigalpa sent him a letter of thanks, Jova responded in a letter, "I am an admirer not only of the Society of Jesus, but also of the work that Padre Guadalupe is carrying out."[36]

In 1969 while Carney was working in Toyos, a tiny town north of Progreso, a tragic accident occurred, in which Carney was indirectly involved. For several years the tension over land in nearby Guanchías had persisted, and at this time *campesinos* in ANACH began to occupy the lands of a wealthy man from El Progreso. Carney had been attempting to organize the peasants into cooperatives but was not actually a witness to these particular land recuperations. Nevertheless, the landowner from El Progreso told a nun that he held Carney to blame for the occupations and that he kept a bullet in his pistol at all times "to put into the mouth of this communist priest." Events took an ironic turn, however. One day while the gentleman was out of town, his two teenaged sons and some companions found the gun in a drawer and proceeded to play Russian roulette, leaving one bullet in the cylinder. The man's younger son pointed the pistol at his brother's head and slowly pulled the trigger. The bullet entered his older brother's mouth and came out the back of his head, killing him instantly. The other boy then collapsed at the sight of his brother's limp body.

Carney happened to be visiting in El Progreso that day and, being the only available priest, went to comfort the family. When he arrived, the father was crying, slumped over next to his son's body, and the younger son was recovering in the hospital. Carney tried to console the sobbing man as best he could. The irony was not lost on either the landowner or Carney that the bullet meant for the priest's mouth had wound up in the mouth of the son. Carney later heard that this landowner experienced a spiritual conversion as a result of this tragedy and became "a friend of the poor *campesinos*," although he retained his land and business interests.[37]

Carney's love of justice brought him that same year into yet another controversy. This time, in a Sunday sermon, he came to the defense of Salvadoran *campesinos* living in Honduras, who were being evicted from their homes by soldiers and often beaten or raped in the process. It was unimportant to Guadalupe that it was a very inopportune time for him to be criticizing Hondurans for mistreating Salvadorans, for this was the year of the so-called "Soccer War" between El Salvador and Honduras. Tensions over land scarcity in tiny, heavily populated El Salvador had gradually caused thousands of Salvadorans to slip over the Honduran border. But, as we have seen, competition for land in Honduras was increasing dramatically in the 1960s. The landowners' organization, FENAGH, had complained that Salvadoran immigrants were the ones responsible for the peasants' land seizures and growing militancy. These accusations were one of many reasons for the "Soccer War" of 1969, during which Honduras was humiliated by the occupation on its soil of Salvadoran troops. Nevertheless, El Salvador was forced to allow thousands of its citizens to re-enter their homeland. At this time, the level of patriotic fervor naturally rose in Honduras, and for Carney to criticize the maltreatment and expulsion of Salvadorans earned him the temporary label of "anti-Honduran."[38]

In 1970 Padre Guadalupe was transferred to Sulaco, but because the conservative priest he was to have replaced refused at first to relinquish his post, Carney spent five months laboring in nearby Yorito. There, as ever, he continued working with ANACH in the struggle for land, but also became involved in organizing the Hicaque Indians. He succeeded in bringing a good part of the tribes into ANACH, hoping to aid these poor and down-trodden native Hondurans in regaining some of their ancient lands, which had by now become the cattle ranches or coffee plantations of wealthy landowners.[39]

It is becoming evident that controversy followed this Jesuit from Missouri wherever he went. If he was not defending Honduran *campesinos*, he was speaking out for the rights of Salvadoran immigrants or demanding justice for all but forgotten Indian tribes. It is perhaps tempting to dismiss his actions as a perverse desire to agitate Honduran society, or even as an attempt to gain the national spotlight. But the memoirs of this man reveal a dedication of mind and soul that could only be found in one who sincerely tried to follow the difficult path his religious faith set forth for him:

My spiritual life is firmly founded on the solid rock of being sure that God exists. I believe this not only because God has to exist as the magnificent architect of the universe; but I believe this because I have experienced God and because I continually feel the presence within me of a Father who loves me and of the Spirit of Jesus who directs me. . . .

My favorite prayer, one that I have sent to many of my friends, was written by Foucauld when he lived alone among the pagan *bedouin* in the African desert about fifty years ago: "Father, I abandon myself into Your hands. Do with me whatever You want. For whatever You do, I thank You. I am ready for, I accept, all. Let only Your will be done in me and in all your creatures. And I'll ask nothing else, my Lord. Into Your hands I commend my soul; I give it to You, Lord, with the love of my heart. For I love You, my God, and so need to give, to surrender myself unto Your hands, with a trust beyond all measure, because You are my Father."[40]

But his life among the poor in Central America caused him to reinterpret that prayer to include his understanding of the meaning of his own existence:

During all these first years of my Jesuit life I had the idea of Charles de Foucauld, that for loving the poor it was enough to just be one of them, share their life with them, be present among them as a witness of Christ, helping them in their sicknesses, etc., without getting involved in politics, without criticizing or denouncing the injustices that they suffer. Later on I learned that a Jesuit has to love his neighbor more efficaciously. . . .

If I love a poor person, I'll help him get out of his poverty; if I love a sick person, I'll help him find a cure: not just give him a tranquilizer, but go to the cause of the sickness in order to completely get rid of it. In the Spiritual Exercises of St. Ignatius a Jesuit learns that he should use all the means necessary to achieve the goal. And so, for a Jesuit to love the poor, he has to do all he can to help eliminate the poverty of the poor masses of the world.[41]

Perhaps the compelling drive behind Padre Guadalupe's relentless pursuit of justice is best outlined in his description of his love for the poor—and his hatred for the forces that keep them that way:

I'm really a lover, even though I often don't act like it. I love people, all kinds of people. Also I'm a contemplative. My greatest joy is to contemplate what God's loving Providence does in this world, especially in people I meet or read about and in my own life. I think I sincerely love the poor, not only out of pity for what they are forced to suffer and out of rebellion against the system that forces them to be poor, but as lovable persons in themselves, as bits of God, of Christ. . . . To love Christ really is to try to live as He lived. If I love the poor as Christ did, I, too, freely choose to become one with them, live with them, share their lives, besides trying to use my talents to help and teach them. . . . He freely chose to become one of the masses of poor people of the world, of the eighty percent of the world who "have not," rejecting the comfortable life of the twenty percent who "have" (even though he loved them too).

And he tore into the system and those that held the masses in the bondage of ignorance and poverty. He cursed them, and said "Woe to you hypocrites, you priests, and to you rich, and to you who are honored and accepted by the world." And he was killed for it. To be killed for my following of Christ would be my greatest joy too. . . .

But besides this great driving force of love . . . the other great driving force in my life is hate. I hate injustice, and I hate hypocrisy. . . . I hate the bourgeois, American way of life, keeping up with the Joneses, the sophisticated cocktail party, Playboy Club, comfort-seeking "Great Society." I hate the way blacks, Indians, dark-skinned foreigners are treated and kept marginated. I hate the way the United States tries to control all the countries of the world, and world trade, for its own benefit, trying to export our materialistic way of life to other countries. I hate and resent the way the rich and middle-class Americans *and* Hondurans can live in big, comfortable houses, have cars, land, and education, while my brothers and sisters, the poor, are forced to live as they do. . . . I don't hate the "haves," but I hate the system that not only allows but forces society to be made up of the "haves" and the "have-nots." . . . This hatred . . . is a driving force in my life that *makes* me do many things that I do, like go live in another country, by myself, risk my life, be looked down upon, misunderstood, considered kind of crazy. But what can I do? I feel moved by the Holy Spirit in all the important decisions I make.[42]

Between 1973 and his downfall in 1975, President López Arellano allowed Carney to continue his work with peasants without being harassed. This, of course, was during López's reformist period, when he was turning over lands to *campesinos* on a temporary basis, while striving to enact a plan for permanent land reform. Moreover, in 1973, López Arellano, the same military strongman who had tried to deport Carney in 1968, actually conferred on him Honduran citizenship. For ten years Carney had been requesting permission from his order to become a naturalized Honduran. Finally, with this permission and with the help of a Christian Democratic lawyer, his application was approved by the Honduran state, although the staff at the U.S. embassy tried to dissuade him from taking this unusual step. But, as Guadalupe explained it, he wanted the privilege of being a Honduran in order to become one of the world's poor, as Christ had been, and to fight side by side with the peasants for liberation; he also felt he would be more effective in the struggle for justice in Honduras as a citizen of that country.[43]

It was also during this time—after 1973—that Carney's "metamorphosis" finally ended, and he became what he termed a Christian Marxist. His transition from a traditional priest, however, had begun much earlier. In his autobiography he relates that when he had first come to Honduras, he, like most missionaries, was unable to see the oppression of the poor caused by multinational companies. Indeed, U.S. missionaries saw the United Fruit Company as their ally since it allowed them to travel on its ships without charge. Yet Carney also noticed that the U.S. priests not only made little headway in proselytizing the Honduran poor, but were actually often resented by them. Eventually he came to realize why:

> Most of them [the banana workers] are completely indifferent to religion. . . . After the strike [of 1954] many more of them became anticlerical. . . . The priests lost their golden opportunity to win over the workers when they did not back them up in the strike, and did not openly denounce the transnational banana company for its exploitation of the workers and repression of the incipient labor union.
>
> Instead of preaching against the injustices of the U.S. company, they preached against the dangers of communist infiltration in the unions. So once again religion served (unconsciously, perhaps) to justify the repression of the workers, to support the capitalist system of exploitation.[44]

Priests saw themselves as dispensers of the sacraments, not as advocates of social justice, and for this reason they actually sanctioned the oppressive status quo without meaning to do so. Carney had begun to understand this in the early 1960s while serving in Yoro:

> The pastor there put great pastoral emphasis on the Eucharist, on daily visits to the Blessed Sacrament, and on receiving Holy Communion. We even had to carry a hand counter with us as we gave out communion in order to mark down the number on a sheet after mass. . . . As if this were the sign of Christianity in a person! As if this should be the apostolic, pastoral priority in Honduras!
>
> I now recognize that this was an alienating kind of religion. . . . The parish of Yoro was (and still is) one of the regions of Honduras where the *campesinos* and workers are the most exploited and least organized to defend themselves. . . . Big landowners live in Yoro and control everything that happens in the region. All the military and other local authorities obey them. . . . They used to receive Holy Communion every Sunday; they liked the religion of Jesus in the Blessed Sacrament, because it legitimized their lifestyle, soothed their consciences and *made them feel Christian without having to act Christian.*[45]

He noticed that the pastor also remained silent when the large landowners fenced in the lands of the Hicaque Indians residing within the boundaries of his parish and forced them off the land. Instead, the priest and his parishioners prided themselves on helping the "poor little Indians" by giving them food and used clothing. Carney felt anger at the hypocrisy of the church-attending landowners and concluded that the missionaries needed to redirect their priorities. It was still unclear to him, however, how this should be done: "I still did not know how to analyze Honduran society to recognize the social sins," he relates in his autobiography. "We only denounced the personal sins, which also were abundant, of drunkenness and living in concubinage, of having a family without getting married." He did realize, however, that the church, to be more effective, had to identify with the poor. Consequently, when his new pastor decided to paint and remodel the rectory, Padre Guadalupe suggested that instead they move into a smaller, poorer house not unlike those of the majority of the people of Yoro. Not only did the pastor disagree, he also became quite angry as Carney persisted in his view.[46]

This was only one of many times when Guadalupe insisted that U.S. missionaries identify with the poor, only to infuriate his fellow Jesuits as well as other priests and missionaries. One such episode proved extremely humorous—at least for the uncompromising Jesuit. Carney learned that the School Sisters of Notre Dame, who operated a girls' high school in El Progreso, had decided that they needed a swimming pool:

> I heard that one of our Brothers was going to build them a private swimming pool, not for the students, but for the nuns, in the large yard behind their convent. The cost would be twenty-four thousand dollars. . . .
>
> I was scandalized and unbelieving, and so I went to ask Sister Superior if it was true. She admitted it but added that I had no right to stick my nose in her affairs. I told her that, like Christ, I had to denounce sin and try to save people from their sins. I said that building a swimming pool for the sisters' recreation here in Honduras where most of the people did not even have enough to eat would be a mortal sin. I told her to look through the window at the poor shacks in which their neighbors lived . . . and asked her if she was not ashamed to live here in this residence that was their convent and high school. . . .
>
> When the Brother was just finishing the Notre Dame swimming pool and before they filled it with water, I went up to the big cement block wall around the pool and cursed the pool, asking God to destroy it, not to let it ever be used. . . . When they filled the pool with water for the first time, the bottom of it split, the water ran out, and the black sewage waters of Progreso seeped up into the pool. How I rejoiced, and how I praised our God who can play such a joke! It makes no difference that afterward, with another sinful waste of a large sum of money, they fixed the pool. . . . Everyone knew that the pool was cursed and that God did not want it. Today this swimming pool is never used, and many of the sisters wish it had never been built.[47]

Guadalupe not only noticed that few priests and nuns were willing to share a life of poverty with the Honduran majority, to say nothing of actively working with them for justice, he saw moreover that those who did struggle for social change seemed most often to be Marxists—adherents of an ideology he had been taught to despise.

I started to read . . . all the books I could find about Marxism. . . . My contacts with Marxist worker and *campesino* leaders were slowly stripping me of my prejudices and leaving me, rather, with an admiration for the Marxists who struggled for justice. They had more courage and, it seemed to me, more love for the poor than most Christians. . . . My metamorphosis was advancing by means of my struggle for the poor.[48]

When, as a result of the Second Vatican Council and the Latin American bishops' conferences at Medellín and Puebla, the church declared its "option for the poor," Carney was pleased. He soon concluded, however, that the church had not gone far enough.

Some of my American Jesuit brothers are an example of how most bishops and priests interpret this "option for the poor": loving them, serving them, spending their time and money for them with housing projects, Radio Schools, health clinics, and so on. They try to alleviate their miserable poverty, helping a few of them to overcome their poverty by means of a good high school education that will assure them a good-paying job. My hope is that they would also enter into conflict with the *exploiting system* that produces so many poor people. At times they fearlessly denounce the injustices against some poor persons, but they do not attack the root cause of these injustices and of the poverty. They are reformists, developmentalists.[49]

To Padre Guadalupe, the church was deficient because it refused to side with the poor class against the rich, hoping instead to be friends to all:

The great majority of the bishops and priests still want to be on good terms with everyone, with the rich and with the poor, with the oppressed and with the oppressors. They want to avoid this conflict, or class struggle; they do not want to choose one class against the other. That means that their option is for the status quo. This is the same as choosing the social class that is in power, the bourgeoisie, the exploiters, against the exploited class. Christ did not try to be on good terms with everyone. He plainly made his choice for the oppressed class and was killed by the oppressors.[50]

Yet Carney had always been a pacifist, an admirer of the methods of Mahatma Gandhi and Martin Luther King, Jr.; as such he had problems with Marx's assertion that only through violent revolution could meaningful social change become a reality. An event in another Latin American country in 1973, however, caused him to alter his views and complete his development into a Marxist:

But what caused the biggest leap forward in my metamorphosis . . . was the military coup d'état in Chile, with the murder of Allende and tens of thousands of "leftists" by the army, and the later revelations of the dominant role that the U.S. embassy in Chile, the CIA, and the transnational U.S. companies, like ITT, played in all this before and during the coup. The U.S. economic blockade, the CIA's fomenting of the counterrevolution inside of Chile, spending hundreds of millions of dollars for this, and the fact that Allende did not control the whole army made it impossible to carry out the Chilean revolution peacefully, following the rules of bourgeois democracy. . . .

I now seriously doubted that the nonviolent methods of Gandhi, of pacifism, of active resistance, of civil disobedience, of peaceful mass demonstrations, could change the capitalist system and liberate a country from imperialism. After the bloody military coup of 1973 in Chile, *it was obvious that the United States would never allow a country that is economically dependent on it to make a revolution by means of elections*—through the democratic process directed by the majority—at least as long as the country has an army that obeys the capitalist bourgeoisie of the country.[51]

To Carney, CIA involvement in the Chilean coup was only the latest evidence that the United States would not allow peaceful democratic change in Latin America: "The intervention of the CIA to overthrow the revolutionary military officers in Peru, and the invasion by the U.S. marines . . . to brutally smash the popular revolutionary insurrection in the Dominican Republic in 1965 were other obvious proofs confirming the Marxist-Leninist theses."[52] Padre Guadalupe nevertheless realized that most U.S. citizens would find his conclusions incomprehensible. Thus, he writes in his memoirs:

It is hard for North Americans to understand, much less appreciate my continual condemnation of capitalism. This is because few North Americans have personally experienced the cruel, oppressive, "19th century" capitalism of the third world, where workers live in economic slavery, where the rich landowners often value the *campesinos* as only cheap arms and legs, necessary inconveniences for production and profit.

It is also hard for North Americans to listen when I attack "yankee imperialism" but most North Americans seldom see the faces of the men, women, and children in the third world who are cruelly exploited by the multinational corporations. These giant organizations look for cheap land, cheap resources, cheap help. They want a stable environment (most often enforced by fascist military dictatorships) where safety regulations are few or nonexistent, where consumer products (medicines, pesticides, etc.) are tested without accountability for human and environmental consequences. And always enforcing this capitalistic and imperialistic exploitation is power, the economic, political, and especially military power of the United States, one of the strongest nations in history.[53]

Although now a Marxist, Carney was certainly no defender of such oppressive regimes as that of Soviet Russia:

> Socialist and communist systems have "institutionalized sin" at times, as when the party or state takes too much power from the workers, when human rights are not respected, when religious freedom is denied. People need to work, fight, and die for liberation from the injustices of these systems even as they do against raw capitalism. The concentration of power in the state in socialism or communism has in itself a danger that people begin to exist for the party and state rather than the party and state existing for the people. Such corrupted socialist and communist states also become imperialistic. A good example is Stalin's Russia. . . .
>
> We Christian revolutionaries dream of a socialist society in Honduras unlike any society presently existing in the world, "a quantitively [sic] distinct society." We do not want to copy the model of the Soviet Union, China, Cuba, or any other country. We want to create a socialism, fully true to Christ's teachings, born in and of Central America for Central Americans.[54]

But for Padre Guadalupe, Marxism alone—as a self-contained, total ideology—was insufficient.

> For me, Marxism explains a lot, but needs the Christian vision to complete it. It explains the world already made, but it does not explain where it came from, why it exists and evolves as it does, where the laws of dialectical evolution came from; it needs metaphysics.
>
> Marx rejected religion and God because he correctly concluded that religion has historically at times been used as an "opium of the people," an ideological instrument of the exploiting minority to help dominate and control the exploited masses. . . .
>
> Thanks partially to the Marxist criticism of religion, the Holy Spirit has finally been able to lead many present-day Christians to an under-standing of the gospel of Christ as the "good news for the poor" about their liberation from the yoke of exploitation. Only in recent years has the understanding of the teachings of Christ . . . evolved sufficiently to enable us to arrive at a renewed understanding of the gospel (with help from modern science) regarding the salvation and the transformation of this world into the Kingdom of God.[55]

In 1976, Padre Guadalupe was transferred to Saint Isidore Parish in Tocoa, in the Aguan Valley. His close collaboration continued with ANACH, but Carney, along with many of the union members, became disenchanted with

ANACH's president of long-standing, Reyes Rodríguez Arévalo, who was widely believed to be corrupt. They therefore threw their support behind another man. In October 1978 when it became apparent to Carney that the union's recent re-election of Rodríguez had been fraudulent, he wrote a public letter to "all the honest *campesinos* of the ANACH" explaining his position:

> After fourteen years of struggling side by side with you in the ANACH with all my heart, this year for the first time I did not go to the National Convention of the ANACH to ask for God's blessing, because I knew that there was going to be more foul play than ever. Before the convention, I heard that some of the delegates to the convention were being influenced by agents paid with money from AIFLD, from the U.S. embassy, and from the CIA (the U.S. spy agency). I also imagined that the army would intervene to assure the victory of the candidate that the U.S. embassy wanted. . . . [56]

These were not idle accusations. Philip Agee, former CIA agent and author of *Inside the Company: CIA Diary*, describes AIFLD as being "CIA-controlled"; and others besides Carney mention the considerable influence exercised by AIFLD on ANACH.[57]

Once again, Carney's forthright words incurred the disapproval of those in power, and once again he was expelled from the country, this time for good. Decree Number 360 of the governing junta of General Policarpo Paz García accused Carney of "propagating dissociative doctrines and ideas," and, referring to the priest's letter of October 1978, the decree claimed that he "embarrasses the North American Government and its accredited Embassy."[58] Thus, in November 1979, Carney was called in by Honduran immigration officials. He was stripped of his hard-won Honduran citizenship; he was handcuffed, brought to the airport, and locked in a closet for several hours before he was put on an airplane bound for Miami.

The reaction to Guadalupe's expulsion was widespread. Hondurans, from peasants to bishops to students, protested the government's arbitrary action. The Episcopal Conference of Honduras stated:

> We profoundly lament this mode of procedure of condemning a man without a hearing and without giving him an opportunity to defend himself. We believe that such a proceeding goes against one of the principal and basic norms of all law, recognized in our Constitution when it says: "The right to defense is inviolable" (Article 57). The very least we can do is denounce this action and present our formal protest. Contrary to all that might be claimed, actions of this nature do nothing to help the tranquility of the country, something which we ardently desire.[59]

The bishop and clergy in the diocese of Santa Rosa de Copán came to the much stronger conclusion that anyone who mistreats a priest is immediately excommunicated ipso facto and this includes the "intellectual authors of such maltreatment," a comment which set off a nationwide debate over whether or not Paz García, the military junta, and police agents involved were all excommunicated from the church.[60] The Jesuits also issued a public communication condemning the action of the military government and demanding that Carney be allowed to return to Honduras to defend himself against the charges.[61]

While bishops and priests were making formal declarations of protest, students, laborers, and *campesinos* in at least forty-seven church organizations and fifty-three popular organizations were denouncing the regime's action in newspapers nationwide.[62] A group of peasants occupied the Cathedral of Tegucigalpa and demanded that Carney be allowed to return to Honduras. The "Ballad of Padre Guadalupe" was written and sung in many churches all over Honduras:

> Out of pain I am going to sing about a prophet
> Who was thrown into exile in handcuffs by the soldiers.
> Even bullets will not keep me quiet.

> His dream was of liberty,
> Of living together in communal life.
> He followed in the footsteps of Christ;
> He was always ready to carry the cross.
> Guadalupe is a fighting man who listens to the poor.
> He is poor with the *campesino*,
>   living the destiny of the working man.
> He confronted the bought-off leaders and was persecuted . . .

> Padre Lupe, you have left our land,
> Ejected by those beasts.
> You are exiled as are all the valiant
> Who raise high their heads in the face of oppression.
> And we are ever conscious of your love of the people.
> (Refrain): That's enough, that's enough,
>   That's enough of death and lying
>   That's enough, that's enough,
>   Is the cry of the land.[63]

One Honduran commentary declared:

The powerful in Honduras today are correct in viewing Padre Guadalupe as a dangerous enemy, because of his preaching and even more so because of his example; because of him many people in Honduras believe that "the *campesino* of today is not like the *campesino* of yesterday." We are assisting at the birth of a new man, whose prototype will not be determined by exterior appearances but by his character, by his knowledge and not by his possessions. Today in Honduras there is a Padre Guadalupe in each *campesino*, in each worker, student or committed professional.

It is in vain for the regime or for those who have manipulated this affair to believe that the expulsion of Padre Guadalupe has resolved the problem. The causes of the injustices have not gone away with him; they remain with us.[64]

There was one positive result of Carney's expulsion; Dr. Ramón Custodio López, head of the Committee for the Defense of Human Rights in Honduras, has stated that a major inspiration for his founding of this organization was the forced exile of James Carney in 1979.[65]

Back in the States, Carney was touched by the demonstrations of support given him by those he had tried so hard to help in Honduras and was also grateful to his fellow Jesuits for their warm understanding:

My dear brother Jesuits,

I feel very humble and unworthy, and very grateful for the many magnificent demonstrations of solidarity and affection of so many people and popular organizations of Honduras, but principally for the friendship of you, my dear brother Jesuits. I am appreciating more and more how wonderful is this brotherhood we have, called the Society of Jesus. Also here in the U.S. I have received such affection and comprehension from the Jesuits that it has left me confused. I just finished my Retreat here in Jesuit Hall of St. Louis University, during which I meditated on Luke 15 and felt just like the prodigal son who returned . . . after so long an absence, and instead of being criticized and questioned about this lack of contact, I was embraced and feasted. . . . [66]

But the support that touched him most was the simple protest of five Hicaque Indian tribes:

Meeting together in Subirana, we representative members of the Tribes of Subirana, Tablón, Mataderos, Las Vegas de Tepemechín, and Santa Marta, asked ourselves why it would be that Padre Guadalupe was expelled from here? We are not in agreement with this. Padre Guadalupe is the only one who has our confidence and has backed us up in everything, and we need him.[67]

At this time, Carney obtained a U.S. passport and in early 1980 began a new phase of his life. Exiled from the country he loved, he spent the next three and a half years in Ocotal and San Juan de Limay in Nicaragua, and there endeared himself to the peasants, just as he once had to those in Honduras. After his death, many Nicaraguans expressed their grief at the loss of a man whom they had come to love as a brother. Some *campesinos* recalled how shocked and embarrassed they were when Padre Guadalupe first began to visit their "old, poor houses" that had never seen a priest before.[68] But he quickly made it obvious that he was used to dirt floors and happy with meals of beans and tortillas. The testimonial of the community of El Horno is typical of the bond of friendship that grew during these few years:

> Before Padre Guadalupe came to this community, it was in sad shape; but from the time he began to form our Base Community we saw a great change. We remember how he instructed us to prepare our children to receive their First Communion. We remember how he would take his food, principally in the houses of the lowly, because it was not to his liking to eat in the houses of the rich. We remember how he was so caring with the poor people and with the children. . . . [69]

And a woman, Dona Tránsito, recalled:

> Lupe always fought for justice, and he was our brother, most sincere. In our eyes Lupe has not died. His word will always be present to our people. He was a symbol of unity. He had patience when he came to our simple homes. He was a Jesus, who came to live with us for a time.[70]

Nevertheless, Carney was apparently a deeply troubled man in Nicaragua. Frustrated at being banished from Honduras, he never relinquished the hope that he would some day return. He often seemed preoccupied; one time he even proposed to a startled church committee that midnight mass on Christmas Eve be moved up to eight o'clock. He spent many reclusive hours in his small hut outside of town, where some discovered that he worked at unusual times; never a deep sleeper, he would nap in the evening, work in the middle of the night, then catch some sleep in the pre-dawn hours.[71]

There were probably many hidden battles being waged within this middle-aged priest. For one thing, he was busy writing his autobiography; recording his memories of past struggles in Honduras intensified an already strong desire to return to his adopted land and see through at least some of the projects he had left there. Yet he had no means at his disposal to overturn the decision that had sent him into exile. Even more frustrating was his inability to communicate effectively with and to lead the peasants he had left behind.

Moreover, Father Carney had arrived in Nicaragua at an exciting time—only a few months after the Sandinistas had overthrown the dictator Somoza and his National Guard; and Guadalupe was impressed by the strides being made by the young Sandinista government to better the lives of Nicaraguan *campesinos*. They had more food and better health care, and illiteracy was being tackled and conquered. Carney was convinced that his prayer for dignity for the Central American *campesino* was being answered in Nicaragua, but only because the oppressed had been willing to fight and die to overthrow their oppressors. He likewise felt certain that the time was right for the peasants and workers of Honduras to follow the Nicaraguan lead. If he had any lingering doubts that Christianity prohibited one from embracing revolution when all other attempts to achieve a just system had failed, the Nicaraguan revolution terminated them.

As he sat in his primitive hut laboring over his autobiography by candlelight and pondering his future, Carney was well aware that Honduras was being increasingly militarized by the United States. Carney vehemently opposed the U.S. military buildup in Honduras and used very forceful language condemning it in his Christmas message to the Honduran people, broadcast on December 23, 1982, via Radio Venceremos, the clandestine Salvadoran guerrilla station:

> Honduras now is a country surrendered and completely supervised: It is under the control of the Department of State of the United States. The Armed Forces are directly under the direction now of the "military advisors" of North America and their helpers. . . .
>
> . . . I call upon all true Christians, and all Honduran patriots, to unite themselves, without distinction of social class or ideology, . . . for the liberation of our country from Yanqui imperialism, as the revolutionaries speak of it.
>
> We cannot permit our Honduran Armed Forces to help the somocista ex-Guards [contras] against the people of Nicaragua, nor to help the governments and armies of El Salvador and Guatemala in their genocide against their own peoples.[72]

It is not surprising that one effect of this militarization on a country like Honduras, which had just held elections in 1981 after a decade of military rule, was an increase in human rights violations. As described by Leyda Barbieri in a statement before Congress, Honduras's military regimes, unlike those in El Salvador, Guatemala, and Somoza's Nicaragua, had been relatively "benign"; yet "since 1981, reports of torture, clandestine cemeteries and jails, extrajudicial killings and disappearances have increased."[73] Guadalupe, while in Nicaragua, kept himself up-to-date on developments in Honduras: "Every day I get filled with sorrow and anger to hear of the brutal repression, torture, and murder of more and more leaders of the popular organizations by the police, or by paramilitary squads who are secretly under the police."[74] The following story, told by Guadalupe's friend, Father Fausto Milla, relates one such case:

> Take the case of . . . a married man with three children. He was a magnificent man who worked intensely in the Celebration of the Word and, as a practical Christian, worked also in *campesino* organizations, trying to unite the people and get them moving to improve their situation. . . . After I was myself kidnapped, there was in my parish a

demonstration of solidarity and protest. This man was one of the leaders. He and the other leaders were subsequently kidnapped by the army or the police. I call it "kidnapping," because there is no judicial warrant, no charge, and seldom any witness to the arrest. This man was tortured until he had suffered the equivalent of many deaths. His head was stuck to the floor by his own coagulated blood. . . . Then he was taken to a clandestine jail in Tegucigalpa, the capital. His companions there said that from that basement no one ever emerged alive. . . . He did not want to believe that he was to die there, but the police convinced him when, before the eyes of the cellmates, they tortured a child to death. This is the DNI [security police]. . . . [T]he DNI is the perfect death squad! It was his first night, he thinks, that they took out three men who never returned. . . . Some two or three days later, . . . my friend heard his name called. . . . From the door he was pulled by the hair to the interrogator's office. That was his salvation. The interrogator discovered in the questioning that my friend was a relative of his, and, without saying anything, resolved to free him. . . . The details of this case are so monstrous that they are almost incredible. When I heard him tell his story, he trembled from head to foot.[75]

Carney, by the end of 1982, had resolved to return to Honduras even though to do so was illegal and dangerous. When his sister and brother-in-law, Eileen and Joe Connolly, visited him then in Nicaragua, he informed them that he would eventually cross the border; he further told them what they should do if he were killed.

It was not until mid-July of 1983 that he finally entered Honduras with a tiny band of Honduran guerrillas. Before he left, Carney handed over to his friend Fausto Milla, who was living at that time in Managua, his U.S. passport and also his few possessions—a chasuble, his mission crucifix, and the earplugs he used to help him sleep. Later, in an interview with Bob Adams of the *St. Louis Post-Dispatch*, Milla tried to explain the thinking of Padre Guadalupe:

He was a great enemy of war. But he was very much convinced that the legal and civic channels of change were worthless. One thing I can assure you: Even though he might have accompanied guerrillas, he never got any military training or handled any guns. . . .

When he was faced with two kinds of violence—one, the violence of repression and poverty, and two, an armed insurrection—he preferred the second as the lesser evil. At least it promised a better life in the future. . . .

He was a man of very strong convictions. He had a very large heart toward the people. And he had an advanced vision of Christianity—one that sometimes scandalized the bishops.[76]

Padre Guadalupe resigned from the Jesuits a few weeks before he joined the revolutionaries. He remained a priest, however; it was in fact as their chaplain that he joined the band. Carney had often said that since 90 percent of all Central American guerrillas are Catholic, they too are entitled to have priests to give them the sacraments and to help them reflect on their lives in combat, just as the soldiers fighting for governments in power have historically had. The dangers inherent in joining this expedition were not a matter of concern to Guadalupe.

> Since my novitiate, I have asked Christ for the Grace to be able to imitate him, even to martyrdom, to the giving of my life, to being killed for the cause of Christ. And I strongly believe that Christ might give me this tremendous Grace to become a martyr for justice.[77]

The ninety-six-member guerrilla band, led by José María Reyes Mata, was actually doomed from the moment it crossed the border into Honduras; whether Carney suspected this or not is not known. There they would be in the presence of four armies: the Honduran and U.S. armies, as well as Nicaraguan contras and Salvadoran troops being trained by the American army. In less than a month two guerrilla deserters informed Honduran troops of the whereabouts of Reyes Mata's band; the guerrillas therefore split up into two groups. Several skirmishes ensued; and a few weeks later thirty-eight guerrillas, including their leader, were said either to have been killed in the fighting or to have perished by starvation. The guerrilla "menace" had been destroyed.[78]

The official story released by Honduran army officers was that Father James "Guadalupe" Carney and nine others had starved to death when the Honduran army cut off the food supply to the guerrilla band. His corpse was not provided, but at a press conference, held on September 19, 1983, vestments, a wooden chalice and Bible, and a pair of sandals—all said to belong to the priest—were displayed.[79]

Immediate skepticism—on the part of the Jesuit Superior in Honduras, journalists, friends, and especially the Carney family—greeted the announcement of Padre Guadalupe's alleged death by starvation. Where was the body of Padre Guadalupe? Why was the family not permitted to interview the prisoner who had told Honduran army officers of the priest's slow death by starvation in the jungle? Why, indeed, was the army so certain that the priest was dead, if Carney's body had not been located and the army had only the testimony of a captured guerrilla? In fact, why would Father Carney have starved to death: he was known to have been in excellent health when he left Nicaragua, was rugged, well disciplined, and so familiar with the Honduran countryside that, as his sister Eileen said, "he knew every berry."[80]

With regard to the vestments, it was claimed that they had been buried in an arms cache, but they were not damp or musty; Jesuit Superior José María Tojeira believes it ridiculous to think that the priest would have buried his vestments—he would have had them with him to the end. And why, he questions, would Carney have suddenly begun wearing sandals, which are not really suitable to the Honduran terrain, when for twenty years he had worn sturdy black oxfords?[81]

The Honduran army's press conference seemed to many observers to be merely an elaborate show. The editor of the San Pedro Sula newspaper *Tiempo* was called and invited to attend the conference in Olancho around 2 P.M. on September 18; that would have been several hours *before* the battle occurred in which the guerrilla leader Reyes Mata supposedly died.[82] Nonetheless, the main purpose of the conference was to announce the death of Reyes Mata and the resulting defeat of the revolutionary band. Moreover, although Reyes Mata's body was said to be beyond recovery in the jungle, somehow photographs had been taken of his corpse. (It has since become generally suspected in Olancho that Reyes Mata's body was never revealed because he did not die in battle on September 18, but had been captured alive and horribly tortured prior to that date; this prevailing conception is based on the fact that Honduran workers in early September had seen Reyes Mata brought under guard to El Aguacate air base.)[83]

When members of the Carney family spoke to U.S. embassy officials in Tegucigalpa about these inconsistencies in the Honduran story of their brother's death, they were asked if they would keep confidential any information revealed to them. They refused to agree to this, and were then given the questionable Honduran version.[84] Believing that U.S. officials had no intention of assisting them in pursuing the truth about Guadalupe's death, the Carney family decided to conduct their own investigation. They made several trips to Honduras and other Central American countries, where they were aided by human rights advocates and churchworkers; they later stated that they had evidence that their brother had been captured by the Honduran army, that he was subsequently interrogated and perhaps tortured, then executed, probably on September 16, 1983.[85]

These findings of the family were corroborated several years later by Florencio Caballero, a former sergeant in Honduran Army intelligence. Caballero reported to the *New York Times* in May 1987 that the "Honduran Army high command maintained a network of secret jails, special interrogators and kidnapping teams who detained and killed nearly 200 suspected leftists between 1980 and 1984." The group was trained and advised by the CIA, which had access to the clandestine jails, as well as "to written reports summarizing the interrogation of suspected leftists."[86] The ex-sergeant added that several rebels including Father Carney had been captured by the Honduran military and turned over to his unit.

Hoping to uncover more information on their brother's fate, two members of the Carney family questioned Caballero themselves in mid-1987. The Honduran then revealed that he had been present at a meeting that was held to plan the military operation which would eventually defeat Reyes Mata and his guerrilla band. According to Caballero, General Gustavo Alvarez Martínez, then the commander of the Honduran armed forces, told the group, "When you capture Guadalupe or Reyes Mata, kill them after interrogation." Also present at this meeting were U.S. personnel.

Caballero confirmed that Guadalupe had indeed been captured, alive, although in a weakened condition. The little band of guerrillas had surrendered quickly without a battle when confronted by the superior firepower of the Honduran army. As for Guadalupe, said Caballero, "His weapon was his bible." He then went on to say that he himself had not been present at the priest's interrogation and execution, but some of his ex-comrades had been. One had joked about how Carney, after being tortured, had knelt, extended his arms in the form of a cross, and forgave those who were about to execute him. Others in Caballero's unit had then taken the priest off in a helicopter. As the aircraft hovered near the Río Patuca, the soldiers attempted to throw Carney from the chopper. Guadalupe struggled with his captors, but in vain. He was then hurled, alive, to meet death on the mountainside below.[87]

James "Guadalupe" Carney had given twenty years of his life to some of the poorest *campesinos* in the Western Hemisphere. He loved the Honduran people, suffered and strove with them, and both before and after his death has been regarded by them as a folk-hero. He was a compassionate man, driven by a consuming sense of justice and drawn by the spiritual insights of more than thirty years of religious life.

A Honduran Jesuit assigned to Nicaragua describes the legacy Guadalupe Carney bestowed upon Honduras:

For me there is no priest who holds a higher place in my memory than Padre Guadalupe. . . . My family . . . is not very religious. . . . Besides this, my father had a certain disdain for priests. But when he spoke of Padre Guadalupe, he always referred to him as "Padre," as a very special person, who had an ability to listen to the joys and sorrows of poor people, because he accepted them as they were. In this way my father came to accept all priests. . . .

I have passed through Honduras on various occasions, and I have talked with friends who are *campesinos* there, and I believe that . . . the memory of Padre Guadalupe continues to be converted into a renovating and transforming force. I say this because, each time I visit, in spite of the disinformation of the news media of Honduras about him, the memory of Padre Guadalupe gains momentum and brings hope. And I believe that his point of view and his struggle, his image and his figure is becoming vindicated. Given time, I do not have the least doubt but that we are going to give Padre Guadalupe a place in the vanguard of our history as inspiring us to bring about change.[88]

PART II

GUATEMALA

You should know that throughout Guatemala there . . . exists a deep and pervading sense of fear. The week before we arrived a whole village of over fifty people was annihilated by the army. It is not an uncommon occurrence. No one knows which villages will be next. People are killed by burning, shooting and torturing. Most are Indians, who make up the majority in a country of over seven million people. They are quiet, peaceable, almost naively straightforward and honest. Lists are published at the university naming those professors and students who are to be killed. Many are already dead, many more driven into exile in neighboring countries. In the villages all local leaders, especially those who have some form of leadership in community organizations, unions, schools and churches are destined for death.

National Council of Churches
"An Epistle to the Believing Communities
in the United States"
May 13, 1981

William Woods

3

William Woods

Maryknoll Missionary

In early November 1976, after vacationing with his family in Houston, Texas, Maryknoll missionary William Woods flew to Austin to spend two days with his long-time friend, Father John McCarthy. Father Woods was returning to Guatemala, where he had served as a missionary for the last eighteen years. "[Bill] was in a mellow and tense mood, if that's not a contradiction," recalls McCarthy, who today is bishop of the Diocese of Austin. "We talked long and late into the night. He said that [in April] he had been called in by the U.S. embassy in Guatemala City and given this advice: 'Father, you should get out of the country, and if not, at least move here where we can keep an eye on you.' " The warning was given by Ambassador Francis E. Meloy (who was himself murdered by terrorists in the summer of 1976, soon after his arrival in Lebanon as U.S. ambassador).

Obviously troubled, McCarthy asked: "Bill, what good are you to your people if you're dead?" Woods replied that he had thought about this himself and concluded that his work was too important to abandon; in about three and a half months his Ixcán jungle project would be completed and he would then move to the capital city.

The next day McCarthy drove Bill to the airport. "As I was driving away," recalls the bishop, "I saw him taxiing to the main runway. I turned back, got out of the car, walked to the fence and watched until the plane was out of sight. I had never done that before."

Three weeks later, McCarthy and a friend were jogging; at the end of their workout, they were met by his friend's wife, who called out: "Did you hear about Bill Woods?" Instinctively the priest asked, "Is he dead?" When he received an affirmative answer, he added, "Was he murdered?" The woman responded that she did not know.[1]

William Hervey Woods was born in Houston on September 14, 1931, the second child and oldest son of William Hervey Woods, Sr., and Anna Charnley

Woods. The family was an interesting blend of Irish-American and Texan stock. His father, a vice president of Gulf Oil, was an ordained deacon and is described by Father Alfred Smith as "rugged, hard-working, yet so tender he would kiss each of his stalwart sons on the lips well into their late teens."[2] He is depicted by others as a "nice guy" with a strong religious faith, but also as a hard-headed Irishman who could be "a real grouch" at times. His mother is characterized as courageous and serene. Bishop McCarthy remembers that when he first met her she had taken into her household an elderly, unmarried aunt and that later she cared for another needy relative in the same manner.[3] Father William McIntire, who had dinner with her in Guatemala just after Bill's death, recalls that she "as always was remarkably calm, most concerned about the other families" whose loved ones had died along with her son.[4]

Bill was, beyond a doubt, a composite of both his parents. Author Ron Chernow reports, "Woods could be bull-headed" and "had an Irish temper."[5] McCarthy also mentions the Maryknoller's quick temper but adds that "he was very generous; he would give away anything he had and perhaps much of what you had. . . . He had the biggest heart in Western civilization."[6] Bill was raised with his sister and four brothers in the then rural area of Bellaire, just outside of Houston, where his family belonged to Holy Ghost parish. While attending Saint Thomas High School he resolved to become a priest. Father Smith, who opened and directed the Maryknoll Promotion House in Houston, recalls Bill's first visit with amusement:

> He wanted to know if I wanted the grass cut. I was agreeable and we arrived at a satisfactory price. The next morning he arrived with his brother to begin work. After two hours or so he came to the door for his pay. I went out to look and said, "but you didn't do the back." "Aw," he cried, "that wasn't in the price." "To me it was, what good is a half done job?" Grumbling loudly he and his brother got back to work. He took his money and left, but was back that evening very irate. "Father, I think you cheated us today." "Bill," I replied, ". . . how can you speak of being cheated?"

The argument continued until Father Smith, on an impulse, silenced the young man by asking if he had ever thought about becoming a priest.

> Thoroughly shocked he backed out of the house. Two weeks later he came back. "All right, where do I sign up?" . . . [Later after his ordination] he would say, now with a grin, "you cheated me on my first job here, now I work for nothing."[7]

In an undated, hand-written essay, probably composed during his first year in the seminary, Woods describes his decision to enter the missionary order, conveniently neglecting his run-in with Smith:

I made up my mind to be a priest when I was in the first year of High School. At that time I wasn't sure just what kind of order of priest I wanted to be. I didn't talk to anyone about my vocation except my parents. Then one day, when I was in the second year of High School, I met Fr. Al Smith by accident, and he asked me to come see the Maryknoll's [sic] new house. I went over there one day and he explained to me what I didn't allready [sic] know about Maryknoll. I liked the idea because I would be able to teach the people just like Christ did. Then to [sic] I liked it because I would represent the American people on the mission field. From then on I went to see Fr. Smith every week, and I met other boys who were planning to be Maryknollers too. We formed a club, or nucleus as Fr[.] called it, and we all went to see Fr[.] together and he would advise us on the different things that came up. We brought our friends over to the Maryknoll house and then we would talk about the priesthood and Maryknoll. This turned out pretty sucessful [sic], and I think its [sic] the best way to find vocations.[8]

In hindsight, Bill's essay reveals much about his character. First, his carelessness in spelling, grammar, and style betrays a flaw which often annoyed those who would later work with him. Although his thoughts were filled with grandiose plans, he displayed little concern for the mundane, but often essential, details. He constantly exasperated his religious superiors by forgetting to send reports out on time or by neglecting to fill out bureaucratic forms in triplicate. And, although he was successful in obtaining generous contributions for his projects, he could never be described as a polished fund-raiser. As a fellow priest commented, he never bothered to compose those sophisticated "personal touch" letters that adept fund-raisers do so well. Instead, he opted for a short cut—the form letter—and frequently forgot to respond to a donation with a note of thanks.

Woods's statement that he wanted "to represent the American people in the mission field" testifies to a conservative patriotism that he never lost. Unlike so many of the North American priests and religious currently in Third World countries who have voluntarily chosen to share the poverty of their charges, Bill lived almost by U.S. standards. His home in Barillas, Guatemala, was almost like a Texas ranch house, equipped with a small refrigerator and record player. While traveling, he thought nothing of sleeping on the ground and making whatever sacrifices were required; he did this, however, because he had to, not out of a conscious option to live like the poor. To Woods, the North American lifestyle was something to be proud of; he made no apologies for it and hoped that someday his Indians would come to share in something similar. Bishop McCarthy remarks that Bill would in fact have been unsympathetic with much in recent liberation theology: "[He] had a small view of the world; [he] wasn't concerned about multi-national corporations [or] about what is going on in Africa." In other words, his thoughts did not extend beyond a concern for the Indians. "He even said good things about the United Fruit

Company: 'Boy, those people who work at United Fruit have a super clinic and electric lights; my people don't.' What price Guatemala paid to have United Fruit put electric lights in houses he never thought about or talked about."[9]

After graduating from Saint Thomas High School in 1949, Woods entered the Maryknoll seminary at Glen Ellyn, Illinois, along with several other young men from Houston. Included in the group was his close friend, Rafael Dávila, today a member of the governing General Council for the missionary order. The Glen Ellyn seminary had just been opened and Dávila remembers that several buildings were being hurried towards completion when they arrived. Bill was a bright but undisciplined student. A smooth talker, however, he managed to convince his Maryknoll teachers to send him to Mexico in the summer of 1956 to study Spanish, although his grades were too low to merit such a privilege. This glib ability to persuade the most unlikely people to support his views would prove to be a useful asset in his missionary days in Guatemala.

Bill received his bachelor's degree in 1953 and next spent a year of novitiate in Bedford, Massachusetts. He was then sent to Maryknoll, New York, where he completed his theological training in 1958. There, Father Dávila remembers, he, Bill, and a few other seminarians formed a study group. While the rest of them would be discussing the complex theories derived from their lectures and textbooks, Bill would invariably apply the material to hypothetical, but practical, situations that apparently had nothing to do with the course matter. Somewhat irritated, his classmates would tell him condescendingly that his "off-the-wall" theology would prove useless in helping them pass their courses. Years later, however, Dávila repeatedly found that he was forced to face practical problems in his priestly duties which Woods had introduced in these study sessions and which had then seemed so ridiculous.[10]

It was the practice of the Maryknoll Fathers to have seminarians who had completed the novitiate spend at least one summer before ordination working in the active ministry. Consequently, Bill was sent in the summer of 1956 to San José, California, where he assisted Father Donald McDonald in his apostolate to migrant farmworkers. McDonald, a friend and adviser of union leader César Chávez, was a rugged, aggressive priest, who refused to accept the poverty and misery of the Hispanic farmworkers as an unchangeable fact of life. Bill was greatly inspired by him and incorporated much of his style in his later missionary work in Central America.[11]

In the summer of 1957, Bill, by then a deacon, was sent along with Rafael Dávila to Houston where they assisted hospital chaplain Father Joseph Fiorenza in his ministry. Dávila recalls one incident during this time which reflects Bill's character and later approach to conditions in Guatemala. Two babies had been shot and brought to the hospital; both had lost much blood, but their parents belonged to a religious sect which forbade transfusions. The parents refused to listen to the pleadings of the hospital staff; as a result, the children died, one in the arms of Dávila. Bill was furious; pounding his fist on every object in sight, he simply could not accept the fact that two human beings had been allowed to die because of what he considered to be the stupidity of their parents' views. Stubborn anger in the face of injustice, which he later displayed continually in his missionary work, would inspire him to achieve wonders, but it would also incur the wrath of the authorities.[12]

Woods was ordained to the priesthood on June 14, 1958, and was immediately assigned to Barillas, a town in the western part of Guatemala, near the sparsely populated Ixcán and Quiché jungle regions.

About the same size as Tennessee, Guatemala—from a geographical and cultural standpoint—could be a tourist's haven. Among its lures are beaches and lush rain forests, lakes visited by mysterious noonday winds, and magnificent mountains interspersed with volcanoes. Pilfered ancient ruins dot the countryside and provide a visible link in time with the colorful fiestas and market days of today's Mayan Indians. The political and socioeconomic problems of Guatemala, however, have transformed paradise into a land of bloodshed.

To understand Guatemala's problems, one must realize that about 55 percent of its 7.1 million people are Mayan Indians. Living mostly in the southern and western highlands, the Mayas constitute a rural society of isolated villages in which life has changed little with the passing of time. The various communities display a wide range of cultural and linguistic differences, including distinctive costumes. The Mayan economic mainstay is subsistence farming, with some regional specialization in handicrafts; their annual per capita income is about $81. They are, writes the historian Walter LaFeber, among the poorest and most isolated people in the Western Hemisphere.[13]

Of the remaining 45 percent of the population, the vast majority are *mestizos*, a mixture of Indian and Caucasian. Four percent are of European descent and dwell in urban areas; politically conservative, this class controls the country. Over the years, however, some *mestizos* have entered their ranks. Ron Chernow sums up the status of the elite succinctly:

> The trinity of generals, landowners and entrepreneurs that reigns over Guatemala turns out, on closer inspection, to be three faces of the same all-powerful class. Many of the military are also major landowners and businessmen, and employ mobile military units as their private armies. "In Guatemala, the army doesn't just defend the interest of the private sector," said one Guatemalan journalist. "They are the private sector."[14]

The landowning, business, and military elite consider the Mayas to be inferior: The more "Indian" persons are, the less civilized they are thought to be, and Indians are equated with laziness, dishonesty, and biological inferiority. Thus, to persecute and oppress the Indian population is socially acceptable to many of the privileged class. For outsiders to come to Guatemala to labor for the spiritual welfare and material improvement of the Indian is incomprehensible and therefore greeted by the elite with suspicion.[15]

In the sixteenth century, when the Spanish led by Pedro de Alvarado conquered the Mayas, thousands of Indians died. The conquerors soon established the feudal-like *encomienda* system, virtually enslaving the Indians and working them to death. Due to unceasing complaints from Spanish friars led by Bartolomé de Las Casas, the brutal *encomienda* was replaced by the New Laws of the Indies in 1542. These laws permitted the Mayas to live in their own villages while obligating them to perform labor services—by law usually one week a month, but in practice often more—for the Spanish landowners. From the sixteenth century to the present, Mayan descendants have been forced to work the large plantations of the non-Indian elite.[16] "Crews of Indians," writes Phillip Berryman, "are brought down from the highlands. It happens that the fallow time for corn and beans coincides with the harvest period for coffee, sugar, and cotton (October–February) and large numbers of Indians are chronically in need of cash—in fact, in debt, and usually to the labor contractor—so that there is guaranteed a seasonal labor supply."[17] Thus, the Mayas are essential to the Guatemalan agro-export economy. Several times in history they have rebelled, only to be brutally suppressed.

With the coming of independence from Spain in the early decades of the nineteenth century, the Guatemalan elite, like that in the rest of Central America, split into two factions that competed for control of the country. The Liberals envisioned themselves as progressives who favored emphasis on coffee production; they were anti-clerical and when in power passed laws aimed at confiscating property of religious orders and communal lands of Indians, so they could be incorporated into the agro-export economy. The Conservatives, on the other hand, favored the aristocratic ways of the past, when the Catholic church worked in harmony with the privileged. Although neither faction concerned itself with ameliorating the condition of the Indians and poor *mestizos*, the Conservatives at least provided the Indians with a modicum of paternalistic protection. In the last years of the nineteenth century, a new agricultural product, bananas, began to play a major role in the socioeconomic structure of Guatemala. Whereas the coffee plantations were owned by local elites, the banana business was controlled by large U.S. companies bent on making as large a profit as possible for their North American stockholders. Thus, a new foreign dimension was added to the country's power structure.

Until 1944 Guatemala was ruled by dictators who paid little attention to meaningful reform. When General Jorge Ubico was forced to resign in July 1944 and his military colleagues were unable to form a lasting government, elections took place. Juan José Arévalo Bermejo, a Liberal, won with 85 percent of the vote. Modeling himself after U.S. President Franklin Roosevelt, he was seriously interested in turning his nation into a twentieth-century democracy. His inauguration as president on March 15, 1945, ushered in a decade of social progress—a decade which serves as a reference point for all subsequent Guatemalan troubles. The right to vote was granted to women and the illiterate; political parties (with the exception of the Communist Party) were allowed to organize; unions were permitted to form and encouraged to grow; freedom of speech and assembly was genuinely allowed; social security programs were created; and governmental health and education programs were expanded. In 1951, Colonel Jacobo Arbenz Guzmán was elected president with 63 percent of the vote, promising to continue the politics of Arévalo and create a modern capitalist country. In 1952 he had a major land reform law passed. Over a thousand plantations were expropriated and turned over to more than a hundred thousand *campesino* families. Peasants were to pay for the land and former owners were to be compensated according to its declared tax value. Approximately 400,000 of the 550,000 acres owned by the United Fruit Company were expropriated, 85 percent of which were uncultivated. Since this U.S. company had had its property drastically undervalued for tax purposes, it stood to lose from the government's redistribution program. Working with the Central Intelligence Agency (CIA) and with the blessing of President Eisenhower, United Fruit succeeded in having the Arbenz democratic government declared communist and toppled it, replacing it with an oligarchic dictatorial regime more to its liking and headed by Colonel Carlos Castillo Armas.

By 1954, Guatemala's brief era of political progress was over.[18] It should be noted that Arbenz had removed the prohibition against the Communist Party and that a minority of his officials were communists. It must also be stated, however, that several members of the Eisenhower government were linked to United Fruit. Anne Whitman, the president's personal secretary, was married to Edmund Whitman, United Fruit's public relations director; Secretary of State John Foster Dulles and his brother, CIA Director Allen Dulles, were members of a law firm which did extensive work for the banana company. Thomas Cabot, the brother of Assistant Secretary of State for Inter-American Affairs John Moors Cabot, had been president of the company in 1948, and the family owned stock in the company, as did United Nations Ambassador Henry Cabot Lodge. The most blatant conflict of interest, however, can be attributed to Under Secretary of State Walter Bedell Smith, who applied for a major executive position at United Fruit while he was helping to plan the overthrow of Arbenz. Later, he was named to the corporation's board of directors.[19]

With Castillo Armas in office, land reform ended and repression began. Over 99 percent of the expropriated land was returned to its prior owners; *campesinos* and labor union leaders who objected were murdered. Within a year of his taking office, union membership dropped from 100,000 to 27,000. Literacy programs were terminated.[20]

The corrupt Castillo Armas was assassinated in 1957, only to be followed by a series of military dictators or civilians collaborating with the army. During this time, agricultural exports expanded dramatically along with the landholdings of the elite minority. From 1960 to 1974 the total annual value of the five major agro-export products increased from $105.3 million to $367.5 million. This dramatic growth took place at the expense of subsistence farming; so, as the population of Guatemala rose, there was less land available to provide *campesinos* with the corn and beans necessary for the survival of their families.

Within the army there was also dissatisfaction, which led to an incipient guerrilla movement. In 1966, President Mario Méndez Montenegro commissioned Colonel Carlos Arana to search for and destroy the rebels; assisted by U.S. training, advisers, and equipment, his troops killed between six and eight thousand people within the next two years, nearly all of whom were innocent peasants, since, according to various sources, the guerrillas never numbered over three hundred. U.S. pilots in American planes even dropped napalm on *campesinos,* and one thousand Green Berets participated in the counterinsurgency operations. It was also at this time that right-wing death squads were formed to assist the army; a U.S. colonel, John Webber, played a role in their formation. Finally, in 1970, Colonel Arana was elected president, and kidnappings, torture, and murder intensified; from 1970 to 1975, fifteen thousand people disappeared.[21]

In the 1960s, in an attempt to alleviate the problems stemming from land shortage, the Guatemalan government began a program of colonization in the largely uninhabited, steamy jungles of the Petén, Quiché, and Ixcán. The purpose of the project was to provide landless peasants with small family-sized plots. In 1978, Michael McClintock of Amnesty International reported that "ten years ago, there was nothing, just Indians quietly moving in and setting up little farms. They cleared the land and sent out their goods by mule."[22] The situation changed dramatically, however, in the 1970s when foreign oil companies decided to begin drilling operations in these areas. Army officers were now interested in gaining ownership of these inhospitable jungles and this meant more trouble for the Indians.

This, then, was Guatemala. Bill Woods, newly ordained and enthusiastic, arrived in 1958 and would labor there until his death in 1976. He came with a mixture of optimism, religious faith, skill, generosity, and naiveté. These qualities would soon enable him to undertake tasks that appeared impossible; yet he would often—inexplicably—succeed. As Bishop McCarthy states, he was a "Texas cowboy for Jesus," ready to enjoy the open spaces of Guatemala, to ride horses, jeeps, airplanes, and motorcycles, and to teach the Indians about the Catholic faith.[23]

Bill's assignment at Barillas was perfect for a "cowboy" with big Texan ideas. After arriving and surveying his new environment, he decided he needed a good horse for visiting the scattered Indian families in his large parish. He wrote to his friend McCarthy asking him if he could raise the necessary funds in his U.S. parish. The future bishop, eager to help, acquired over five hundred dollars and Bill got his horse. Before long, however, Bill informed McCarthy that the animal was useless and he had been forced to find additional funds elsewhere for a second horse, one which proved excellent. Today, the bishop laughs at the incident, noting that his friend could have been a bit more sensitive to his feelings.[24]

McCarthy quickly became a major supporter of Woods's missionary work. Between 1962 and 1970 he personally made no less than five visits to Barillas, three to deliver jeeps bought or remodeled in the United States for the Guatemalan mission. He remembers his first visit with special clarity: Bill had driven an old jeep to Houston in 1961 for the three-month vacation that Maryknoll gives to its Central American missioners every three years. He had the vehicle overhauled and asked McCarthy to accompany him on the ride back to Guatemala. The two drove through Mexico, past Huehuetenango in Guatemala and up into the mountains to Santa Eulalia, from which it was a twelve to fourteen hour ride by horseback over rugged mountainous terrain to Barillas. When they arrived at Santa Eulalia, they were met by some of Bill's Indian parishioners who brought them two horses. The Indians then returned to their village by foot, using a shortcut unsuitable for horses and a visiting urban padre from North America. After a few miles, Woods realized he had carelessly forgotten to get food, water, and flashlights from the Indians. McCarthy tells the rest of the story:

> The sun went down on us but we had to go on. My horse collapsed, got up, and soon collapsed again on top of me. I told Bill to go on and come back for me the next morning. It was raining hard and I just laid back as if I was drowning. Bill had a terrible mouth when he was mad. He cursed my horse and beat it until it got up. He put me on his horse, the lead horse, took its tail and wrapped it around one of his hands. With the other hand he held the reins of the other horse; it was the useless one we had bought for him. It was pitch dark and we were on a mountain trail. I was in the lead but I couldn't hold back my horse going down the hills. Bill, walking between the two horses, would be pulled and stretched, cursing all the way. When we finally got to his parish the Indians came out to greet him. They carried torches and led us in the rain into town. They were singing and it was a beautiful sight.[25]

It was a Saturday night when they reached Barillas. Had it been another night they would not have been greeted in such a festive fashion. Bill had built a hostel for the Indians so they could come into Barillas from the surrounding villages on Saturday, stay overnight, then attend a Sunday morning mass, complete with marimbas, hold a market after the service, and return home Sunday evening.

McCarthy recalls a later trip with two other priests in 1965. Woods invited all of them to join him in celebrating mass with the Indians:

> Everybody was hot and stinking in this crowded hut, [with] rain coming through [the roof]. Bill divided the vestments up among us [and] said, "I'm the principal celebrant, so I get the chasuble." We priests died laughing. It was very unliturgical but a great mass, the Indians singing their hearts out. We were all jammed in there, covered in mud, but the church was alive.[26]

Life in Barillas was hard, however, and Father Woods saw his parishioners suffering in ways he refused to accept. Perhaps he could begin a small wood-carving cooperative for them and set up outlet markets in the United States; such an undertaking would be a source of welcome revenue. The fact that neither he nor they knew anything about this skill was inconsequential. He determined to learn this craft and within a short time he had become an excellent wood-carver.[27] He next proceeded to pass on this newly acquired knowledge to his Indian parishioners. Within a few years, the project proved to be a successful money-making venture, in spite of letters like the following that well might have discouraged a few would-be customers:

Dear Father,

I have been advised by some cultivated men that it might be of help both to you and to us, to tell you about a mail order business we have here. In this parish we have had a carving co-op in operation for the past six years, in which we carve various religious articles and some typical things. We have 25 families living off this co-op and their work is exceptionally good. We have begun shipping crucifixes and small statues direct to the U.S. by regular mail.

We have a standard type (10 inch corpus) out of rare and precious wood, which we ship by regular mail anywhere in the U.S. for $10.00. There is no duty charged on arrival and it is delivered to the address as any letter would be. Also we ship a resurrected Christ statue (10 inches high) something like the Christ of the Andes for $8.00. The only disadvantages to the deal are that: (1) It takes over a month to arrive; (2) The crucifixes are shipped apart, the arms have to be glued and the corpus screwed on the cross, the statue of the Risen Christ is shipped in one piece. . . .

Please forgive this impersonal and form letter. Things are fine down here. Guatemala is still the best damn mission Maryknoll ever had despite of [sic] revolutions or any other indications to the contrary.

Thanks for the stateside help.

In Christ,
Bill[28]

The wood-carving cooperative was just a small part of Father Woods's indefatigable labors for his people. He opened a clinic for them and served as their doctor for minor ailments and even when necessary, for more serious problems. He would suture a badly bleeding machete cut, leaving an ugly scar but saving the victim's life. He extracted teeth, actually a rather easy job since the Indians' teeth were often horribly decayed. No health problem was too complex for him at least to attempt to solve. Father Dávila remembers a situation in which a sick Indian needed more help than an amateur like Bill could provide. Woods promptly got on the short-wave transmitter he had installed with a gas generator for electricity, contacted a doctor in New York, related the symptoms to him, and received the advice necessary to help the patient.[29]

Father Woods knew, however, that his hard work touched only a small minority of the poverty-stricken Mayas. For truly meaningful reform, the Indians needed their own land and plenty of it. Had not the government begun a program allowing poor peasants to settle in the inhospitable Ixcán? Perhaps he could harness his energies in this direction. Always thinking on a grandiose scale, he felt that with a few good ideas he might even be able to save the entire Mayan population from a life of misery.

While still brainstorming on how best to develop an Ixcán project, he and another Maryknoll priest went for a vacation to Guatemala's Pacific coast. There, as he watched crop-dusters at work, he formulated his plan. He would fly Indians into the inaccessible jungles where they could carve out farms for themselves; he would then fly out their produce so it could be sold at markets. The fact that he knew little about flying was irrelevant; he would learn.

Woods immediately introduced himself to the pilots and explained his plan to them. They were so intrigued that they began at once to give him flying lessons. By the end of his three week vacation he was ready to apply for a pilot's license.[30]

Bill next obtained permission and a substantial donation from his order to undertake this project. However, because he wanted to purchase one hundred square miles of land between the Ixcán and Xalbal Rivers, much more money was needed. Before long he had received a $10,000 donation from the Strake Foundation; later, in 1974, it would provide him with an additional $20,000. His friends in Houston could also be counted on; one parish pledged to provide him with $250 per month.

The project was officially begun in 1965. The Ixcán was separated from civilization by the 4,500-foot Cuchumatanes Mountains. At first, Bill and his associates journeyed for a few days by horseback into the jungle to clear land and build an airstrip. Woods would next return to Barillas and then fly Indian families back into the jungle, where they would begin carving out a settlement. The Indians would initially sleep in makeshift shelters close to the airstrip; before long these same peasants, who more often than not arrived in their steamy new home with little more than the clothes they wore, would be the proprietors of small productive farms.

Realizing that Guatemalan *campesinos* were ignorant of the legalities of land ownership and often had their small holdings confiscated by the powerful elite, Woods determined to follow the law to the letter in obtaining land titles. At his request, Callan Graham, a prominent Texas lawyer, flew to Guatemala at his own expense to provide the Maryknollers with professional legal counsel. Graham also chose a competent Guatemalan lawyer to act as co-counsel.[31] The Indians were given individual, equal-sized plots of land; however, all titles were to be registered in the name of the cooperative. This would make it impossible later on for the rich to buy them out individually once the land was fully developed. It would likewise make it more difficult to steal their land through intimidation or violence. The government was fully aware of this and consequently made every effort to stall Woods in his attempt to secure a title to the cooperative's land.

Life was difficult for the members of the project. Used to cool mountain breezes, they now occupied a humid jungle area where temperatures were often above 110 degrees. When the rains came, the Indians would sometimes be forced to carry their crops for two or three hours knee-deep in mud to reach the airstrip. As Dave Hollstegge, Woods's chief assistant for the Ixcán project, remarks:

> To me, the project is very revolutionary in so many ways. . . . It's not customary within Indian culture to just pick up and go away and set up new residence in another town. Here these people picked up and hauled off to this unknown, godforsaken land, completely different in climate from what they were accustomed to. The whole idea of their having the opportunity to acquire land—of living with other Indian groups with different languages, culture and customs—is revolutionary in the best, nonviolent sense of the word.[32]

Nevertheless, the project proved a greater success than anyone could have imagined, anyone, that is, but Bill Woods.

By 1976, the tireless missionary had three Cessna 185s servicing five cooperatives and was about to add a fourth plane, a twenty-five passenger model worth $500,000. He and his associates had flown over twelve thousand trips to and from the area. Approximately two thousand families had been settled in the jungle, forming five towns; thus, about eight thousand *campesinos* were living lives of independence and dignity, many for the first time in their lives. Five schools were built and staffed with thirteen teachers; each of the five cooperatives had its own clinic run by a grand total of fifteen certified paramedics and two nurses. Guatemalan doctors were flown in periodically and student doctors made regular visits as part of their training program. An air-ambulance service was set up for serious medical emergencies, making over six hundred flights. Two full-time agronomists assisted the Indian peasants; nurseries were set up and new plants introduced. The project had over a thousand head of cattle and was producing annually 80,000 cwt. (hundredweight) of corn, 10,000 cwt. of beans, 500 cwt. of coffee, and 200 cwt. of cardamum. The project leased a hangar from the government in Guatemala City and bought a storage room in Huehuetenango. Excess crops were airtransported to these two cities where they were sold at market; the Indians paid the co-op three cents a pound for shipment.[33]

Woods was also interested in making the Indians better Christians. The project, therefore, had a small hilltop church and meeting hall. Bill provided the people with radios, which were used for religious instruction. He also had religious comic books printed and distributed to the Indians. The project was so successful from a religious and material point of view that other missionaries talked of using it as a model for similar structures elsewhere.

While the Indians and Father Woods were laboring to create their success story, others were finding the Ixcán of interest, but for entirely different reasons. Foreign oil companies had known since the 1950s that this jungle area contained oil deposits. Nonetheless, the global price of this fuel was too low to merit the expenses of exploration and drilling. The tremendous rise in oil prices by the 1970s, however, changed their outlook, and they were now ready to invest heavily in the Guatemalan jungle. As the Guatemalan government made ready to auction off drilling rights to the highest bidders, the military and landowning elite began a mad scramble to gobble up this territory that they had once considered worthless. Soon-to-be-president General Fernando Romeo Lucas García eventually acquired 78,000 acres west of the Indian cooperatives. But he and others wanted even more. Land speculation was such that by 1978 (one and a half years after the death of Bill Woods) the jungle lands had increased fifteen times their 1965 value.[34] It was now inevitable that the brutality suffered by the poor throughout the more populated areas of Guatemala would soon come to the isolated Ixcán.

In May 1975, Luis Arenas was murdered by two men, probably members of a small guerrilla band living in the jungles since 1972. Arenas, who owned a large plantation not too far from Woods's project, was known as the "Tiger of Ixcán" for his unusually harsh treatment of his workers.

Within a week of his murder, four planes dropped more than a hundred paratroopers over the Ixcán. The soldiers began arresting Indians and hauling them off in helicopters. Some were later released but many were not. Many of the Indian *parcelistas* (members of the cooperatives) left their wives and children and fled into the jungles, promising to return when the army departed. But the army remained.

Bill approached the colonel in charge of the operation but the officer refused to discuss the reason for the military's presence.[35] Father Woods reports the rest of the episode:

During the month of June the army kept milling around in the Xalbal area. On June 10th the helicopter landed in Xalbal and Miguel Sales Ordoñez, a health promoter who worked for the project, was carried away for questioning. To this date he has never been heard of [January 14, 1976]. At this point I began to see lawyers asking them what rights we have and what we could do to find out what happened to these people. I went to Santa Cruz, Quiché, which is the center of the operations of the army and asked to see the boss. I was referred to the second in command who when I explained the situation, told me to mind my own business and preach the love of God to the people. His attitude was threatening, insolent and disrespectful to the religion. Later I went to see a lawyer in Quetzaltenango who advised me to send a telegram asking for habeus

corpus from the judge of the first courts in Santa Cruz, Quiché. I also
went to see the Bishops of Huehuetenango and Quiché explaining the
situation. They mentioned that I ought to have nothing to do with the
situation, let the people handle it. I returned to the Ixcán and had the
wives of the missing men write the telegrams and I took them by plane to
Huehuetenango to be sent. As I was leaving Huehuetenango I realized
that I had forgotten to send the telegrams, so I decided to land in Quiché
and give them to someone to mail. The head of the army camp was at the
field and saw me land. The next day I was informed by the head of civil
aeronautics that the planes of the project could not fly anymore since we
were a danger to lives and property. This telegram came from the head of
the army in Santa Cruz, Quiché. I immediately got word to the President
of the Republic and the order was rescinded within two days. . . .

Among the many people captured one man was released and came in
to tell me of his experiences. He had lost about 30 pounds, had two
busted ribs, and claimed his front teeth were loose. He was carried away
in the helicopter around June 10th and taken to a nearby strip for
questioning. He claims the main idea of the questioning was to find out
how I was involved in the guerrilla activity. He was beaten and finally
flown up to Quiché. In Quiché he was closed up in a dark room for what
he thought was three days, no food and water were given to him. Later he
was beaten again, questioned and after a few weeks in Quiché was flown
back to the area and given a green uniform. He went along with a small
group of soldiers . . . in [to] the jungle. For around two weeks this man
was kept prisoner and made to haul things around for the soldiers.
Finally he was released and returned on foot to Xalbal. He could give
us no information of the eight to ten men [still] missing from the project. . . .[36]

Around this time, Woods contracted hepatitis and was forced to fly to the
United States, where he spent two months recuperating. When he returned to
Guatemala he continued his fight to find out what had happened to the
desaparecidos (disappeared).

Soon Woods had to face two additional crises. On February 4, 1976,
Guatemala was rocked by a devastating earthquake; 22,000 people were killed
and 77,000 injured while more than a million were left homeless. Around the
same time, Bill received word that his father had suddenly died of a heart
attack. He immediately returned home to Bellaire for the funeral mass, where
he delivered the homily before a church filled with oil executives and co-
workers of his father. He related the grief evoked by this one man's death to the
suffering of thousands of the Guatemalan poor because of the earthquake. He
then announced that there would be a collection in his father's name for the
displaced victims in his missionary land. Over the next couple of days, word
spread and an incredible sum—between $18,000 and $20,000—was collected.

The phenomenal priest was able to acquire even more, however, for after his return to Central America he was appointed to a four-member Maryknoll committee that distributed approximately one million dollars worth of corrugated roofing to homeless victims of the earthquake.[37] He also began making plans for a housing project on the outskirts of Guatemala City to alleviate the housing shortage.

Bill Woods was becoming a legend in Guatemala, a champion of both the rural and urban poor. On the other hand, the powerful were beginning to perceive the dynamic priest as a troublemaker.

It was only two months after his father's death that the incident occurred which is mentioned at the beginning of this chapter: Bill was invited to dinner by U.S. Ambassador Meloy and warned that he was in danger from right-wing government officials, including Minister of Agriculture, General Fausto Rubio Coronado; Minister of Defense, General Romeo Lucas García; and Military Commandant of Quiché, Colonel José Sandoval Torre. The ambassador told Woods that these officers accused him of being supported by Cuba, of robbing the Indians of their money, and of disregarding the laws of Guatemala.[38] It was around this time too that his planes were grounded and his commercial pilot's license was suspended; the government, however, was permitting him to fly one of the Cessnas, but only for his priestly duties. Frustrated, Woods went to see the Minister of Agriculture and, along with Bishop Martínez of Huehuetenango, he also met with General Vassaux, the Minister of Interior.[39] Moreover, he decided to complain directly to General Laugerud, the president of Guatemala. In a letter dated May 17, 1976, he wrote the following:

Dear Mr. President:

I am writing this letter to ask for your help, as I don't know what to do and I need the support of the Guatemalan government and especially your support.

During Holy Week, the American Ambassador asked me to visit with him and we talked for four hours about my work in Guatemala for the last 18 years. He asked me what I did in the Ixcán area; what my relations were with the guerrillas; and what my political ideas were. I answered all his questions, indicating that I have never had any relationship with the guerrillas and I have no political ideals.

After hearing what I had to say . . . he told me two things. First, that he was well impressed with the Ixcán Project and would do all he could personally to help me, and second, that he had reasons to fear for my personal safety. He indicated that there were some high officials in the government, probably members of the armed forces, who were against my work and myself. This troubles me a great deal, not only personally, but also because of the effect it could have on my work.

After describing his Ixcán project he tells of his latest setback:

> On the 7th of May, Aerixcan and I were grounded. The reason for this was due to a report from various military men, and although I consider the report exaggerated, I acknowledge that one of my pilots was carrying, at their request, seven INTA [National Institute of Agrarian Transformation] employees, when the plane's capacity is five passengers. . . .
>
> I love Guatemala and especially those peasants who are putting so much effort into developing a new life in the Zona Reina. It would break my heart to have to leave the country. I repeat, my only interest is to help make the peasants better Christians, better Guatemalans, and thus help them produce more for themselves and for their country.
>
> Mr. President, the Ixcán Project and I need the help of the Guatemalan government and especially yours. . . . I am sure that if you could personally see the achievements the project has made, you would agree that it cannot be abandoned, and therefore, I extend a most sincere and cordial invitation to honor us with your visit to the Ixcán Project.
>
> Hoping to hear from you soon, I remain at your wishes to offer further information if you so require it.
>
> Very truly yours,
> Fr. William Woods[40]

Needless to say, Laugerud did not accept Bill's offer. Woods soon received a letter, however, from Hans Laugerud, the president's brother and second highest official of INTA, the government land-distribution agency. The letter advised Woods

> . . . to remove his people from certain areas in the colonization project which were being designated forest areas. Father Woods felt that he was being used to remove people from lands they had been legally living on for several years. [He], therefore, wrote a letter to INTA explaining that this organization should deal directly with the Cooperative, that he was in the Ixcán to take care of the spiritual needs of the people, and that the Cooperative was the responsible body. Since his planes . . . were grounded and he wished to avoid being used politically, Father Woods left for the U.S. [in September].[41]

This would prove to be his final vacation. He received word in early October that his airline's suspension was lifted and his commercial pilot's license restored.[42] After the short visit with his friend John McCarthy referred to earlier, he returned to his mission on November 5, 1976.

A short time later, reports McCarthy, he confided to his mother in a cassette tape that he was in trouble again with the authorities. A plane had crashed over the border in Mexico just north of the Ixcán project. The survivors radioed for help; when, after a long time, no one answered their distress call, Bill decided to fly to their rescue, even though he was not given a clearance to do so. He told his mother that from the time he landed with the survivors, there had been constant surveillance on him. He guessed that the government would certainly take his license away again and feared that this time it would be permanent. But during the short time it took for his message to pass through various postal clerks and make its way from Guatemala to Houston, Bill had died, the victim of a plane crash. Mrs. Woods, therefore, heard her son's last words to her after her return from his funeral in Guatemala. For reasons that will be unfolded below, Bishop McCarthy notes tersely that "they took away far more than his license."[43]

On Saturday morning, November 20, Father Woods had breakfast at the Maryknoll House in Guatemala City. Brother Bob Butsch then accompanied him to the International Airport. He and his American mechanic serviced and gassed one of the Cessna 185s, which had recently been overhauled in Houston. The mechanic later indicated that the plane had been in fine condition. Bill was to fly to the Ixcán with four passengers: John Gauker, a construction specialist who had come to Central America in August with his family to work with Woods on the Guatemala City housing project; Selwyn Puig, a mother of four who was flying to the cooperative to take photos to accompany an article on the Ixcán project that had recently been accepted by *Maryknoll* magazine; Ann Kerndt, a worker in the Ixcán for Direct Relief Foundation, a small California-based organization; and Dr. Michael David Okado, a Japanese-American intern who decided to fly out with Ann to see the Ixcán. Kerndt and Okado had apparently paid Bill a small fee for transportation.[44]

The Cessna, after weighing in to assure that it was not overloaded, took off at 10:01 A.M.[45] Just as it cleared the last ridge through the canyon leading into the jungle, when the aircraft was only abut 150 feet above the ridge, witnesses saw the plane begin to plummet towards the earth, then twist around and smash into the mountain it had just cleared. According to his sister, Dorothea Woods Wedelich, Bill, while on vacation in Houston, had spoken to parochial school students in September and predicted that if the Guatemalan elite ever planned to kill him they would plant soldiers on the last mountain ridge since his low-flying plane would be an easy target.[46] As more questions than answers began to unfold concerning the crash, Bill's prediction would assume an ironic significance.

The crash took place at about 10:15 A.M. Several witnesses reported that the weather that day was perfectly clear in that part of the country. In fact, another pilot, Guy Gervais, related that on that day he made several trips over the same area as Woods without seeing a cloud in the sky.[47] Nevertheless, Colonel Roberto Salazar, commandant of the Guatemalan Air Force, later told Father Ron Hennessey "that he had been at the scene of the accident, that the Father was accustomed to flying in bad weather, and that he had gone through a cloud and run directly into a mountain."[48] One might legitimately ask why the colonel would give the impression that the weather was bad when it was not. More questions arose. It was later discovered by Father Hennessey that a few days before the crash Salazar had instructed the governor of Huehuetenango, who was planning to travel to the Ixcán, not to go with Woods. The governor obeyed, but after waiting in vain for three days for the Air Force to arrive for his return flight, he called Woods by short-wave radio and the priest piloted him safely back to Huehuetenango. Salazar likewise insisted that those working for the Direct Relief Foundation cease flying with Woods. When foundation officials replied that arrangements had already been made for some of its members to be flown by the American priest from Guatemala City to Huehuetenango, the Colonel reluctantly allowed the flight to take place, warning the officials, however, to make sure that no one in the future should fly with the priest into the Ixcán. Ann Kerndt, a member of the Direct Relief Foundation, evidently ignored the Colonel, for she died with Woods on her second trip after the warning.[49]

When Bill's plane did not arrive in the Ixcán, the Maryknollers in Guatemala City were notified by his associates at the project. They called the civil aeronautics authorities but could obtain no information; the following morning they finally were given news of the "accident" by a colonel. Yet Maryknoll found out later that the Guatemalan military had actually arrived at the impact site just a few hours after the crash and had had the pieces of bodies removed to a nearby town plaza by 8:00 P.M. that night. This was a clear violation of Guatemalan law, which stipulates that a judge must view an accident scene before the bodies can be removed.[50]

From the above, several puzzling questions and contradictions arise: Woods had made this trip hundreds of times before, often in inclement weather; it seems odd that on a perfectly clear day, a plane in excellent condition would suddenly crash. Why did the military remove the bodies when to do so was a clear violation of law? Why were the Maryknollers not informed of the "accident" until well after the army had taken away the bodies? The military obviously knew of the crash, so why the secrecy? Was it a coincidence that Woods died in the exact spot where he had predicted that the military would murder him if they so desired?

Certain additional problems soon became apparent. A military official had reported to the priests at Maryknoll House that Woods's plane had plowed directly into the mountain and was immediately consumed by fire.[51] Yet when Father Hennessey went to identify the remains of the passengers, which were sent to Guatemala City the day after the crash, he found they were not burned. In early December the Maryknollers decided to investigate the site themselves. They found that the plane was a pile of rubble; its engine, at first wedged six feet into the side of the mountain from the impact, had been pried loose and rolled down a hill. There were certainly no signs that the aircraft had been consumed by fire, so why had this been reported? Moreover, it was obvious that the aircraft had not plowed straight into the mountain, for the way the engine was impacted and the way the surrounding weeds had been cut by the plane indicated that the aircraft did not crash in a near horizontal position, as had been affirmed by the official report. There was also no evidence that the plane had struck any tree in the vicinity.[52] The windshield and side windows, all made of plastic materials, were missing from the wreckage.[53] Had snipers fired through a window as the low-flying aircraft cleared the ridge, the remains of the windows might have borne evidence of bullet holes.[54] Is this why they were missing? Finally, Hennessey spent three days completely disassembling the engine. From his investigation "it was evident that the pistons and valves had all been functioning," and had Woods not been disabled he could easily have landed in a nearby pasture.[55]

A few days after the "accident," the Guatemalan civil aeronautics authorities sent a team of investigators to the crash site. They noted in their report that the plane's parts had burned up. Later, when Maryknollers questioned the accuracy of this statement, the report was quickly rewritten with the information on the fire deleted. Ron Chernow, who conducted a personal investigation a year and a half after the crash occurred, found that the civil aeronautics investigators had never set foot on the crash site; they had merely flown by helicopter to the area, hovered over it for a few minutes and returned to the capital to draw up their conclusions. He also learned that when Armand Edwards of the U.S. National Transportation Safety Board flew to Guatemala to lend his expertise to the investigation, the Guatemalan government made every effort to prevent him from reaching the site. First they attempted to frighten Edwards off by informing him that he should arm himself when he went to the crash area because it was a haven for dangerous guerrillas. When he asked to be flown to the site anyway, which was a fourteen-hour automobile trip from the capital, Edwards was told that all helicopters in Guatemala were grounded for maintenance and therefore he could not be flown to the area.[56] Since it is doubtful that this could be true, one can safely conclude that the Guatemalan government did not want a U.S. expert on air accidents exploring the scene of the crash. From this and the several other points stated above, it appears that the Guatemalan authorities had something to conceal.

Maryknoll missionaries by tradition are buried in the country where they die. Thus Bill Woods and John Gauker were the first laid to rest in the order's niche in the Huehuetenango cemetery. Gauker, at the order's request and with his wife's approval, was buried as a Maryknoll lay missioner.

On November 23, a funeral mass was concelebrated in Guatemala City before a large congregation of mourners. Mrs. Woods, her daughter Dorothea, and sons John and James attended; all expressed strong doubts that Bill's death was accidental.[57] Phyllis Gauker was present along with her newborn daughter and three-year-old son. The following morning the bodies were driven by hearse on a four and a half hour journey to Huehuetenango, where a second funeral mass was said. A number of people, especially among the Indians, murmured that Father Woods and his passengers had probably been murdered. Many priests and several bishops expressed similar feelings, one even correctly predicting that Bill would be the first of many missionaries killed in Guatemala.[58]

As might be expected, the Ixcán was soon occupied by the Guatemalan army, supposedly to root out guerrillas. Union leaders, peasant organizers, tourists, foreigners, and journalists were no longer permitted to go there. Less than two years after Bill Woods's death, to the east of the Indian project a labyrinth of dirt roads had been built by Basic Resources, a European oil conglomerate. A highway crossing the Ixcán cooperatives was being constructed under the personal supervision of President Lucas García; when completed it would connect his newly acquired lands with the operations of Basic Resources.[59] Father Karl Stetter, sent by the local bishop to replace Woods, was expelled from Guatemala in 1979.[60] In March 1982 over three hundred people were murdered by the army at La Unión, one of Father Woods's *pueblos*. Similar massacres were carried out by the military throughout the Ixcán project from March to June. There were also a few individual assassinations committed by the guerrillas.[61]

This caused the evacuation of all of the Ixcán Grande—all of Fr. Bill Woods' centers (and their *aldeas* [neighboring villages])—in the spring of 1982. The people made it back to their pueblos of origin or, the majority, 20,000 people maybe, fled to Mexico which was an hour's walk for some or even up to two months or more for others, having to live and hide in the jungle on the way.

   Today 4th Pueblo, La Unión, Maylon, La Resurrección . . . and Los Angeles *are still abandoned*. First Center and Xalbal are again functioning . . . not with the original inhabitants but with other Guatemalans, Indians and Ladinos, brought in from other pueblos by the army.[62]

Today the jungles of the Ixcán and Quiché are so heavily owned by the Guatemalan military that the *campesinos* have sarcastically dubbed the area the "Zone of the Generals."[63]

Was Bill Woods murdered by the generals? The authors asked this question of several missionaries. All feel certain that he was. But most telling is the claim of one priest. According to him, some Guatemalan friends, after having attended a social function with military personnel, told him that they actually heard a few inebriated officers boasting about having killed Woods.[64]

Most thought-provoking, however, are the words of Bishop McCarthy, who notes that Bill and his four companions were not the only victims: "He was murdered, though I can't prove it. He made the difference in thousands of people's lives. He was snuffed out when he could make the difference in thousands more."[65]

4

Stanley Rother

Diocesan Missionary

It was July 1981, fiesta time in Santiago Atitlán, a picturesque Indian village on the southern shore of Lake Atitlán in Guatemala. In the past, tourists would be arriving, crossing the deep, dark blue lake by launch, enchanted by the surrounding volcanic mountains and refreshed by the cool, "eternal spring" temperature. But there were very few visitors this year; their numbers had dwindled as word had spread that the Guatemalan army was abducting, torturing, and murdering Indians in the vicinity.

The Mayas who live in Santiago Atitlán—the Tzutuhil Indians—had made the usual preparations for the festivities on July 25 centering around the feast of Saint James, their village's patron saint and namesake. But the nine-month-long presence of the army, camped in a nearby field, having taken its toll in human lives, had seared the soul of the village with fear, and the fiesta could only allay this tension temporarily.

The pastor, a tall Oklahoman in his mid-forties, called "Padres A'plas" in the Indian tongue, had suffered through months of sorrow with the villagers. Like them, he had grown fearful as he witnessed the surge of repression. Like them, too, he had helplessly watched a close friend being kidnapped; Diego's muffled screams, "*Ayúdame! Ayúdame!*" (Help me! Help me!), had rung in the priest's ears for weeks. But unlike the Guatemalan Indians, Padre A'plas could have departed for another world, the safe haven of Oklahoma, where North Americans, unaware of the barbarity that stalked Guatemala, were planting their wheat, tending their cattle, and drilling for oil. There he could have become Father Stan Rother again, pastor of a respectable middle-class congregation; his thoughts could have returned to the concerns of the "real" world—like the parish building program and the escalating air conditioning bills. In Oklahoma, he would not have been tormented by the "unreal" screams of an abducted friend or the sight of a mutilated parishioner by the side of the road.

But Stan, aware of the risks, remained in Guatemala among this group of Tzutuhil Indians. Not one to court martyrdom, he once echoed the sentiments of a fellow priest: "I like martyrs, but just to read about them."[1] He also told several friends that he hoped to stay alive by doing nothing foolish to antagonize authorities. Nevertheless, he also wrote that "at first signs of danger, the shepherd can't run and leave the sheep fend for themselves."[2]

So in July 1981, Padre A'plas was with his people for their annual fiesta. As part of the celebration, he blessed 101 couples in marriage, an all-time village record, and over 200 parishioners received first communion. But festivities had been dampened by army "recruiters" who went from door to door forcibly rounding up teenage boys for military service.[3] Like the Indians, Rother knew that to protest was not only futile but dangerous. However, in spite of his careful avoidance of any political entanglements, Stanley Rother was murdered, shortly after midnight on July 28, in the rectory where he slept.

Although the three tall, masked intruders at first attempted to abduct him, Rother knew that torture lurked ahead for kidnapped victims, and he feared not only the ordeal itself but what he might "confess" under interrogation. Whatever he said might have been used as evidence, however warped, to torture and kill others. True to his resolution, revealed earlier that year to friends, that he would never be taken alive, Rother fought alone against the three armed men, yelling "Kill me here!"[4] The kidnappers, unable to subdue the desperate priest with kicks and beatings, finally complied; two shots reverberated through the sleeping village and the last struggle of Padre A'plas was over.

Stan Rother was the seventh North American missionary to be killed in Central America, after Cypher in Honduras, Woods in Guatemala, and the four churchwomen in El Salvador. How had this Oklahoman, a politically cautious and reserved missionary from a traditional Catholic farm family, apparently become some kind of a "threat" to the power structure in Guatemala?

Stanley Francis was born during a dust storm to Franz and Gertrude Smith Rother in a farmhouse near the tiny town of Okarche in central Oklahoma on March 27, 1935. Two days later his father brought him to their parish church, where the authoritarian pastor insisted that "Stanley" was not a fitting Christian name and baptized the baby "Francis Stanley" instead. Afterwards, the Rothers, just as stubbornly but without any fanfare, switched the names around again.[5] But, in time, the old German priest would finally have his way: the Tzutuhil Indians that Stan would live and die with years later had no word for "Stanley" and called him "Padre A'plas"—"Father Francis" in their Mayan dialect.

Stan's great-grandparents on both sides had migrated to the Oklahoma Territory around 1893 after the historic land runs that opened up two million acres of Indian territory to settlers; and the Rothers and Smiths had staked out their claims to part of the prairie land. They were staunchly religious "sod busters" of German ancestry. Oral tradition, passed down from generation to

Stanley Rother

generation, tells of one-room houses and screenless windows where rattlers and bull snakes often slept on the sills. Life was difficult, but the Rothers and Smiths struggled through the bad times and prospered through the good times, and eventually their tenacity paid off. By 1926, the Rother branch of the family owned about two thousand acres of farmland.[6]

Over the years the family had its share of trials: a granduncle of Stan once accidentally drove over his own child with a cattle truck; Stan's grandfather was struck by lightning (but lived); his cousin, a marine, died in combat in Korea; and Stan's younger brother Jim died of leukemia in 1974, leaving a widow and two youngsters.[7] Stan's death in 1981 was not the family's only tragedy.

Stanley was Franz and Gertrude's firstborn; Elizabeth Mary, James, Carolyn Ann (who died soon after birth), and Thomas completed the family. The Rothers belonged to Holy Trinity parish in Okarche, and Stan attended Holy Trinity elementary and high school. Although he had academic difficulties in his college years, his sister remembers that all through grade and high school, Stan was an average to good student who sometimes made the honor roll with no grade lower than a "B." He had many chores on the family farm, but Stan also found time to be an altar boy, president of the Future Farmers of America, boys' athletic manager and a member of Young Christian Students. The Holy Trinity High School yearbook of 1953, the year Stan graduated, notes beneath his photo: "Noise is not his specialty. Cooperation marks his personality."[8] Although he was an active teenager, with a wide range of interests, he was quiet-spoken, not an aggressive leader, and this was a life-long character trait. Two weeks before his murder, he jokingly would remark in a letter to friends that he could use a course in "assertiveness training."[9]

After graduation from high school, Stan told his family he wanted to study for the priesthood. His parents were happy to learn his decision, but Franz, the down-to-earth wheat farmer, betrayed a bit of exasperation at the teenager's lack of foresight: "Why didn't you take Latin instead of working so hard as a Future Farmer of America?" he asked his son.[10] This question would prove more perceptive than the elder Rother knew at the time.

In the fall of 1953, Stan entered Saint John's Seminary in San Antonio, Texas. He completed four years of college there, but began to have trouble when he started his theological studies at San Antonio's Assumption Seminary in 1957. Stan's academic problems were not the result of below average ability: his future intellectual achievements would include earning a bachelor's degree in history, becoming proficient in Spanish, and mastering a difficult, unwritten, Mayan Indian dialect. His sister Elizabeth (now Sister Marita Rother, A.S.C.) sheds some light on Stan's academic problems as a seminarian:

> When he got to the seminary he found a lot of diverse activities that gradually took precedence over his studies. He grew up on a farm and he had his responsibilities and chores to do from little on. Like all farmers, he learned to do many things, from building, to repairing machinery, to

raising crops, and he took a lot of pride in his work. When something around the seminary needed repairing, Stan would volunteer. When the trees needed trimming and the hedges needed attention, Stan volunteered. The farm boy was coming out; after all, that was the life he had known, lived and loved for 18 years. (As soon as he got home in the summer, he would be on the combine harvesting wheat or on the tractor plowing up the soil.) Consequently, his studies did suffer. . . .

I do know that his desire to be a priest was great enough that he was willing to overcome the adversity of "not making the grade" and proving that he could do it.[11]

In those pre-Vatican II years, extensive training in Latin was still crucial for the seminarian; in fact, theology and philosophy texts used in the seminary were at that time written in Latin. As his father had sensed, Latin proved particularly difficult for Stan, since he had no background whatsoever for it. After one year at Assumption, he was informed that he must repeat the courses; the following year, when the faculty did not see enough improvement, he was told to leave at the end of the first semester. Marvin Leven, a classmate and friend of Stan at Assumption Seminary, remembers clearly—and with some annoyance—the events of Stan's last year in San Antonio: Although Stan struggled quite a bit with his academic work, he was often asked by faculty and staff to do odd jobs around the seminary. The young man seemed to be able to do anything; he could fix tractors, do electrical work, and repair buildings and furniture. Stan was asked to do these projects not only during the recreation time but also during study time. Still he never complained that he was getting behind in his studies. When he was told that he could not continue his studies for the priesthood, but that he should consider serving as a brother, Stan was greatly disappointed. Marvin, who was a few years older than Stan, called Victor Reed, Stan's bishop in Oklahoma City, and explained the situation to his secretary.[12]

His pastor back home in Okarche, Edmund Von Elm, also interceded on behalf of the crushed ex-seminarian. He went with Stan and Franz Rother to visit Bishop Reed, who asked Stan if he still wanted to be a priest. Stan answered, "Yes, but it's all over for me, isn't it?" The bishop answered, "No, it isn't; it's not my smart priests that are my best priests." Reed then arranged a second try for Stan at Mount Saint Mary's Seminary in Emmitsburg, Maryland, after some tutoring in Latin at a minor seminary in Oklahoma City.[13]

At Mount Saint Mary's, Stan still could not completely resist the temptation to use his wide variety of skills. Before his first year was over, he had become one of the three leaders of a group of seminarians working on the renovation of the grotto. Their work, according to Father Harry Flynn, then a deacon at the Mount, gave the grotto "a beauty which was really unknown before and which is so splendid today." Stan's classmates there remember the time he was working in the grotto, and suddenly jumped down from a tree he was pruning and ran toward a tiny stream nearby—pursued by a swarm of angry bees upset by the proximity of his saw to their humble hive. Oblivious to the scene he was making, Stan finally got some relief from their stings by rolling over and over in the mud and water. The story of Stan's close encounter with the bees swept the seminary and provided his classmates with a few days' worth of hilarity.[14]

But whatever work he volunteered to do while at Mount Saint Mary's, this time a more mature and persevering Stan did not allow himself to be diverted by too many manual tasks. Just before Stan's graduation, the rector of the seminary wrote Bishop Reed: "Mr. Rother has made excellent progress at this seminary and should be a very valuable parish priest."[15] Fortunately for Stan, the change of atmosphere had succeeded. Within twenty years, the man who had entered Mount Saint Mary's with the rather dubious academic record would receive—posthumously—the Mount's cherished Brute Award for meritorious service.[16]

On May 25, 1963, Stanley Rother was ordained in Oklahoma City. Ordination cards, which he had designed himself, read: "For my own sake I am a Christian; For the sake of others I am a priest." Father Stan spent the next five years as associate pastor of various parishes in Oklahoma. While at his first assignment, Saint William's in Durant, he took the opportunity to earn a bachelor's degree in history from Southeastern State University. He then became associate pastor at Saint Francis Xavier and Holy Family Cathedral in Tulsa, and at Corpus Christi in Oklahoma City. He also spent seven months of that time turning quonset huts on church property near Lake Texoma into a complex of cabins for a youth camp. By then, he may have sensed a bit of irony that his ministry was not always sacramental; as he once confided to Father Dave Imming: "Here I am doing carpentry when others are doing priestly work. But these cabins will be good for others; so I don't mind."[17] But his longtime friend Father Leven believes that these years in Oklahoma were not the happiest for Stan. Rother, perhaps as a result of his academic problems in the seminary, had a "poor image of himself intellectually" and consequently did not feel secure in his ability to serve his American parishioners. Leven, however, says that Stan's parishioners did in fact appreciate their quiet and reserved pastor, but that some of his fellow priests criticized him for being too matter-of-fact, too unassuming and unemotional.[18]

While he was at Corpus Christi parish, Rother heard that a priest was needed for Oklahoma's mission in Guatemala. He volunteered for the job, was chosen by Bishop Reed, and arrived in Guatemala in June 1968. Where else but among a distant and needy people, like the Tzutuhils of Guatemala, could a priest like Rother have combined carpentry and liturgy, agriculture and Eucharist, teaching the alphabet and preaching the gospel? Whatever doubts the thirty-three-year-old priest may have entertained in Oklahoma about his abilities as a pastor would evaporate over time as he served the Indians of Santiago Atitlán. It was not until Stan left his native land, became immersed in a remote culture, and learned to speak two foreign tongues that his ministry finally began to fit his character and diverse talents.

The mission had been founded four years before, one of many in Latin

America developed at that time in response to the call of John XXIII. The pope had made a particularly emphatic appeal to North American Catholics, through a speech delivered by Monsignor (now Cardinal) Agostino Casaroli at the University of Notre Dame in August 1961. As Gerald M. Costello describes it:

> The speech he delivered that day would rank as one of the most significant in the history of the U.S. church. It served as a blueprint for the United States' full-scale mission involvement in Latin America; its words set in motion a series of events that were to alter thousands of lives and change the face of the church on two continents. There was a bit of gimmickry to it, and the charismatic appeal of Pope John was close by in the background. But few talks of its kind in the modern church have been as successful in dramatizing a need and drawing forth the desired response to meet it.[19]

Oklahomans had responded to this call by founding "Micatokla"—the Catholic Mission of Oklahoma—in Santiago Atitlán, Guatemala.

Not a few of the early North American missioners were unrealistic in their expectations. With the best of intentions, they believed that somehow their American know-how, efficiency, energy, and resources would make noticeable inroads against desperate poverty, ignorance, and disease. In a few decades or so, they thought, the memories of long centuries during which many poor Latin Americans had come to identify the church with the wealth and power of an oppressive elite would be wiped out. Many returned to the United States disillusioned.

If Father Ramon Carlin, Oklahoma's original missionary to Santiago Atitlán in 1964, had ever entertained such notions, by 1966 he certainly had confronted the reality of life in a Central American mission. Father David Monahan, now editor of *The Sooner Catholic*, recalls a visit he made to the mission in 1966:

> [Father Carlin] was the short fat man with the brush haircut who sat next to me, flicking the ashes off his cigarette into the water. . . . [He] had eyes trained to see the double reality there. He relished the complex native culture, and he had even more appreciation of the goodness and comeliness of the Indians. He admired the spunk and tenacity of his people. And the natural splendor of the area moved him. But he understood the awful reality that the Indians were slaves . . . to malnutrition, to an astounding array of diseases, to ignorance, to superstition, and to traditions which had them shackled with a thousand different chains. . . .
>
> He talked about the conscience problem of living in the rectory, modest by U.S. standards but far and away the best house in town, while close by women were giving birth in the dirt, and families were parceling out meager portions of corn and beans, and malnourished babies were

dying of a flu they had not the wherewithal to resist. Yet, he realized that North Americans could not survive there over a long haul under other terms.[20]

Santiago Atitlán was a very popular tourist attraction. Visitors came by the boatloads across the ten-by-fourteen-mile lake to see the "quaint" village and its "quaint" inhabitants, the Tzutuhil Indians who wore colorful, beautifully woven clothes. There was also an open market where Indian handiwork could be purchased and a sixteenth-century church that had been built by Spanish monks and had been declared a national historic monument by the Guatemalan government.

But some tourists surely must have sensed the hardship of life in the village that existed beneath the charming facade. They could not overlook the malnourished children, the lack of sanitation, and the meager food; perhaps a few even wondered why so many of the women had racking coughs. And, prior to the coming of the Oklahomans in 1964, some visitors may have commented on the obviously inadequate school and the absence of any type of medical care.

The population of Santiago Atitlán, the largest of twelve towns around the lake, numbers about 30,000 Tzutuhils and several hundred Ladinos of mixed Spanish and Indian descent.[21] Scanning the village from a higher vantage point, a visitor could see myriads of small cornstalk huts with reed-thatched roofs grouped in clusters around open yards. Three generations are crowded into one tiny hut, so each open-air yard is extensively utilized, weather permitting, for all kinds of activities. The entire village is divided up into six smaller neighborhoods called *cantones*. Paths of volcanic sand transect and surround the village; volcanic rocks are strewn everywhere. The village, only one square mile in area, seems crowded to the outsider, for the Indians must conserve their land for farming, not for spacious dwellings.

At daybreak, one could see the men, all wearing their customary hats, leaving their huts to go work in the fields; the boys will join their fathers an hour or so later. Their "fields" are small plots of land of two or three acres that the men till and plant using only a hoe and stick; because of the land shortage, there is also a patchwork of small plots on the steep slopes of nearby mountains. But not all the men till the village fields all year round; some are working on large *fincas* (plantations) along the Pacific coast or in the nearby mountains, earning twenty-five to seventy-five cents per day (during the 1960s) for backbreaking labor.[22]

Before the women and girls leave the huts, they use a small amount of wood to take the early morning chill off the hut and to cook the day's ration of black beans. Wood is carefully conserved; it is being consumed faster than nature can replenish it, and it is frightening to the Tzutuhils that their only source of warmth and energy will not last forever. Because there is no ventilation within, smoke has blackened the walls of the hut; it is thought that so many of the women have tuberculosis partially as a result of cooking tortillas and beans in these smoky, unventilated huts.

Now the women, all wearing colorful shawls and most of them barefoot, are gathering in the yards; the ones with huge baskets of dirty laundry on their heads will take the path to the lake to do the family wash. Others also go in that direction, carrying large, empty clay jugs or plastic bottles on their heads to fill with drinking water from the lake, not far from where the other women are washing. This practice, along with the heavy runoff from the village during the rainy season that washes human and animal filth into the lake, accounts for most of the dysentery and intestinal worms that afflict the people. Before the Oklahoma missioners arrived, diarrhea, flu, measles, and malnutrition killed half the children under five.

Back in the village yards, grandmothers are passing on the art of weaving on the backstrap loom to their granddaughters. Some of the girls may be still in the practicing stage, using palm leaves; others are making a tentative start on their first garment, using the brightly colored threads. Once a young woman becomes proficient, working at the loom will consume the major portion of her day; one of the traditional garments takes about two months from start to finish.

A few of the youngsters will head for the little school. There they will spend two years learning Spanish from a woefully inadequate teacher. The children have spoken only Tzutuhil at home; but Spanish is the official language of Guatemala and for any progress at all to be made in education, this tongue must be mastered. Reading and writing will come later. Unfortunately, only a very few will complete more than two or three years of school; the fourth grade graduate is an educated man or woman in Santiago Atitlán.

So this was the reality that Father Carlin faced. The Oklahoma mission team began to tackle some of the most glaring problems by developing a credit union and a clinic, a radio station, a weavers' cooperative, and an experimental farm. Illiteracy among the Tzutuhils was nearly universal; therefore Carlin almost immediately initiated a project to have their native language put into written form; in the meantime, catechists were trained to help in religious education. Four remote plantations also came under the wing of the Micatokla mission. A radio station, called the "Voice of Atitlán," began to educate the people around the lake on topics of health and catechism, while also providing the villages with news and music. In time, the radio station was turned over to some of the Indian leaders, who continued its endeavor to educate and inform. In 1980, when the kidnappings, tortures, and murders began, the manager of the station was one of the first victims; and the army forced the "Voice of Atitlán" off the air.

When Father Stan arrived in 1968, there were five priests, a nurse, three nuns, and two papal volunteers on Micatokla's mission team. As Monahan says in *The Shepherd Cannot Run*:

Some team members of Micatokla apparently had formed a prior judgment on him: a nice enough guy but not so bright, conservative, and basically a "Mass priest." There were doubts about his ability to master Spanish well enough to be effective at the mission.[23]

But Carlin, the practical pastor, realized that Rother's open attitude and willingness to work would go a long way in this Indian village that had been adopted by the Catholics of Oklahoma. The two men were able to give to one another: the older priest became "mentor and model" to the younger; and when Carlin could no longer remain at Micatokla because of his health, Rother took his place as pastor. By 1974, the only North American remaining on the mission team was Stan Rother.[24]

Stan adapted so well to mission life that on a 1971 archdiocesan personnel form he commented, with typical brevity, "[I] plan to stay here for some time."[25] Two inter-related factors contributed to his realization that he had found his niche as pastor. First of all, his remarkable array of abilities was not just an asset at Santiago Atitlán; it was a necessity. Here Stan could be architect, carpenter, chauffeur, repairman, technician, purchasing agent, accountant, banker, teacher, counselor, agronomist—and priest. And Rother was a careful, thorough craftsman who took great pride in his work. All around the mission one would encounter his handiwork—the cabinets and tables he made, the medical equipment he repaired, the hospital he helped build, the stained-glass windows and mosaics of wood he installed in the church, the farm he cleared and cultivated so that he and the Indians could experiment in growing wheat, corn, beans, vegetables, peaches, avocados, and strawberries. In the weavers' co-op, the villagers even made a stole with a pattern that Rother himself had designed; the garments were then sold at a profit in the United States. Even bookbinding—a skill with seemingly limited usefulness that Stan had learned in the seminary—was quite valuable in this country village; Stan was thus able to make Catholic teaching and devotions available to his parishioners in the form of a prayer book called "Prayers for the People," written in Tzutuhil.[26] At the time of his death, an index of baptismal names for parents-to-be was almost completed and a translation of the New Testament into Tzutuhil had just been finished.[27]

The second factor that made Santiago Atitlán seem more and more like home to Stan was the affection that grew between him and the Indians. Stan soon found that just as he had much to share with these farmers and weavers, so did they have simplicity and patience—a certain purity of spirit—to offer him. Rother was not the first North American, and certainly will not be the last, to be irresistibly drawn to the Mayan Indians of Guatemala. In his letters, he called them "these beautiful people of God,"[28] and with genuine humility referred to himself over and over again as their shepherd. A few months before he was killed he wrote to the Catholics of Oklahoma:

This is one of the reasons I have for staying in the face of physical harm. The shepherd cannot run at the first sign of danger. Pray for us that we may be a sign of the love of Christ for our people, that our presence among them will fortify them to endure these sufferings in preparation for the coming of the Kingdom.[29]

Rother seemed to be able to draw from an inner source of rapport with the Tzutuhils. Was it their patience and perseverance, traits that he himself had had to develop in his struggle to become a priest? Was it the humiliation of poverty that they experienced daily? Stan had certainly known humiliation when he had stood before his bishop after failing in two attempts at his theological studies. Or was it simply their common agricultural ancestry? Whatever drew the two together—the North American priest and the Tzutuhil Indian—it formed a strong bond that could not be severed, even by the fear that set in with the coming of the Guatemalan army in October 1980.

Over the thirteen years that Rother spent among the Tzutuhil, the ties had grown stronger in many ways. Stan had a custom of eating a Sunday meal with a different family each week after he celebrated mass; by 1973, he had realized that the benefits of this tradition were mutual:

It is quite satisfying and revealing, satisfying for the contact and interest, and revealing as to the poverty that exists so close to us here and the great faith and spirit they [the Tzutuhils] manifest. Maybe it does me more good than it does them.[30]

Early in his missionary career, after he had learned Spanish adequately, Rother decided to learn the unwritten Mayan dialect spoken in Santiago Atitlán; to do this he went to live with an Indian family for a while and was tutored by a native speaker.[31] He eventually became so proficient that he was able to preach in the Tzutuhil tongue. Learning the language was truly the key to the spirit of the Tzutuhil people; in this way Father Stan was able to understand the subtleties of their culture. In time, he would become a revered addition to their society.

Rother valued Tzutuhil traditions that others may have overlooked. One unique aspect of worship, for example, was the "cacophony of prayers," as Rother called it. Right before and after the consecration of the mass, the Tzutuhils would spontaneously lift up their voices in individual prayer. The prayers, beginning sporadically, would grow louder and more rapid, until the church resounded with hundreds of personal entreaties directed heavenward. At such times, Rother said, he felt the presence of God.[32]

Other customs centered around sharing.[33] The village was divided into six *cantones* and on Thursdays the women of one of these neighborhoods would take turns gathering corn and bringing it to the altar of the church to be blessed; it was then the men's responsibility to distribute the corn among the poor and sick of the village. Rother was especially touched by the community's sharing one Christmas Eve. The collection was counted, and it amounted to twenty-three quetzals, fourteen of which were entirely in centavos. This meant that 1,400 families had given just one centavo each; their pastor, however, realized that each penny was actually a generous donation from a family who was giving not from abundance but in order to share with others whose need was even greater than their own.

Stan also enjoyed watching some of the Tzutuhil courtship customs. The girls and boys would gather around the village—girls in one cluster, boys in another—and then parade around the village in groups. If a boy was interested in a girl, an entire group of boys would ease over to the girls, and the boy who had his eye on a particular girl would yank on her shawl. The girl then had a choice: she—and her group of girls—could stop and she would smile and chat with the young man; or, if she was not interested, she would simply flip her shoulder sharply and jerk her shawl out of his grasp. The boy then knew she was not exactly smitten with him. Rother always hoped to catch some of the courting on film, but was never successful.

The customs that most impressed Rother were the celebrations that had developed around Holy Week and Easter. He was not an overtly emotional man, but these ceremonies, he often said, brought tears to his eyes. It is no coincidence that in 1981 after he had been warned that he was on a death list and had managed to escape to Oklahoma, he chose to return to Guatemala on the eve of Palm Sunday, so that he would be with the people for Holy Week.

Rother's particular fondness for the Tzutuhil celebrations during Holy Week reveals a great deal about the bonds of affection and understanding that existed between him and the Indians. While most of the village's rituals during this most significant week of the liturgical year followed orthodox Catholic traditions, there were also several key events that centered around a cigar-smoking idol named Maximón. For Rother, who was rather conservative in his religious views, to tolerate these deviations from orthodoxy shows his love for these people and his insight into their spiritual needs.

The week of celebrations began, as usual for Catholics but with a dramatic flair in Santiago Atitlán, with a re-enactment of the triumphal entry of Jesus into Jerusalem on Palm Sunday. A drumbeat first announced the event, as the Indians, dressed in their colorful best, gathered in the courtyard behind the church around six in the morning. Waving palm branches, they surrounded Jesus on the donkey; the processions then wound through the narrow streets of the village and finally entered the church for the celebration of mass. Monday and Tuesday of Holy Week in the traditional Catholic liturgy are uneventful days, but not so in Santiago Atitlán. On Monday night, after the villagers had cleaned the church from altar to entrance, the ceremonial washing of Maximón's clothes occurred. But it was on Tuesday evening that the idol actually entered into the liturgical calendar. Frankie Williams, a Methodist and a frequent visitor to the mission, felt it was an honor to witness this ritual and describes it with some awe: The customary drumbeat preceded this important event, and the people gathered in the home of the *télenel*, the head of the small group of Indian elders called the *Cofradía*. As they awaited Maximón's appearance, excitement built to a crescendo of intensity inside the crowded hut; by the time the figure of Maximón emerged from its place of hiding in the rafters, the tension was truly electric. The Tzutuhils then carefully dressed Maximón in layers of freshly laundered clothing. The next morning Maximón, accompanied by a crowd of Indians, would pay his annual visit to the mayor's office.

Afterwards, he was brought to his private little chapel near the entrance of the church where he would "hold court" until his next dramatic appearance in Holy Week ritual on Good Friday.

The Holy Thursday ceremonies were lengthy but serene. In the afternoon, the people gathered in the courtyard behind the church for a reverent re-enactment of the Last Supper. Twelve boys, dressed in colorful kimonos and headdresses, were chosen as the apostles, and several courses of food were served. The food was not eaten, however; it was gathered in a sack after the Supper was over and given to the poor of the village. A procession then wound through the streets, ending up inside the church for the washing of the disciples' feet and the celebration of mass.

On Good Friday, an almost life-size figure of Jesus was nailed to a wooden cross around eleven in the morning, and three hours later was placed in a coffin. Some of the men then lifted the coffin on their shoulders and carried it through the crowded church. Just outside the entrance, the procession stopped, as the figure of Maximón was brought from his chapel next door. There in the archway of the church, the Tzutuhil tradition converged with the Christian tradition as Maximón did a unique little dance before the coffin of Christ. His attitude and gestures seemed to say to Jesus, in the words of Frankie Williams: "Ha, ha, ha, you young upstart! They caught you, but they didn't me!" Maximón was then carried off to await next year's Holy Week.

The culmination of the week's events was Easter Sunday, and this was one occasion when the usually reserved Rother was often visibly moved. At 4:30 in the morning, a bonfire was lit in the middle of the plaza in front of the church. From each of the four directions, villagers came in the darkness, bearing lighted candles and singing songs of joy. They each extinguished their candles; then the light from the bonfire was transferred by Stan to a single large candle—the paschal candle—from which the other candles were gradually relit. Once inside the dark church, the only source of light was the flickering candles, until at a certain point in the ceremony the first rays of daylight shone through the open rear door of the church. By this time, everyone was tense with excitement, and at that very moment, the church's bells would ring out, the organist would begin to play loudly and joyfully, and a huge, colorful banner portraying the risen Christ would arise from the floor of the church.

The intrusion into the holiest week of the year of the idol Maximón and his little dance of triumph before the dead Christ may have appeared to some outsiders to be a mockery of Christian ritual and tradition. However, Penny Lernoux, in *Cry of the People*, sheds some light on why customs like these are still prevalent:

Their [Latin Americans'] religion was fatalistic, syncretic, and paternal-istic: God was like the large landowner, to be appeased and bribed; his son, Christ, who appears everywhere in Latin America as a crucified man, epitomized the suffering and death of the poor. . . . For them,

Christ had been beaten down, tortured, and killed by a higher authority, just as they had been and their fathers before them. . . .

. . . The Christ they know is a poor guy without influence, like themselves, not the teacher or the leader who defeated death and who inspired his people with a new vision of heaven and earth.[34]

Rother may not have been aware of the psychology behind the existence of Maximón, but he certainly did realize that a few years of catechism by North American missionaries were not going to wipe out centuries of doctrinal ignorance in Santiago Atitlán. Prior to the coming of the Oklahomans, the village had been without a resident priest for one hundred years; an impatient attempt by a new pastor to eliminate the Tzutuhil ritual could have had disastrous effects on the culture, unity, and spontaneity of the people. Because of his unique ability to comprehend the villagers and because of his great affection for them, the twentieth-century Catholic priest patiently tolerated the mysterious Maximón.

As time went on, Rother was more and more accepted into the inner circles of village life. The Tzutuhils and Stan exchanged many "treasures." Rother began the custom of presenting each couple he married with an instant photo of themselves after the wedding ceremony, a gift that was greatly valued by the Indians. The Tzutuhils made beautiful, hand-woven vestments for their pastor, which Father Stan treasured and wore on special occasions. Eventually, he would be honored by the Tzutuhils as no other priest, no other North American, was ever honored: The people conferred on Stan his Indian name, "A'plas"; and the Indian elders of the *Cofradía* presented him with the symbolic *perraje*, a colorful neckstole, and accepted him as one of them.[35]

And Padre A'plas reciprocated. The rectory was open to the people night and day. Stan was often asked to be the arbitrator in property and trespassing disputes. To do errands for the people, he made innumerable trips to Guatemala City—by no means a pleasant journey, since it was fifty-six miles away over awful roads. He offered his friendship to old Nicolás whose slobbery habits disgusted many; Rother ate lunch with him every day, cutting his meat and making sure he had plenty to eat and some extra to take home. He also offered him a bed in the rectory for an afternoon nap. This practice continued for years, until one day Nicolás failed to show up for lunch and was found dead in his hut.[36] Stan also once saved the life of an Indian who was repairing a pump in a well and had been overcome by fumes. Rother, risking the fumes himself, jumped into the well and pulled the half-conscious man to safety.[37]

A memorable event for Rother—and one that indicates the great respect he had earned from the Tzutuhils—was the death of an old Indian named Tomás in 1979. Tomás had become a close friend of Stan; over the years the old man had counseled the young priest on the Tzutuhils' customs and beliefs. Tomás, called the "Bishop" by some because he always followed the priest in processions, was revered by the villagers for his wisdom. One morning, Stan was called to Tomás's bedside to give the old Indian the last rites and his blessing.

Although the "Bishop" was very weak and death was only a few hours away, when Stan had finished, Tomás suddenly sat straight up in bed, put his hands on Rother's head and chanted a blessing in Tzutuhil. Frankie Williams, who was present but could not understand the language, knew that both Tomás and Stan were profoundly moved during this exchange. After she and Rother had left the little cornstalk hut, she asked him what old Tomás had said. Stan would not tell her, saying only that it would embarrass him and that he hoped it wouldn't happen.[38] When he later mentioned this event to his sister Marita and others, he wrote in his laconic way: "A high point in my life here was when [Tomás] raised up from his death-bed to give me his blessing. It was partly sung, and I regret that I didn't have a recorder with me."[39] But what exactly the old "Bishop" sang remains a mystery.

Father Stan also gave his time, energy, and money for the welfare of the villagers. Although the illnesses caused by malnutrition and lack of sanitation must have overwhelmed him at times, he did what he could to alleviate them. Out of a trust fund left him by an uncle, Rother arranged to have a little boy with cancer of the mouth treated in a private hospital in Guatemala City; the boy was eventually cured and returned home.[40] He once had found this boy's father doubled up in his shack, dying of dysentery; Rother had brought him to the mission hospital where he gradually recovered.[41] When Stan heard of a woman who was suffering from a high fever and could not nurse her newborn twins he made arrangements for the adoption of one of them by a fellow missionary and his wife, Jude and Julia Pansini. The family had found a wet nurse for one twin; the other, weighing only three pounds, had been fed sugar water for six days before she was brought to Rother. Stan made several trips to Guatemala City to buy formula for her and little María gained in strength before joining the Pansinis.[42] Father Leven, who made seven trips to the mission while Rother was there, remembers several occasions when Stan transported seriously ill parishioners over rocky roads to the national hospital in Sololá; the entire family would go along, and Stan's pick-up would be crammed full of relatives.[43]

Stan also worked closely with Project Concern, a private, nonprofit organization based in San Diego, California, that provides health and nutritional care and training in Third World countries. Through the efforts of Jude Pansini, Project Concern began to staff the little hospital in Santiago Atitlán in 1975; it was the dedication of this group, as well as that of the original Micatokla clinic staff, that gradually forced the 50 percent infant mortality rate down to about 20 percent.[44] But all diseases and medical problems could not possibly be treated by the tiny staff, and the Guatemalan government provided no medical care in the Indian village. Although there was a public hospital available in Guatemala City, according to Rother the poor did not receive "proper care" there[45]; moreover, most of the Tzutuhils were terrified to venture away from their village—the city was a world away to them—and were also hampered by the language problem, since no one outside of their little community spoke Tzutuhil. They simply learned to live and die with their diseases, often dragging themselves to work in the fields in obvious pain. Malnutrition was so vicious that the skin of children would often drop off in layers. To alleviate some of this misery, Rother arranged on two occasions for a team of six doctors from Guatemala City to volunteer their services to the people of Santiago Atitlán. They arrived late Friday or early Saturday and worked almost non-stop with only a few hours sleep, all weekend long, treating the Indians who waited patiently for their turns.[46] In the last few months of his life, Rother expressed concern on many occasions for one of the villagers, a man who had been picked up by a death squad and returned injured but alive to the village a few weeks later; the man was hobbling around the village on crutches and thought he still had a bullet in his hip. Stan presented the man's case to an Oklahoma doctor who was spending his vacation treating needy Guatemalans in the nearby town of Sololá. The physician agreed to treat the Indian, and as it so happened, on the day Stan was murdered, this bone specialist operated successfully on the man.[47]

Stan's life in Santiago Atitlán, though not as austere as the villagers', was certainly difficult and full of physical and spiritual challenges. As the years passed, the clothes of Padre A'plas began to acquire "more patches on patches." Whenever Stan traveled, he chose poor accommodations, simple food, and cheap transportation. Father Leven recalls one trip he made with Rother during which they spent the night in a hut that was "worse than a chicken coop" in the United States. Their meals were so meager that Leven asked him why he ate such simple fare; "because the people are so poor," Stan answered.[48] Through his ministry among the Tzutuhils and perhaps from their example, Rother had grown in simplicity, compassion, and inner strength. But as Frankie Williams puts it: "He was not perfect; he could be angry, blunt, tenacious, and cross—a real bear at times. He was an ordinary man, who became extraordinary."[49] And Jude Pansini, who worked for several years with him at the mission, gives this portrayal:

> Father Rother grew like I've never seen anyone grow in the priesthood. He went from being an ordinary person like the rest of us to someone very special. Most of all, he knew the law of Christ. He was a transformed wheat farmer. . . . [50]

For twelve years, the life of Stanley Rother in Santiago Atitlán, although challenging, was essentially peaceful. But the peace was shattered in October 1980 when the Guatemalan army set up camp on the mission farm. To understand why the Tzutuhils' lakeside village was invaded by fear and violence, one must understand the repression that had permeated Guatemala since 1974.

As the ruthless presidency of Colonel Carlos Arana moved toward an end, the armed forces announced that no one outside the military would be permitted to run in the 1974 presidential contest. They then confidently put forth as their candidate former defense minister General Kjell Eugenio Laugerud

García. A coalition calling itself the National Opposition Front gave its nomination to General Efraín Ríos Montt. When the early election returns gave Ríos Montt a surprisingly large lead, the government immediately suspended the vote count. A few days later Laugerud was declared the victor with a 41 percent plurality.[51] When the military, in spite of such obvious fraud, refused to permit a recount, Ríos Montt proved himself a loyal soldier, quietly accepting the military's decision as well as an ambassadorship as a consolation prize. To those who hungered for a better life, it now appeared obvious to everyone, even the most naive, that Guatemalan elections were a sham, not meant to bring meaningful reform.[52]

Government-sponsored violence continued at such a level under Laugerud that U.S. President Jimmy Carter felt compelled to end military aid to Guatemala in 1977. Nevertheless, Laugerud did not prove as compliant as had been expected. When he permitted Indian settlement of the jungle areas, the wealthy landowners labeled him a communist. A confrontation was avoided when the country was ravaged by a catastrophic earthquake in February 1976, which diverted the attention of politicians and military officers.

As in 1974, only military candidates were permitted to run in the 1978 presidential election. When no one received a majority of the vote, the oligarchy's candidate, General Fernando Romeo Lucas García, was declared the winner by the Guatemalan Congress, even though only 35 percent of the congressmen took part in the voting.[53] The election was notable, however, for another reason; remembering the fraudulent contest of 1974, 60 percent of the electorate refused to vote.[54] In an ominous prelude to the next four years, on the day before Lucas García's inauguration, Father Hermógenes López was shot dead in San José Pinula after championing the cause of his parishioners in their struggle with a company that was attempting to divert their water supply; he had also taken out an advertisement critical of the army in a local newspaper.[55]

Lucas García lost no time reversing Laugerud's policy of tolerating minor reforms. On the contrary, he inaugurated what proved to be the most repressive period in modern Guatemalan history. Death squads, recruited from the army and police, killed political opponents, union members, students, *campesinos*, Indians, catechists, and religious leaders in unprecedented numbers. By the end of the new president's grisly term in March 1982, over 13,000 people had been murdered, while countless others were kidnapped and tortured. As Jon Cozean reports, "Lucas García's regime was widely regarded as the most repressive and corrupt in Latin America."[56] Rother would be one of its victims.

In May 1978 over a hundred Kekchi Indians were massacred at Panzos by the army for attempting to defy powerful landowners who had ordered them to leave an area that they had lived on for ages. A few months later, thirty demonstrators were shot dead and three hundred wounded for protesting a 100 percent rise in busfares. On January 31, 1980, Lucas García's cruelty shocked the world. Twenty-eight peasant, university, and labor leaders occupied the Spanish embassy to protest the increased violence of Lucas García's regime. When the police made ready to storm the building, the Spanish ambassador ordered them not to intervene, reminding them that the embassy enjoyed diplomatic immunity. Nevertheless, the police attacked and the building caught fire. As Guatemalan authorities stood by, the embassy was permitted to burn to the ground, killing twenty-seven of the occupiers and twelve others. The one protestor who survived was kidnapped from his hospital bed and murdered by security forces the next day. The Spanish government was so incensed by such disregard for international law that it immediately broke off diplomatic relations with Guatemala.[57]

Nevertheless, protests from around the world did nothing to temper the brutality of the Lucas García regime. Convincing himself that foreign missionaries, rather than increased repression, were responsible for the growing demonstrations of the masses, the president vowed that he would rid his country of such troublemakers within two years. A Filipino priest, Conrado de la Cruz, and a lay assistant were kidnapped by a death squad in Guatemala City and murdered on May 1, 1980. A few days later a Belgian priest, Walter Voordeckers, was also killed. Government-sponsored violence against the church, however, was only beginning. On June 4, Father José María Gran, a Spanish missionary, and his lay assistant were followed by an army helicopter as they attempted to return to their residence from a parish visit; ambushed along the deserted road in Chajul, Quiché, they were shot in the back and died. The following month, a Spanish priest, Faustino Villanueva, was gunned down in Quiché. After the murder, several witnesses saw the two gunmen enter the local barracks of the treasury police. The following day these same two men searched the area for an Irish priest and two nuns, who fortunately escaped detection. Moreover, when Bishop Juan Gerardi of Quiché learned that the police had planned to murder him on July 19, 1980, and failed only because he had been unable to keep a scheduled appointment, he decided to leave the diocese. After announcing his decision to the priests and nuns of Quiché, he suggested that they do likewise. They did. Soon, Bishop Mario Ríos Montt was forced to go into seclusion when he found that his name had been put on a death squad's assassination list because he condemned the kidnappings of union leaders in his diocese. Finally, hand grenades were hurled at a convent staffed by Canadian nuns in Morales, Izabal, but the sisters were not injured.[58] Right-wing terrorism was then turned against the moderate Christian Democratic Party. Its October demand that all political parties be permitted to take part in the next presidential election was answered with the assassinations of seventy-six of its members.[59]

The accusations of subversion and communism directed toward anyone who spoke out for reform and human rights were not immediately perceived as threats to the community on the shore of Lake Atitlán. But Stan Rother was watching these developments very carefully. In ten years his outlook on Guatemala shifted from one of hope to one sensing impending evil. In 1969 he had written: "This peace [of Christmas] is a comfort to us who live in a world beset by unrest—political, social and religious. Happily, this is not so evident here in Guatemala." By May 1979, however, apprehension was growing:

An anonymous hate sheet . . . made its debut a few Sundays ago. The mayor, the school director, teachers, and anybody of importance in town made the list. I was number 8. . . . The political situation here is really sad. . . . Guatemala is systematically doing away with all liberal[s] or even moderates in government, [and] labor leaders[;] and apparently there are lots of kidnappings that never get in the papers. There are something like 15 bodies that show up every day in the country and show signs of torture and [of being] shot.

I haven't received any threats as such, but if anything happens, that is the way it is supposed to be. I don't intend to run from danger, but at the same time I don't intend to unnecessarily put myself into danger. I want to live like anyone else.

By early 1980, he sensed an even more ominous future for Guatemala:

There were the killings by police and army in the Spanish Embassy in [the City at] the end of January. . . . Last Sunday the army killed four spectators at the end of a soccer game. . . . On the Coast here, fields are being burned, [there are] strikes at sugar mills, buildings and equipment on the fincas being destroyed, even trucks loaded with cotton bales being stopped and burned. . . . Everyone blames everyone else and the tension builds, more killings, repression. Don't know when it will all stop. It will get worse before it gets better.[60]

Whether he realized it or not at that time, by 1979 Rother had actually backed himself into a no-win, "Catch-22" situation. He had expressed his intention not to "unnecessarily put myself into danger." But did this mean that to play it safe he should close the doors of his rectory to those on death lists? Should he help the widows and hungry children in his parish who had lost their husbands and fathers, their only source of income or food? Yet to help these so-called "subversives" and their families was itself seen as subversion by the army and oligarchy. Before he died, this man, who had studiously avoided controversy, had to respond in all honesty to an interviewer's question concerning his political involvement: "To shake the hand of an Indian is a political act."[61]

For a while in 1980, life proceeded normally in Santiago Atitlán. There was anticipation in the air because a group of nine nuns, Carmelite Missionaries of Saint Teresa, eight of whom were Guatemalan Cakchiquel Indians, were coming to work at the mission. They would eventually become well integrated into village life, contributing their many talents to education, music, and health care. Stan, in his usual low-key way, translated his excitement at their arrival into intense activity getting their house ready for them. He spent a month laying linoleum, installing cabinets, a sink, and a brick flower box; then he wrote his sister that he had not finished it all—he still wanted to paint, build work tables, and install a refrigerator and stove.

There were other preoccupations too. The summer of 1980, which broke records for high temperatures and killed scores of North Americans in the Midwest, was also hot and dry in Guatemala. Although the bean crop in Santiago Atitlán was threatened, the major concern was Manuel Tum's accident. Tum was a Cakchiquel Indian, a layworker who was hired to help out at the mission. In late summer after an evening of drinking, he took, without permission, a Bronco that was in Rother's name and set out with a companion for San Pedro, about ten miles away. They veered off the road and plummeted fifty feet down a steep incline into Lake Atitlán. Manuel escaped with a few bruises, but his companion, a school teacher who left a wife and one-year-old daughter, was killed. Manuel deserted the scene of the accident and went home to bed. The Bronco and the body were discovered the next morning and Manuel, although suspected, denied it all. That evening, Rother and Father Pedro Bocel, his associate, talked with Manuel and inspected the bruises on his arm and shoulder. Manuel finally confessed, but still did not turn himself in to the authorities for two more days. Rother then found a lawyer for him. Tum went to prison to await trial; Stan, up until the time he was murdered ten months later, visited Manuel once or twice a month.[62]

This whole episode took on a deeper meaning after Rother was killed. In several letters, Stan mentions his visits to the prison to see Manuel, and always adds that the layworker was actually safer there awaiting trial than he would have been in Santiago Atitlán; for it was only a few weeks after his arrest that the army encamped on the mission farm, and the abductions and disappearances began. Obviously, Stan believed that Manuel would have been one of the villagers targeted by the army. Nevertheless, he visited the prisoner faithfully, paid for his defense, and was quite concerned about the outcome of the case. Although this is not the only reason why Rother was eventually placed on a death list, some believe it was a contributing factor.

It was also around this time, the end of the summer of 1980, that fear began to infiltrate Santiago Atitlán, as the spreading repression finally touched the lives of the Tzutuhils directly. In September, Rother wrote a frank letter, carried out of Guatemala by a friend, to Archbishop Salatka of Oklahoma City:

> The Diocese of Quiché . . . has been abandoned completely. The Bishop even left. . . . Two priests were killed[;] catechists, lay people, etc. were killed and the rest of the priests left to stay alive. . . . The repression continues there and at one place there were about sixty men of the Church lined up by the wall and they killed every fourth person.
>
> The Country here is in rebellion and the government is taking it out on the Church. The low wages that are paid, the very few who are excessively. rich, the bad distribution of land—these are some of the reasons for widespread discontent. The Church seems to be the only force that is trying to do something (about) the situation, and therefore the govt. is

after us. There are some that say the Diocese of Solola, where this mission is, is the next area on the list for persecution.[63]

Indeed it *was* next on the list.

The pastor and residents of Santiago Atitlán began to notice some unusual occurrences in their village during the annual fiesta. The midsummer festivities had been marred by soldiers dressed in camouflage fatigues carrying submachine guns. In the same letter to Salatka, Rother describes the apprehension that descended on the rectory and on the village:

[The army] didn't do anything but put everyone on edge, walking around in groups of three or four, standing on the corners watching everything. Since then we have had strangers in town, asking questions about the priests, this catechist or that one, where they live, who is in charge of the Cooperative, who are the leaders, etc. Because of this intimidation, several of the leaders of the different organizations are out of town or in hiding. It has changed our style of life here in the rectory too. The doors and gates are being made more secure, the front door is now locked all the time and people just can't enter at will. These twelve years I have slept in the same room that overlooks the plaza in front of the Church, but since a rectory and convent were attacked with grenades in the Eastern part of the Country, I sleep elsewhere now where the walls are rock instead of wood.

I am aware that some of our younger catechists are working with those that are preparing for a revolution. They are young men that are becoming more and more conscientious about their situation and are convinced that the only option for them is revolt. . . . [Recently] the President gave a speech. . . . One remark made was that he wanted to expel all those religious who were catechizing the people. . . .

The reality is that we are in danger. . . . For a month or so now, all classes and group meetings have been cancelled. We are working in smaller groups. My associate and myself are seen less in the street, and almost never leave the rectory at night. The tactic of the govt. has been to kidnap those they think are leaders, torture them and then kill them. Two days ago a young man from the neighboring parish was taken in the middle of the night, . . . a cousin of one of our nuns. He is not expected to be found alive.

. . . If I get a direct threat or am told to leave, [then] I will go. But if it is my destiny that I should give my life here, then so be it. . . . I don't want to desert these people, and that is what will be said, even after all these years.[64]

In late October 1980, several hundred soldiers camped in fields outside the town and began a lengthy stay. Although their camp was partly on the mission's farm and Rother received complaints that troops were stealing corn and avocados, the cautious priest wrote his archbishop: "I have no intention to go ask them to move either."[65]

Within five days of the army's arrival, four villagers were abducted, one of whom Rother knew quite well. This was Gaspar Culán, the director of the radio station and a former deacon. He was to have been the first Tzutuhil Indian ordained a priest, but before ordination he had received a dispensation to marry; at the time of his abduction he had a daughter of about ten months. Concerning the presence of the army in Santiago Atitlán and Culán's kidnapping Phillip Berryman offers this insight:

> From the army's point of view the immediate motivation may have been the fact that some time previously a group of ORPA [Organización del Pueblo en Armas] guerrillas had come into the town and held a meeting. Some said Culán had spoken favorably of what the guerrillas said. In a more general sense this army occupation seemed to mark a new stage in which whole towns could come under siege and in which the prior presence [of] the guerrilla organizations could be the pretext for retaliatory actions against people in towns and villages. Such had been the situation in Quiché for years, and it now became characteristic of large parts of the Indian highlands.[66]

By January 1981, thirty of Rother's parishioners would be abducted.

It was Rother's custom to address the Catholics of Oklahoma in a Christmas letter that was published annually by the *Sooner Catholic* of Oklahoma City and the *Eastern Oklahoma Catholic* of Tulsa. In his Christmas letter of 1980, Rother, after relating the happier highlights of the year, attempted to introduce Oklahomans to the fear and sorrow that had become a part of daily life at Micatokla:

> I am sure that many of you have heard rumors and [seen] articles about our area during the past month or two. Some are true, sad to say, some exaggerated, some false and some that hasn't been told. The purported reason for the presence of the army in our immediate area is to drive out and protect us from communist guerrillas. But there aren't any around here. A group did come into town in early June for about 2 hours and made some promises to those who were around. There seemed to be interest on the part of some in their presence here. So far we have ten men that have disappeared. The director of the radio was one of the first and then later the station was broken into and looted. There is no set pattern for those being taken. In our town are a number of informers who are paid by the authorities to be spies etc. They are paid for names turned in if they are later captured. The denunciations are sometimes because of envy, vengeance or just downright greed. A good friend of mine just happened to be in the wrong place when several others were picked up. He left a wife and three children. The wife and one child have active TB and the baby is only six weeks old. Another man left seven children.

The Sisters, the other priest and myself have not been threatened. My associate has felt that he has been followed etc. but no direct threats. We have to be careful where we go and what we say to anyone. A nice compliment was given to me recently when a supposed leader in the Church and town was complaining that "Father is defending the people." He wants me deported for my sin.[67]

The village "informers" seem to have touched a raw nerve in the priest's soul. Rarely does Rother ever have an unkind thought to share in his correspondence, except in the case of friends turned into spies: "I don't know if I could offer help to one of these informers. I know quite a few of them and some had been apparent friends."[68] And after Rother's murder, an Indian parishioner observed: "Padre Francisco [Rother] couldn't bear to see some (informers) pull in money by selling their brothers. He said that, and for that they killed him."[69]

Although Rother in his Christmas 1980 letter does not go into detail about just what the accusation "Father is defending the people" refers to, it could have been any one of a number of things. For one, when terror struck the people, Rother opened up the doors of the church for them to sleep there; as a result, hundreds of Indians came every night to the church for protection. Several of the catechists of the village even sought refuge in the rectory itself; they took turns standing watch through the night. It also became a well-known fact that Padre A'plas was helping the widows and children left destitute by the disappearance or murder of the breadwinner. He used his own Christmas check to help these victims' families; he was training some of the widows to take their husbands' places at the professional loom of the weavers' co-op and was trying to open up more markets in the States and in Guatemala City for the sale of hand-woven Indian stoles. But in Guatemala, even the simplest act of charity could be labeled "subversive"—if it was directed toward a family with a name on the death list.

To make matters worse, at one point an officer in the army called a meeting of the villagers to try to convince them that the soldiers were there to protect them against guerrillas. This may have been the one time that Rother confronted the army directly: He asked the officer how he could claim the soldiers were protecting them since there had been only fear and kidnappings after the army's arrival.[70] Surely the officer did not forget the gringo pastor's audacity.

Not all of the catechists in Santiago Atitlán believed that sleeping in the church or the rectory was enough protection; several left their families and went into hiding. One of these was Juan Mendoza, who had been instrumental in converting the Tzutuhil language into written form and who, in the fall of 1980, was working on a translation of the New Testament into Tzutuhil, a project held dear by the Oklahoma missionaries since the days of Father Carlin. This village leader left for Guatemala City soon after the army encamped at Santiago Atitlán; he came back once in a while to see his family, and Rother visited him every time he went into the city. Leaving town may have prolonged his life for a few months; however, in June 1982, on one of his occasional visits to his family, Mendoza was dragged off a bus by soldiers near Santiago Atitlán and disappeared, never to be seen again[71]—a common occurrence in Guatemala.

Diego Quic, "probably the most sought-after catechist," according to Rother, chose to remain in Santiago Atitlán with his wife and two little boys. Diego had a key to the rectory and ate and slept there almost daily, visiting his family in the late afternoon. Frightened and puzzled over the reason his name was put on a death list, he once asked Stan, "I have never stolen, have never hurt anyone, have never eaten someone else's food, why then do they want to hurt me and kill me?"[72]

The fact is that those who were kidnapped were *not* guilty of crimes; they were never accused, arrested, brought to trial, or convicted. They were simply labeled "subversive," their names were put on a death list (this method was used to terrify them and everyone else in a given area), and they were executed usually after torture and interrogation. The few mutilated bodies of the disappeared that did show up in ditches or in fields testified to the gruesome treatment the abducted were made to endure before death. It was Diego's fate to join the thousands of *desaparecidos* in Guatemala.

Rother describes the moment of the catechist's kidnapping in a letter he wrote in early January 1981[73]:

As [Diego] was approaching Saturday night about 7:45, he was intercepted by a group of four kidnappers. Three apparently tried to grab him at the far side of the Church as he approached on the porch that fronts the Catholic Action offices, the Church and the rectory. He got to within 15 feet of the door and was holding on to the bannister and yelling for help. The other priest heard the ruckus outside and stepped out to see them trying to take him. He considered trying to help, but was scared by their height. He called me from the living room where I was listening to music but also heard the noise, and by the time I realized what was happening, grabbed a jacket and got outside, they had taken him down the front steps of the Church and were putting him in a waiting car. . . . I just stood there wanting to jump down to help, but knowing that I would be killed or be taken along also. The car sped off with him yelling for help but no one able to do so. Then I realized that Fr. Pedro, Frankie Williams from Wichita and I had just witnessed a kidnapping of someone that we had gotten to know and love and were unable to do anything about it. They had his mouth covered, but I can still hear his muffled screams for help. As I got back in the rectory I got a cramp in my back from the anger I felt that this friend was being taken off to be tortured for a day or two and then brutally murdered for wanting a better life and more justice for his pueblo. . . .

Sunday morning we heard that all the passengers of the late bus from the City heard the kidnapped yelling for help as they met the four-door sedan led by a military jeep and followed by a military ambulance. Soon after the kidnapping that night we went out and found his hat in front of the Church and his right shoe at the bottom of the steps. . . . He was 30 years old, left a wife and two boys, ages 3 and one. May he rest in peace!

About 20 minutes after the kidnapping, I went to the telephone office and asked the police in San Lucas to investigate a car coming their way. I told them it was a kidnapping and that they were armed. They said they would see about it, but they probably hid instead. We heard yesterday that four or possibly five were kidnapped there that same night.

. . . That makes 11 members of this community that have been kidnapped and all are presumed dead.

. . . For these 11 that are gone, there are eight widows and 32 children among the group. These people are going to need emergency help. Others have had to flee also to save their lives and to find work in exile is almost impossible. They will also need help. . . . Letters asking for help are on their way right now to London, two different places, and they will very likely send some money. . . . I accepted the task of funneling the money to where it is needed. Since helping these people could very easily be considered as subversive by the local government, we have asked that the money be deposited directly in the bank there, and that there be no direct communication between the donors and me. . . . Be careful about sending letters here mentioning relief etc. We never know when the mail may be intercepted and read. This letter is being hand-carried to the States. . . .

I am not ready to call it quits yet. What happened last Saturday was indeed scary and happened at our doorstep, but we don't know if his presence here with us will affect us directly. . . .

Just say a prayer on occasion that we will be safe and still be able to be of service to these people of God.[74]

Soon after the kidnapping, Mrs. Williams and Rother scanned the nearby fields for Diego's body, but with no success. According to Frankie, on one of these searches Stan, who was usually reserved and composed, appeared deeply agitated remembering Diego's muffled screams for help and asked her, "Do you think Diego understood that I could not help him?"[75] After Rother himself was killed, Mrs. Williams testified to the House Subcommittee on Human Rights and International Relations that Diego had "made the mistake of complaining to the local police" that they were lax in helping to locate kidnap victims.[76] But the answer to Diego's question "Why then do they want to kill me?" lies deeper than that.

The Indians who were usually targeted for abduction and torture were those who had made some advancement in their communities. Any Indian in a leadership role, like Diego, was suspect; victims and potential victims included teachers, catechists, cooperative leaders, and directors of radio and medical programs. The reason these people were singled out is a product of centuries of prejudice toward the Mayas in Guatemala, a racism which is so extreme that

Indians are considered to have no more dignity than "mules," a term often used to describe them.[77] Such violent racism can ultimately lead to genocide and, in fact, this word has been used to describe the attacks by army and death squads on many Indian villages where the elderly, women, and children are massacred.[78] Hatred against the Indian can also be transferred to those, like Rother and many others, who treat the Indians with respect and attempt to alleviate some of their hardships.

Four days after Diego's kidnapping, the army killed sixteen people at a plantation near Santiago Atitlán, using the usual excuse that guerrillas had been spotted in the area. Then, on January 12, apparently while Rother was in Guatemala City, he received warning that he was now in immediate danger. He went into hiding in the city for sixteen days, until a visa could be obtained for his associate, Father Pedro Bocel; for Rother felt that Bocel, a Cakchiquel Indian, was much more likely than he was to be kidnapped. On January 28 the two priests left Guatemala, and arrived in Oklahoma City on the 29th.[79]

Rother's family was relieved at his safe return. Although Stan had tried not to overburden them with the details of repression in Guatemala, they were nevertheless aware that life at Micatokla had become precarious. Stan remained on the family farm in Okarche for about two and a half months. As he usually did on visits, the industrious missionary helped out with chores and particularly with the housework while his mother was ill, but this time his brother Tom noticed a difference: "Stan would sit at Mom and Dad's and just stare for an hour at a time. His body was here, but his mind was there."[80]

While in the States, Rother received numerous requests to speak but declined most of them. One reason for this was an unfortunate incident that resulted from one of the few talks he had given on a prior visit. In Edmund, Oklahoma, Stan had given a sermon at Sunday mass in which he spoke of oppression in Guatemala and mentioned that the Guatemalan reality did not correspond to the propaganda issuing from the U.S. government on Central America. A man in the congregation, infuriated by Rother's lack of "patriotism," had fired off a "vitriolic and vicious" letter to the Guatemalan ambassador in Washington, D.C., with a copy to the archbishop, charging the priest with promoting the overthrow of the Guatemalan government.[81] Rother, who had done everything short of renouncing his priesthood and his human compassion to stay out of trouble in Guatemala, was deeply upset by this accusation. He had shown no sympathy for guerrillas whatever. Perhaps a fellow missionary in Guatemala, Father Ronald Burke, describes Stan's attitude best:

> Some American government officials have suggested that missioners are killed because they become political activists. These officials should have known Stan Rother. He had always been the quiet one, cautiously restricting his pastoral work to non-controversial areas. The last priest we expected to be killed by the Guatemalan government was Fr. Stan Rother.
> Stan was impatient with priests he thought were too political in their analysis of the country's problems. An unabashed conservative, he never

referred to any new theology. He said that the Gospel of Jesus was enough. . . . [82]

Another reason for Rother's low profile while in Oklahoma was that he hoped one day to return to Guatemala. Consequently, he turned down a request by Mark Gruenke, a Christian Brother in Minneapolis, to go on a speaking tour of the United States; he also declined to get involved in liberation theology meetings in Mexico.[83]

Sometime in March, Rother and Bocel heard that it was safe for them to return. Bocel left on March 11, but did not return to Santiago Atitlán. Stan stayed in Oklahoma another month, agonizing over, as he himself described it, "the big question . . . should I take a chance and go back?"[84]

Stan, of course, did decide to return; when asked by his family "why?", he answered simply that they were his people. He returned to the Tzutuhils on April 11, the eve of Palm Sunday, to celebrate Holy Week and Easter with them. He was enthusiastically welcomed back to the village and things appeared to settle down to normal. No villager had disappeared for certain since February, and one had actually returned, although he was wounded; some still seemed to be missing, but whether they were in hiding or not was unknown. After Easter Rother called a general meeting of all the catechists to discuss future classes in preparation for marriage, first communion, and confirmation. Most were reluctant to stir up any reprisals by organizing and holding classes again, for the army was still encamped in nearby fields. Finally, one catechist told Rother that if it was up to the catechists nothing would ever get done and that A'plas just ought to order them back to work. Rother took his advice, ordered classes to begin, and was truly pleased at the reinvigorated spirit of his parishioners. Stan also could not praise the sisters enough for the warmth and vitality they were contributing to mission life: It was they, he wrote his cousin, who had kept the mission work alive while he and Bocel were away; "and to think," he added, "that they just got here last September."[85]

But on the national scene, mayhem continued. In early 1981, Amnesty International issued a study, *Guatemala: A Government Program of Political Murder*, which charged that repression was *not* the work of private right-wing groups, but could be traced to the army, working from a communications center annexed to the presidential palace. Systematic attacks on peasant villages were becoming commonplace. *Campesinos* were defenseless against machine guns, grenade launchers, and helicopters. In one village, the people fought back with rocks; the estimated dead numbered between 150 and 300, mainly women and children.[86]

Rother's final visit to Oklahoma, a very brief one, was in mid-May to attend the ordination of his cousin Don Wolf. At that time, he gave his chalice to his parents—it had been a gift from them—and visited briefly with friends. After his return to Micatokla, in a letter dated June 1, 1981, to Father Don McCarthy, an old friend from his seminary days, Rother revealed that he was concerned about his safety and was considering a compromise between leaving the Indians altogether and remaining in Santiago Atitlán in constant fear:

> Maybe you can come down here on your vacation this summer? I am looking for a replacement. I am here for 13 years now and am too well known. After being on the list, I can never be real safe again. I don't know how long their memory is. These are just thoughts, but I would like to have someone to keep things going and I could be in and out on an irregular basis. I would like to have some time to help two catechists get the New Testament ready for printing. They are doing this work while in hiding.[87]

It is probable that Rother, by June 1981, realized he was still a potential death-squad target. In an interview for the *Los Angeles Times* that month he said: "I have found that I am on a list of those to be killed. . . . I talked too much when I was in Oklahoma, and some of it got back to Guatemala."[88] By this time, Rother often slept with his clothes on, hoping that if the death squad came for him he could make a quick escape. He once joked with friends that he was "sleeping with his boots on," and he told Father Leven, who expressed concern for his safety, "don't worry, don't worry, I have my way to escape."[89] Perhaps Rother thought he would be given a warning beforehand. And in fact that is exactly what occurred. Just after midnight on July 28, three tall men, their faces covered by masks, broke into the rectory. They could not immediately find Rother, probably because for safety he no longer slept in his own bedroom. Instead they found Francisco Bocel, brother of Pedro Bocel, and told him to take them to Rother. Thus when Rother was aroused from sleep that night, it was not by the intruders but by the voice of Francisco on the other side of the bedroom door. "Father, they are looking for you," the young man said. This was not what he had been instructed to say by the kidnappers; he was supposed to trick the priest into opening the door on some minor pretense, but instead he had offered Rother a warning.[90]

Stan could have escaped, for there were windows; probably he had even anticipated a couple of possible routes. But what he had not anticipated was that Francisco would be in the custody of members of the death squad. Given their record of brutality, Francisco would have then been the one to die. Rother opened the door. A struggle began with the three masked men, as they tried to drag him out. Francisco, who left the immediate area, heard the priest yell, "No, I won't go with you! You'll have to kill me here!" The fighting continued for perhaps two more minutes, and then Rother lay dead on the floor, bruised, with gunshot wounds in the temple and jaw.[91] The sisters heard the shots, then waited thirty minutes before they went to Stan's room and found the body. Four of them took the 3:00 A.M. bus to San Lucas Toliman to report the murder.

Later that morning, the people of Santiago Atitlán brought Rother's body to the church, and villagers gathered there throughout the day. On the same day he was killed, two masses were celebrated there by more than twenty-five priests, and on July 29 the mission church was packed with three thousand parishioners, thirty-five priests, and two bishops for the funeral mass; a thousand or more villagers stood outside. During the funeral mass, the priest's heart was buried in the floor of the church sanctuary; the Tzutuhils had been so distressed to learn that A'plas was to be buried in Okarche that they had requested this compromise from the family and church and government officials.[92]

At the funeral mass on August 3 in Oklahoma City, Archbishop Salatka called Rother "a great man and an uncommonly good priest," "the Beautiful American." He said: "I trust that the government will not rest until the truth of his death is brought to light, including the realities of life in Guatemala which conspired to harm him."[93] Father Stan was buried in the little cemetery in Okarche. He wore the colorful *perraje* on his shoulders, the treasured stole from the elders of Santiago Atitlán; in large letters on the headstone are inscribed the words "Padre A'plas."

Not surprisingly though, the archbishop's plea for the truth was ignored and a real travesty of justice began in Guatemala, for shortly after Rother's murder three local Indians, two of them close friends of Stan, were arrested and charged with the crime. Guatemalan authorities stated that Sister Ana María Gonzales Arias had related that the three had been surprised by Rother while they were robbing the church. Later Sister Ana María fled to Mexico, where a spokesperson for her religious order told the press that she had never made the above statement.[94]

Salatka and the Rother family protested these arrests to the U.S. State Department, and the three men were eventually released after General Ríos Montt seized control of Guatemala. The true murderers, however, were never arrested, never even pursued.

Even in the United States, the outcries of Salatka, the Rother family, and the concerned citizens of Oklahoma, as well as the testimony of Frankie Williams at Congressional hearings, were not enough to prevent the Reagan administration from lifting restrictions on the sale of trucks and jeeps to the Guatemalan army. Furthermore, one year later journalists Bob Rivard and Tanya Barrientos reported:

> . . . In Guatemala the U.S. embassy did not even send a representative to the memorial mass for Rother. Only one American reporter attended. There have been no congressional fact-finding teams. Sources within the U.S. embassy in Guatemala indicated the incident had a low priority.[95]

For three years, Santiago Atitlán was without a resident priest; the nuns continued to hold the mission together, training catechists, teaching children, helping the sick, and leading prayers on Sundays when a priest from a neighboring parish could not come for mass. In July 1984, however, the Oklahoma archdiocese sent Father John Vesey and later Father Thomas McSherry to serve the Tzutuhil Indians.

It may never be known exactly why Rother was marked for murder by

Guatemalan death squads. In the United States, he had spoken out for the rights of Guatemalan Indians and had been condemned by a fellow country-man in a letter to the Guatemalan embassy; his friend Father Leven believes this could have brought Rother's name to the attention of authorities.[96] In Guatemala, he had visited a parishioner in prison; he had opened up his church as a sanctuary for those parishioners who found out their names were on the death list and had offered the catechist Diego Quic the hospitality of the rectory for the same reason; he had comforted the victims' families; he had tried to obtain food, money, and clothing for the widows and children left without support; he had asked an army officer why persecution had begun when the soldiers came to town; and he had denounced those village spies who would betray their brothers. The priest's "crime" was that he applied the gospel to his daily life in a village under attack.

He had had the chance to return to the safety of Oklahoma. Tom Rother had read his brother's thoughts as he watched him brood and stare into space during the spring of 1981; and at Stan's funeral he tried to console another mourner: "It's better this way than for him to have come back here and lived to be 90 years old, always knowing that he should've been there."[97] In the end the Tzutuhil Indians had beckoned patiently from the shore of Lake Atitlán and Padre A'plas had simply returned to them.

5

John David Troyer

Mennonite Missionary

John David Troyer was only one of many Protestant churchmen brutally murdered in Guatemala. Marco Antonio Cacao Muñoz, an evangelical pastor and a founding member of a journalists' union, was beaten to death on July 5, 1980; three days later another evangelical, a deacon named Roberto Ortiz Morales, was killed by machine-gun fire. Four months later four more Protestant churchmen lost their lives through violence. On November 11, while returning from a prayer service in Jutiapa, preachers Apoliciano Albeno López and Raúl Albeno Martínez were ambushed and murdered. Four days later Pedro Caal was killed in the Petén, and on November 21 Santos Jiménez Martínez, a pastor of the Brotherhood of Evangelical Churches of the People, was shot dead after leading a religious service in Santo Domingo Suchitepequez near the Pacific Ocean.[1] Troyer is unique, however, in that he was the first and, as of this writing, the only Protestant missionary from the United States to be murdered in Central America.

Protestants first appeared in Guatemala in 1882 when Liberal president Justo Rufino Barrios invited the Presbyterians to open a church in Guatemala City. By the end of the 1970s there were sixty-seven different Protestant denominations in the country, many of them recent arrivals. About 15 percent of the population was Protestant. Some Protestant churches were dedicated to the eradication of institutional violence and injustice. Most sects, however, restricted their concerns to the spiritual development of their members and to evangelizing others. They took great care to separate themselves from political controversy and the struggle for human rights.[2] The Conservative Mennonite Fellowship Mission, of which Troyer was a member, certainly falls into this category. The views of its members are summed up by Dallas Witmer in his book, *The Guatemalan Cry*:

Each soul is precious. . . . For Christ places the worth of each soul at more than the whole world. And how costly the loss each time an

John David Troyer

impenitent soul slips off into eternity before the Gospel reaches him! Millions in Guatemala are living wasted lives, dead while they live, many are passing into eternal torment daily. Thousands of these would respond to a full Gospel witness.[3]

In other words, the Conservative Mennonites, like most other fundamentalist missionary churches in Guatemala, feel that every adult who dies without "finding Jesus," without being "saved" in the conservative evangelical manner, is destined to burn forever in hell. If such is the case, they conclude, it seems far more important to concentrate on saving non-believers' souls than to waste time in the struggle for physical well-being in this world. This is not to say that material help should not be extended; it should, especially when it provides contacts for evangelization.[4]

The origins of the Mennonite Church can be traced back to Zurich, Switzerland, where in 1525 Conrad Grebel and his followers became estranged from the reformed movement begun by Ulrich Zwingli. Believing that Zwingli had compromised his original program in order to win support from the Zurich senate, Grebel established a faith based on allegiance to the Bible above the senate and on baptism limited to "true Christians" who had consciously "received the Spirit." In other words, only adults were to be baptized, for they alone are accountable persons, capable of repenting and being "born again." Innocent children would be saved due to the atonement made by Christ through his death and resurrection and therefore had no need for baptism. Because of their belief in adult baptism the followers of Grebel became known as "Anabaptists," a word that actually means "ones who are rebaptized." The term "Mennonite" eventually came to be used after Menno Simons, a former Catholic priest, became a leader in the Dutch Anabaptist movement in 1536.

The Mennonites, from the beginning, rejected the intertwined church-state system of the day. In the early years they spread rapidly in urban centers, but severe persecution contributed to their development into introverted, quietist enclaves of believers, who withdrew *in toto* from the world of unbelievers. Condemning individualism as sinful, they attempted to live the life of spiritual as well as economic fellowship found in the Acts of the Apostles. This sense of brotherhood formed a strong bond and has been inherited by their members today. The pamphlet *Who Are the Mennonites*? explains: "Because of their love for each other Mennonites also practice what they call mutual aid, that is, they come to the rescue of each other in any and every case of need, even when such assistance proves costly from a financial standpoint."[5] The brethren, as they called themselves, also eschewed the hierarchical and class structures of sixteenth-century society, fostering instead egalitarianism:

Since the Church of Christ is to be a brotherhood, no distinction based on any earthly factor is to have significance. Neither wealth, nor education, nor ordination may blur the truth of the equality of the saints. Hence the ministers are regarded basically as teachers of the Word of God rather than as professional pastors, much less as priests. All titles are avoided because of the Brotherhood character of the church. Whether ordained or unordained all the members think of each other as brothers and sisters in the Lord.[6]

Finally, the Mennonites professed strict pacifism:

The waging of warfare . . . puts one's obligation to the state above his obligation to the church, for professing believers from warring nations kill each other as soldiers of their respective states while professing to love one another as fellow members of the body of Christ. It is also impossible to explain how a Christian can claim to love the unsaved of all lands, desiring their salvation with all his heart, and then attempt as a soldier to hurl such unsaved persons into a Christless eternity. Mennonites, therefore, stand for unconditional love and for nonresistance to those who would do them evil.[7]

Even though the Mennonites were small in number, withdrawn from secular society, and pacifists, they were nevertheless viciously hunted, persecuted, and martyred into near-extinction by Calvinists, Catholics, and Lutherans alike. In the eighteenth and nineteenth centuries many of the brethren from both the Swiss and Dutch branches emigrated to North America in hopes of finding religious toleration, peace, and freedom. There, in a new environment free from persecution, they have grown steadily. Today there are over 200,000 in the Western Hemisphere.[8]

The Conservative Mennonite Fellowship was begun in 1956 by a small group of churchpeople who were disenchanted with the major Mennonite church bodies—most notably, the Mennonite Central Committee—which they considered too doctrinally and politically liberal. One obvious difference between the majority of Mennonite churches and the Conservatives is over clothing. The Conservatives believe the contemporary clothing worn by the more liberal Mennonite women to be "unscriptural"[9] and "immodest."[10] Women are required to wear plain, full-length cape dresses which hang just above the ankles, have long sleeves, and fully cover the shoulders. It is also compulsory for the men to wear the straight-cut, Nehru-type collar suit coat.[11] There are likewise significant political contrasts. Members associated with the Mennonite Central Committee, on the one hand, participate at times in non-violent protests; some of its affiliated churches have declared sanctuary for Salvadoran and Guatemalan refugees; and some of its U.S. members have taken part in such activities as Witness for Peace in Nicaragua. The Conservative Mennonites, on the other hand, claim to adhere to absolute separation of church and state and therefore refuse to play any role whatsoever in partisan politics, even when human rights issues are involved. They seem, throughout their missionary years in Guatemala, to have accepted at face value the claim of that country's government that "communist guerrilla terrorism had reached [such] levels" that it was forced "to mobilize all means possible to pull it out by the roots."[12] Indeed, after the murder of Troyer a delegation from the Conservative Mennonites met with the governor of Chimaltenango, presenting him with a paper "explaining our work and that we are in no way to be identified with the MCC [the Mennonite Central Committee] in organization or operation, especially in political views."[13]

In 1964, the Mission Board of the Conservative Mennonites inaugurated an evangelical project in Guatemala aimed primarily at the Indians. Its activities were centered in Chimaltenango but by 1981 branches were extended to the villages of Las Lomas, El Rodeo, Palamá, and Paquib.[14] The brethren by that time had approximately eighty members regularly receiving communion and about 175 attending services.[15] The twenty-fifth year of the Conservative Mennonite Fellowship and the seventeenth of the group's Guatemalan commitment would be marked by the tragic and senseless murder of John David Troyer. As his fellow missioner, William Bear, remarked: "The book of the martyrs is opened again."[16]

John was born on March 7, 1953, at Talfree Memorial Hospital in West Branch, Michigan. He was the first child of Alvin and Luellen Graber Troyer, who, fourteen months later, presented him with a brother named Nelson. The close-knit family was completed with the births of two more sons, Dwight in 1958, followed by Mark three years later. During their preschool years, John and Nelson were inseparable; their parents recollect with amusement the confusion of their second son on his older brother's entrance into kindergarten: "The first day John was gone, Nelson didn't know how to play alone; he kept wandering around and then came in the house and said, 'Mom, I am just like a lost dog.' "[17]

The Troyer family were simple, hard-working, religious folk who ran a grocery and butcher business in Mio, Michigan. Seth Troyer, John's grandfather, owned the store and taught his son Alvin the butcher trade. As their father worked, all four boys watched with fascination; it was not long before they began to imitate the elder Troyer's skillful actions. Using their toy animals, they pretended to butcher cows and pigs: "They had stuffed animals and a [toy] monkey," recall their parents, "that many times over were killed, dressed out, and hung up in the cooler."[18] The four youngsters eventually followed their father in the butcher trade and assisted him in running the grocery business. Later, in his mission work, John would kill and dress out the meat consumed by the community, thereby saving the group a considerable amount of money.[19]

John attended school from 1958 to 1970 in the small community of Fairview, a village about nine miles northeast of Mio. During the spring break of his senior year of high school, he decided to accompany his minister, Floyd Yoder, and the Yoder family on a trip to a Mennonite mission in Costa Rica, where the Yoders' son Jason served. John returned convinced of the great need for more missionary workers. He did not yet feel, however, that such a calling was for him.[20] Before long, he began to change his mind, and by 1972 he had reached a decision. He then entered Messiah Bible School in Holmesville, Ohio, to take courses aimed at preparing him for the missions. After completing the first half of a twelve-week program,[21] he committed himself to a two-year term in Guatemala.

On May 11, John began his journey to Guatemala City from the small airport in Traverse City, Michigan. He was to serve the mission program as bookkeeper and treasurer and assist the community in any way he could.[22] Landing with Troyer on the same plane was Marie Schrock, a young Conservative Mennonite missioner from Mississippi, who would later become John's wife. She, like her future husband, had made her first commitment, also for two years. She was to run the clinic in Palamá, one of the more remote outposts of the mission program, about thirty miles from Chimaltenango. The *clínica* had been opened in 1970 by Norma Zehr, a registered nurse and member of the mission team. At first, only church members made use of her services, but eventually non-Mennonites from throughout this isolated area brought their sick for treatment.[23] When, at the end of her two-year commitment, Norma returned to Canada to be married, Marie replaced her as head of the clinic staff. After seven months, however, Norma returned to Palamá with her husband and again took charge.[24]

Like Norma, Marie found malnutrition was the major cause of sickness among the Indians who came to her for help; unlike in the United States, people were on the verge of death from lack of treatment for such common maladies as measles and whooping cough.[25] Many Indians suffered from pneumonia, primarily due to a combination of poor housing and cold mountain nights; and infant mortality was scandalous. The *clínica* served as an excellent means for proselytizing; when men came suffering from the aftereffects of drunkenness, Marie would refuse to give them pain-relieving medicine. Instead, she admonished them "to give [your lives] to Christ and let Him cure you."[26] Each patient who sought help at the clinic was given religious literature and invited to attend Mennonite church services.

In May 1974, when their two-year commitments were completed, both John Troyer and Marie Schrock returned to the United States. They were married on June 22 and settled down in Michigan. Guatemala had gotten into their blood, however, and they felt called to return. They did so in September 1975, pledging themselves to three years of service in Palamá, which they extended for an additional three months. After John and his family, which now included three children, returned to Michigan in December 1978, he became an ordained Mennonite minister.[27] He and Marie returned to Guatemala for the third time to serve another three-year term; this time, John became pastor of the church at Palamá and overseer of the Paquib mission, about six miles across the mountains.[28]

True to the Conservative Mennonite tradition, John devoted his efforts primarily to the spiritual realm; his pastoral work entailed preaching, counseling, and visitations.[29] The Palamá community consisted of about thirty-one communicants, with an additional ten to twenty Guatemalans attending services. There were eleven local communicants at Paquib, but an average of twenty-five to thirty came to chapel on Sundays. A native deacon under Troyer's direction was charged with the care of the Paquib community. The mission board, however, hoped eventually to replace him with an ordained minister and his family.[30]

Palamá had become a permanent mission site in 1970 when a house was constructed for a resident missionary family. Aside from the clinic, a chapel had been built in 1971 and a Christian school in 1972. Since the local public school was inadequate, many children attended that of the mission. Infuriated, officials at the public school tried but failed to have the Christian school closed by the government.[31] When Troyer served as ordained minister at Palamá, the school was directed by a Mayan teacher, Domingo Tubac, who had about twenty young students. Classes were coeducational and absenteeism was a problem.[32] Students are on vacation in Guatemala from October through December, so during these months vacation bible school was held for children, adolescents, and adults. The missionaries also conducted adult reading classes, as well as classes in child care and sewing.[33]

As far back as 1968, the Conservative Mennonite Fellowship Mission (CMFM) realized that some priority had to be given to alleviating the poverty of its Guatemalan members, the majority of whom were hard workers who earned only sixty to eighty cents a day. Consequently, most of them lived in one- or two-room adobe homes with dirt floors, and few could afford anything better than homes made of cornstalks. The mission opened a factory in Chimaltenango which produced wooden stepladders, but it proved unprofitable and was closed after two years. Two large chicken farming operations were also begun in the same town but likewise proved unsuccessful. Meanwhile a special board was set up in the United States to oversee material aid projects; under its authority, the missionaries launched a business venture called Small Farm Enterprises. A small egg-laying project proved more successful, and soon the enterprise felt confident enough to expand to Palamá, where four Indian church members were supplied with fifty hens each and adobe chicken houses with netting and corrugated steel roofs. Eventually, the Palamá operation was expanded to include hog, goat, and broiler projects. Later, the material aid program was extended to all mission points; small vegetable growing projects were tried, and interest-free loans were made to needy Guatemalan church members who, prior to this time, were forced to borrow money at as high an interest rate as 18 percent per *month* in order to purchase the fertilizer and seeds necessary for survival.[34]

The mission's no-interest loan project, although quite helpful to the Indian recipients, could at times have most unattractive side effects for the North Americans. John Troyer made several loans from his own pocket, losing approximately $700 when some of the projects failed. Dale Miller, describing his duties at Chimaltenango, writes:

I also had the less pleasant job of collecting payments from those that owed the Small Farm Enterprises. This had a few unpleasant aspects such as trying to collect when they didn't have money, and having to refuse to help them with a project or money when they asked sometimes.[35]

Much of Troyer's and the other missionaries' time had to be devoted to such mundane tasks as building projects, traveling from one mission to another by jeep or motorcycle, maintaining the dirt road to the main highway, and making mechanical repairs. Due to the rugged terrain, a fender or two were always in need of fixing, and punctured tires were a common occurrence.

The all-day workers' meeting held once a month at each mission was a welcome change from the usual daily routine. The North American missioners would gather together in the morning for a church service conducted totally in English. Business matters would be addressed in the afternoon and, if concluded early enough, there would be time left over for a volleyball game. The entire mission team in each area would also meet once a month for special evening services. Prayers would be said for private intentions and for the needs of other individuals.

Life at Palamá was rigorous, more so than at most of the other Mennonite missions in Guatemala. Dale Miller, who assisted Troyer at Palamá for a few months, reported that in that outpost there was much less time available for social pleasantries and fellowship: The road was extremely bad and in need of constant attention; also due to its remote location, the community had to wait longer than usual for mail to be delivered from family and friends in the United States. Nevertheless, Miller adds, a few hours could always be found for hiking and good conversation and, although forever busy, the group was content.[36]

As devout Conservative Mennonites, the Troyers were always careful to divorce themselves from politics and its repercussions on the Indian people. Nevertheless, as the following letter from John and Marie brings out, they could not help but notice the harsh realities of life in Guatemala:

Dear Christian friends,

Greetings from our home to yours. . . .
It appears that the dry season has finally come to stay. With it, of course, comes the dust. The mud on our road, which caused us so much slipping and sliding in the rainy season, has now dried and billows in our narrow dirt road between the rainy and dry season.

The people here have nearly finished harvesting their beans and some have started husking corn. Their patios have turned into drying areas for beans and corn. After it has been dried, the majority will be stored away for the family's use during the coming year and the rest will be sold. Often the money from this corn will have to go on debts incurred during the past year.

During these months, work is scarce for the people in the outlying areas. And so, as the custom has been for years, the men and sometimes the whole family will go to the coastal areas of Guatemala looking for work. There they work on large farms (fincas) picking coffee and cotton and cutting sugar cane. The pay is fairly good but life there is rather miserable. Often sleeping quarters consist of only a blanket under a tree, sometimes the food is scarce, and there are many diseases ready to plague the workers and their families. A number of the brethren from Palamá and Paquib are at the coast working now. Please remember them in your prayers.

The Troyers next talk of news from their community at Palamá:

> We praise the Lord for a number in the community who are showing a renewed interest in the church. These were members at one time but for various reasons had left. One family in particular . . . has attended a number of the services and has expressed some desire in becoming part of us again. Pray for them and others as well.
>
> There is a lot of sickness around right now, possibly due to the colder weather we are having. Often in the morning there will be frost on the ground. Our family has had its rounds with colds and "grip." Our youngest, Timothy, spent a night in the hospital because of pneumonia. We are grateful that the Lord is healing his body again.
>
> Thank you for your prayer support. . . .
>
> In Christian love,
> John and Marie Troyer
> John Ray, Marilyn, and Timothy
> [the three Troyer children][37]

The Conservative Mennonite mission board had assigned Paul Strubhar to live with the Troyer family and assist John both at Palamá and Paquib. He stayed well past his commitment but eventually was no longer able to delay his return to the United States. Since Marie Troyer was pregnant, John was in critical need of help. Observing the Mennonite tradition of "mutual aid" in times of exceptional need, the board transferred Dale Miller from Chimaltenango to Palamá for the duration of his commitment. Miller's arrival at the mission was indeed fortunate, for on March 31, 1981, Marie gave birth to twin girls, Sharon Joy and Karen June. The Troyers now had five children, the oldest being only six years of age. Before long, the board also sent Gary Miller, Dale's brother, to help out in Palamá. His commitment was for two years and although his and his brother's service at Palamá and Paquib overlapped at first, he was being groomed to take on Dale's responsibilities, which he did when the latter shortly returned to the United States.[38] This then was the little Mennonite group at Palamá as time drew them closer toward the violent events of September 13 and 14.

The small band at the mission outpost on the evening of the 13th consisted of John Troyer, the twenty-eight-year-old pastor; his wife, Marie; their five young children; Gary Miller; and a young Indian woman, Emiliana Cristal, a member of the church who had come to stay a few days at the mission house to lend Marie a hand with the babies. All were simple people who attempted to live a quiet, unassuming, prayer-oriented life in the midst of a country torn by injustice and violent oppression. All were pacifists who would not even strike back in self-defense; they belonged to a church which demanded such a strict separation of church and state that no political involvement whatsoever was tolerated. Gary Miller recalls in his own words the horrors of that night:

I had somewhat of a premonition Sunday night that something was going to happen to me, personally. And I did not know when it would happen or what it would be. I was sitting at the kitchen table writing letters after everyone else had gone to bed. About 9:30 I finished my letters, but somehow I had a restless feeling. I didn't feel like going to bed, although it was the time I normally retired for the night. I just sat there for a long time with my head in my hand on the table. As I thought into the future I wondered what plan God might have for my life. Of course, I didn't have the answer.

But then my mind turned to the past. I thought about many, many memories from my childhood. It seemed to me that I was coming to a halfway point in my life, somewhat of a dividing point. As I was thinking, words for a poem about my childhood came to my mind, and I wrote them. For two hours I wrote, and the thought came to me that this might be the last work of writing I may ever do, so on the top corner of the paper I wrote the date: September 13, 1981. I thought, if this is found in my possessions people will know that this is the last work I ever did. When I finished writing, it was 11:30. I read briefly in my Bible for a devotional meditation and blew out the light and went to bed.

I had lain in bed for about five minutes, perhaps, when I heard loud, angry shouts outside the house. Immediately following the shouts I heard terrible hard blows being rained with some instrument on the door. I jumped out of bed quickly and looked out the window. I saw three men on the front porch of the house. My first thoughts were, "They're a band of drunks. They are assaulting our house. They don't know what they're doing."

I knew by the force of the blows that the door wouldn't hold out long, so I pulled on my clothes and hurried over to John Troyer's room at the opposite end of the house. On the way I heard three shots outside. That is when I guess my fears were bordering on terror. To think that a group of armed drunk men were about to enter our house! I knew there'd be no mercy—they would not be rational. When I burst into John's room they were already out of bed, as they had heard the noise.

John asked, "Who is it?"

I said, "It's a bunch of drunks out there. Let's pray."

We threw ourselves across the bed and John said, "Gary, will you pray for us?"

So I prayed, asking the Lord's protection, but most of all that His will would be done for us. When we got up from prayer we weren't sure what we should do next. We were still afraid, of course. The thought entered my mind that maybe we could escape out the back door. But just that quickly I thought, "They'll be guarding the back door, too."

We went to the window and looked out. The three men were still on the porch. There were four men out on the driveway lying on their stomachs with their rifles leveled at the house. All this time the men were yelling angrily.

John opened the window and called out, "Sirs, you can have anything that's in the house."

They said, "That's all right. Come out! Immediately! With your hands above your head! There won't be any loss of life."

John said, "Very well, we'll do it."

We quickly awakened the children. Also staying with us for a few days was a girl, Emiliana, a member of the church. She was helping Marie with the babies. I went to her room and told her briefly what was expected of us. Then I went to my room and put on my shoes, and we all gathered by the front door which the men had beaten open but had not entered. Each of us took a child in his arms. I picked up four-year-old Marilyn and stepped outside the door first. All this time the men outside were saying, "Keep your hands up! Hands up!" I had my hands above my head and Marilyn was clinging to my neck and crying.

There was very bright moonlight, for the moon was full. This was unusual for Guatemala at this time of the year as it is usually raining in the night. We could see everything about our captors very clearly. There were about ten men, all in green uniforms. Each man had an automatic rifle strapped to his shoulder. One man was carrying a machete, possibly used to beat down the door. Three men wore stocking masks over their faces, but the others were unmasked.

The first question they asked was, "Is there gasoline?"

After that they quickly dispersed. We were ordered to be seated on the porch with our legs dangling over the edge. One man, presumably their leader, stayed with us to guard us. Some went into the house. We could hear them rummaging around and things being overturned and crashing to the floor. Several men got on the car. They opened the hood, took off the air cleaner, were doing something to the carburetor. I thought they were probably getting gas out of the car. Maybe they didn't know that they couldn't get gas without having the car running.

After this they ordered me back into the house. They said all the time, "Keep your hands up! Keep your hands up!"

They seemed fearful. They wanted to know where my camera was, and I showed them.

"Do you have a recorder?" they asked.

"Yes, there are two recorders." I showed them where they were.

"Do you have binoculars?"

I didn't understand the word for binoculars. I was afraid they wouldn't be able to make me understand what they wanted of me and would become angry. At that point they were stern but they seemed to be rational.

They said, "The thing that you can see a long way away with."

"Yes," I said, and showed them where they were.

They said, "Go back outside the house," and I turned to go.

I guess I didn't go fast enough, for one of them kicked me from behind, but not too hard. That was the only time they actually laid hands on me, if I may use that term.

I sat down outside again where the guard was lecturing. I couldn't understand everything, but he had two major points. First, he accused us of teaching things that are not good for the people, deceiving them. He did not specify; I believe because he didn't know what we were teaching. He said we were teaching the people evil things.

John Troyer's answer to that was, "It certainly is not our desire in any way to deceive the people. Rather we are here to bring them the Gospel."

The second theme, which they spent most of the time talking on, was the rich versus the poor. He said, "You are rich. You are coming in and taking advantage of our poor neighbors. We are poor. We are Indians. How much money do you have in the house?" he asked.

We gave him the approximate figure of $160.00.

"I have one cent in my pocket," he went on. "I am poor. This is why I am out here. We are the Army for the Liberation of the Poor. If anybody asks you who did this, tell them that. We're not out here killing people for the fun of it. There's a reason for it."

The girl that was with us, Emiliana, was eighteen, and a Christian. He asked her, "Aren't you tired of being oppressed by the gringos? Aren't you poor? Why are you here?"

Her answer came back, "Sure, we're poor, but we believe in getting out and working with our hands to earn our living." They didn't say too much more on that subject.

Another question they asked was, "Is it fair for you to have this nice car? And this nice house?"

The house we lived in was moderately nice compared to the cornstalk huts and mud huts that are the homes of the natives. But it was not an elaborate house.

He said, "Is it fair that you have these things when your neighbors don't have enough food, don't have enough clothes, and don't have shoes?"

I told him that these things are serving for a purpose. I said, "Without this car we couldn't even be here. We couldn't come in here to hold services and help the people. Our primary emphasis is to give spiritual help and then the material."

John pointed out about that time too that we do help the people in the form of interest free loans, for example. When they need to buy fertilizer and don't have money to buy it, they can't afford to pay interest on loans. Out of his own pocket he had loaned them money, and a lot of it he never saw again. He told me just a couple nights before, "I lost something like seven hundred dollars loaning it to these people." He had a concern for their needs and was doing everything he could to help.

However, it seemed that the men were not in a mood to listen to us. They had talked nearly an hour, and also had the inside of the house pretty well ransacked. Piled in front of the house were our two-way radio communication system, flashlights, recorders, and cameras—small valuable things easy to carry.

The leader was joined by a small, aggressive man who asked us several times, "How do you feel about what we're doing? Is it fair what we are doing to you?" One time he brought his gun up to me and clicked off the safety to add emphasis to what he had said.

John said in a soft voice, "Naturally we feel very sorry for what is taking place."

The nights in Palamá are very chilly at 8,000 feet, and we had brought out just a few blankets for the little ones. We were shivering, and John said, "Will you please let me go inside the house and get a few blankets for the little ones?"

"No," he replied. "Now you know how we feel. We don't have enough blankets either. We're poor."

By this time I could hear from the inside that they were splashing a liquid around the house. I thought it was probably gas, but it later turned out that they splashed kerosene all over the floor, up to the ceiling, on the walls and over the furniture. They opened the drawers and poured it on the clothes, and I thought they were going to light the house. They poured it all over the car, too (gasoline, I suppose) and started getting ready to light it. The car was right by the porch, close to us, and we started edging away when we saw what was going to happen.

The guard said, "No, stay there."

John said, "Well, it's going to go up with a poof! Let's move. It's dangerous here."

Finally, reluctantly, he said, "O.K. Go down in the driveway just a little way."

So we moved down, and pretty soon the car went up in flames and really burned hotly. We were seated on the grass by the driveway, and pretty soon he said, "Leave the children here and go on down."

Marie began to sob and say, "Oh, please! Oh, please! Don't take the children from us!"

Right away I had visions of them shooting and killing the children while we were watching, and I thought that would be more than I could take. Marie pleaded and pleaded, but he didn't say too much. He just fiddled around and watched the car awhile.

Pretty soon he said, "O.K., go on down."

We didn't ask any questions. We just picked up the children and moved down the driveway to the front of the church nearby.

Then he said, "Leave the children here."

The children all sat down in the grass at one spot. Then he told John and me to move over to one side. We stood there and watched. About that time all the men except two started up the road carrying in sacks on their backs the things they had taken from the house.

One of the two men with us turned to me and said, "O.K., stand over here."

My stomach was knotted up in fear. When I saw how they lined us up I sensed what was coming, so I turned. The man maneuvered close in front of John and I heard a shot. But John didn't fall. He just bowed his head and hunched up a bit and turned sideways. The man shot three more times, and John still didn't fall. Between the shots, I could hear John saying "Please, sirs, please, please."

Marie was sitting over there with the children crying, "God, don't permit it! God, don't permit it! Please, sir, don't do it! We'll leave tomorrow; we'll go to the States."

The man looked at Marie and smirked a bit and said, "You'll leave tomorrow, will you?"

All this time I was standing there just clenching my fists and saying softly to myself, "Lord, your will be done; Lord, your will be done." I didn't know what else to say. I was just paralyzed. I thought first when they were shooting at John that maybe they were trying to really scare him to make sure he'll leave. I thought maybe they wouldn't kill him.

But then the second man came up a little bit closer. He took good aim and shot, and my heart just sank to the bottom of my toes when I saw John slump down backwards. I thought, "No! They got him!" My hopes were dashed to the ground when I saw him fall. They shot once more after he fell. In the end there were five bullets found in his body.

Then in one quick motion he turned and fired at me. It seemed like a giant impact had struck my shoulder. Twisting as I fell, I landed on my chest with my face turned away from him. Because they shot John more than once I expected another bullet to come ripping in from behind me any minute. I thought, "This is what it feels like to die." It just flashed through my mind, and I said, "Lord, into thy hands I commend my spirit." I lay there and waited for the bullet to come, but it never did. There was just silence, and I didn't move. I didn't say anything, because I was afraid that if I would move they would see that I was still alive and they would shoot me again.

One of the women called to me, "Gary!"

I didn't say anything, because I was afraid they were still there. Pretty soon Emiliana came over real close and looked at me and turned to leave. As she turned I said, "Emiliana, are they gone?"

She said, "Yes, they're gone."

So I got to my feet and looked around. John was still lying on his back. I went over—I had to walk stooped over—and looked at him. His breath was coming in jerky little gasps, and I thought he didn't look good. I thought, "He won't make it."

Marie was bending over him and examining him closely. She said, "He's really bleeding badly in his arm."

I said, "Here, take my shirt and use it for a tourniquet," and I pulled it off.

By this time I was getting weak and the pain was coming. (At first it was a shock and there wasn't much pain.) After a few minutes it got worse and worse, so I lay down on the ground nearby.

As Marie worked over John's body she said, "John, don't die, don't die. John, you can't leave us. John, we have five children; you can't leave us. You have to stay with us."

But John didn't hear. He was just lying there unconscious. I don't believe he ever knew anything that happened.

Pretty soon Marie turned to me and said in a calm voice, "Gary, he's gone, I'm afraid. He's just sleeping so peacefully."

I said, "I'm sorry, Marie. May God give you strength."

I then rested there awhile, fearing in my heart that the men would return and see me alive and kill me. Yet I didn't want to leave Marie, and Marie didn't want to leave her husband. You can understand that.

I said, "Marie, I'm going to leave. I'm going over to a neighbor's house."

There were no neighbors home. When they had heard the gunfire and commotion they all fled into the fields. There was no help to be found.

So they helped me to my feet. By that time I could hardly go. I proceeded slowly to the house of a church member living within about a quarter of a mile of the church.

I opened the door and went inside and lay on the floor wrapped in a blanket. Pretty soon Marie and her children came and we stayed there until morning.

About two o'clock the owner of the house returned and wanted to go for help. We lived seven miles off the main highway, back a winding, rugged dirt trail, accessible only to four wheel drive vehicles. He would have to go out that road for help and he was afraid, for he knew the men who did the shooting were still at large, and he didn't know where they were. Finally he gained courage and left. He caught the five o'clock bus for Chimaltenango and told the brethren there what had happened. They hurried as fast as they could, but it was 8:30 in the morning before they could possibly get there.

As we waited for them we talked. Marie took a marvelous attitude. She must be a very strong woman is all I can say. I remember that several times she took her little six-year-old John Ray and held him close and said, "John Ray, you have to help Mama now. Daddy's gone."

The children didn't really comprehend what had happened. They asked, "Where's Daddy?"

She said, "He's in heaven now."

They wanted to know, "Why did those men have to shoot my daddy?"

Marie told them, "Children, we have to love those men."

About 8:30 I was taken out, and admitted to the hospital in Guatemala [City] about noon. My pain had become less severe, and there were no complications.[39]

Shocked by the Palamá episode, the Conservative Mennonites agreed to a rendezvous at mission headquarters as soon as possible, where they would decide what future actions should be taken. On Tuesday, September 15, Merle Yoder notified the United States embassy of John's murder, and embassy representatives were sent at once to Chimaltenango to interview Marie. The next day hundreds of mourners attended a memorial service for their slain friend, and on Wednesday the Troyer family accompanied John's body on a flight back to the United States. A funeral service was held on September 19 in Fairview, Michigan. Over seven hundred people gathered to pray and pay their last respects to Troyer; about forty of them had served with him at one time or another in Guatemala.[40]

After much soul-searching, it was decided that all the North American missionaries should return to their native country rather than chance more senseless violence. Gary Miller, whose rapid recovery was incredible, flew home on Thursday, only four days after he was shot. He soon took a teaching position in Grandin, Missouri, at a Mennonite Christian day school. Nearly two years later, in July 1983, Gary married Marie Troyer, John's widow. Today they live with the five Troyer children in North Carolina. The children's psychological recovery, however, was not as remarkable as Gary's physical progress: for a long time after their father's murder, the oldest children were haunted by nightmares of the ordeal they had witnessed.[41]

By September 25, 1981, the last of these North American missionaries had left Guatemala. The five mission outposts were left in the capable hands of the native Conservative Mennonites, one of whom was an ordained minister while two others were deacons. The missioners' decision to leave Guatemala proved to be a wise one, for shortly after their departure armed men arrived at the Chimaltenango church headquarters demanding to see the "gringos." Soon this scene was repeated at Las Lomas, where strangers came and questioned the Indians as to the whereabouts of the North Americans. When Herbert Ebersole, a U.S. citizen and member of the Mennonite Messianic Mission, received death threats along with a demand for extortion money, his board decided to withdraw all but two of its workers. The Messianic Mission maintains close ties with the Conservative Fellowship, which had helped it organize its mission at San Juan, about a hundred miles from Chimaltenango. Finally, a Guatemalan Conservative Mennonite was forced to flee to Mexico after receiving death threats.[42]

In October 1981, the Conservative Mission Board resolved to send a two-man team back to Guatemala each month to give counsel and direction to the native community. William Bear and Merle Yoder formed the first team charged with this responsibility and spent a week visiting the brethren at all five mission locations. As mentioned earlier, the two also met with the governor of Chimaltenango, presenting him with a written statement explaining the beliefs of the Conservative Mennonites and that they are in no way connected with the more politically involved Mennonite Central Committee. Having heard this, the governor "warmly encouraged" the Conservative Mennonites to return to the country and continue their work.[43] In early 1983 the Mission Board decided to do so and today U.S. Conservative Mennonites again serve at all five mission outposts.

One question remains to be discussed: Who killed John David Troyer? At first glance, the answer seems obvious; the assassins announced, reports Gary Miller, that they were the "Army for the Liberation of the Poor." Moreover, they lectured the Mennonites on the poverty of the local population and the unfairness of the North American missioners' wealth. Consequently, one could not help but conclude that the murderers were leftist guerrillas. Upon closer examination, however, the answer is not so cut and dry. Could the right-wing death squads have committed the crimes of September 13 and 14, while purposely making it appear to be the work of the left? If the guerrillas were responsible, which group of them perpetrated the deed and what was their motive? These questions will be treated in the remainder of this chapter. However, before doing so, it should be made quite clear that such matters are of more concern to the authors of this book than to the Conservative Mennonites. The latter, as has been stated throughout this chapter, believe in complete separation of church and state. They are a spiritual, "other-world" oriented group who merely want to be left alone by the right and left so they can practice their religious beliefs in peace. Although they mourn the death of Troyer, they are reluctant to become involved in investigative questions which might jeopardize their current missionary work.

Perhaps because of their strict adherence to the separation of church and state, the Conservative Mennonites are politically naive. They seem to accept at face value whatever is said by the Guatemalan government. That this is so is brought out by the description of the 1974 presidential election in Dallas Witmer's *The Guatemalan Cry*:

National elections in March caused excitement and apprehension for the missionaries, as well as all Americans residing in Guatemala. The pro-American party governing for four years was re-elected to power, but the opposing party also claimed the victory and threatened to make its claim good by force. There was a strong communistic element backing the opposing candidate, which vowed to nationalize Guatemala, and among other things dismiss Americans from the country. . . . A recount of the votes was ordered. For awhile it appeared the opposition would win after all. But when the votes were all tallied at last, it was confirmed that the party in power would remain there.[44]

Evidently, the Conservative Mennonites, in spite of the irregular vote tallying procedures, seemed not even to have thought of the possibility that the recount may have been called to rig the election in favor of the "official" candidate. But when one realizes that the unnamed "communist backed" candidate was Efraín Ríos Montt, a general in the Guatemalan army, the political innocence of the Conservative Mennonites becomes still more apparent. Although Ríos Montt was considered less conservative than General Laugerud, the government's candidate, he could in no way be construed as the communists' candidate. Several years later, after becoming a member of the fundamentalist California-based Church of the Word, Rios Montt would declare himself president. In his first televised speech he would warn Guatemalan guerrillas: "Subversives take note, only the army has the right to carry arms. You must drop your weapons, because if you don't, we are going to take them from you." To link such a man with communists is inconceivable and to accept such a connection without question shows a lack of knowledge of Guatemalan politics.

The authors asked several people, Conservative Mennonites and others, if they had received any additional information on John Troyer's death. Gary Miller replied:

I am afraid I cannot help you much about who the killers were or what became of them. As I stated in my report, I understood them to be leftist by what they said at that time. Someone has suggested that the disciplined manner in which they carried out the operation would be characteristic of a leftist group. You would likely know better than I if that has any merit. To my knowledge no action was ever taken by anyone to identify the killers.[45]

John's parents, Alvin and Luellen Troyer, replied in a similar fashion:

No, we never received any further information on the group that killed John. If the Mission Board heard anything they didn't let us know. As far as we know they were never identified. There were some arrests after John's killing but not identified with John's death. We were told that back in the hills of Palamá they found enough food hidden to supply 100 men for a year.[46]

Harry Hertzler, editor of the Conservative Mennonite Fellowship's monthly newsletter, *The Harvest Call*, commented likewise that the assassins seemed to be guerrillas from their statements to Gary Miller but that neither the Guatemalan nor U.S. government has provided them with any further information on the case. He added that rumor has it that the attack on Palamá was a mistake, that the killers were actually after another group. Whether or not this is true, however, he has no idea, nor did he say who the other group might have been.[47] One possibility is that the murderers might have been from a right-wing terrorist group and mistook the Conservative Mennonites for the more socially active Mennonite Central Committee, which began mission work in Guatemala in 1976. This, however, is mere speculation.

Delton Franz, of the Mennonite Central Committee, told the *National Catholic Reporter* that the armed men said they were guerrillas; " 'but they were dressed in army uniforms . . . and we've been told that this is rather a common ploy' for one faction to pose as its opposing faction when carrying out violence."[48] In a letter from Franz to the authors, he noted: "There are some sensitivities in how our agency deals with the debate over whether Troyer was killed by the left or the right. As your own inquiry with the Conservative Mennonites has revealed, their interpretation may be different from that of others who interpreted the situation."[49] Rich Sider, the Mennonite Central Committee's secretary for Central America Programs, responded to the authors' inquiry by pointing out that:

After Troyer was killed all of their missionaries left the country and we tried to extend a helping hand during that difficult time. Our efforts were not appreciated and, in fact, created real problems for them and as a result we backed off.

At the time of the killing the U.S. State Department, I believe, made some effort to investigate the killings but likely didn't get very far. In Guatemala these kinds of killings are very seldom solved. We have no access to information because of the lack of a relationship with [the Conservative Mennonites] and so can only speculate on who did it and why.[50]

From the above, it is clear that no direct evidence exists linking the left to the murder of Troyer except the fact that the killers said they were the "Army for the Liberation of the Poor."

At the time of Troyer's death there were four major guerrilla organizations. The oldest were the communist-dominated Rebel Armed Forces (Fuerzas Armadas Rebeldes, or FAR) and Guatemalan Workers Party (Partido Guatemalteco del Trabajo, or PGT); the other two groups, the Organization of the People in Arms (Organización del Pueblo en Armas, or ORPA) and the Guerrilla Army of the Poor (Ejército Guerrillero de los Pobres or EGP) were not communist-dominated but were composed primarily of Indians. Although there is no "Army for the Liberation of the Poor," it seems safe to assume that the armed men at Palamá identified themselves as the Guerrilla Army of the Poor, and Miller, being completely unfamiliar with the leftist organizations, remembered the name incorrectly when he later attempted to recall the events of September 13 and 14. The EGP was the largest guerrilla group in Guatemala at that time and its membership was about 80 percent Indian. Since the group seems to have been active in the Palamá area and since the assassins of Troyer identified themselves as poor Indians, it is probable that they were either members of the EGP or tried to pass themselves off as such.

On the other hand, a large percentage of the lower echelon of the Guatemalan army also included Indians, and it is quite possible that some of them killed Troyer. The fact that these conscripted soldiers willingly take part in much of the right-wing violence is perhaps best explained by the techniques reportedly used at times in basic training:

> When a young man was inducted, he was first subjected to several days of starvation. Then a group of starving recruits would be gathered in a circle. A few tortillas would be placed in the center in front of them. They were then made to fight and brutalize one another to see who would get the tortilla to eat.
>
> Similar "training" would then be given with live animals for bait. They would be taught to dismember the animals and eat them raw. At night they would be subjected to the blaring of loud-speakers telling them that the peasants were communists and the enemies of the country. After months of this kind of treatment, soldiers would become like brutes, with no sense of their humanity, and willing to perform any atrocities against their own people.[51]

Indeed, many conscripts openly bragged to writer Phillip Wearne about how they shoot villagers and burn their homes and crops; some claim to have taken part in as many as eighty such operations.[52]

The fact that the assassins of John Troyer constituted a unit of ten men, all in green uniforms with automatic rifles, indicates that they may have been from the Guatemalan military. For one thing, EGP units are usually made up of both men and women and seldom do they wear neat uniforms as Troyer's killers did.[53] Indeed, Indian villagers claim they can identify military death squads because their members usually wear Guatemalan army jungle fatigues and even when they arrive in civilian dress, they wear the military boots of the army and have military haircuts and weapons.[54]

Moreover, virtually every impartial source reports that the guerrillas, who could not survive without the support of the rural populace, are usually careful not to kill innocent civilians. Their tactic is to carry out surprise attacks on government installations or utilities; they kill soldiers, government officials, landowners considered exploitative, and government informers (*orejas*).[55] Since the Conservative Mennonites do not fit into these categories, it is highly unlikely they would have been singled out for death by the guerrillas. In fact, as far back as 1967, when some Mennonites expressed fears concerning a flare-up of guerrilla activities in Guatemala, Conservative missioner Herman Hershey insisted that the guerrillas only went after rich people and therefore would not bother the North American missionaries. He proved correct and the Mennonites were not bothered by guerrillas.[56] Nevertheless, it should be noted that left-wing violence did increase beginning in 1981,[57] and it is possible that the EGP could have mistaken Troyer for someone else and killed him, or thought that he and his group were collaborators with oppressive forces.

On the other hand, right-wing violence had rapidly escalated since 1977, peaking in 1980–81. Amnesty International estimated that approximately 3,000 people labeled subversives by the government were killed between January and November 1980 alone.[58] Fred Sherwood, former president of the American Chamber of Commerce in Guatemala and a firm supporter of the Guatemalan military government, admitted his belief that the right was responsible for these murders when he remarked in 1980: "Why should we be worried about death squads? They're bumping off the commies, our enemies. I'd give them more power. . . . Why should we criticize them? The death squads—I'm for it."[59] Government violence so escalated that in September 1980 the Guatemalan Vice-President, Francisco Villagrán Kramer, decided he could no longer remain associated with the government; he flew to the United States where he startled the world by announcing that he was "left with no option but to resign, after all efforts to ensure the respect of human rights in the country had failed."[60] Shortly thereafter, in 1981, Amnesty International related the findings of its study on Guatemalan death squads in no uncertain terms. Its report, *Guatemala: A Government Program of Political Murder*, concluded: "The selection of targets for detention and murder, and the deployment of official forces for extralegal operations, can be pinpointed to secret offices in an annex of Guatemala's National Palace, under the direct control of the president of the republic."[61]

One final observation is in order. Since several Protestant religious leaders, hundreds of Catholic catechists, and eleven priests were murdered by the army and rightist terrorist squads between 1978 when Lucas García became president and September 1981 when Troyer died, it seems apparent that clergy and other religious leaders were high on the government's death list. Likewise, since many of these Catholic and Protestant victims were not involved in the struggle for human rights, and many were foreign missionaries, it is safe to assume that foreign clergy were in particular peril, whether or not they were "political activists." Thus, John Troyer could well have been a victim of government-sponsored murder.

With the above in mind, the authors feel that no conclusion can be reached in attempting to answer who killed John Troyer: he could have been murdered by either the right or the left; there is simply too little concrete evidence to conclude anything further. However, one fact can be stated with certainty. Regardless of who was responsible, the murder of John Troyer, a twenty-eight-year-old father of five, was a cruel act of violence perpetrated on an innocent man who only wanted to live in peace. As such, it was no different from countless other murders committed in tormented Guatemala.

James Miller

6

James Miller

Christian Brother Missionary

Brother James Alfred Miller was the last North American missionary-victim of the violent Lucas García regime.[1] Like Cypher and Rother, Jim was raised on a farm; the practical and wide-ranging knowledge he absorbed in his early years later infused his missionary work in Central America with a farmboy's unique blend of jovial cooperation, hard work, and no-nonsense pragmatism.

James was born on September 21, 1944, the first child of Lorraine and Arnold Miller. Jim, along with sisters Patty and Louise and brothers Ralph and Bill, was raised on a dairy farm near Ellis in central Wisconsin, not far at all from where young Michael Cypher was growing up in Medford. As a youngster, Jim was inquisitive, outgoing, and energetic; he had the "gift of gab" as friends put it, and was self-assured enough to befriend neighbors regardless of age. Jim's father says: "He was sensitive to people of all ages; he understood their moods. He was close to his neighbors and he often went to help them on their farms." One close friend was Wilfred Steffanus, a farmer who lived across the road. Jim offered to help Steffanus clear his fields of rocks; it struck his neighbor that the boy seemed to enjoy this uninspiring task and never complained. Jim later chose Steffanus as his sponsor in confirmation, and the two always remained close friends. Two months before he himself was killed, Jim spent some time at the bedside of Wilfred's elderly mother, who was dying. Jim prayed and read from the Psalms; his cheerful presence was a great consolation to Mrs. Steffanus, her son remembers. Miller too was impressed by the dignity of the old woman; he told his mother: "If death is always like hers, then I don't know what people are afraid of."[2] Although Wilfred at the time was grateful to Jim for comforting his mother, it seems that Mrs. Steffanus's peaceful acceptance of death was a gift for which Jim, aware of the violence that pervaded Guatemala, was also quietly thankful. Mrs. Steffanus died on the day Miller left Wisconsin for the last time to return to Guatemala.

Jim went to elementary school in Ellis. The public school he attended was a one-room schoolhouse, a picture from the past of rural Americana. There, Jim's small class was taught, along with seven other grades, by one teacher.[3] Jim used to walk the mile and a quarter between the Miller farm and school-house every day; when he arrived home he had the habit of giving the rest of the family a detailed description of all he had observed that day. His parents and siblings were far from bored with this daily rendition—in fact, they found his garrulous descriptions quite entertaining.[4]

Although some would classify Jim, rather ambiguously, as an "average" student, he did have a notable facility for language and an enthusiastic interest in geography and science. When he graduated from the one-room schoolhouse in Ellis, his parents presented him with a *World Book* encyclopedia, which he read from cover to cover trying to absorb everything he could.[5]

As a youngster growing up in the forties and fifties, Jim was not self-conscious about his religious beliefs. He once forgot to say his penance after confession; when halfway home from church, he realized this and knelt down to pray on the road. Throughout his pre-high-school years, he dreamed of one day being a priest; his brother Bill recalls how he made a toy tabernacle from an old clock and pretended he was saying mass. The inventor of Tinker Toys probably never envisioned the use that young Jim would find for his product: with great imagination, he devised a monstrance and added benediction to his repertoire. On his parents' property, Jim even built a model church, that still stands today, where he played priest.[6]

In 1958, he began his freshman year at Pacelli High School in Stevens Point. Impressed by the eleven Christian Brothers who operated the school, he gave up his dreams of the priesthood, deciding that the life of a teaching brother was more to his liking. He entered the order's junior novitiate at Glencoe, Missouri, in September 1959. "In one day," he later recalled, "I left the state of Wisconsin for the first time, took my first train ride, and saw a building over four stories high."[7] He was transferred to Christian Brothers Prep in Saint Paul, Minnesota, for his second year in the juniorate. "There were 36 of us," he wrote in 1978, "and we attended classes at Cretin High School. I believe I am the last surviving member of that historic group."[8] After being sent back to Glencoe for his final year of high school, Jim graduated in 1962.

Even in those early years of formation, the young farmboy from Wisconsin impressed his teachers with his simplicity, energy, generosity, and good humor. Brother Bernard LoCoco remembers that:

> He was very outgoing, emotional, [and] offered bear hug greetings. We never discovered in him any duplicity. He was an average student, applied himself, but was always thinking about how to help others. Whatever he did, he had to be into it fully—almost like a young colt.[9]

Brother Gerard Pihaly, who also taught him at Glencoe, has similar recollections:

He was a good student, but also a very generous person. He would sign up for the most challenging jobs. He liked to work with machinery very much, having come from a farm. He would take the garbage down to the farm by tractor, grade the gravel roads, dig up large flat rocks for flagstone walks. He was a joy to be with during recreation because he was always a very optimistic person and generally had a lot of interesting stories or jokes to tell.[10]

After completing his novitiate year in Winona, Minnesota, Jim entered Saint Mary's College, also in Winona, where he majored in Spanish and English, earning a B.A. degree in May 1966. Greg Robertson, today an administrator at the College of Santa Fe, taught Brother James during those undergraduate years. He remembers him as a cheerful and outgoing student, intelligent but not an intellectual, a down-to-earth young man who would, as often as not, turn in his term papers late and who, although prayerful, would occasionally fall asleep during daily meditation.[11] Brother Theodore Drahmann, who supervised Jim at Saint Mary's, recalls that "he was interested in Spanish . . . because he always seemed to have the idea that he wanted to go down to the missions in Latin America."[12]

Indeed, upon graduating, Brother James asked to be assigned to Latin America. The foreign missions would have to wait, however, because a semester before graduating he was asked to substitute for an ailing brother at Cretin High School in nearby Saint Paul. Although the position was supposed to be temporary, he stayed at Cretin for three and a half years. There, he taught Spanish, organized and coached a soccer team, and took on the task of maintenance supervisor, a job which appealed to his practical nature.

During these years Brother James impressed many people, but no one more than one of his students, Don Geng, who today likewise teaches and coaches at Cretin:

As a student and later as a fellow faculty member at Cretin High School, I was privileged to know this humble, committed person. He was a man who knew the true meaning of service; no task was beneath his efforts. During my high school days we admired his simple dedication; after spending his day in the classroom teaching Spanish, he would spend countless hours in the halls as a janitor and maintenance man. No work was unworthy of his dignity; he mopped the floors, scoured the toilets and cleaned the school furnaces. His students . . . behind his back . . . labeled him "Brother Fix-it" as he lumbered through the halls, tools strapped to his belt, and wielding some object needing repair.[13]

Jim's generosity and humility extended beyond the Christian Brother communities. Jane Campbell, his cousin, was one of many to whom he gave his time:

I . . . remember the time he spent most of a day putting up a gutter and downspout on our house, with my husband's assistance, and how he persisted and would not give up, re-building some parts until he had it right; and then, not even taking supper with us because the "Brothers" were having something special on that night that he didn't want to miss.[14]

Miller was happy throughout his stay at Cretin. He once remarked to Don Geng's parents that he would have been content spending the rest of his life serving the middle-class students at the high school, but he felt God was calling him to work with the Central American poor;[15] so every year he re-applied for an assignment in the foreign missions. He participated in an intensive summer session studying Spanish in 1968 and in July 1969 finally got his wish. He was sent to Bluefields, Nicaragua, where he taught both elementary and high school for the next three and a half years. He also organized a soccer team, ran the bookstore, and did extensive work on the brothers' residence, including the replacement of almost the entire plumbing system. In 1973, he returned to Saint Mary's College for a year to complete a master's degree in Spanish.[16]

Sent back to Nicaragua in March 1974, this time to Puerto Cabezas, Brother Miller began to reach his full potential as a teacher and administrator. But to understand the events of the four years that Brother James served in Puerto Cabezas, one must first briefly review a portion of the troubled history of Nicaragua; for Jim's work would involve him directly with the Somoza dictatorship, causing some to view him as a "typical *yanqui*," a Somocista collaborator.

United States involvement began in Nicaragua in the 1850s when Commodore Cornelius Vanderbilt established a company which transported North Americans anxious to get to California for the gold rush across the narrow Nicaraguan territory. Soon another North American, the adventurer William Walker, was invited by the Liberal branch of the elite to help them overthrow the Conservative branch then in power. Walker, however, had other plans; with his army of three hundred U.S. nationals, he not only defeated the Conservatives, but also proclaimed himself president, declared English the new official language of the country, and legalized slavery. His regime even gained diplomatic recognition from the United States.[17]

Soon the Liberals joined with the Conservatives and with the governments of the other Central American states in an attempt to drive out the American intruder. When Walker made the mistake of antagonizing Vanderbilt, the Commodore used his massive fortune to assure his defeat. After two additional incursions into Central America, Walker was finally executed in Honduras in 1860. The Walker fiasco so disgraced the Liberals that the Conservative branch of the elite was able to hold power until 1893. When the international demand for coffee rapidly increased in the last quarter of the nineteenth century, the elite decided to expand their coffee-growing operations. Beginning in 1877, a number of laws were promulgated requiring Indians to sell off their communal lands. As historians Benjamin Keen and Mark Wasserman report:

These laws effectively drove the Indian and mestizo peasants off their land gradually transforming them into a class of dependent peons or share croppers. The passage of vagrancy laws and laws permitting the conscription of natives for agriculture and public labor also ensured the supply of cheap labor needed by the coffee growers. These oppressive laws provoked a major Indian revolt, the War of the Comuneros (1881); its defeat was followed by a ferocious repression that took five thousand lives.[18]

In 1893 Liberal José Santos Zelaya overthrew the Conservative regime and ruled as dictator for the next seventeen years. He allowed U.S. investors into his country in such numbers that by 1909 they controlled the sources of Nicaraguan wealth. Becoming alarmed by the growing U.S. control of the national economy, Zelaya rejected overtures from North American bankers and instead accepted a large loan from the British.

These signs of independence convinced the United States . . . that Zelaya must go. With American encouragement, a conservative revolt broke out in 1909, American marines were landed at Bluefields on the Atlantic coast, protected the conservative forces there against government attack, and turned over the collectorship of customs to the conservatives. Under military and diplomatic pressure from the United States, Zelaya resigned. . . .

The conservatives installed Adolfo Díaz, an obscure bookkeeper in an American mining firm in eastern Nicaragua, as president of a puppet regime that hastened to satisfy all the American demands. An American banking firm, Brown Brothers and Seligman, made loans to the Nicaraguan government, receiving as security a controlling interest in the national bank and state railways and the revenues from the customhouse.[19]

Needless to say, the government of Díaz was unpopular, so much so that in 1912 some Nicaraguans tried to oust him and his U.S. supporters. This caused President Taft to send in the Marines, who remained for twenty years, until 1933. In 1927 Augusto César Sandino began a guerrilla war of liberation which lasted for seven years and proved costly to the North Americans, both monetarily and in lives. The United States eventually decided to equip and train a security force, the *Guardia Nacional*, to replace the Marines. When American forces withdrew, Sandino, by now a national hero, put down his arms and ceased to fight. Not long after, in 1934, on orders from the U.S. handpicked commander of the *Guardia*, Anastasio Somoza García, Sandino was kidnapped and executed. Finally, in June 1936, Somoza overthrew the Nicaraguan government, and as historian Walter LaFeber points out, "for forty-three years he and his two sons ruled the country as a private fiefdom."[20] Throughout this period the Somozas had the support of the U.S. government.

In 1974, when Brother James returned to Nicaragua, after receiving his master's degree, Anastasio Somoza Debayle, the younger son of Somoza García and a West Point graduate, was "elected" president. The Somoza family at this time owned five million acres of land—an area the size of El Salvador—while 200,000 peasants were landless. Somoza Debayle likewise owned the twenty-six largest businesses in the country and had a personal fortune of about $300 million.[21] But the dictator's fiefdom was beginning to crumble. On December 23, 1972, an earthquake destroyed much of Managua, killing ten thousand people and leaving hundreds of thousands homeless. As international aid poured in from around the world, Somoza and his *Guardia* officers simply pocketed it. Such blatant thievery caused more and more of the middle class to join with the poor in opposition to Somoza. The Catholic church began to speak out:

> On the first anniversary of the earthquake the Church hierarchy held a commemorative mass in the central plaza of Managua. Somoza . . . invited himself to the Church celebration. Meanwhile, the Christian [base] communities of Managua . . . made hundreds of hand-held placards and carried them secretly into the plaza. As the ceremony unfolded, Somoza and his officials were deeply offended by the statements of the bishops and angered by the display of anti-regime slogans. Abruptly he got up and walked out, while national guardsmen disconnected the loudspeakers carrying the Archbishop's speech to the audience.[22]

On December 27, 1974, shortly after James Miller arrived in Puerto Cabezas, a small rebel group from the Sandinista National Liberation Front (FSLN) crashed a party in Managua, taking a number of important Nicaraguan officials hostage. After three days of negotiations, during which the rebels received considerable international attention, Somoza was forced to pay them $5 million in ransom money and allow them to flee the country. The audacity of the Sandinistas did much to popularize their cause; but Somoza, furious at his humiliation, responded with increased brutality.[23]

Thus, James Miller returned in 1974 to a Nicaragua which was on the verge of revolution. However, Puerto Cabezas and the Atlantic Coast in general— being far removed from Managua and the other centers of political activity in the west where most of the fighting would take place—played little part in the events leading up to the overthrow of Somoza, and Miller was not unduly concerned with the political situation.

Brother James's assignment was to teach high school at the Instituto Nacional Bartolomé Colón. As soon as he arrived in his new home, he threw himself completely into his work—to the utter amazement of his community. Just as in Bluefields, he began single-handedly repairing the brothers' residence, when he was not teaching. Before long he decided to resurrect the defunct Puerto Cabezas volunteer fire department and turn it into an efficient unit. He visited many of the fire stations in Managua, where he was able to beg hoses, nozzles, and—surprisingly—a fire truck; he even came up with fire-men's uniforms, which the volunteers proudly wore in local parades. He arranged a training course for the fire fighters and personally scored the highest grade on the final examination. Needless to say, he served as local fire chief until he left Nicaragua in July, 1979.[24] Brother Bob Walsh, who served with Jim, was amazed at the level of his energy:

> For Santiago [James], I think manual work was play, was recreation. I could not even attempt nor could I ever do all the things he was doing here in Puerto Cabezas for the people—teaching, administration, parish catechetics, civic projects, and good old-fashioned manual labor. Sunday literally had to be a day of rest for his over-worked body.[25]

Brother Cyril Litecky, his provincial and former teacher, was more impressed, however, with his rapport with the townspeople. "I vividly recall visiting him in Puerto Cabezas, riding in a jeep with him and stopping several times in one block so he could greet and visit with the people of the town."[26]

In Nicaragua the schools, including those of the Christian Brothers, were run by the state. The Somoza government, in the mid-1970s, inaugurated a program requiring basic industrial arts at the junior high school level. When the government began building small additions to some of its schools for this new program, Brother James proposed a more elaborate scheme for his school; he drew up plans for an industrial arts-vocational education complex which would cost about $175,000. He then lobbied at the Ministry of Education for his proposal and received approval. In 1977, he was appointed principal of the Instituto Nacional Bartolomé Colón, which at that time, had an enrollment of 550 students. Finally, the Somoza government asked him in 1978 to supervise the construction of ten new rural elementary schools being built in the Atlantic Coast region.

Brother Cyril Litecky explains Jim's dealings with the Somoza government in the following manner:

> [Brother James would get] exasperated at the red tape. In Managua (Nicaragua's capital), he would go to people and lean on them until he got things done for the school. That is why he was identified with the people in power; not because he was in concert with them, but just because he would get them to get things for him.[27]

Brother Stephen Markham sees Miller's political involvement in the same way, as purely pragmatic:

> Yes, Jim's perspective on Church, theology, politics, etc. was basically conservative. In fact he seemed to glory in projecting himself as a

conservative. However, he was not a traditionalist. His conservative
perspective was basically a pragmatic and utilitarian approach to life. If
he set out to do something he did it and he did not hold back from
exerting influence, even pressure, on those who stood in his way. Jim was
not one to bother about philosophical discussions or worry about political ideologies. He focused his energies and attention on accomplishing
the task at hand and it didn't matter if that task was a construction
project or an educational endeavor. . . . He had a way of dismissing
[political] questions by saying "I don't get into that" or "it's real complicated but we are there to teach them (the youth) to farm or read,
etc."[28]

Brother James in many respects was similar to Father Bill Woods. He did not
view the problems of Central America in global or complicated terms. In other
words, he was unable, or perhaps unwilling, to dwell on economic dependency
theories or problems caused in the Third World by multinational corporations.
He would have been hesitant to accept the need for a theology of liberation
within the Latin American church. In Brother James's view, the people in his
mission community were poor and uneducated; a good school with quality
equipment and a practical educational program would help alleviate poverty
and thereby improve the people's lives. Therefore, what counted was obtaining
such a school and program; and he would concentrate all his energies in this
direction. Jim—always practical—did not waste valuable time and energy
dwelling unduly on theoretical matters.

Like others, Brother Nicholas Geimer, who worked and lived with Miller in
Puerto Cabezas from the fall of 1977 until July 1979, sees the relationship
between Jim and the Somoza government as pragmatic, but he also views it as a
complex issue not easily defined:

What were Jim's relationships with the Somoza government? You have to
realize that in Nicaragua most directors of schools were political appointees. Many were completely unqualified—retired military officers, for
example. . . . Education was, and is, controlled nationally. A director
had to lobby for his fair share of the educational budget, especially if he
wanted more than his share, as did Jim. Jim cultivated the friendship of
the president of the senate (Somoza's righthand man) and a member of
the lower house (also vice-minister of education). These two were from
the Atlantic Coast and were concerned about improving things in this
neglected part of the country. So Jim was quite successful in getting more
for his school through these two. However, his relationship was on a
business, not social, level.

Jim told me he knew these two were personally profiting from the
government money spent on the coast, through kickbacks on building
contracts, high pay/low work jobs for relatives, etc., but he felt that was
the way the game was played and couldn't be helped.[29]

After his appointment as supervisor for the construction of ten rural schools, Jim would go every month or so with the contractor to assess progress and make sure corners were not being cut. After one such trip, Miller told Brother Nicholas that the contractor had said he would never again bid on a government job, since he had to kick back all his profit to the two above-mentioned politicians. This revelation of blatant corruption bothered Jim considerably; yet he realized he was in no position to do anything to stop it.[30]

Being, in general, ideologically apolitical, Brother James tried to avoid direct political involvement. Being a pragmatist, however, he felt some concessions were necessary. Thus Geimer notes:

> As director, Jim was expected to attend a reception or two . . . for these two politicians when they visited Puerto Cabezas. These receptions were really political rallies for Somoza's Liberal Party. Many of the teachers attended also, fearing their jobs depended upon it. Jim announced the meetings but did not force us teachers to go.
>
> The only other political activity on Jim's part that I am aware of is the following incident. When he returned from one of his trips to the capital he told me that when he went to pay his respects to his two friends in the legislature, he was called into a "smoke filled room" situation, and his recommendation was asked about whom they should nominate for mayor of Puerto Cabezas. Needless to say, the nomination was equal to election. Jim was quite excited about this episode of backroom politics.[31]

When the Sandinistas intensified their revolutionary activities, Brother James refused to permit any political activism in their favor among the students. Since nearly all the fighting was confined to western Nicaragua, far from Puerto Cabezas, and, according to Brother Nicholas, the Sandinistas had little support in this town, there were very few attempts among the students to demonstrate on behalf of the FSLN. Geimer recalls only two incidents: When a student attempted to organize a pro-Sandinista activity at school, Brother James talked to his father. Consequently, the father stopped his son, who then became Jim's bitter enemy. When Miller was in the United States after the ouster of the Somoza regime, this student bragged he would kill the gringo brother if he ever returned to Puerto Cabezas. On another occasion, the school's night watchman discovered that someone had slipped a letter under each classroom door making ridiculous accusations concerning Miller and threatening him. Jim picked up all the copies before anyone arrived at school. "At one time the Sandinista clandestine radio read a list of people in Puerto Cabezas who were to be dealt with when they took over," reports Brother Nicholas. "The names must have been supplied by their local sympathizers, and Jim's name was included."[32]

In truth, throughout the Nicaraguan revolution, Miller was neither pro-Somocista nor pro-Sandinista. To him the political struggle was an annoyance which interfered with the running of his school. Such an attitude explains why at times he was not reluctant to oppose the will of the Somoza regime. On one occasion, as the fighting escalated in Nicaragua a local militia was organized by the National Guard commander in Puerto Cabezas. All public employees, including teachers, were expected to "volunteer" and participate in scheduled drills. Members of the militia were also supposed to stand night guard duty, thereby relieving the *Guardia Nacional* of this odious task. The teachers at the Christian Brothers' school did not want to take part, and Jim strongly supported them, arguing that it would interfere with their school duties. Only one teacher participated and there were no reprisals taken against the rest.[33]

On another occasion, all the teachers, upon arriving at school, were called by Miller to the faculty room for a meeting. He informed them that he had received a radiogram from the Ministry of Education ordering the suspension of all classes because of the expansion of violence in Nicaragua. Since the fighting was confined to the Pacific area and Puerto Cabezas had been completely peaceful throughout these times of struggle, Brother James suggested that the command from Managua be ignored. Many of the teachers, perhaps sensing a chance for time off with full pay, argued against him. Since the students were milling around the hallways without supervision, Jim reluctantly agreed to decide the matter by democratic vote. He was far from happy when the majority went against his position. Nevertheless, he instructed the faculty to hold their first class and then bring their students to the assembly hall, where they would then be dismissed. After a short time, however, the faculty was surprised to find that another meeting was to be convened immediately. There they were told by Miller that the local military commander had just notified him that if school was suspended all teachers would be expected to report at once for "volunteer" militia duty, since it would no longer interfere with their teaching. A new democratic vote was called for, and not surprisingly the decision to suspend classes was reversed. "Most of the teachers thought Jim had 'suggested' this policy to the commander," notes Brother Nicholas, "and I think they were right, although Jim never said so."[34] Ironically, that very afternoon the National Guard commander received an erroneous report that several fishing boats filled with Sandinistas were on their way to attack Puerto Cabezas. The commander panicked and shut down the school along with virtually everything else in town. The teachers were not conscripted into the militia but obviously there were some very uneasy moments on their part. The events of that day resulted in some bad feelings toward Brother James on the part of the faculty, bad feelings that remained.[35] Once again, Miller had demonstrated that the school was his foremost concern.

In July 1979, Brother James left Nicaragua, never to return. The facts that his departure coincided with the final victory of the Sandinistas over Somoza and that he left as the supposed guardian of an elderly nun caused many to conclude that he was forced to flee the country clandestinely. Geimer explains, however, that this was not the case:

Jim had been planning a visit to the States for some time. He had always had to go during school vacation, in the middle of Wisconsin's winter, and Jim hated cold weather. The country parish where his mother's family came from was going to celebrate its centennial, and Jim planned a vacation for this time because all his relatives would be gathered for the event. As the time approached the fighting and chaos shut down regular means of transportation, and he had to beg a ride to Managua on a Red Cross flight. Getting out of Managua was even harder. All the Somocistas were trying to get out, too. He finally did get on a plane as a guardian for an old nun. But he was not fleeing. He had every intention of returning and left a few copies of a letter clearly stating this intention. It was his religious superiors who decided, wisely I think, that it would be better for him not to return. Had he tried, I do not think the Sandinistas would have harmed him, other than a possible short detention and then expulsion. More likely they would not have let him [re-]enter the country. Had he not gotten out in the first place, I think he would have been deported.[36]

Brother Cyril Litecky, Miller's provincial, also maintains that Jim left to visit friends in Wisconsin: "He left all his belongings in Nicaragua, planning to return; but we determined it would be prudent for him not to return until things settled down." The decision was made "because we had questions about his 'safety' under the Sandinistas because he had worked at the Somoza-run school."[37] After a few months, Miller asked his superiors to allow him to return to Puerto Cabezas, but a new Sandinista provision stipulating that only native Nicaraguans could henceforth be school directors caused Litecky and others to deny his request.[38]

After spending one hundred days in a program of spiritual renewal at the Sangre de Cristo Retreat House near Sante Fe, New Mexico,[39] he returned to Saint Paul where he again taught Spanish. Once more his immense energy impressed his fellow workers. Brother H. Lewis Twohig marveled at how he often "put in as many as sixteen hours, working for the students, or for the school and his religious community."[40] Twohig recalled also how, in the few free moments he had, he found time to take a course in welding at Saint Paul Technical-Vocational Institute because he felt it would be helpful when he went back to Central America.[41]

Upon his return to Saint Paul, Brother James and Don Geng renewed their close friendship, but this time Geng saw an added dimension in Miller's personality:

He was, first and foremost, a man of great simplicity. I remember in 1979 giving him a ride to his TVI welding class because his ride fell through. In making conversation with me, he bragged that he wore the same pair of pants each week so that he would not ruin his blue jeans with some careless welding mistake. Some students even made fun of his simplicity and yet one of the most apparent changes I noticed in James after his return to Cretin in 1979 was his impatience with the high standard of material wealth in America that we take so much for granted. He would ruffle the students' pride by criticizing the students' lack of commitment to their studies. He would say, "How can you waste your opportunity for an education—in Nicaragua . . . education is a privilege for only the most privileged. And you students don't study—you just fool around. It's a crime and a sin to waste such a gift from God and your parents."[42]

Jim was pleased when in January 1981 he received word that he was being sent to Huehuetenango, Guatemala, where he would join six other brothers— three North Americans and three native Guatemalans—working with impoverished Indian boys. When Don Geng expressed concern about his friend going into a violence-filled environment, the somewhat overweight Jim just laughed: "Well, at least I have some incentive to lose some weight. I can then dodge the bullets more easily."[43] His levity, however, was probably tempered by the knowledge that he was replacing a brother who had received warning from a right-wing death squad to leave the country or be killed.[44] He must have hesitated at least momentarily knowing that throughout 1980 in Guatemala "repression reached a new level of intensity in the number of people killed and in the openness with which repression was carried out" and that "while the attack was directed at all sectors of society for the first time there was a systematic and virtually indiscriminate attack on church pastoral agents."[45] Whether he read the statement issued by the Guatemalan bishops in June 1980 is not known, but any missionary would have become unnerved at the following words:

-As we have denounced on previous occasions, there have already been numerous catechists, prayer leaders, and other Christians kidnapped, tortured, and murdered.

-We pastoral agents are continually watched, our sermons are taped, and our every activity is checked.

-In a basically Catholic country, three priests have recently been murdered and another kidnapped. Several other priests and religious are threatened with death, and others have been expelled from the country. . . .

-A part of this religious persecution is the campaign to discredit and slander certain bishops, priests, and religious, a campaign that tends to create a climate of distrust in the body of the faithful towards the legitimate pastors. . . .

-The very priests who have offered their lives as martyrs for Christ, in preaching the Gospel, have been afterwards the objects of insidious calumnies meant to blacken their obvious Christian witness.[46]

Yet Miller knew that he and his fellow brothers at Huehuetenango were needed by Indians whose life expectancy was 45 years—16.4 years less than the rest of the country—and whose infant mortality rate was as high as 100 per 1,000 live births. Surely he realized that his teaching and agricultural expertise was sorely needed in a nation where 82 percent of the Indians were illiterate and virtually all Indian children suffer from malnutrition and parasites, where in 1979 the worst land distribution ratio in all of Latin America existed and where 90 percent of rural Indian families owned no land or less than the minimum necessary to support a family at the subsistence level.[47]

Miller's Guatemalan assignment was twofold. He taught English and history of Mayan art and served as a guidance counselor at the Colegio De La Salle, a school of about nine hundred students opened by the Christian Brothers in 1960. He also maintained the entire physical plant and worked three after-noons a week as assistant director of the Casa Indígena De La Salle, an educational experiment which was the pride of the brothers. The Casa was added to the Colegio in 1974 at the suggestion of a young Guatemalan brother, Rolando López, who convinced his superiors that since the greatest social problem facing the church in his country was the poverty and mistreatment of the Indian, the brothers must aim at the eradication of these evils. The Casa Indígena consisted of an experimental farm and a boarding house, where from 100 to 150 Mayan boys lived. The youths were chosen on the basis of their leadership potential from the mountain villages surrounding Huehuetenango. They took the full curriculum of classes at the Colegio, but in the afternoon worked on the model farm learning modern scientific agriculture. After com-pleting their schooling, the pupils were encouraged to return to their villages, where it was hoped they would teach their newly acquired knowledge in their native dialect to others.[48]

As Jim worked with his Indian students he developed a great respect for them. He realized, however, that the atrocities inflicted on them at the hands of the military and the death squads were increasing daily. It was while he was in Huehuetenango that terrified *campesinos* began to pour over the Mexican border. In May 1981 about five hundred entered Chiapas, but were forced back to Guatemala a few days later; it is unclear what became of them. Then in June 4,000 peasants crossed the border; they were permitted to remain and Guate-malan Indians thus began their miserable sojourn in a foreign land. By the end of 1983, they would number at least 100,000, living in unbelievable squalor and subject to raids from Guatemalan troops crossing the border.[49]

Tens of thousands more were forced to flee the military attacks on their mountain villages, thereby becoming internal refugees. Their pathetic situa-tion caused journalist Phillip Wearne to write:

Without identity papers, whole families live in total fear, trying to hide themselves in provincial cities or the capital. Many stay only a few weeks in the same place. Indian dress and language are quickly discarded so as to prevent being identified with a subversive area. Many are simply starving. "I know whole Indian families living on 30 cents a day," says one nun in Guatemala City.[50]

Others fled to Belize and Honduras, most arriving sick and starving after a perilous journey in which "many braved bullets along the border where the Guatemalan army allegedly created a free-fire zone."[51] Some eventually crossed into the United States, where they were often helped by religious and other groups who chanced arrest and imprisonment in an attempt to hide them from immigration authorities intent on forcing their return to Guatemala.

Brother James also understood that in Guatemala U.S. citizenship no longer served as protection against torture and death; the murders of Stanley Rother and John Troyer—both occurring while Miller served in Huehuetenango—made this apparent.

At any rate, it must have been with mixed emotions that Brother James returned to the United States in late November 1981 for surgery on the cartilage in both knees. Reluctant to leave the Indians he had learned to love, he could only have felt a sense of relief at the thought of returning to a peaceful society. While recovering from his operation at Saint Mary's Hospital in Minneapolis, Jim was barraged by family and friends with questions concerning the violence in Guatemala. "I asked Jim if he wasn't frightened at the thought of returning," remembers Brother Steve Markham. Miller responded, "You don't think about that; that's not why you're there. There's too much to be done; you can't waste your energies worrying about what might happen. If it happens, it happens."[52]

Jim's family had the good fortune to have him home with them for Christmas 1981. During this time they tried to dissuade him from returning to Guatemala, but he would have none of it, saying time and again that his place was with the Indian boys. Finally, perhaps exasperated, he told his sister Louise: "One of two frightening things could happen to me in Guatemala. I could be kidnapped, tortured, and killed, or I could simply be gunned down." If he had to die, he said, he prayed it would come through the second alternative.[53]

When his knees were once again strong, he left the United States for the last time. Brother Gerard Pihaly took him to the Twin Cities Airport. On the way he asked him if the violence in Guatemala was really as bad as had been reported. Miller replied:

> "We never know when we rise in the morning if we will be alive by nightfall. We are teaching human rights to these poor Indians and after they start demanding them, it leads to bloodshed." I asked him how it was possible to live under such horrible psychological situations. He answered: "We just don't allow ourselves to dwell on it. The need to help these poor uneducated people is so great that it is the all-consuming motive for being there."[54]

Miller's words to Brother Gerard are certainly consistent with his earlier attitude as principal in Nicaragua toward the education of his students. There, he had fought to keep the school open in trying times and had maneuvered with Somoza's officials to obtain extra funds for his school. There, Miller the pragmatist had put education above all and had consequently been considered by some to be a Somocista collaborator. Rather than dimming his overall emphasis on education, his experience in Guatemala had matured it. His willingness to sacrifice for the education of the underprivileged was developed in Guatemala to such a degree that Brother Jim was even able, in spite of personal risk, to put the education of young Mayan Indians above all else.

Just a few short weeks after his return, on Saturday, February 13, 1982, late in the afternoon, Brother Miller was preparing to patch a wall at the Casa Indígena. Not one to relax when an odd job beckoned, he had just returned from scrubbing floors at the new convent of six Poor Clare nuns, recent arrivals in Huehuetenango from Memphis, Tennessee.[55] Suddenly, four men wearing face masks sped by in a car; Brother James was shot seven times in the chest and neck by submachine-gun fire. No longer welcome in Nicaragua, where he had been perceived as a rightist collaborator, Miller died instantly at the hands of what almost certainly was a Guatemalan right-wing death squad. It was an ironic turn of events.

Bishop Victor Hugo Martínez of Huehuetenango celebrated a Mass of Resurrection for Jim on Sunday, February 14, at the Casa Indígena De La Salle, after which well over a thousand Indians accompanied the body on its four-mile journey to the local airport. All along the way his students took turns carrying the coffin on their shoulders. The body was flown to Guatemala City where Bishop Eduardo Fuentes celebrated a memorial mass at the Christian Brothers' residence. On February 15, a third mass was concelebrated by the papal nuncio, another bishop, and several Guatemalan and U.S. priests.

On February 16, after his body reached the United States, a memorial mass was celebrated at Saint Paul's Cathedral before about six hundred mourners. Archbishop John Roach, president of the National Council of Catholic Bishops, gave the homily. After expressing his thoughts on the commitment and martyrdom of Brother James and other missionaries recently killed in Central America, the archbishop paused; gripping the podium, his voice rose:

As I prepared this homily I promised myself that I would not politicize this celebration of life and death. It is impossible, however, to ignore the conditions which lie at the base of this tragedy.

Last November the bishops of the United States issued a statement on Central America. We were criticized in some quarters . . . with saying too much. Tonight in my mind and heart I feel we said too little.

Must those who serve in Guatemala and places like it live in the constant fear that at any moment they may be the victims of violence by irresponsible people who respect neither others nor themselves? In God's name this must stop. There will be other deaths. There will be other persecutions. The tragedy will be compounded if the day comes when the world is calloused in facing the death of the James Millers of this world.

We cannot allow that to happen. We must challenge the political and economic structures which not only keep people under oppression but condone deliberate violence. . . .

If liberty is not treasured, if life is not valued, then violence will flourish.

In this crisis of civilization, it is not possible to remain neutral or detached either as persons or as a nation. We are linked as brothers and sisters in Jesus Christ with those who struggle to be free. We are also linked with them as citizens of a country whose government policy affects development, and in some instances non-development, in their countries. . . .

You and I must support those who fight the oppression of the poor, fight for the rights of those who have no rights . . . but we cannot afford the luxury of being spectators in that struggle. We must hold up the arms of our sisters and brothers who speak for and who work for God's poor.[56]

Don Geng was one of the mourners at Saint Paul's Cathedral that day. Later, he expressed his emotions upon leaving the religious service:

As echoes of the final hymn . . . rang in my ears and moistened my eyes, my exit from the Cathedral was blocked by several activists disseminating information against our U.S. involvement in Latin America. My initial reaction was one of anger: I didn't want politics to get in the way of my grief. I wanted those activists to leave. However, I suddenly realized it was precisely politics which killed James Miller.

As I skimmed the brochures, I understood the violence . . . which pervades Central America. In Guatemala . . . 80% of [the] people make less than $79.00 per year, the average city dweller can afford only $.13 a day for food (eggs are $.08 a piece, chickens are $1.79 per pound) and Amnesty International has documented over 9,000 politically motivated murders by government-supported death squads. . . . Then I thought of the international scoffing which received Reagan's announcement that "human rights policies are improving in El Salvador." I realized how it took the brutal and shocking murder of this humble, committed Christian Brother to awaken me to the injustices that prevail in our hemisphere. I imagined for one split second the terror of not only starvation and poverty, but the brutal, inhuman fear that so many of our poor Latin American neighbors must face when confronted with powers (be they from the right, middle, or left) that do not respect human dignity. . . . I imagined myself as a father living in squalor, without a job and unable to adequately feed, clothe or house my wife and children. I felt for a moment the stark terror of a peasant of Indian heritage in some isolated mountain village who suddenly feels a cold, automatic steel barrel jabbed into his ribs by some faceless enemy of unknown origin.[57]

Brother James was no leftist. Why then was he killed? The answer may lie in the relations between the brothers at the Casa Indígena and the Guatemalan army. The government, to meet its quota of conscripts, often rounded up Indian boys who happened to be on the streets, forcing them into the army. Even though students were supposedly exempt from military service, those from the Indian school were often impressed into the army. When this would happen, a brother would present proof to the authorities that the particular boy in question was a student. The military would then reluctantly release him.

Two days prior to the shooting of Brother Miller, a Mayan pupil was forced into the army in accordance with the above pattern. A Christian Brother, but not James Miller, went to the authorities to obtain his release. This time the military refused to relinquish their catch. Apparently the brother, adamant in his demands, infuriated the soldiers. The murder of Brother Miller was probably meant as a warning to the brothers at the Casa Indígena to cease interfering in governmental affairs.[58]

A short time before his death Brother James wrote a letter to his friends, Greg and Maura Robertson. In it James reveals his love for the Mayas, a love that overcame fear and bound him to a violent land. Greg read it at a memorial mass celebrated by Father Loren Koziol at the College of Santa Fe:

> After nearly 10 years of service in Nicaragua and a year and a half in the States, I arrived in Huehuetenango, Guatemala, in early January 1981. . . .
>
> The days were often long, and many demands were placed on my time at the Indian Center, but I thoroughly enjoyed my work with the Indian boys. Through my close daily association with them, I have come to respect and love them all and to have a deep respect for the many centuries of Mayan history and tradition that is their cultural heritage.
>
> Guatemala is a beautiful country of mountains, valleys, lakes, lush tropical forests and fertile coastal plains. It is probably one of the most colorful countries in the world. The ancient Mayan modes of dress and customs blend with those of the Spanish conquerors to form a rich panorama of colors, sounds, and special traditions. The Indians still speak their traditional Mayan tongues (seven or eight Indian tongues are spoken among the boys at the Indian Center—Spanish has to be the common language).
>
> The Indians are industrious farmers, honest, peace-loving, simple people whose hospitality is proverbial. I always find it a joy to visit the homes of the boys from the Indian Center. The Indians of Guatemala form about 50 percent of the seven-million-plus population of the country; but they are the poor, the oppressed, the forgotten ones of Guatemala. Many of them are desperately poor, the majority are illiterate, and malnutrition and infant mortality are endemic problems.
>
> Our apostolate at the Indian Center has for its principal purpose the

formation of educated leaders among the Indian population. We have hundreds of requests each year from priests, sisters and village leaders to accept boys from their towns and villages, but we can accept only 150, including those who are already in the six-year high school program. The selection process is difficult, but we try to accept those with the most leadership potential. We ask the families to pay $12.50 a month for their sons' room and board and schooling, but many can pay only a fraction of that (real costs are $50 per boy per month). The rest of our funding comes from donations of the Christian Brothers in the United States, the Maryknoll Fathers and Brothers and from many generous relatives and friends in the United States and Europe. CARE provides some rice, wheat flour, cooking oil, etc., each month. God must smile on our venture with those fine lads, because somehow we always manage to receive help from someone just when we need it most.

I can't end this letter without asking for your prayers for Guatemala (and for all of Central America). The level of personal violence here is reaching appalling proportions (murders, torture, kidnappings, threats, etc.), and the church is being persecuted because of its option for the poor and the oppressed. The Indian population of Guatemala, caught defenseless between the Army and rebel forces operating in the country, is taking the brunt of this violence. We pray and long for peace and a just solution to Guatemala's many social and economic problems (most of which date from the Conquest in 1524), but until now peace and justice elude us.

Aware of the many difficulties and risks that we face in the future, we continue to work with faith and hope and trust in God's Providence. Please join your prayers with ours *every day*. Many selfish, blind and hardened hearts must be converted to the love of Christ before a lasting solution can be found. Armed force will not solve the problems; only dialogue and mutual understanding can be viable solutions.

I am personally weary of violence, but I continue to feel a strong commitment to the suffering poor of Central America. "God's ways are not man's ways," says the Bible. God knows why He continued to call me to Guatemala when some friends and relatives encouraged me to pull out for my own comfort and safety. I have been a Christian Brother for nearly 20 years now, and my commitment to my vocation grows steadily stronger in the context of my work in Central America. I pray to God for the grace and strength to serve Him faithfully by my presence among the poor and oppressed of Guatemala. I place my life in His Providence; I place my trust in Him.

I hope you understand my position. The intensity of the past year in Guatemala has come out in these last paragraphs. Please pardon so many personal references, but I can't take the situations and experiences of the past year out of a personal context.[59]

7

Frank Xavier Holdenried

Ecumenical Missionary

Frank Xavier Holdenried never called himself a missionary. He did not belong to any religious order; in his work, he was not even formally affiliated with any particular religion. He was simply "an American living in Guatemala."[1] After his murder there in April 1983, Frank would be genially remembered by friends and relatives in the United States as "a real operator," "a man with a lot of *savoir-faire*," "a down-to-earth guy who drank, smoked, cussed, and argued," "a flamboyant character," "a captivating storyteller."

Frank Holdenried was an unusual man. His biography is the chronicle of a half-century-long search for spiritual meaning in his life. This quest took him on a roundabout journey: from the fruit orchards of northern California where he was raised, to a monastery in Portugal and to a tiny coastal village in Spain, and thence back to California. He was married, had a child, and was soon separated from his wife. His checkered career included seminary training under the Jesuits and monastic life with the Carthusians, a short stint in the Air Force, some training in law and journalism, studies in mysticism, and various business enterprises that ranged from publishing a successful international magazine to ventures in oil and jukebox supply. But it was in a barrio in Guatemala City that Frank finally found the elusive meaning he had sought. He wrote his cousin Dick Smith from Barrio Santa Luisa in December 1978 after two years in Guatemala:

> The mystery of it all is that following Christ, 2000 years dead, and trying to take his advice can produce in the person a sense of happiness and well-being that no other type of commitment seems to be able to produce. For me, He is the ultimate reality. I always suspected this from my youngest years, but of course, could not express it. That's why I managed to hold onto my faith through a lot of personal trials, and was willing to risk going to novitiates and monasteries in search of the true meaning of life. Here, the search for me is ended.[2]

Frank was born December 7, 1932, in the Los Angeles area, the only child of Joseph and Hazel Holdenried.[3] Joseph was the president of Daniel Industries, an oil fields service business that made components for measuring the flow of oil and gas. His parents separated when Frank was about twelve, and the boy went to live in Lake County in northern California with his father's brother, Oscar Holdenried, and his wife Thressa. There he attended Lakeport High School and graduated in 1950.

His aunt and uncle owned a large pear ranch near the town of Kelseyville. The Holdenried clan could trace its family tree back to the original pioneer stock that had settled in Lake County in the mid-nineteenth century. Frank's numerous relatives in the Kelseyville area were farmers and ranchers—staunch Republicans, mainly Presbyterians, and rather well-to-do. Frank, however, was raised a Catholic because this was the religion of his mother; Frank's father had no religious affiliation. Although as a teenager and young man Frank did spend some time with each of his parents, he considered Lake County his home, and there he would return as a young adult for lengthy summer visits. As an older man, a self-styled lay missionary in Guatemala, Frank spent time there resting, writing, and soliciting funds for his many projects in Guatemala. Sometimes he would visit "Unk" and Aunt Thressa on his own initiative, but there were also times when Frank felt threatened in Guatemala and had to flee that country's political madness for his own safety.

While still at Lakeport High, Frank plunged into a rather remarkable occupation, one which grew out of a childhood interest in raising and showing Great Danes. During high school and later on after serving in the military, Frank would attend dog shows and write reviews for a London-based magazine called *Dog World*. According to his cousin Dick, as chronicler for the dog show circuit, Frank made the acquaintance "of many rich and famous people; most notable were Mrs. Edgar L. Kaiser and Prince Y.N. Troubetzkoy, whose wife was a wealthy heiress."[4] When the owner of *Dog World* died, Frank bought the magazine from his estate and published it himself for four or five years. However, Reverend David Leeper Moss, a Methodist minister who later became one of Frank's closest friends, explains that, although *Dog World* was a successful business venture for Frank, he eventually sold the magazine "because of the emptiness he saw and felt" in this line of work.[5]

After high school Frank was drafted and served two years in the Air Force; when his time was up, he attended Loyola University of Los Angeles, where he studied pre-law and earned a bachelor's degree. At this time, Frank lived in Los Angeles with his father, who was gravely ill with brain cancer. He was also writing for *Dog World* then, so Frank's college years were busy ones. When Joseph Holdenried died, Frank inherited part of his father's estate, investing some of it in Clinton Oil and in Melody Music, which supplied jukeboxes and cigarette machines. But, as his cousin states, these investments were eventually lost because Frank did not keep up with them over the years.

During the 1960s, as a young man in his late twenties and early thirties, Frank spent several years searching for a spiritual niche for himself in two

Frank Xavier Holdenried

religious orders—the Carthusians and Jesuits. Frank entered the Carthusian Order, living for six months in a monastery in Evora, Portugal, but could not adapt himself to the strict discipline. He contracted hepatitis and was forced to leave the order.[6] He also tried the Jesuits, entering their novitiate in Los Gatos, California, where he studied for two years. About this experience Frank's cousin states: "He liked the Jesuits, but didn't or couldn't take the rigors of their order."[7] Dave Moss elaborates: "He joined the Jesuit Order for a few years. His superior though recommended he not take his vows."[8]

Frank would remain dissatisfied—unfulfilled—spiritually for several more years. He studied, wrote, and pondered for a year in Benidorm, Spain, a little coastal town on the Mediterranean. His mother was with him then, and they wrote a story together. Frank's wife Fara, in a newspaper interview after his death, remarked that he had always felt a deep spiritual call to action and that his European sojourn was in part a search for spiritual rejuvenation.[9]

Frank, too, alludes briefly to his years spent in Spain in a letter he wrote from Guatemala City in 1978: "I have tramped around Spain, studied mystical theology under Spanish and English theologians, and am thoroughly familiar with Teresian spirituality, Spanish mysticism, etc."[10]

While in Spain, Frank embarked on a new business venture; he and two friends acted as sales intermediaries between some of the developing African nations and First World industries. This job took him to Switzerland, Paris, and Africa. It was in Paris that he met Fara, an airline dispatcher from Oregon, who was twelve years younger than Frank. After a short courtship, they were married in 1970. They had hoped that in marriage they could share their mutual love for travel. Both were drawn to the European scene; they wanted to live in a foreign country where Fara could realize her dream for a career in international relations.[11]

None of these hopeful plans materialized, however, for various reasons. Frank's many business interests in the United States needed his attention there, and a daughter, Lisel, was born the first year. The Holdenrieds therefore settled down in Los Angeles instead of in Europe, and were soon beset by financial problems. One stroke of bad luck was the collapse, due to an earthquake, of a successful restaurant that Frank and a partner had opened in Saugus, California. As Fara explains it, "We were left sitting with a lot of commitments. We had to scramble fast."[12] Frank did some writing for the *Los Angeles Mirror* and took on the demanding job of running the delicatessen and catering service of a large grocery store. While managing the delicatessen, Frank became spokesman for the retail clerks' union—and was fired by the store.[13]

Frank and Fara's marriage did not survive the problems they confronted. They separated, but neither wanted a divorce. Fara and Lisel simply went one way and Frank went another. About their marriage, Fara stated in an interview with the *National Catholic Reporter* after Frank's death:

At first we had our differences, but once they came out in the open, we developed respect for one another. We worked separately, but sometimes together. It was an unconventional way of doing things. I don't apologize for it. That's just the way we did it.[14]

After Frank and Fara separated, Frank found himself in a midlife crisis. By now in his forties, he still seemed unable to find the path in life that would give him the inner peace and direction for which he yearned. He had roamed the world searching for ultimate meaning in his life, and his wide-ranging mind had dabbled in law, mysticism, journalism, Great Danes, and money-making schemes. Almost like an adolescent after a bewildering first taste of freedom, Frank returned to his boyhood home, the pear ranch of Aunt Thressa and Uncle Oscar in Lake County, California.

It was at this time that he became close friends with the pastor of his aunt's Presbyterian church in Kelseyville. Reverend Dave Moss[15] describes the Frank Holdenried he met then as a "lonely and lost man," overwhelmed by financial problems and unhappy over his separation.[16] Frank later described this period of his life to another friend, a Methodist minister named Gerry Phelps. His life was in a turmoil after his separation, Frank told her; he was convinced he had failed and was severely depressed. Never one to ignore for long the spiritual dimension of life, Frank decided to spend some time on a retreat. As he examined his past and its apparent failures, Frank decided the only thing left for him to do was to give his future to God. Reverend Phelps recalls Frank's rather unorthodox prayer: "Look, Lord, I'm giving the rest of my life to you. Now whatever goes wrong, it's *your* fault."[17] In fact, it was not long at all before the "lonely and lost" middle-aged man began to find new meaning and direction in his life.

Around this time, the event took place which would change the rudderless course of Frank's life forever. In February 1976, a severe earthquake rocked Guatemala. When it occurred, Frank happened to be visiting a friend in Los Angeles, who employed a Guatemalan housekeeper, an undocumented alien. When the first sketchy reports of the catastrophe hit the air waves, the housekeeper became distraught and anxious for news of her family's fate back in Guatemala. Frank, in his characteristic role as a "real operator," offered to try to get more information than was then available from the news services on the extent of the earthquake's devastation. He soon found a local ham radio buff who was able to link up with another amateur operator in Guatemala. Before long, news of the tragedy was being transmitted to Frank through this hastily contrived connection. When Frank told this story, he was fond of claiming that he had known the true extent of the Guatemalan earthquake hours before either UPI or AP could get through.

Frank's involvement did not end there. His friend's maid desperately wanted to locate her children in Guatemala and bring them money, but since she was undocumented, there was no way she herself could go to them. Frank volunteered for this mission of mercy. Although he knew little Spanish, he figured that his past worldwide travels and his familiarity with border hassles and international red tape qualified him for this task. The housekeeper and twenty-five of her friends, also undocumented Guatemalans, chipped in to purchase a round-trip ticket for Frank; they also gave Frank money for their children and relatives back home, which he would attempt to deliver personally.

When Frank arrived in Guatemala City, the Jesuits there assisted him in locating the children and families of the Guatemalan maids. He followed his instructions and parceled out the money entrusted to him in Los Angeles. But then Frank decided to remain a while. He offered his services in areas ravaged by the quake, working as an ambulance driver and an emergency medic, or helping out in any way he could.[18]

Frank's recent soul-searching indicates that at this time he would have been deeply receptive to the immense human need that surrounded him. Instead of being overwhelmed by the plight of the victims of the earthquake, however, Frank began to feel that perhaps this was where he was needed, that Guatemala might offer him the meaning in his life that had eluded him. But Frank was still not sure exactly what, if anything, he could offer these unfortunate people. As he told his friend Gerry, he simply prayed, "Lord, show me what you want me to do." Later he related the following to his friends and obviously considered this unusual experience to be a foundation stone of his future ministry in Guatemala; as Gerry Phelps recalls Frank's story:

> One day Frank was walking alone down a mountain path when an Indian boy approached him from the opposite direction. As the boy passed Frank on the road, he looked directly into the youth's eyes—and saw Jesus. Stunned, Frank stopped in his tracks, totally immobilized. He turned toward the boy but the Indian youth had vanished.[19]

In October 1980, nearly five years later, in a long, intimate letter to Dave Moss, Frank alludes to this "mystical" experience, as Moss calls it.[20] By this time, the political turmoil in Guatemala had mushroomed and Frank was beginning to sense that he himself was a potential target:

> The grace I am constantly receiving—with greater intensity each day—is to see Christ in the eyes of everyone. The spiritual tension in my life can best be expressed as Christ within me, trying to get out, and Christ outside me trying to get in. . . .
>
> The Christ I see in others is Christ resurrected; only in my own eyes do I see Christ crucified. That is the mystery of this great grace I am receiving. And I am terribly afraid. . . .
>
> God never infuses the gift of His Presence into the soul—as He did to me 5 years ago in the mountains above Comalapa—unless the Faith that results from that infusion will be called upon to protect the soul in some final moment of Passion. I understood that clearly 5 years ago—even when I was walking so blindly and fumbling around trying to learn just what it was He wanted.[21]

After the earthquake of 1976, Frank eventually returned to the States. Prepared to tell his friends about the desperate need he had seen in Guatemala, he arrived with his suitcase filled with slides and his heart full of enthusiasm. He immediately sought Moss and asked to speak to his Presbyterian congregation. Frank hoped to interest them in offering their help to the Guatemalan people. Frank also spent this time re-thinking his own future and talking it over with friends. The year 1976 had not yet come to a close when Frank made his final decision: he would return to Guatemala.

Frank arrived in Guatemala City with very little money. He decided to make his home in Barrio Santa Luisa, one of the slums that ring the capital city; he had become familiar with this particular shantytown on his prior trip, when he had located in its crowded streets the missing child of one of the Guatemalan maids of Los Angeles. Frank himself describes the people and the barrio in an article published in *America*, July 17, 1982:

> . . . My newly adopted people had fled from a deep ravine where they had been living and were squatting on land owned by a local bank. The sandy escarpment under which they had been living gave way during the quake and poured tons of dirt upon them, killing hundreds and wiping away most of their few possessions.
>
> An episode that local psychiatrists were calling "post-earthquake depression" had settled over our provisional community creating an atmosphere of incredible fear and anxiety among everyone. This psychological condition was further aggravated by the 2,200 aftershocks that followed during a three-month period.
>
> Although they lived in the city, these people went for years without being visited by a priest. Their parish had been carefully carved out to separate them as shantytown dwellers from the nearby middle-class residents, and one priest was assigned to care for all 150,000 of them.[22]

Many of the older people had refused to move from the ravine, in spite of the quake danger, so the barrio had a core group of younger families with leadership potential in the community. Frank hoped to be of some use to them, but did not want to interfere by bombarding them with his suggestions and help.

At an early point in his ministry, Holdenried decided on what he called the *sin caras* approach, or "facelessness." As Dave Moss describes it, this technique involved several dimensions. For one thing, it defined his relationship with God. Frank saw himself as God's instrument, the "faceless one" through whom God would bring justice and love to the poor of the barrio; Frank therefore strove to be a servant to the people, avoiding the temptation to be the paternalistic Yankee. Another aspect of *sin caras* was ecumenical. A Catholic himself, Frank did not want to be constrained by being identified with any particular religious order or church. When a group of nuns who had sponsored his visa developed some problems with authorities, Frank "simply turned his collar around," as he put it, and was granted sponsorship by a Protestant organization. Still another phase of *sin caras* developed later on, when Frank began to feel threatened; he hoped that a "faceless," or apolitical, approach would prevent him from being singled out by either right-wing terrorists or guerrillas for reprisal.[23]

So in 1976 Frank moved into a tin shack, similar to the shanties of the other slumdwellers. He shared the inconvenience of communal outhouses with the other inhabitants. He ate the same food as they did. Having brought only a pair of sandals and two changes of clothes with him, his attire soon began to resemble his neighbors'—well-worn, with holes and patches; and the soles of his feet developed deep cracks.[24] Holdenried, once a wealthy, globe-trotting young man who had dined with the rich and worldly and counted royalty among his friends, had become one of millions of "faceless" inhabitants living in a filthy, teeming Third World slum.

Frank hoped, once he was accepted in the barrio, to listen to the problems of his neighbors, and give advice and help when asked. But the middle-aged stranger was not respected or welcomed at first. He was way overcharged in the marketplace, because he was an outsider, a gringo at that. Fortunately, one neighbor, an old woman named Doña Nelia, soon befriended Frank and began to teach him Spanish. Residents of the barrio, having no sewerage or sanitation facilities, would throw their garbage out into the streets, where it was piling up, increasing the likelihood of vermin, rats, and disease. Frank went out into the street to rake up the putrefying refuse that was accumulating and cart it off to the dump. His neighbors found some kind of perverse humor in this and taunted him for his efforts. But Doña Nelia scolded them sharply; shaking her finger at Frank's tormenters, she cried, "Can't you see he's trying to clean this mess up? Don't you understand he is afraid an epidemic will break out and kill everyone?" This gesture of Doña Nelia's broke the ice. A few days later when neighbors saw Frank cleaning the filthy public latrines, they did not laugh. Instead, they asked to borrow the disinfectant and took on the responsibility themselves. But the newcomer, hardly the stereotypical North American, continued for a while to baffle his neighbors. One day a group of them came to Frank's house and handed him a purse with about $14 in coins. "Take it," they said, "We all contributed something. We know this must be hard for you here. Please go to a hotel and enjoy a good meal and some drinks. Spend it on yourself."[25]

Eventually, neighbors began to confide in him, and Frank, as he had hoped when he arrived, was then able to offer what aid and advice he could. He began to deluge his friends and relatives in the United States and all over the world with letters requesting money to help the inhabitants of Santa Luisa. In order to handle the money that began coming in for Frank's work in Guatemala, he asked Dave Moss if his church could be used as a non-profit clearinghouse. Frank's organization was called Ayudantes de los Pobres, "Helpers of the Poor." Frank's cousin Dick Smith, a member of the congregation, was its treasurer. According to Gerry Phelps, Frank's ministry was run on a shoestring budget, with funds never exceeding $5,000 to $10,000 at a time.[26] When Frank needed money, he wrote his cousin. With the mail service in Guatemala somewhat erratic, Frank was often close to panic over funds. He once wrote Dave:

Did you receive a check from me for $500 about a month ago? Prince Troubetzkoy sent it. I am almost out of money and have the terrible feeling that you or Dick never got the letter. We seem to be losing mail this year. Please advise me right away, so that if there is a problem, I can advise the Prince to stop payment. Maybe he will send another.[27]

Frank's intention in involving the folks back home with his work in Guatemala was twofold. Obviously, one reason was to obtain money for the poor of Barrio Santa Luisa. But to Frank, a second reason was just as important; Moss describes still another aspect of *sin caras*:

Frank believed that the only way to change things was for these conservative Republican Protestants to meet, through him, another person face to face, the person of Santa Luisa. So he encouraged us to help one individual or family in Guatemala, an orphan child or a single parent. In this way, [Frank worked] locally both in Kelseyville, CA, through a small church, and . . . locally in Santa Luisa, as a helper to those who would come to ask him for help with a specific need. He was the "faceless one" in between. . . . He tried to be a bridge of understanding and compassion between Kelseyville and Santa Luisa.[28]

Although Frank was a Catholic and had studied in a seminary and monastery, he had been raised by a Protestant aunt and uncle. His intelligence and background were expansive and his outlook broadened even more so in the context of his ministry in Guatemala. As Frank saw things, no one should excuse himself or herself from helping the poor. His appeals knew no limit; prince or congressperson, conservative or liberal, Protestant or Catholic, Democrat or Republican, union official or employer—any acquaintance at all could expect at some time or another to be bombarded by an entreaty from Frank Holdenried on behalf of his people in the barrio. A letter to a friend, however, would include not only a request for support, but also a brief analysis of Guatemala's economic, social, and political problems; for Frank believed North Americans had to become aware of the tremendous need in order to effect any long-term changes. Some of his Protestant relatives had once said that since most Central Americans were Catholic, their problems should be up to the Catholic church to solve. Frank could not have disagreed more, and when he sensed a change in his own family's views because of his intercession he could not conceal his happiness—tinged with a little pride.[29]

Yet Frank realized early in his ministry that the problems of Guatemala were widespread, complex, and frightening. In December 1976, he wrote Dick:

More of my people are becoming absolutely destitute every day. . . . I will be here a long time—it is inevitable. I'm starting a new work and I would only be kidding you if I said that there was an end to it. The work will outlast me. You really come face to face with life here and it makes some of the things at home seem superficial.[30]

With the donations coming in, Frank embarked on several barrio projects. His friend Doña Nelia was one of the first to benefit. The enterprising old lady had had a shower rigged up in her home and was charging ten cents to her neighbors who wanted to get clean; unfortunately, though, the shower only provided cold water. This was her only income; on it she was supporting herself and a grandson. Frank was touched by their plight and wrote his friend Dave:

She is housebound because her 16 year old grandson suffered a head injury at 6 months of age, and he is now just a baby—withered, because his muscles have never been exercised. It is pathetic. He must be turned every few hours, etc. I don't have to draw you a map.[31]

Frank frequented Doña Nelia's shower regularly, but after three chilly months went by in which he had only one hot shower, he hit upon a brilliant idea. With money begged from friends, Frank bought her a shower head that heated water. Now, for fifteen cents he and other barrio residents could buy a hot shower. The old grandmother, whose business had dwindled during the cold months, would once again have enough income to scrape by.

It may as well be mentioned early on that Frank Holdenried was no Stan Rother when it came to the mastery of technical skills. He was easily frustrated by mechanical projects—like installing a solar stove. At one point he wrote his cousin Dick that his elderly Aunt Thressa was handier than he was:

Yes, I got that instruction on solar cooking. Why don't you come down here and put that damn thing together. Everything it calls for has to be imported and you know me—I can't drive a nail. Thressa could do it fast.

Not too convincingly, but probably not wanting to seem ungrateful, the baffled mechanic concluded: "Thanks—we'll give it a try anyway."[32]

But Frank's lack of technical expertise did not dampen his enthusiasm. On one trip to California, he filled up an old van with shovels, books, treadle sewing machines, and other practical objects. The machines were destined for a newly painted shack Frank called the "Galera," where barrio women would be trained in sewing. He also helped open a day-care center. Living and working nearby was a group of Mother Teresa's nuns. These women volunteered to "outfit" the center, as Frank put it:

These sisters have some tin sheets to give me. They are really wonderful and spiritual women. Their foundress is Mother Teresa of Calcutta, who was on the cover of Time a year ago Xmas. My own views of life square perfectly with hers and what unforeseen luck that they should live so close by. They are good and generous friends.[33]

Frank eventually met Mother Teresa and would visit with her when she was in Guatemala. (In a later letter, however, he seems not to be in quite the same accord with Mother Teresa's views: "She is quite a lady," Frank writes, "even though we don't always agree on things."[34])

Another project in which Frank took pride was his maternal/infant nutrition program for 225 children under six years of age. He took an active interest in this program—active in every sense of the word. When he learned that one mother, pregnant with her fifth child, was anemic, he spent $70 on injections for her. When she went into labor in the middle of the night, he hurried with her to the hospital, through a rainstorm and mud. Almost as proud as the baby's father, Frank wrote Dick:

[Olga] had a girl (8lb. 7oz. an hour and a half later) and was so happy. . . . She was in top shape obviously. That's one of our biggest babies—now I will watch over her for the next two years and she will be smart and we can educate her later on. And, Dick, there is practically no infant mortality in [Santa Luisa] today. Quite a change in three years [since his arrival] in a country with the highest I-M rate in Latin America.[35]

Other letters were not quite so cheerful, however. He mentions the pneumonia that was rampant in the youngsters in the mile-high barrio, and one poignant notation to his cousin was the "donation" made by a medical doctor of "hospitalization to death without charge" of Mateo (age two) and Esmeralda (age five).[36]

Quite soon after he took up residence in the barrio, Frank became aware of the "street kids" of the shantytown who needed guidance and support in their undisciplined young lives. Perhaps Frank's spiritual encounter on the mountain path encouraged him to come to the aid of these youths; certainly, his contact with the barrio grandmothers influenced him in this direction, for they often spoke of the despair that invaded their grandchildren's spirits when they faced the reality of dire poverty in the slum. Many of them would take to the streets and turn to drugs and alcohol, because they saw no job opportunities for them in the future.[37]

Frank approached this aspect of his barrio ministry like the others. He thought it wise not to intrude too quickly into the lives of the street youth. But Frank began to take note of some of the neighborhood teenagers, particularly the ones who appeared to be bright and to have leadership potential. Paco was one such youngster. Without actually confronting Paco with a grandiose plan for his future, Frank gravitated into the boy's life. He began to turn up, conveniently, at a neighborhood hangout when Paco just happened to be there.

After about three months of simply making Paco aware of his presence, the boy approached Frank, asking him what he wanted from him. Frank saw his opportunity and after a long conversation struck a bargain with the boy. If Paco would agree to return to school, if he would live by some practical rules and guidelines, Frank would provide him with a home, clothing, food, and support until he completed his education and was able to find a job and live on his own. Paco decided to give it a try.[38]

This was the beginning of Frank's Escuela de San Iñigo, an aspect of his work in the barrio which Reverend Moss terms "a stroke of genius."[39] Gradually, with funds donated by friends in California and elsewhere, Holdenried expanded his little shanty to accommodate six or seven boys who had ended up on the streets; most were orphaned or abandoned, but some, like Paco, were not. He hired a tutor to teach them the very basic subjects they needed in order to return to school or to enter school for the first time. He provided his growing foster family with material support, as well as a caring parent-child relationship with a structured home life. Frank offered the boys security, with a strong admixture of loving discipline. Like any conscientious North American parent of adolescents, Frank was strict about the boys' study habits and the use of drugs and alcohol. Unlike most North Americans though, Frank had to get his boys into good physical condition before any progress could be made in other aspects of their lives. This meant providing the youths with a healthy, though simple, diet; it meant medicine to rid them of worms and parasites in their intestines; it meant visits to a dentist to have teeth fixed that had been neglected for years.[40]

Frank's efforts paid off rapidly. To the surprise of many observers, these street kids did not return to their former way of life. They stayed in the home Frank provided them and studied hard; when they went back to school, they fit in well in the academic environment. Paco, for example, within three years of his re-entry into school, was elected president of the student body. Frank had proved to be a good judge of potential.

Frank's long-range goal in the education of these boys was to provide a future source of leadership in the barrio. Therefore he insisted that his foster children live and study within the barrio environment and attend the public schools. Although there were some scholarships available at parochial schools, Frank did not attempt to take advantage of them because his boys would have had to board there. Frank was convinced that once a boy left the barrio to attend school, he would be easily swayed and impressed by his rich schoolmates and would soon be imitating them and become ashamed of his own barrio heritage. Upon graduation, he would leave the barrio forever; his education, while a source of escape for him, would never provide a "leadership pool" for the poor of the barrio, which could be drawn upon in the future and one day help interrupt the cycle of poverty for others in the shantytown.[41]

Although Holdenried was no expert on social work, or parenting for that matter, he was confident that his work with the boys was being guided by someone wiser than he:

Saturday, I found another boy in the streets. He asked if he could watch my car. Carlos is 13, never been to school—is very bright—and amazingly well mannered. His mother died in the streets during the earthquake, and his father (who drinks heavily) ran off with another woman. It is always the same story. He is the most peaceful kid to be around. With so many in the streets and so few I can really help—I am always grateful to find children who are able to thrive on care—some don't.

I believe very deeply that these kids are being handed to me by God Himself, Who loves them. Since He is making me responsible for them I know He will give me the means to do the job—but in His own way.[42]

As Frank's little family in the barrio grew, his letters began to reflect his new role as "proud papa":

Today Victor gets baptized and from now on July 4th will also be his birthday—so today he is 13. . . . The kids are doing well in school—showing honest effort in all ways. They are popular with the other children and with the teachers—making a positive influence in very negative surroundings.

By Golly, I think we've got something here![43]

A later letter shows the active part Frank took in the education of the boys under his care; it also reveals that Frank was not enamored with the quality of schooling in Guatemala City:

Mario is doing really well in school. I am pushing him (with his consent and approval) and he is receiving a beautiful education—more from me than the school. He is first in his class in everything and has read Hemingway's *Old Man and the Sea* and liked it. He loves soccer. . . . [44]

As in any large family (particularly with teenagers), Frank had his share of disciplinary problems. He used his ingenuity, a firm, guiding hand, and his flair for dramatic appeal in the following episode:

[Mario] broke up with his first girl friend, and Saturday night came in loaded on beer for the first time. It was quite an experience for both of us. The older guys gave him beer at a fiesta and he got too much. I poured hot coffee down him and he emptied his stomach 4 times—then I took him for a long walk at 1:30 in the morning. He said, "Father, I am so embarrassed—forgive me." He could think alright, just couldn't get his knees to work! Well, the next morning he was fine and I had a short talk about—not booze—but the lesson that our companions are not necessarily our friends and they try to bring us down for perverse reasons of their own.

I was mad as hell at the men [who had provided Mario with the beer] and they apologized to me—saying that Mario was a marvelous example for the others, and they felt terrible about what they had done. I told them that the next time they tried something like that—please come to me first and cut my throat. That shook 'em.[45]

But along with the usual difficulties one might expect to encounter when raising several rambunctious youths, Frank also had to face an unforeseen ordeal no North American parent would ever have anticipated: the nabbing and torture of a child by the secret police. In January 1980, Paco, the youth whom Frank first persuaded to leave the streets, was picked up for interrogation one night as he returned home alone. Unknown at the time to either Frank or Paco, the strangled body of a policeman had been found behind Frank's shack. The secret police had grabbed the first person they saw in the vicinity—seventeen-year-old Paco.

Paco's brother and other family members spent twenty-eight hours looking for the boy in various police stations. Finally, a guard at one station admitted that Paco was there; the desk sergeant, however, routinely denied it. Frank tells what then happened in "Terror in Guatemala," an article that later appeared in *America*:

Guatemala has a well-established habeas corpus law, but local lawyers tell me that to use it often means certain death for their clients. Police do not like admitting when they have someone under investigation. Because their methods for extracting information sometimes cause death, they prefer to finish an interrogation before acknowledging that a missing person is in their custody.

Paco's family and I knew what was happening to him at the police station. And although he did not say so, Carlos [a Jesuit priest who was a chaplain at the police station and a friend of Frank] also suspected the truth. When we called him, he left the dinner table mid-meal and rushed to meet us on the steps of a nearby church. While awaiting him, I began thinking of a defense for Paco; something that had a chance of working under the serious circumstances and absence of law.

"This is no ordinary slum kid," I told Carlos. "You've got to get this story to the secret police before it is too late." Then I carefully recited events leading up to his arrest. On the previous evening Paco and I had an early dinner downtown, and on the way home we stopped at the Pan American Hotel to buy an evening paper. The lobby was filled with officials from the American embassy who were accompanying Congressman Robert Drinan . . . to a national press conference. Father Drinan was in Guatemala on a human rights investigation. When we met him we were asked how things were going. Based upon my experience in the slums up to that time I said that the pressure seemed to be easing a little. The next afternoon, the day of his arrest, Paco turned up to make himself some lunch before leaving to play soccer. I was giving a background interview to the Caribbean correspondent for a major American newspaper. After meeting him, the journalist, fresh from covering the Nicaraguan civil war, commented prophetically that boys Paco's age were the cannon fodder in revolutionary wars and were always the major victims of the violence all over Central America.

"Carlos," I said, "Tell the secret police that this boy is known to half the staff at my embassy and to a famous newspaperman as well as Congressman Drinan. But you must be careful not to scare them into denying that they have him under interrogation, or they might kill him in order to cover up their mistake. Tell them that I won't make any trouble over what they have already done to Paco providing they stop immediately. Otherwise, I will make sure that the whole world knows about this incident. Put it to the detectives that they have a chance to do something positive for Guatemala's image in the world community. But good or bad, it's up to them. The boy is innocent because he was with me in front of witnesses during the time of the murder."

When we entered the police station, the desk sergeant still would not admit that Paco was in their custody. Carlos located the senior officer in charge, and after a lengthy conversation he returned and told me that "they have him." At that moment, I knew that Paco's life would be spared and we owed it to Carlos's intercession.

Carlos was allowed to enter the interrogation room, but I, a foreigner, was not. "He's been touched," he stated matter-of-factly when he rejoined us. "He's been touched" meant that Paco had already been subjected to the dread "capucha" or hood. The capucha is a piece of rubber inner tube cut to fit over the face. The victim lays [sic] prone on his back. One detective straddles the thighs, and the other straddles the head. His job is to pound the ears with doubled fists, then place the hood over the face. The first man then delivers a heavy blow to the diaphragm, knocking the wind out of the victim. As he gasps for air, the rubber inner tube stops the ability to inhale.

As a variation the capucha is sometimes dipped in water then sprinkled with ant powder before use. The greatest danger, according to popular report, is to a victim who had been drinking. Such a person is not always aware of the moment when death approaches and thereby fails to signal in time that he is ready to talk.

Carlos arrived as they were preparing to put the capucha on Paco for the second time. As a result the torture was halted immediately.

The next day one of his interrogators was machine-gunned down by terrorists in front of the police station as he was leaving for home after work. The slain man's family asked Carlos to say the funeral Mass, and I had to wait until he finished before he could take me to another detention center where Paco had been transferred.

By then 72 hours had passed since Paco's arrest, and I was becoming increasingly anxious to see him. Since it was after visiting hours in the new jail, Carlos used his considerable influence to gain our admission. I was allowed to talk to Paco for only a few minutes through a small window cut out of an iron door. He had easily lost 10 or 12 pounds during his ordeal, and I could see that his ears were swollen and filled with caked blood.

"Why didn't you tell the police that you were with me?" I asked.

"I was afraid that if I did, they would come and get you too," he replied simply.[46]

Paco was finally released after seventy-nine days in jail.

Although Paco became one of the few in Guatemala to reappear in relatively good shape after interrogation and torture, the tragic story does not end here. In August 1981, Father Carlos Pérez Alonso, the Spanish-born Jesuit who had made Paco's release possible, disappeared. He was kidnapped by two armed men as he left a military hospital after saying mass. As Holdenried points out in "Terror in Guatemala," the disappearance of Father Carlos was possibly related to the fact that he, along with other Guatemalan Jesuits, had signed a statement denouncing the human rights abuses of the Lucas García regime.[47] However, it is also possible that Carlos's intercession on Paco's behalf may have been a cause of his disappearance; another reason may have been that the army and police felt "betrayed" by Carlos's criticism of the government's human rights record, since he had worked closely with them as chaplain for the military hospital and for the National Police. But even the disappearance of the Jesuit did not bring the cycle of evil to a close; less than nine months after his article criticizing Guatemalan police methods appeared in *America*, Frank Holdenried himself would be found beaten to death on a Guatemala beach, quite possibly by a paramilitary right-wing death squad.

From January to March 1980, while Paco was being held in jail, violence in the barrio increased to alarming levels. Two drunk off-duty policemen came to Frank's house one day, enticed one of the boys out of the hut and put handcuffs on him. They hoped that Holdenried would pay them a bribe for the fifteen-year-old's release, so they could continue their carousing at a local cantina; but Frank was not home at the time. Fortunately, they freed the boy anyway. Other policemen accused Frank of buying stolen property and selling glue and paint thinner to barrio teenagers to get high on. On an even more ominous note, Frank related:

They are killing teenage boys everyday, for one reason or the other. I read about it in the local papers everyday. And it is worse in our barrio. Every night the detectives enter and do a body search on everyone they meet, beat some of the kids and arrest others, on whatever charge they feel like making. It's not for nothing that Guatemala is considered one of the five most repressive regimes in the world.

Concerning Paco, Frank continued:

I am very fearful for the first time in Guatemala. But how can I leave? Considering that while Paco was being tortured, he refused to say that he was with me for fear they would do the same to me—I could never turn my back on that kind of love. I'm stuck and know it.[48]

By the time Paco was released from jail, Frank had decided to leave the barrio, at least temporarily, taking the boys with him. He was offered a place to stay where, he wrote Dick, "there is no violence . . . and in other revolutions this area has always been secure. It is at the foot of a volcano, on the shore of Atitlán. So beautiful."[49] Little did Frank know that within months the mountains around Lake Atitlán would become silent witnesses to disappearances, torture, and murder.

By May 1980, Frank and his little clan of six boys were settled in San Lucas Toliman on Lake Atitlán. They called their new home Casa Javier. The boys attended grammar or high school; two of them entered a trade school. Frank's health had deteriorated considerably during his four years in the barrio, and he believed in the country he would recuperate. He, like so many in the barrio, had developed a nagging cough. At San Lucas, Frank intended to catch up on correspondence (he was an avid letter writer), work on a book he called "The Politics of Joy," and take frequent naps. Although he could really feel his age creeping up on him (he was now forty-seven) and in a low moment believed no one would ever know all the hardship he had been through in Guatemala, he still claimed, "I have never been happier."[50]

During his years in Guatemala, Frank often returned to California to visit with family, rest a bit, and raise funds for his organization, Ayudantes de los Pobres. In the summer of 1980, Holdenried enjoyed a particularly pleasant visit with Fara in Los Angeles and on the spur of the moment, Fara decided that she and Lisel would meet Frank in Mexico City for an extended weekend. Gradually, after the separation that had been so painful for Frank, he and Fara had been able to establish a satisfactory relationship that actually deepened even though they were separated. Kathleen Hendrix, writing for the *Los Angeles Times* after Frank's death, spoke with Fara and offers these insights: "The marriage per se ended, but their relationship deepened. . . . In that sense, they remained a family, and lived as one when Holdenried would come on visits. Fara, however, regretted that although they had a good understanding of each other, she was unable to share in Frank's spiritual side."[51]

While his relationship with Fara seemed to stabilize during the years Frank spent in Guatemala, his relationship with Thressa Holdenried, the aunt who had raised him, was a bit volatile. Gerry Phelps, who stresses that there was a healthy bond of love between Thressa and Frank, also notes that the two personalities often clashed. Thressa believed that Frank was "wasting" his life in Guatemala, that his efforts on behalf of the poor showed a lack of responsibility toward his own family. And, since Frank was nearing the age of fifty, what would become of him when he reached retirement age? Aunt Thressa was not too impressed by Frank's conception of how he would spend his sunset years: "I'll peel potatoes in Mother Teresa's kitchen," he told his aunt, relishing her dismayed reaction.[52]

As has already been established in the chapter on Stan Rother, the fall of 1980, only a few months after Frank and the boys moved there, saw a dramatic turn of events in the Lake Atitlán area. At this time, Frank's letters home reflect his deepening spirituality and his fear that his life would be cut short before he could accomplish his goals. In the following letter to Dave Moss, Frank discusses his fears, his hopes for a pending fund-raising trip in the States, and his spiritual development:

> The situation here is getting very hard—a soldier shot a guy right in front of my house the other night. It is difficult for me to put my feelings down on paper. . . . I just cannot abandon these people in the face of danger. I understand what that might mean. I have close contact with our diplomatic mission and am watching the situation closely. They know where I am at all times and have a copy of my schedule when I am on the road. That's about all I can do.
>
> [In the U.S.] I intend to look for money to support my work. . . . I just have to get the Ayudantes off the ground somehow. I intend to write a spiritual testament . . . as I want my ideas to exist for others, should I not get a chance to complete my work as I envision it. This will contain a resume of two overriding themes—the Presence of Christ in Man and the Politics of Joy which is summed up in me as I live and work.
>
> More important, Dave, are the things happening to me deep inside the soul. There are profound changes occurring in me. A purification of the heart. With this comes an increasing capacity to suffer patiently and with joy and hope. My prayer is so simple, because I have nothing more to say to God but "Teach me to love You more and more." . . .
>
> Dave, if we are really true believers in Christ (as opposed to "faithful Christians without faith") can we really expect in the long run a better deal than He Himself got? It is not some masochistic death wish I'm talking about. It's just walking with Christ—searching for the lost ones—as the Good Shepherd did—scolding the powerful for their injustices—as He did; running with the lowest element of society, as He did; being praised by some for the wrong reasons and being condemned and misjudged by others. . . . Love grows in this life—only accompanied by an increased capacity to suffer for others. There is less and less of self in it all the time—until the end, when finally God takes all for Himself, and there remains nothing left of self-will. . . .
>
> One of the reasons I am so afraid these days is that I feel that I have lost control over my life and my destiny. It's as though I am no longer captain on this flight—but that God is—and He's neglected to tell me where we're going. I'm going along for the ride now, and won't—can't is truer—get

off until we land somewhere. It's the love experience I am having—what is there to exchange it for? Why should I get off? St. Paul tells us that we must measure our life—not by years—but by what we have become and by what we do. Three people have said things to me: Fr. Mooney, before coming here the first time—"God wants something from you. He has set a trap for you—He always does when He wants something." Fr. Healy, my master as a novice, called me God's chosen one and says Mass for me everyday of his life; and Sister Primilia told me, "You, like Charles de Foucauld, may have to die first, before this is over," then they will discover your work and thought. This and the charisma that is my gift to function as I do are all signs of hard things to come to me in the future.

Christ's presence in the soul—that's what makes us Christians and followers. We call ourselves Christians for a lot of other reasons that make absolutely no personal demands on us.

There are some things I would like to add—but I just cannot from here. I'll tell you when I see you. But it's not for nothing that I have written to you as I have.[53]

Frank's presentiment of hard times to come was well-founded. According to his cousin Dick, about a year after he and the boys moved to San Lucas Toliman, Frank received death threats from the right.[54] Consequently, he left the boys in the care of the North American mission team there and went back to Lake County for a prolonged stay in 1981 and 1982. During this time, Frank was able to visit with his Aunt Thressa, who was suffering with cancer and who died while Frank was in the States. He missed his boys in Guatemala though and kept in touch with them regularly; they would write Frank often giving him progress reports on their school work.

On March 7, 1982, while Frank was in California, still another fraudulent election was held in Guatemala, in which no liberal or moderate candidates dared to run and an estimated 65 percent of the populace abstained from voting. Since there was no clear winner, the Guatemalan Congress backed General Aníbal Guevara, Lucas García's candidate, who had received only 16 percent of the vote. The other three right-wing candidates protested in a street demonstration and were tear-gassed and arrested. Because of the resulting dissatisfaction, Lucas García was overthrown in a bloodless coup on March 23, and a junta led by a born-again fundamentalist, General Efraín Ríos Montt, took over the government.[55] Lucas García's notorious presidency had been widely considered the most repressive in all Latin America, and Holdenried became optimistic that there would now be a change for the better in Guatemala. Frank began to consider returning to his boys.

In the five years that Frank had spent in Guatemala, he had developed a lively interest in the political situation there and its relationship to U.S. foreign policy. No profile of Frank Holdenried would be complete without a discussion of his political views, which are revealed in his extensive correspondence.

When Frank first went to Guatemala he knew little if anything about the history or problems of Central America. He could not have even pointed out the location of Guatemala on a map, he would later tell his friends with a laugh. He was a patriotic U.S. citizen, who firmly believed that the American way of life—God, democracy, and capitalism—was the surest recipe for both success and happiness. The major obstacle to world peace and prosperity was communism and therefore the United States had an obligation to do all in its power to save the world from the Marxist cancer. As his wife Fara commented at his funeral, Frank had not been a politically oriented person; nevertheless, the environment in which he placed himself forced him to question the system, to become politicized.[56] So the registered Republican, the former businessman and son of a corporate executive, began an intense self-education program, hoping thereby to learn the causes of and the solution to the harsh realities he saw all around him. It did not take him long to conclude that the greed of large North American corporations, working in collaboration with the U.S. State Department, were in no small part to blame. "It will come as no surprise to you," he wrote to a friend, "that there are 177 U.S.-based multi-national corporations operating in Guatemala. Even though they pay better than the local companies and the jobs they offer are coveted—still many of our problems can be traced back to their businesses."[57] When his cousin, Dick Smith, asked if the United Fruit Company might allow them the use of some of its land for Ayudantes de los Pobres projects, Frank left no doubt about his negative views of this corporation:

> Remember that in the fall of '75 the chairman of the board of United Brands (Fruit) jumped from the Pan Am building in New York after it was learned that he authorized payment of a $2,000,000 bribe to the president of Honduras for the purpose of maintaining the 25¢ tax per carton on bananas. All high class guys. But with a 50¢ tax the [Honduran] government would have been able to increase its revenues to pursue its own national interests and the development of its people.[58]

On big business in general, Frank added: "It would take a book to explain all the things that the multi-nationals are, how they circumvent the law, how the word 'supra-national' better identifies them."[59]

Holdenried became convinced that U.S. middle-class workers were forced to finance with their taxes the cost of State Department intervention, yet only big business profited:

> When you consider the money State gives away comes mainly from the American middle-class worker, one is forced to ask what benefits accrue to him? The truth is that the benefits go first to the banks, then the multinational entities, leaving the sting to the workers.[60]

The average North American laborer, thought Holdenried, suffers in another way. When U.S. policy is aimed at preserving a status quo enabling North

American corporations operating in Latin America to pay extremely low taxes and salaries, many impoverished workers illegally enter the United States in search of better economic conditions. Thus, the North American laborer is forced "to face the daily competition of illegal aliens, who are entering the U.S. each year at an increased rate."[61] If life is made livable for the Latin American poor, thought Frank, they will no longer be forced to come North. Consequently, unions must pressure the State Department to stop fostering the unfair colonial policies advocated by big business: "Labor has a real stake in the solution to this problem"; it must realize "the ultimate cynicism [of] the idea that 'what is good for General Motors is good for the country.' "[62]

The U.S. government too must be made to see that an enlightened Latin American policy would best serve its own interest. An honest, benevolent approach to its southern neighbors would bring to an end the long-held Latin American view of the Yankee as an imperialistic exploiter. Instead, North Americans would be seen as friends. This, in turn, would destroy any plans the Soviet Union has of establishing a foothold in South and Central America. By continuing its current myopic policy, however, the State Department was playing into the hands of its communist rivals. Sooner or later these policies would lead to a third world war, a struggle in which the masses would certainly not support their northern oppressors.[63]

Frank saw great potential in President Carter's human rights policy: "It is working, creative, and coherent," he wrote to a friend, "but it is only a first step."[64] Although a Republican, he found little to applaud in Reagan's Latin American program. "Personally, I don't think he knows a hell of a lot about foreign policy," he lamented in a letter to his relatives.[65] He was especially upset when Reagan attempted to reverse Carter's ban on helicopter shipments to the Guatemalan army.[66] Although he supported Reagan's Caribbean Basin Initiative, a plan to bolster the region's shaky economy through $750 million in aid over a three-year period, he doubted that it would succeed "as long as RR thinks bullets are the answer to Marxism."[67] He was especially critical of Secretary of State Alexander Haig and of Jeane Kirkpatrick, whom he nicknamed the "Dragon Lady."[68] For the latter he reserved some of his harshest and most sarcastic words: "Although she is no coquette, United Nations Ambassador Jeane Kirkpatrick has been flirting with fascism since her appointment . . . in January 1981."[69]

But ironically, like those he criticized, Frank too was fiercely conservative in his attitude toward communism, so much so that many of his friends felt he was actually paranoid on the subject. He believed that one of the Soviet Union's major foreign policy priorities was the export of communist revolution to Central America, especially to Guatemala, which borders the presently "safe supply" of Mexican oil, oil the United States would need in case of war with Russia.[70] With words that could have issued from the most right-wing businessman or politician, he warns that if Guatemala falls to the Russian and Cuban Marxists they will use it "as a springboard for incursion and disruption of Mexican oil production in times of world crisis. Thus, the Soviet Union will

have finally completed the noose it has been weaving for the American neck."
He throws in a reminder for any skeptical reader that indeed Nicaragua is
already falling to the Marxists.[71] In a form letter sent to patrons of Ayudantes
de los Pobres, he becomes more extreme: "THE RUSSIANS ARE COMING!
I just got confirmation that the Soviet embassy in San José, Costa Rica, has
more than 300 native Russians on its staff. The American embassy has 46 [U.S.
citizens]."[72] The same theme is repeated in an eighteen-page report drawn up by
Frank in January 1981 to be used by Ayudantes de los Pobres' members in
lobbying the California state legislature:

> Conditions are so bad in Guatemala that all Castro has to do is wait,
> while at the same time furnish the organizing talents and moral support
> for the left, planting agents and dyed-in-the-wool Marxists among them,
> who will eventually emerge as the real brokers of power. There is little
> cost and a lot of benefit to Latin American Marxist movements by
> planning and operating this way.[73]

Frank's emphasis on "the communist menace" tended to alienate some more
liberal individuals who feared such statements could be used out of context by
the State Department and others to justify military support for repressive
right-wing dictatorships. On trips back to the United States, he would endlessly
frustrate his friend Gerry Phelps, who would argue vehemently with Frank on
whether international communism played a major role in Guatemala's internal
political problems. Frank never relinquished his fears of creeping communism
and Gerry eventually consoled herself by concluding that it was probably best
that he did not become more "leftist" in his views, for such a "radicalization"
would undoubtedly antagonize the Lucas García regime in Guatemala and
leave Frank vulnerable, a potential death-squad target.[74]

David Moss, however, sees a cleverly thought-out rationale in Frank's continual emphasis on global communism. He points out that aside from his direct
contact work with the poor, Holdenried felt his primary mission was to make
the average American aware that it was in his or her interest to demand that
U.S. political leaders take a more humane approach to Latin America. Frank
believed that average North Americans lack even a basic knowledge about the
affairs of their neighbors to the South; they fear communism, however, and
this fear can raise their interest in alleviating Latin American poverty, if only to
stall the advance of that dread ideology.[75] In a letter to Dick Smith, Frank
himself says as much: "If we make people aware of world poverty and their
role in solving this problem in terms of U.S. interests, we will be doing a lot, not
only for the poor in the Third World countries, but for America."[76] Holdenried
likewise emphasizes the importance of making Americans cognizant of the
needs of their Latin neighbors in a letter to union leader Ken Edwards:

> From the beginning I have always said that the ultimate validity of my
> work in Guatemala must be measured in terms of the effect it has on my

own countrymen. . . . *Concientización* of the general U.S. population, it seems to me, is both the patriotic and pragmatic duty of every leader in America at this moment in history. . . . There are Latin American states that are 50 and 100 years behind Mexico. Yet, in Mexico there are 3 million people a day who don't eat. . . . At the same time, over the border in the U.S., Purina is advertising nationally a dog food created for overweight dogs. This is a concrete example that cries for the *concientización* of our people.[77]

Holdenried argued that communism could be defeated in the Third World countries of the Western Hemisphere only if the United States developed a viable alternative to Marxism, an alternative based on a fair policy of free trade—U.S. capitalism with a conscience. He evidently placed no faith in the view that the United States should refrain from intervening in Latin American internal politics, letting the various countries solve their own problems; to him the threat of international communism made this unthinkable. But before all else the United States must act forcefully to stifle the oppression of the poor at the hands of the security forces. He suggests that the United States provide funds to professionalize the national police; money should not be used, however, to enlarge these forces. The army, too, which has always supported the rich and powerful "could be changed to come down on the side of the people; everyone would benefit quickly and with a minimum of bloodshed."[78] He does not say how this "change" could come about.

In another of his writings, he focuses on an important problem and its possible solution:

Guatemala, living off an agricultural economy, is exporting too much food, and diverting food production lands to cash crops (cotton, for instance). This is a nation that every expert says can feed itself, yet we have more hunger here than in most places in Latin America. The pressure to earn foreign exchange exists in order to support a large army and an imported lifestyle for perhaps 10% of the people—and [to] maintain the status quo.[79]

He mentions to Ken Edwards, president of the retail clerks' union local 770, of which Frank was a member, that "it would go a long way if American labor had a policy designed to recognize that Third World countries should first feed themselves, and limit their exports to surpluses."[80] The United States must change to "a politics of 'settling for less.' " Nothing would benefit the Latin Americans more than for the United States to accept "a little less on our multinational investments" and to insist instead "that Third World countries first feed themselves before entering the international business world."[81] He sums up his feelings succinctly in a letter to Dick Smith: "Guatemala has the ability to feed itself if it were allowed to. In a word—we [the Guatemalan people] don't want gifts of bread from you; we want the right to grow our own bread. And you must help us win that right."[82]

Once the people are fed, the United States must use its power, money, and technology to educate the poor and create jobs for them; this in turn will bring into being a new middle class emanating from the lower class.[83] "One of our larger goals," Frank tells Dick, "is to convince American business that it is worthwhile to invest in helping marginal people."[84] And to Betty Campbell, a Sister of Mercy and prominent activist on behalf of the Central American poor, he adds: "It would be very hard to convince a kid to hate the U.S. and become a Marxist, if he knew he was living because the U.S. took his side in an effective way."[85] In the fund-raising newsletters of Ayudantes de los Pobres and in numerous interviews, Frank always stressed this theme of human resources: "The children of the poor are the greatest underdeveloped natural resource in the world today," he would claim, "they are the richness of a country."[86]

Against the advice of some of his friends, Frank decided to return to Guatemala City in the fall of 1982. The boys were not able to join him for several weeks, however, due to intense military activity in the Atitlán region, where they were still living. Besides this initial disappointment, Frank also wrote of growing economic hardship in the barrio: The children Frank's nutrition program had helped remained healthy, but the little ones coming up who did not have that benefit were showing effects of malnutrition. Moreover, jobs for the men were even scarcer than before, and Frank was especially disheartened when one young family man told him, "It is our destiny to suffer." Three hundred fifty families had been unable to meet their house payments, for a year, and the bank was threatening to expel them from their homes. Frank sadly recalled the "high hopes we all had during the building program" after the earthquake.[87]

However, Frank was encouraged by the overall political situation in Guatemala under Ríos Montt. On January 10, 1983, he met with Congressmen Jim Leach (R–Iowa) and Stephen Solarz (D–New York) at the U.S. embassy and spoke with them and their staffs. He told those present that Guatemala's human rights record was greatly improved under Ríos Montt, but that the war in the countryside was driving more refugees into the city every day and that the "socio-economic . . . situation is both critical and explosive."[88] In the same vein, writing to friends in the States, Frank claimed: "Things are 1000% better here in human rights, but the poverty and suffering from hunger is grinding, serious, and has the potential to destabilize the country even further."[89]

Frank, unfortunately, was greatly deceived with respect to Ríos Montt. Because the new president kept repression in Guatemala City down to a minimum, and because (as Frank admitted) press censorship was prevalent, Holdenried had no idea of the appalling brutality that continued to spread in the countryside under the fundamentalist president.[90]

Frank's last letter home to his cousin Dick is a long and cheerful description of the many achievements of Frank's boys.

Both Mario (21) and Victor (20) have been by to see me. Both have work—Victor a concrete mason and Mario a furniture finisher; and both now have their grammar school diplomas. Mario is in first year Basico at night. . . . They look great, and we can be very proud of what we did for them over the years. Mission completed. Considering that unemployment is so very high here, I think it says a lot that they have steady work, and are getting by—and are thinking of their own futures. That they come back makes me feel good. . . .

Paco is on two soccer teams and one basketball team. That and his studies keep him out of trouble. He has been working very hard at his Computer Institute, and his grades are improving. . . . Paco has a fine mind, and a head for math. He is absolutely dedicated to his studies, and puts in the hours here at the house. . . . My plan for Paco is that when he finishes high school . . . he will be a qualified Computer Programmer, and can work for $450 a month. With those skills, and top education, he can go on to the university if he wants to, but on his own hook. He won't need but occasional backup help from us.[91]

Not long after Holdenried returned to Guatemala, his health began to deteriorate. He developed a staph infection and lost twenty-five pounds; he had pneumonia, a liver infection, and terrible chest pain. On top of everything else he shed a complete layer of skin twice in six weeks. By the end of March 1983, he was feeling stronger and decided to go to Livingston, a resort town on the Caribbean coast, for a rest during Easter vacation. Livingston, although accessible only by boat, is crowded with outsiders during Holy Week. The hotels fill up quickly and hundreds of people sleep on the beach; there are frequent processions and much dancing and consumption of alcohol. At the time, Frank had five young men in his care; most planned to spend Holy Week with relatives, but Carlos was free and decided to accompany Frank.

On April 1 (Good Friday) according to a U.S. State Department report, the two vacationers watched a procession, spent some time on the beach, and then watched people dance in a seaside café. Shortly after midnight they searched for an empty, dry spot on the shore to sleep. Frank slipped into a hole filled with water, getting his clothes wet. When they finally found a vacant piece of beach in front of the Flamingo Hotel, Frank hung his wet clothes on the fence of the hotel, leaving his passport and wallet in his shirt pocket. Dressed in shorts, he fell asleep with his backpack near him. Carlos slept close by.

At approximately 2:00 A.M. the two were attacked by several men. Carlos was almost immediately knocked unconscious. Frank's skull was crushed with a number of blows from club-like weapons. When Carlos regained consciousness, Frank was still alive—but barely. The seventeen-year-old boy panicked and searched for help. By the time he returned with the local police it was 7:15 A.M. and Frank was dead. Carlos was immediately taken into custody by the police; after being held for two days, he was released. He claims to have seen nothing and has since fled Guatemala. According to Gerry Phelps, who traveled to Guatemala just after Frank's death on behalf of Ayudantes de los Pobres, Carlos was tortured by the police and accused of the murder. When asked about Carlos's silence in an interview with a correspondent from the *National Catholic Reporter*, Fara Holdenried commented: "It might be best for him to go underground. If he does know something, why should he speak out if it means torture and death?"

Local authorities concluded that robbery by hoodlum outsiders was the motive for Holdenried's murder. The U.S. State Department, after investigating the matter, agreed, although at first an embassy spokesman had discounted robbery as the motive since Frank's wallet was not taken. The contents of Frank's backpack were scattered along the beach as if the killers had searched it for valuables. Neverthess, nothing appears to have been taken. Frank's passport and wallet were left untouched in his shirt pocket. An official from the U.S. embassy attempted to explain this by commenting that the robbers probably did not notice these items since they were in his clothes by the fence. When asked by the *National Catholic Reporter* if a "politically motivated attack was out of the question," the embassy official answered, "No comment."

The American embassy and local police seemed not to be overly troubled that they were unable to find a single witness to the murder, even though hundreds of people had been sleeping on the beach that night.[92] But this fact compelled Holdenried's friends at Ayudantes to ask Representative Douglas Bosco to write to the U.S. embassy in Guatemala asking for answers to several specific questions. He did so, and chargé d'affaires Paul Taylor's reply to his inquiry further strengthened their doubt that Frank's death had resulted from simple robbery:

> The police reported they had no other reports of violence the same night that Mr. Holdenried was killed. They also stated that although there were frequent arrests for drunkenness and disorderly conduct, generally the incidence of violent crime in Livingston was low. During her April 6 visit to Livingston, an embassy officer, sent to the town for the express purpose of speaking with officials about Mr. Holdenried's murder, was told by one resident that the last case of a non-Guatemalan being killed was about a year ago when a Canadian tourist was killed by an Italian during a fight over an American woman. To the best of his recollection, the deputy police chief said that in the past year there have been no deaths attribuable [sic] to violence.[93]

Dissatisfied with the official investigation of Frank's death, his California associates turned to Father Jim Curtin for help. Curtin, an elderly Maryknoll priest residing in semi-retirement in a parish in San Francisco, had lived in Guatemala for many years and had contacts in Livingston. Through them he was able to find that several eyewitnesses, though afraid to step out and say so publicly, claimed that eight men, wearing masks and army uniforms, beat Holdenried to death with clubs. If this is true, the motive may have been to silence Frank, who in the past few months had put aside his former *sin caras* (faceless) strategy, had written of Guatemalan repression for U.S. readers, and had spoken with influential American congressmen. Or it may have been more simple; as Blase Bonpane, a former Maryknoll priest who had been expelled from Guatemala in the seventies, put it: "Anyone working on behalf of social justice really has no right to live in Guatemala."[94]

Reverend David Moss, who spent twenty-one days with Frank in Barrio Santa Luisa and was perhaps his closest friend, made the following observation:

> As long as [Frank] was in Santa Luisa, he felt protected by the people. If someone entered the barrio asking for him Frank would be notified right away while the visitor would be given some run around. If Frank said it was o.k. the person would be guided to his shack. It not, the person would be guided out of the barrio. Going to Livingston on holiday was a big mistake. He left himself too vulnerable.[95]

Frank was buried in Kelseyville, California, on April 8, 1983. The service reflected the ecumenical nature of his ministry: Methodist pastor Gerry Phelps, Presbyterian pastor Joanne Hines, and Catholic bishop Mark Hurley all spoke at Frank's funeral.[96] In Barrio Santa Luisa, Guatemala, on April 10, two memorial services were held which hundreds attended. And on April 17, another memorial service took place in Pasadena, California. Twelve-year-old Lisel Holdenried spoke of her father to the guests: "I think he's right along there with Martin Luther King, Jr. and all those martyrs. We didn't get to spend as much time as most kids have with their fathers, but he was a great man and I loved him." Blase Bonpane, a friend of Frank, then commented that Lisel had received "a tremendous spiritual inheritance from her father" and challenged more North Americans to cast their fate with the poor like Frank did: "Let's get a little more reckless," Bonpane said, "a little more maladjusted."[97]

PART III

EL SALVADOR

In rural Africa, the roots of poverty lie in the soil and man's relationship with it, the fatal impact of population and farming methods on a poor land. In Asia, poverty and growing inequality are the inevitable outcome of population growth, land shortage and the dynamics of rural society, But in Latin America, the origins of poverty and inequality are in the ancient and continuing inhumanity of man to man, in naked, ruthless and often violent exploitation.

Paul Harrison
Inside the Third World

Introduction to Part III

Of all the murders of U.S. citizens in Central America, none has evoked more indignation than the execution of three nuns and one laywoman in El Salvador on the night of December 2, 1980. The deaths of these four women exposed many Americans for the first time to the bloodshed occurring not only in El Salvador but in other Central American countries as well. And many began to question the fact that the United States was supporting a government that killed not only North American missionaries but tens of thousands of its own people.

On Thursday, November 27, 1980—Thanksgiving Day—Ambassador Robert White and his wife, Marianne, attended an ecumenical service held by the U.S. community in San Salvador. White had been appointed to El Salvador by President Carter in early 1980, and at the reception following the service met for the first time Ursuline sister Dorothy Kazel and layworker Jean Donovan, both of whom were members of the Cleveland diocesan mission team working in the coastal town of La Libertad. After chatting a bit, the Whites invited Dorothy, Jean, and the rest of the team to their home for dinner the following Monday. They accepted the invitation.

At the dinner party on December 1, Jean entertained the Whites with a lively account of how she had left a well-paying job with the Arthur Andersen accounting firm in Cleveland to come work with the poor in El Salvador. Not surprisingly the volatile political situation in El Salvador was another topic of conversation.[1]

The Whites had insisted that their guests bring a change of clothes for an overnight stay, so they would not have to venture out late at night—El Salvador's roads were far too dangerous. So the next morning Dorothy and Jean said good-bye to their hosts. They climbed into their white Toyota mini-van for a few hours of shopping in the city before they were to drive to the airport to pick up their friends, some Maryknoll nuns who were returning from a regional mission meeting in Managua. Before they left the ambassador's, Jean leaned out of the van window and called to Father Paul Schindler, another member of the mission team, who was also leaving the Whites: "Don't forget . . . get back to Libertad early—we'll have a party tonight with the Maryknollers when they arrive."[2]

The next time Robert White saw Jean and Dorothy was Thursday, December 4, as they, along with Maryknoll sisters Maura Clarke and Ita Ford, were lifted by ropes from their common grave in a cow pasture, about an hour's drive from the airport. Their bodies were bruised and bullet-ridden; the ambassador could see from the evidence that they had been raped. Sickened by what he was witnessing, White was heard to say over and over, "They're not going to get away with this; they're not going to get away with it."[3]

Gradually, the sequence of events that had led to their deaths on the night of December 2 began to unfold. In the province of Chalatenango, where Ita Ford and Maura Clarke aided refugeees from both sides in the undeclared Salvadoran civil war, ominous "incidents of harassment and intimidation against churchworkers" had occurred. The Lawyers Committee for International Human Rights reports:

—In the fall of 1980, for the first time, members of the army began coming into the Church building. They came initially in civilian clothes. Soon they began coming in their army uniforms. By late fall, the army had virtually taken control of the Church. Church officials were reduced to asking the Army's permission before ringing the Church bells.

—In early November of 1980, a sign appeared on the parish door in the city of Chalatenango. The sign showed a knife and a head with blood running down its side, and contained a death threat directed against the men and women who were working with the Church in Chalatenango.

—About the same time, Ita Ford and Maura Clarke moved into the parish house in Chalatenango because they felt more secure there. In November 1980, Ita Ford told an interviewer that "The Colonel of the local regiment [Ricardo Peña Arbaiza] said to me the other day that the Church is indirectly subversive because it's on the side of the weak."

—On December 2, 1980, the day after the women were murdered, a priest in Chalatenango received an anonymous threatening letter. That night another member of the Church staff was shown a list and told that the people on it were going to be killed. The list contained the names of everyone on the parish staff (except the cook), including Ita Ford and Maura Clarke. The unidentified man told the parish worker that the killings would begin that night.[4]

There had also been threats in La Libertad where Dorothy and Jean worked: Treasury Police had been overheard expressing a desire to "get them" (Dorothy and Jean) for their work in transporting refugees.[5]

All four of the women were well aware that their work with the victims of the civil war fueled the hatreds of the ruling class, the armed forces and police, and the paramilitary rightist death squads. Each woman had had to face this reality within the past year, and each had made the voluntary commitment to continue her work with the Salvadoran poor anyway. The women also had enjoyed a certain immunity to the evils that surrounded them. Although Archbishop Romero and many Salvadoran priests had been murdered, no nun had been injured or killed.[6] As North Americans, too, they felt protected; Salvadoran

Monsignor Uriost used to say he felt quite secure driving through the Salvadoran countryside with Dorothy or Jean, "because no one in the country was safer" than these two women.[7] In fact, and among the Cleveland mission team, it had become a standing joke that the best safeguard in Salvador was to be blond and blue-eyed, like Dorothy and Jean.[8] All four women had experienced situations in which they felt protected by their *gringa* looks.

During the afternoon of December 2, 1980, Dorothy and Jean headed for El Salvador's international airport to pick up two of the four Maryknoll nuns returning from a missionaries' conference in Managua. Sisters Teresa Alexander, Madeline Dorsey, Maura Clarke, and Ita Ford had been unable to get reservations for the same flight, so when Teresa and Madeline arrived around three o'clock they told Dorothy and Jean that the other two had said not to return to the airport at six—they would simply catch a bus for La Libertad and save Dorothy and Jean a second trip. Dorothy and Jean, however, insisted it would be no trouble.[9]

Unknown to the women, a National Guardsman was watching them in the airport; when he saw the four leave in the white van, he placed a call to his immediate superior, "No, she's not on this flight. We'll wait for the next one."[10] Around six o'clock Dorothy and Jean returned to the airport only to find that Maura and Ita's flight from Managua was delayed an hour. The airport was crowded with foreigners who were arriving to attend the funeral the next day of five leaders of an opposition umbrella group, who had been abducted by Salvadoran police while they were meeting in a Jesuit high school and had later been found slain on a roadside. Dorothy and Jean spent the time talking with members of the Canadian delegation and with Heather Foote of the Washington Office on Latin America.[11] After Maura and Ita arrived, the four friends set off for La Libertad in their white mini-van; again, their actions were being closely monitored by the Guardia Nacional. Judge Harold R. Tyler, Jr., in a report commissioned by the Reagan administration in 1983, describes what then happened:

> At the airport traffic checkpoint, Guardsman Perez Nieto, following instructions, allowed the van to pass through. He detained all other traffic for about ten minutes, and then returned to the National Guard headquarters.
>
> Passing the checkpoint, the churchwomen arrived at Subsergeant Colindres Aleman's position. They were stopped and ordered to vacate the van. The guardsmen searched the van and questioned the women. Thereupon, Colindres Aleman ordered them back into the van together with Guardsmen Contreros Recinos, Canales Ramirez and Moreno Canjura. Contreras Recinos drove the van and, with Colindres Aleman and Guardmen Contreras Palacios and Rivera Franco following in the National Guard jeep, the small convoy started its journey fifteen miles into the hills of El Salvador.
>
> Shortly thereafter the jeep developed engine trouble. After a brief stop

for temporary repair, the two vehicles made it to the National Guard command post at the town of El Rosario La Paz. There, Subsergeant Colindres Aleman telephoned the airport and instructed his second in command . . . to send another vehicle to El Rosario to retreive them. The jeep was then left at the Guard post, with Guardsman Rivera Franco to guard it.

The five other guardsmen crowded into the small van with the four churchwomen and proceeded in the direction of Zacatecoluca. At the intersection of the road to San Pedro Nonualco, the van left the main road and drove for another six kilometers, finally turning off onto a dirt lane. At a deserted site along the lane, Subsergeant Colindres Aleman directed Guardsman Contreras Recinos to bring the van to a halt, and ordered the women out of the van. The guardsmen sexually assaulted the women. Then, at Colindres Aleman's orders, they shot the women dead with their service rifles, leaving the bodies along the roadside as they fell. The guardsmen, upon completion of their grisly mission, then returned to El Rosario La Paz in the van.

. . . [Later] after the guardsmen had removed several items from the van, . . . Guardsman Contreras Recinos opened the middle door of the van and, with the help of Contreras Palacios and Moreno Canjura, poured aviation fuel on the inside and outside of the van and set it afire. . . . Early in the morning of December 3, 1980, villagers from Santiago Nonualco, a remote village fifteen miles northeast of the airport, found the bodies of the four churchwomen sprawled along the roadside. One of the villagers contacted the local Militia Commander, José Dolores Melendez, to report the discovery. Shortly thereafter, two National Guardsmen and three Civil Guardsmen arrived at the scene, and ordered the preparation of a common grave. The local Justice of the Peace, Juan Santos Ceron, was summoned by the Militia Commander, and authorized the immediate burial of the women as "unknowns," an unfortunate practice that had become common in El Salvador.

. . . Word began to circulate in the community that four female Caucasian "unknowns" had been found dead and buried in Santiago Nonualco. A local parish priest heard the news and informed the Vicar of the San Vicente diocese. In turn, the Vicar notified the United States Embassy that the bodies of the American churchwomen had been found.

Upon learning the news, United States Ambassador Robert White went immediately to the murder site, where he found Father Schindler, who also had been notified by the parish priest of the discovery of the bodies. The Secretary of the Justice of the Peace arrived and gave permission for the removal of the bodies from the grave. All four women had been shot in the head; the face of one had been destroyed. The underwear of three of the women was found separately, along with bloody bandanas.[12]

In January 1982, when Contreras Palacios confessed that he had participated in the murders, he said that Subsergeant Colindres Aleman had claimed
the nuns were "subversive."[13]

On Friday, December 5, 1980, the day after the missing churchwomen's
bodies had been unearthed in the cow pasture (scenes of which had been
televised to millions of American viewers), President Carter suspended all
economic and military assistance to El Salvador, "pending clarification of the
circumstances of the killings."[14] The Carter administration was apparently
easily convinced that clarification was forthcoming and a few weeks later, on
January 14, 1981, resumed military aid to El Salvador, citing the Salvadoran
government's commitment to a thorough investigation of the crime.[15] Not
surprisingly, Ambassador White vehemently disagreed: "All the evidence we
have . . . is that the Salvadoran government has made no serious effort to
investigate the killings of the murdered women."[16]

If seekers of justice and truth were dismayed with the Carter administration,
they were stunned by statements made by appointees and would-be appointees
of the newly elected Reagan administration. On December 16, 1980, just two
weeks after the nation was outraged by the murders, Jeane Kirkpatrick, future
ambassador to the United Nations, stated in an interview (which appeared on
Christmas Day) in the *Tampa Tribune*.

> The nuns were not just nuns. The nuns were also political activists. We
> ought to be a little more clear about this than we actually are. They were
> political activists on behalf of the *frente* [Farabundo Martí National
> Liberation Front] and somebody who is using violence to oppose the
> *frente* killed these nuns.[17]

In February 1981, in a radio interview with CBS news, Reagan's appointee
for human rights commissioner, Ernest Lefever (who was later rejected by
Congress), made a comment regarding "nuns hiding machine guns for the
insurgents."[18] But even more slanderous words were in the offing. Anthony
Lewis, writing for the *New York Times*, commented on the derogatory testimony of Secretary of State Alexander Haig:

> Every so often in our open society a public figure inadvertently displays
> his character in a way that, once understood, can never be
> forgotten. . . .
> The Secretary of State was testifying before the House Foreign Affairs
> Committee. He said this:
> "I'd like to suggest to you that some of the investigations would lead
> one to believe that perhaps the vehicle that the nuns were riding in may
> have tried to run a roadblock, or may accidentally have been perceived to
> have been doing so, and there'd been an exchange of fire and then
> perhaps those who inflicted the casualties sought to cover it up. And this
> could have been at a very low level of both competence and motivation in

the context of the issue itself. But the facts on this are not clear enough for anyone to draw a definitive conclusion."

The next day newspapers reported Haig suggesting that the four American churchwomen may have tried to run a roadblock and been killed in an exchange of fire with security forces. That same day Haig appeared before the Senate Foreign Relations Committee, and Senator Claiborne Pell of Rhode Island asked about his comment.

"I'm glad you raised it, Senator" Haig replied, "because I read some of the press reportings, which were of course not what I said."

He explained that an autopsy on one woman showed the death bullet to have gone through glass first. That meant, he suggested, that one soldier might have fired through a car window, and then others panicked.

"I laid that out as . . . one of the prominent theories as to what happened; and I hope that it does not get distorted or perverted emotionally and incorrectly."

Senator Pell asked whether he was suggesting the possibility that "the nuns may have run through a roadblock." With a tone of amazement in his voice, Haig said:

"You mean that they tried to violate . . . ? Not at all, no, not at all. My heavens! The dear nuns who raised me in my parochial schooling would forever isolate me from their affections and respect."

Pell asked about the phrase "exchange of fire" used by Haig. "Did you mean that the nuns were firing at the people, or what did 'an exchange of fire' mean?"

Haig chuckled. Then, with an air of levity he continued.

"I haven't met any pistol-packing nuns in my day, Senator. What I meant was that if one fellow starts shooting, then the next thing you know they all panic."

That was Haig's testimony. What does it have to do with the facts?

From what is known and has been published, the four women were picked up on the way from the airport to their house late in the afternoon. They were killed many hours later, in a different place. They were shot in the head at close range. None of those facts is consistent with a mix-up at a roadblock.

Haig's "prominent" theory has in fact never been taken seriously in the investigation of the killing, according to people involved in the investigation. An early report that glass fragments had been found in one of the bodies was later called erroneous.

The theory sounds, indeed, as if it could have been based on something floated by the Salvadoran right to obstruct a real investigation. From the start the effort to find the killers has run into obstacles in El Salvador. For two weeks U.S. diplomats could not even get local doctors to perform autopsies; the doctors were afraid of finding something that pointed to the security forces. . . . Whatever the effect of Haig's comments in El Salvador, they say a good deal about their author. An American Secretary of State, talking about the vicious killing of four American women, suggested that they were responsible in some measure for their fate. The next day, challenged, he tried to slither away, joking and expressing amazement and blaming the press.[19]

In spite of there being no evidence to substantiate Haig's statements, the efforts of Ita's brother, Bill Ford, and Michael Donovan, Jean's brother, to obtain a public retraction and apology from the Secretary of State were to no avail.[20]

Thus in the short space of three months after their rape and slaying, Sisters Dorothy Kazel, Maura Clarke, and Ita Ford, and lay missioner Jean Donovan were derided as "political activists" and were depicted as concealing guns and as being engaged in an "exchange of fire" while running a roadblock. Excuses had been made by the American Secretary of State for the "panic" of the right wing security forces of El Salvador. It would seem that high-ranking members of the Reagan administration might agree with the view of Subsergeant Colindres—their accused killer—that the women were "subversives." How different would be the eulogies and lamentations of the Reagan administration when four U.S. Marines were gunned down by leftists in a Salvadoran café in June 1985. The American public would not then hear a strained rationale for *leftist* terrorism or an intimation that the Marines had somehow sealed their own fate.

Nevertheless, in spite of attempts by Reagan appointees to minimize—and even at time justify—the execution of Ita, Maura, Dorothy, and Jean, their lives stand as evidence of their integrity, dedication, and compassion. Their commitment to the poor victims of a Salvadoran madness "so diabolical, it just makes you want to weep"[21]—in the words of Dorothy Kazel—challenges Americans to penetrate the haze conjured up by words like "subversive" and "political activist," and confront the irony that in the Central American context of injustice and repression, it is often considered an act of political subversion simply to work on behalf of the poor. In this light then, the disparaging words of Kirkpatrick, Haig, Lefever, and Colindres toward the churchwomen can be seen as a simplistic mechanism to bolster the Salvadoran government and not as an attempt to convey the facts. As Joseph Kazel, Dorothy's father, told the authors: "The Reagan people were looking for something to throw suspicion on my daughter and the other women. If they found anything at all they certainly would have used it. But they could not find a thing—because there was nothing to find."[22]

Dorothy Kazel

8

Dorothy Kazel and Jean Donovan

Ursuline Missionary and Lay Missionary

Born on June 30, 1939, Dorothy Lu was the second of two children born to Joseph and Malvina Kazel, Lithuanian-Americans living in a middle-class neighborhood of Cleveland, Ohio. Blonde and blue-eyed, she was always considered one of the prettiest girls in her class throughout elementary and high school. Early on, Dorothy demonstrated a spontaneous and cheerful approach to life's little obstacles: Caught by surprise in the third grade by a school Halloween party for which she had no costume, she ran home for lunch and cut a dress out of newspaper. After fastening her creation together with pins, she rushed back to school and received first prize for having the most original costume.[1]

Vivacious, fun-loving, and athletic, Dorothy had many friends of both sexes. Roller-skating was a favorite pastime of hers, and she was in several skating competitions and performances. But slumber parties were her great passion, and her parents remember well the many noisy nights when their living room was carpeted with wall-to-wall girls. Although Dorothy had a wide range of non-academic interests, she still managed to earn very good grades in grammar and high school, and with a minimal amount of studying.

Dorothy was close to her older brother, Jim; he considered her a friend and a "great sister to grow up with." He grew to appreciate Dorothy's patience when he and his buddies organized a "swinging fifties band" and used her for an audience during practice sessions. One of the few unhappy moments of Dorothy's childhood occurred when she was about eleven; her father describes the incident: "One Sunday, [the neighborhood theater] had the movie about the dog Lassie, and in the movie, Lassie got killed. Well, Dorothy came home crying her heart out, . . . so her Dad had to explain to her that it really didn't happen—it was only a movie—and Lassie was still alive—and that made her feel much better."

Dorothy's childhood was almost idyllic. Before leaving her high-school years behind in 1957, she capped them off with two final achievements—she was elected president of her senior class and landed a substantial part in the school play, *Cheaper by the Dozen.* If Dorothy had felt drawn to the life of a nun during those years, no one suspected it. In fact, before she finally entered the Ursuline Order at the age of twenty-one, Dorothy was to spend three years in college and become engaged to a young soldier from California.

From high school, Dorothy went on to Saint John's College (now closed), a Catholic diocesan women's institution in Cleveland that trained teachers and nurses. She entered the "cadet" program, which allowed students to earn a teacher's certificate by taking course work for two years, then teaching and continuing studies on Saturdays. To complete her on-site training, Dorothy taught at Saint Robert Bellarmine elementary school in Euclid, the suburb of Cleveland where she lived with her parents. At this school Dorothy came into contact for the first time with the Ursuline sisters and was greatly impressed by them.

While teaching there, Dorothy was dating a young man named Don from Bakersfield, and their relationship was growing quite serious. Dorothy traveled to California to meet Don's family. The fact that he was not a Catholic was upsetting to her; after they talked about this, Don received instruction in the Catholic faith and became a convert. When Don gave Dorothy a "beautiful" engagement ring, as Mrs. Kazel remembers it, it seemed to everyone that Dorothy would marry and settle down, possibly in California, to raise a family. She and Don began to plan their wedding; but then, her mother recalls, Dorothy became very moody, not her usual self at all. She began to spend a lot of time in her bedroom thinking and was suddenly very serious and preoccupied. After about two weeks of this behavior, she told her parents that she did not feel sure about her upcoming marriage and that she thought her true calling was to be a nun. Mrs. Kazel noticed that once she had made this decision, which was obviously a painful one, a weight seemed to lift from her daughter's shoulders. But it still remained for her to break the news to Don, and this was a "heartbreaking" task for Dorothy, her mother recalls. Even though Don tried to change his former fiancée's mind, Dorothy was too determined to be persuaded. "The next thing we knew," Mrs. Kazel says, "she was entering the convent." She joined the Ursulines on September 8, 1960.

Only Dorothy knew how really trying a time this had been for her, but there are indications that some bittersweet memories of Don followed her into the convent. One year later, after her novitiate was over, she was formally "clothed" by the Ursulines as a postulant and received the name "Laurentine." Sister James Francis stopped in to see the newly named Sister Laurentine and relates: "That night when I made the rounds to check on the postulants she said to me that the guy she was engaged to—his favorite name was Laura. 'Isn't that something I would get this name? It's funny how things like that can happen to you.' " And many years later, while traveling up the California coast from El Salvador with her close friend Sister Martha Owen, Dorothy would relate the story of her engagement and her decision to enter the convent; "it was obvious that she still remembered Don with a lot of affection," Sister Martha recalls. Dorothy did not remain Sister Laurentine. After Vatican II, many members of religious orders chose to return to their given names, so in 1970 she became known as "Sister Dorothy."

When Dorothy entered the Ursuline Order, she had not yet earned her college degree; so in 1963 she enrolled as a full-time student at Ursuline College in Cleveland and graduated on June 1, 1965. After graduation, Dorothy was assigned to teach at Sacred Heart Academy in East Cleveland. She spent seven years at this inner-city school and the work she did there in her twenties and early thirties reveals that Sister Dorothy was maturing into a woman of remarkable energy, dedication, and compassion. At Sacred Heart, she taught typing, shorthand, and bookkeeping to the students, although she was not very fond of these subjects and sometimes would jokingly blame her mother for having encouraged her in the first place to take such courses. But it was actually outside the classroom that Dorothy's ability found direction and her highly charged energy found an outlet. Sacred Heart Academy was located in the heart of East Cleveland, an old transitional area of the city which middle-class whites had fled, leaving the underprivileged behind—mostly blacks and a few whites. Dorothy took charge of the school's innovative "Thrust Program," which gave Sacred Heart students an opportunity to provide community service as a part of their school curriculum. The program had a twofold goal— to offer extra pairs of hands to the struggling and needy community, but more importantly, to prepare Sacred Heart students for roles in that community, to try to open up avenues for these inner-city youngsters into business or service related careers.

Because of declining enrollment, Sacred Heart Academy by the late sixties was struggling for its continued existence. Dorothy was chosen, as well as two other Ursulines, to organize an all-out effort to keep the academy open. They went door to door seeking new students, adapted the curriculum to the needs of the neighborhood, and sought grants from agencies to help the school through the crisis. Despite this, Sacred Heart had to close its doors in 1972. Although her efforts failed, Dorothy had demonstrated tenacity, optimism, and a cheerful willingness to contend with the insurmountable obstacles of poverty and neighborhood decay. Dorothy was anything but a defeatist.

During these years, just as she had as a youngster, Dorothy pursued a wide range of activities that would have exhausted a woman of less ability and energy. She went on camping trips with the Girls' Athletic Association and participated in weekend retreats; she was also an active member of an ecumenical group in East Cleveland. Sister Dorothy attended training sessions so she could teach religion to the deaf, and taught catechism on Saturdays in a parish nearby. One summer in the late sixties, she traveled to the Southwest and taught religion on a Papago Indian reservation near Tucson, Arizona, an experience which many think is related to her decision to volunteer for work in the Salvadoran mission. But apparently all these activities were still not enough to satisfy the young woman's drive, so she began work on a master's degree in guidance and counseling at John Carroll University; after a few years of part-time study, Dorothy received her master's in May 1974.

Dorothy's vivacious personality continually drew others like a magnet. A friend from her early days as a postulant, Sister Kathleen Cooney, says, "You were just drawn to Dorothy! She was very pretty, blue sparkling eyes, . . . high energy. Always joking. . . . " Sister James Francis observes: "She seemed so unaware of her beauty. . . . She loved to get involved and jumped right into everything. She was fearless." Dorothy's niece Cheryl Kazel recalls: "There was never a dull moment when our Aunt came to visit on weekends. . . . I remember she liked to go jogging through the parks. She loved the scenery, the atmosphere, and the company. She was always full of pep and vigor!" And Sister Martha, Dorothy's confidante and sidekick for five years in El Salvador tells of her adventurous spirit: "Dorothy had a real genuineness and openness about her. . . . She had a very free spirit. . . . She'd be the first to jump in the truck and learn how to drive a stick shift, or the first to hop on a motorcycle— just fully open and accepting to all new challenges." Dorothy also had what can inadequately be called true sensitivity; Martha describes this well:

> Dorothy could respond sincerely to whatever emotion you were experi-
> encing. She would cry with you when you were sad, laugh when you were
> happy, pray if you wanted to pray, jog if you wanted to jog, even climb a
> mountain with you if you wanted to. If there was someone around who
> wanted to speak in tongues, Dorothy would wind up speaking in
> tongues!

And Dorothy had an unquenchable sense of humor. Barb Sever, a lay teacher then who has since joined the Ursuline Order, taught with her at Sacred Heart Academy for several years and remembers one of Dorothy's brainstorms in particular:

> The rules of the convent at that time included a nightly curfew and of
> course did not allow for individual vacations. But Dorothy had her heart
> set on a trip to Florida. Knowing that this was impossible, she decided on
> a plan to convince the rest of the community that she had gone to Florida,
> and she roped me into it. She had found out that there was a tiny town on
> the other side of Ohio called "Florida," and her scheme was to leave the
> convent early on Saturday morning, drive 300 miles to "Florida," and
> mail postcards back to the convent saying things like "Lovely weather,
> wish you were here." Of course, they would all have a "Florida" post-
> mark! Then we would immediately turn around and head for Cleveland
> to make it back before curfew. Dorothy figured this joke was good for a
> few weeks worth of laughs: she would kid everybody about her trip to
> Florida and how delightful and relaxing it had been. Unfortunately for
> her little scheme, when we arrived in "Florida," we found the town was
> so tiny it didn't even have a post office! Dorothy couldn't believe this and

we had to cruise the two block long main street twice to convince her that we had driven all this way for nothing. We were disappointed, but still we had to beat the curfew, so without resting or eating we drove like mad back to Cleveland and Dorothy just made it in time.[2]

After Sacred Heart Academy closed, Dorothy began to teach at Beaumont High School in Cleveland Heights. This school was in a racially mixed neighborhood, and it was there that Dorothy, as a guidance counselor, began to help youngsters on drugs or troubled by emotional and family problems. Her ability to work with problem adolescents sprang not only from her reserves of optimism and energy, but also from her unique ability to accept a person completely on his or her own terms. A former student who sought Dorothy's advice during her senior year at Beaumont recalls:

> [Dorothy] was . . . 100% present to any person she was speaking with. . . . She was herself—open-minded and funny. She hated the sin, but loved the sinner. She never judged anybody at all. She had a special feeling for people who had been kicked around—the ones that nobody else wants. . . . [3]

In the late sixties, Dorothy heard that the Cleveland diocese was forming a mission team to send to El Salvador in Central America. Like many other dioceses around the country, the church in Cleveland was responding to the call of John XXIII in 1963 to send 10 percent of its personnel overseas. Dorothy volunteered for the team, but was not chosen to go with that first mission. Six years later, however, when it was time to rotate some of the members of the team, the diocese took Dorothy up on her earlier offer. By this time, Dorothy was well into her work as guidance counselor at Beaumont High, a job she liked and had studied four years to obtain. It was not an easy decision to make, but Dorothy finally said farewell to the students and teachers at Beaumont and cast her future with the Salvadoran people.

Only 8,236 square miles in size, El Salvador is the tiniest nation in Central America. But it is also the most densely populated country in the Western Hemisphere with 550 people per square mile. The land has no important mineral resources and at least half of its people are dependent on agriculture for their survival. Yet, less than 2 percent of the people own 60 percent of the entire country, including nearly all the fertile soil. Consequently, Salvadorans have a per capita income of only $680 a year, second lowest in Central America. (Honduras, at $640, is lowest.)[4]

During the latter part of the nineteenth century, El Salvador's indigo-centered economy was replaced by a system based on the production of coffee for export. The oligarchy—often called the "Fourteen Families"—already held most of the fertile land so the transformation was uncomplicated from its point of view. For Indian peasants, however, the transition had serious implications for their future existence, since many *campesinos* began to lose their communal lands to the large landholders. As profits escalated, the wealthy elite expanded by acquiring whatever agricultural holdings it did not already own, thereby creating a subservient population of marginalized, landless wage laborers. Moreover, with their lucrative profits, the rich landowners were able to accumulate the capital needed to establish their own commercial and banking systems. Contrary to the pattern in most other Central American countries, the oligarchy faced few foreign competitors within, such as the U.S. banana companies that permeated Honduras and Guatemala.

Life was indeed comfortable for the oligarchs, but for the vast majority of the population the story was quite different. As historian Walter LaFeber reports:

On the bottom side of Salvadoran society [were] suffering and exploitation which the people endured with remarkable patience—until 1931. The rapid expansion of the coffee plantations had torn apart Indian villages and their communal lands which provided the food supply. Peasants and Indians became little more than a hungry, wandering labor force to be used at will by the oligarchy. As early as 1900 Salvadorans had sought work in Honduras with United Fruit and other U.S. companies. By the early 1920s they made up as much as 10 percent of the Honduran work force. Their numbers rapidly grew during that decade when lower coffee prices further squeezed out smaller growers and concentrated more power in the oligarchy's hands. As coffee took up more and more territory, the staple foods of maize, beans, and fruit grew scarcer. The only Salvadorans who had enough, not to mention a variety, of food, were the few who could import it from other Central American nations or the United States.[5]

Between 1922 and 1926 the suffering of the bulk of the population became desperate as the price of maize doubled and that of beans increased 225 percent. A glimmer of hope appeared, however, when President Pío Romero Bosque, a seemingly typical member of the oligarchy, stunned everyone by refusing to designate his successor, while instead working for a fair, open presidential election in 1931.[6] Caught unprepared, the conservative elite fragmented and offered five of its members as candidates for president. An outsider, therefore, reformer Arturo Araujo, was able to receive just enough votes to win what many call the only reasonably free election in El Salvador's history.[7] Araujo's tenure in office was not long. In December 1931, after attempting to reform the tax laws and reduce the military budget, he was ousted by an army-sponsored coup and replaced by General Maximiliano Hernández Martínez, who had been his vice-president and war minister. General Martínez was a man who dabbled in the occult and rationalized that it was worse to kill an ant than a human, since a human has an afterlife while an ant's death is final.[8] Nevertheless, the "witch doctor" was "an efficient, if somewhat chilling, ruler."[9]

Meanwhile, Agustín Farabundo Martí, a communist who had helped found the Central American Socialist Party in 1925, was secretly planning what he hoped would be a nationwide insurrection. He had returned to El Salvador after spending fifteen months in Nicaragua, where he served as personal secretary to Augusto Sandino. The two had parted ways because Martí was a Marxist and Sandino was not. "His flag was only that of national independence," Martí would later comment, "not that of social revolution."[10]

Campesinos and Indians in the western coffee-producing areas, where poverty was most severe, were easily convinced to join the planned uprising. The revolt was to begin on January 22, 1932, but the plot was discovered and Martí and his communist associates were arrested on January 19. Nevertheless, the Indians, desperate and with their hopes now raised, went ahead with their rebellion. Leaderless and armed only with machetes, they struck out with no real plan of action. They had killed about fifty people, when the army was sent to stop them. After only two days of fighting, they were easily defeated; twenty soldiers died while the rebels suffered about four hundred casualties. But General Martínez was not finished; choosing to emphasize the insurrection as the first communist revolution ever attempted in the Western Hemisphere, the Salvadoran president, with the enthusiastic support of the oligarchy, determined to make an example of the hapless Indians. He ordered the army to pursue and exterminate as many of them as possible. About 30,000—2 percent of the entire population of the country at that time—were executed.[11] This tragic incident, referred to even today throughout El Salvador simply as La Matanza (the Massacre), has left an indelible mark on the Salvadoran psyche: "The massacre of 1932 permanently scarred the memory of Salvadorans. Because it had been considered an 'Indian' revolt and people were killed as Indians, the survivors put away traditional clothes and customs; there are virtually no 'Indians' in El Salvador today."[12]

Although the 1932 uprising is often termed a communist revolution, such a judgment does not tell the whole story. As Berryman notes:

> There was another root to the conflict, . . . that of Indian resistance. The Indians could still recall their communal lands and resented their expropriation by the oligarchy, whom they were forced to serve as a labor force. . . . To what degree the 1932 uprising was a product of the efforts of leftists such as Martí and their organizations, and to what degree it was a spontaneous rebellion arising out of peasant and Indian resentment for the mistreatment of decades and centuries remains an open question. Clearly both flowed together but the proportion is unclear, and it is this writer's impression that the latter factor has been underestimated.[13]

At any rate, La Matanza was exactly what Martínez needed to secure his shaky position as head of state. His willingness to punish the Indian insurgents convinced the oligarchy that after the "failure" of leadership under Romero Bosque and Araujo, they had finally found a capable president, that is, one willing to take whatever actions might be necessary to preserve the status quo. As Thomas P. Anderson points out, the deal between oligarchy and military became permanent, as "the great landholders . . . forfeited to [Martínez] and to the military the lion's share of political power and offices, while retaining for themselves the larger part of the wealth and social prestige."[14] The United States, which had declined to recognize Martínez, had a change of heart. The State Department decided that since General Martínez had strengthened his support among the oligarchy and seemed capable of maintaining order, he should receive U.S. recognition.[15]

General Martínez ruled with an iron fist for twelve years. He was overthrown in 1944, near the end of World War II, because his fascist sympathies seemed out of step with the democratic tendencies of the day and because there was discontent over the fact that wealth and power had become concentrated in a small group of his followers. From that time on, El Salvador was headed by a series of military strongmen, occasionally alternating with more reform-minded juntas of junior military and liberal civilians. The 1960s saw economic growth, but growth that primarily benefited the rich. New, large industrial plants appeared throughout the urban areas as manufacturing grew by 24 percent between 1961 and 1971.[16] For the first time in its history, the prosperous oligarchy welcomed wide-scale foreign investments. Forty-four multinational corporations entered El Salvador during this decade.[17] But the new capital-intensive industries did not absorb the available labor force. Moreover, in the late 1960s, prices dropped for Salvadoran exports, causing economic hardship for workers. Recently formed unions became more active; in 1967 and 1968 strikes occurred with increasing frequency, and with them governmentally sponsored repression increased. In 1967, General José Alberto Medrano, head of the Guardia Nacional and chief coordinator for all Salvadoran intelligence agencies, founded a paramilitary organization called ORDEN (order). Under its direction, a spy system was set up in the countryside to aid the Guardia in controlling rural unrest, much of it stemming from the oligarchy's refusal to grant land reform.

Tensions continued to mount as the 1972 presidential election drew near. The ruling class was again divided and consequently offered two candidates, General Medrano and Colonel Arturo Armando Molina. Sensing an opportunity for victory, several reform-minded groups joined in a coalition, running as their candidate the popular mayor of San Salvador, José Napoleón Duarte. As the votes were counted, it became clear that Duarte had won. But suddenly all election news was suspended; three days later Molina was declared the winner.[18]

When Sisters Dorothy Kazel and Martha Owen arrived in El Salvador in mid-1974, the country was deceptively peaceful. But for many *campesinos*, intellectuals, students, and workers, the fraudulent election of 1972 had proved that the electoral process could never be the means of effective reform. It is not surprising then that older guerrilla groups and popular organizations such as FECCAS, a peasant league, began to expand after 1972 and new groups and coalitions emerged.[19] It was only a matter of time before the unresolved conflicts stemming from injustice would spawn a new round of bitter strife in El Salvador.

In late summer of 1974, Dorothy and Martha arrived at Nuestra Señora de Guadalupe parish in Chirilagua, El Salvador. Neither woman knew Spanish and they spent their first three weeks in El Salvador feeling bewildered and isolated. There were also a few anxious moments one evening about two weeks after they arrived, when Martha and Dorothy, returning from a meeting in a nearby town, were stopped by the Guardia Nacional. Sister Martha has vivid memories of their first encounter with the Salvadoran soldiers:

> It was a pitch-black night and we were driving down this country road, when suddenly the Guardia appeared out of nowhere and made us pull off the road. If I hadn't been so scared, I might have thought it was funny. There was the crazy Guardia, with rifles, helmets, sidearms, motorcycles, and everything, rattling off something in Spanish to Dorothy, who was driving. But she couldn't understand a word they were saying. Luckily we had Rosie Smith, another team member, with us and she had been in Salvador for several years and spoke Spanish. Although I didn't know what it was all about, I figured it had something to do with Dorothy's license, so I wasn't too worried. But before I knew it, I found myself standing in the pitch dark on the side of the road with two *campesinos*, while the Guardia escorted Dorothy and Rosie off in the car. Fortunately, a truck came along soon with other members of our group so I hitched a ride with them. Then the driver of that truck accidentally passed through a checkpoint farther down the road and the Guardia there tried to pull *him* over. One soldier jumped on a motorcycle and the other one jumped into the little sidecar attached, but they couldn't get the motorcycle started. I thought I was watching a Keystone Cops movie! We finally made it home and later on we found out that the whole commotion with Dorothy was because she was driving with an Ohio driver's license—she should have gotten a Salvadoran one but hadn't had a chance. Anyway, the police arrested the *car*, but let Dorothy and Rosie go. The next day we had to go down to the jail and pay a fine to get the car out. After that, we knew we had to learn Spanish—and fast.[20]

Dorothy and Martha were scheduled to begin their studies at a language school in San José, Costa Rica, the next week. Their first three weeks in El Salvador had not been pleasant ones due to the language barrier, so the two women arrived at the Instituto Lenguaje de Español with a strong incentive to learn. This language school was run by a fundamentalist Protestant group, which had just begun to allow a few Catholics in as students; Dorothy and Martha may even have been the first Catholics to attend on an experimental basis, and Martha recalls that they were asked not to wear their habits. Although some might have found such a request a bit intimidating, Dorothy took it in stride and fit right in with the other students; before long she was joining her fundamentalist classmates in uninhibited, revival-style prayer. "It was typical of Dorothy," Martha says, "to be able to meet someone else on his or her own terms spiritually; she had the gift of true empathy. I remember when we were leaving the school, one of the students came up to her and said, 'Dorothy, you may be a Catholic, but in my book, you are truly saved.' She had made friends with everyone there."[21]

Martha and Dorothy returned to Chirilagua around Christmas of 1974, but only remained there a few months. Just after Easter 1975 they began to serve in the parish of San Carlos Borromeo in La Unión, a town in southeastern El Salvador. There the women stayed for about two years.

The missionary work of Sisters Martha and Dorothy was always a response to the needs of the community they served. In the early, more peaceful years their tasks were mainly pastoral. They held classes on baptism for prospective parents, prepared children for first communion, confession, and confirmation, and met with engaged couples to discuss the sacramental nature of marriage, its responsibilities and the need for lifelong commitment. Through such instruction, the diocesan team hoped to achieve one of its main goals—the strengthening of the family unit. But the team had another goal which was just as important, if not more so: they wanted to train *campesino* leaders to take over these catechetical duties in the future. The task of leadership development was called *promoción*, a word that can be translated as "advancement," or as Sister Martha defines it, "empowering."[22] To understand the concept and why it was so crucial to the team, one must understand the Salvadorans with whom Martha and Dorothy worked.

Most were illiterate or had only rudimentary schooling. They had no modern conveniences. They traveled by ox-cart over winding mountain paths that could hardly be called roads. Their adobe houses were little more than the simplest shelters; there were perhaps a table and chair, some cooking utensils, and woven mats of straw for sleeping. The peasants' clothes were hand-sewn, and the food was simple and monotonous, mainly black beans and tortillas. Once, in a museum in San Salvador, Martha saw a display that showed the "ancient" way tortillas had been made by Salvadoran women. "I have news for the museum director," says Martha, "every woman in our parish still made tortillas the very same primitive way."[23] Many of the people suffered from afflictions or diseases because they could not afford the luxury of medical treatment; they simply lived (and died) with the problem. A boy who was severely burned when a lantern blew up in his face, women dying in childbirth, a pregnant woman hobbling around with a varicose vein protruding like a huge bubble in her leg—these were the simple facts of life in a land where less than 2 percent of the people amass 50 percent of the income[24] and there is not enough money for most to feed their children much less visit a doctor. The only "medical" attention the *campesinos* received was that of the village witch doctor, who treated their ailments with herbs, spices, and rattlesnake skins.[25]

And yet the peasants were hard-working, Martha remembers. It was a common sight in La Unión to see women carrying huge heavy bundles on their heads and men doing strenuous manual labor, like digging a roadbed with shovels, during the heat of the day—which could reach 110 degrees. "A North American laborer would have passed out under those conditions, and particularly if he were malnourished like most of the Salvadorans," observes Martha. On visits to the countryside, the team was constantly impressed with the way all members of the family, old and young, did their part.[26]

To turn some of these simple, struggling, under-educated peasants into catechists was the job of the Cleveland mission team. They organized weekend workshops for thirty or forty potential leaders during which team members used games and group dynamics to teach their parishioners how to speak in public, how to lead discussions, how to prepare others for the sacraments. The underlying theme in all the instruction was one which most of these *campesinos* had never been taught and which certainly had not been part of their experience: that they were children of God, born with human dignity and basic individual rights.[27] It was this concept that would "empower" them. They began to see such tragedies as hunger, poor health, and lack of land, education, and employment as injustices to which their society subjected them. But in a country where a small and wealthy oligarchy depended for its continued existence upon the poverty and landlessness of the majority of the people, the consciousness-raising of the *campesino* was not welcomed and had political ramifications. Those who occupied privileged positions feared that a growing demand by the majority for their rights would topple the rotting pillars of injustice upon which their society was based. It is for this reason that when tensions rose in El Salvador the catechists and those who instructed them were labeled immediately as "subversives."

Persecution of alleged "subversives," however, did not begin at once; and when Dorothy and Martha began their leadership-training workshops, they did not immediately see the broad implications *promoción* would have. The first few years of Dorothy and Martha's missionary work were thus rather peaceful, at least from a political standpoint. They read in the papers once in a while about isolated incidents, like a kidnapping in the capital of San Salvador, but their lives "out in the boonies," as Sister Martha puts it, were not affected. They were kept very busy, traveling from village to village to organize classes, give first aid talks, take parishioners to the hospital, or set up libraries. "What I remember most was the constant running around," says Martha.

The two women were quite a contrast. Martha was cautious, fearful sometimes, about tackling the steady stream of challenges they faced in El Salvador, even prior to the heightened political tensions. Dorothy, on the other hand, has been described by many as "fearless"; she thrived on challenge and the unknown was not a threat to her. When the women got motorcycles to facilitate travel to out-of-the-way communities, it was Dorothy, not Martha, who eagerly grabbed the handlebars and tried to figure out the new vehicle. But the two Ursulines complemented each other well: Dorothy would jump in the jeep and head for an isolated village at a moment's notice; it was Martha who remembered to pack a lunch and throw in a canteen and who worried about the numerous calamities that might befall them should the jeep break down on the rocky mountain path.[28]

A major task that fell to the women was to oversee the distribution of food to needy *campesino* families. North American bishops purchased items like flour, rice, oil, and powdered milk from the U.S. government at discount prices and shipped the food to El Salvador through an organization called Caritas. There were certain regulations that the team and the peasants receiving the food had to follow: The recipients were to attend talks given by team members on health and hygiene and on how to cook the food properly. Many had to travel long distances by foot or ox-cart, crossing and re-crossing rivers, to attend these periodic lectures. At each gathering, the children were weighed to see if they indeed were benefiting from the food and that it was not being used to fatten the family's farm animals, as sometimes would occur. "The peasants loved the rice, oil, and powdered milk," Martha recalls, "but they had no idea what to do with wheat flour, since they were culturally accustomed to corn flour. So white flour was a problem—it often ended up being fed to the pigs."[29]

Dorothy was not immune to an occasional display of North American arrogance during her first years in El Salvador. She once received some chickens as a gift and decided she would put them in the same coop with another missionary's chickens; she was not going to let them run wild like the Salvadorans did. "A typical *gringa*," Martha remembers with amusement, "she was going to teach the people how chickens *should* be raised. But unknown to Dorothy, her chicks were diseased, and the disease spread. Soon they all developed lumps in their little throats, went blind, then keeled over one by one and died," bringing Dorothy's chicken-farming venture to an abrupt end.[30]

At one point during these early years in El Salvador, Dorothy invited one of her former students—a young woman with a drug problem—to come visit her and Martha. She believed that the young woman might benefit from an experience with the Christian base communities that the Cleveland team was developing through their efforts at *campesino promoción*. An unexpected turn of events occurred, however: Several times Dorothy had to sit up well into the night counseling the girl and encouraging her to stay off drugs. The next day Dorothy would be up bright and early to face her usual daily tasks and Martha feared she was exhausting herself. "But Dorothy wouldn't give up," says Martha. "She continued to give everything she could to the young woman at night and to the Salvadoran people by day. Eventually I had to go to Guatemala for a language refresher course; when I got back I found Dorothy deathly ill with malaria—and her former student was nursing her around the clock."[31]

In 1976, while Dorothy and Martha were still in La Unión, the Molina regime announced a mild proposal for land reform, called the Agrarian Transformation Plan. A small group within the Salvadoran elite had come to realize that some kind of agrarian reform was necessary, for the agro-export economy of El Salvador was becoming less and less capable of supporting the burgeoning, landless population. They believed that if the plan were drawn up carefully, it could, in fact, benefit the large landowners who, when divested of their land, would be reimbursed at market value and given incentives to reinvest in industry. As Berryman comments: "The Molina government was to call the land reform a 'life insurance policy for our grandchildren,' meaning, one assumes, that it would save them from losing all in a peasant revolt."[32] However, the plan was watered down before it went into effect. Most of the popular organizations criticized it for not offering true agrarian reform; and it was vehemently denounced by wealthy landowner organizations, who called Molina "a communist in uniform."[33] The only significant support for the Agrarian Transformation Plan came from the United States, which was going to send El Salvador a hefty sum of money from the Agency for International Development (AID). As Berryman notes: "The whole process revealed the oligarchy's unity and tenacity when it felt its interests threatened. It also manifested a confidence that its domination of El Salvador was secure."[34]

It was not long after this failure to compromise occurred that tension began to build to the point of explosion in El Salvador. In February 1977 an election was held; and General Carlos Humberto Romero, the favored candidate of the wealthy, claimed the presidency in a contest that scarcely even offered the pretense of legality. In fact, hours of radio conversations were taped by the opposition in which the military police and the Guardia were heard transmitting commands to stuff ballot boxes.[35] When the extent of the fraud became known, there were strikes all over the capital city of San Salvador, and a rally was organized by the opposition that packed the plaza with 40,000 to 60,000 people. The military was called out and more than ninety demonstrators were killed. The opposition candidate prudently opted to flee El Salvador.[36]

What took place during the first half of 1977, the intensity of the confrontation, seems astounding even when seen in the light of later events. In a few months the government began to arrest, torture, and expel priests, two priests were murdered, two top government officials were kidnapped and killed by guerrillas, the official party won elections through widespread fraud and a massacre, Oscar Romero became archbishop, troops launched a military attack on Aguilares, and a terrorist organization threatened to assassinate all Jesuits in El Salvador. This period was a watershed. . . . [37]

One event at this time stands out because of its marked effect on the newly installed archbishop of San Salvador; this is the murder of Oscar Romero's old friend, Father Rutilio Grande. Grande, a Jesuit, had been working for about four and a half years in Aguilares; nearby *campesinos* owned or rented small plots of land that could not even provide minimum subsistence. Grande became one of the first in El Salvador to organize the *campesinos* into basic Christian communities. But the landowners took a dim view of his work with the peasants, many of whom, in total frustration with the government's refusal to recognize even the simplest demand for their right to food and land, were organizing politically. Many joined FECCAS, a peasant federation, and were becoming involved with the Revolutionary People's Bloc (BPR), which was growing rapidly in the area.[38] Father Grande attempted to draw a fine line between activism and pastoral work, saying "We cannot get married to political groups of any sort but we cannot remain indifferent to the politics of the common good of the vast majority. . . . "[39] But this attempt was in vain, for the right-wing groups continually denounced him. Undaunted, Grande gave a stirring sermon in February 1977 (a week before elections), which may have led to his murder just four weeks later. The following is a short excerpt:

> I'm afraid that if Jesus of Nazareth came back, coming down from Galilee to Judea, that is from Chalatenango to San Salvador, I daresay he would not get as far as Apopa, with his preaching and actions. They would stop him in Guazapa and jail him there.
>
> . . . They would accuse him of being a rabble-rouser, a foreign Jew, one confusing people with strange and exotic ideas, against democracy, that is, against the minority. . . . They would undoubtedly crucify him again.
>
> In Christianity today you have to be ready to give up your own life to serve a just order . . . to save others, for the values of the gospel.[40]

Some believe it is more than coincidence that Archbishop Romero, after viewing his friend's bullet-ridden body in Aguilares, began his evolution from the cautious, conservative man who had just been installed archbishop to the outspoken critic of governmental injustice who himself would be assassinated just three years later.[41]

It was during this escalation of violence that Martha and Dorothy had to leave La Unión, for the simple reason that there were no priests left in the town. One priest, a Salvadoran named Miguel, lost his voice out of fear when his name appeared on a death list; he then left El Salvador. His colleague, Father Leonel, also a Salvadoran, fled La Unión when a close friend of his was tortured by army commandos and strung up by the thumbs.[42]

After leaving La Unión, the two Ursulines went to the port town of La Libertad to work with other members of the Cleveland diocesan team. Martha and Dorothy settled down about two miles outside of La Libertad in the tiny hillside village of Zaragoza, which was cooled by delightful breezes off the Pacific—a refreshing change from the stifling heat of La Unión.

La Libertad, located about fifteen miles southwest of San Salvador, right on the ocean, is a small town of about 15,000. In the central plaza stands the church, as well as buildings housing the Guardia Nacional and the National Police. Many of the town's inhabitants earn their livelihood from fishing; they venture out to nearby islands in the Pacific in rickety boats for their daily catch. They are by no means prosperous, since the fishing is not really very good and there is little commercial activity. The docks are busy, however, with the men hoisting up boats and mending nets, and the women carrying large bundles on their heads. Salted fish are laid out everywhere in the sun to dry. Everyone in the family helps out on the dock; this means that children rarely go to school. The beaches near La Libertad are wide strips of black volcanic sand, and the area was once an attractive haven for surfers. Not far inland are large cotton and sugarcane plantations where poor *campesinos* work as day laborers.[43]

The team divided the La Libertad district into two zones, with Martha, Sister Christine Rody, and Father Ken Myers working the western section, and Dorothy, Sister Cindy Drennan, and Father Paul Schindler the eastern section, which included the plantation areas. There were about thirty-five church communities in the parish, quite a large number for six people to manage. Although Ken and Paul crisscrossed the two sections, it was impossible for them to celebrate mass in every *canton* (community) each week, so individual team members were assigned to different communities; and it was their responsibility to organize "Celebrations of the Word" in each *canton*. During the Celebrations, there would be bible readings and discussions, and the eucharist would be distributed.

In order to spot the natural leaders in a community, the team would often announce that a "mission" would take place in the *canton*. Three team members would work together on these "missions," which lasted a few days. "We called them 'missions,' although they weren't," says Paul Schindler, "because if we called them 'leadership training workshops' no one would have come. But they could sure remember the excitement and emotion of those old-style Redemptorist missions!" Peasant leaders, male and female, emerged during these missions; these *campesinos* would then be given special training by the Cleveland team to lead *charlas* (talks), and as it had been in La Unión, *promoción*, "empowering," was emphasized. These catechists would eventually take over in the Celebrations of the Word, but a Cleveland team member was usually present. The reading and reflection groups that formed around the Celebrations are also known as basic Christian communities. The team members also tried to organize youth groups, women's groups, and choirs, so they often developed close ties with individual women and men in the communities. When some of these carefully trained catechists were later visited by death squads and left mutilated and murdered, the team grieved as if a relative or old friend had been struck down.[44]

Besides the time-consuming traveling to outlying communities and organization of the Celebrations, Dorothy and Martha also continued their work with Caritas in La Libertad, distributing food from sixteen centers to the needy. They were always busy and could have used extra pairs of hands, for as the repression grew, many native priests were forced to flee and gradually five additional *cantones* were added to their parish.[45]

But there were also many diversions. Since they had no television, they amused themselves by reading long, involved novels well into the night—those of Michener and the Bicentennial Series were favorites. They both enjoyed music, and Dorothy would sing, while Martha played the guitar. Dorothy, who loved animals, was easily entertained by their two cats, Paja and Boogers.

("Dorothy didn't want a run-of-the-mill cat's name like 'Fluffy'," explains Martha, "so as a joke she picked the rather disgusting name 'Boogers.' "[46])

Dorothy's sense of humor had not dimmed over the years. A North American visitor to Zaragoza recalls that Dorothy was totally unable to resist the opportunity for a good laugh.[47] When a newcomer to El Salvador was spending her first night in the little house where Martha and Dorothy lived, Dorothy took it upon herself to explain the facts of life in El Salvador to the woman. Since their house had no indoor bathroom, the visitor was shown the way to the outhouse. "But listen," Dorothy warned, "it gets really dark here at night and in order to scare away the roaches, rats, and dogs, you have to make a lot of noise. So on your way to the outhouse, beat the ground and bang on walls, trashcans, anything at all, to keep away the animals." Once back in the house, as she settled into her sleeping bag, the guest was informed that she had better zip it up all around—to keep the roaches out. If the visitor had the misfortune of awakening during the night to use the facilities, the whole house would know, for everyone would hear the loud clanging and banging going on outside, as Dorothy's unwitting victim cautiously wended her way to the outhouse. And Dorothy would also warn an unsuspecting North American: "This is malaria country, you know; you *have* had your shots, haven't you?" (There is no vaccine to prevent malaria, as Dorothy knew very well from harsh experience.) But such harmless jokes seemed to put her guests at ease, for those who visited her unanimously recall how welcome she made them feel in what was for many an uncomfortable and strange new environment.

At times, Martha and Dorothy did some traveling and sightseeing. Dorothy went to Antigua, Guatemala, for a refresher language course one spring just a few weeks after the earthquake of February 1976 that devastated Guatemala. On that "vacation," Dorothy spent most of her time helping the people in a little town outside Antigua dig foundations, using pitifully inadequate tools, for new shelters. A major excursion for the two Ursulines was a trip home to Ohio taking the scenic route up the West Coast of the United States and Canada as far as British Columbia. But the one trip Dorothy had for a long time had her heart set on was a visit to the Machu Picchu Inca ruins in Peru, and she finally realized this dream in January 1978. The long train journey was somewhat marred by an intense headache that beset Dorothy for several days due to the high altitude, but Martha's photographs of the trip show a smiling Dorothy who refused to let a little inconvenience like a splitting headache ruin the trip of her lifetime. Martha and Dorothy also took several one or two day excursions within the borders of El Salvador, often visiting volcanoes and other sites that were of particular interest to Martha, who was intrigued with geology.[48] Joseph and Malvina Kazel visited their daughter in October 1977 and Dorothy gave them the grand tour; as Malvina comments:

Those were the happiest two weeks we spent together. She showed us all the most beautiful spots there. The Izalco volcano was one of the highlights—a very narrow winding road—but beautiful when you got to the top. And flowers—she couldn't get enough of their beauty. She would get up close to try and catch their beauty. She loved nature.[49]

Once, when Dorothy and Martha visited the spot where the controversial Miss Universe Pageant had been held in 1975, Dorothy seized the opportunity to ham it up. Jumping up on the rocks and parading around, the Ursuline nun did an unforgettable impersonation of a beauty queen contestant. "She liked to clown," says Martha, "and she was kind of cute, you know. She just couldn't resist."[50] There was one excursion they made together which Martha now recalls with irony:

> It was back in 1976, during the Bicentennial. . . . Dorothy and I were so proud of our country's two-hundredth birthday that we climbed the tallest mountain in El Salvador and hoisted a big American flag there. Dorothy . . . was a flag-waver. She was terribly proud to be an American.[51]

Later, this memory became particularly painful for Martha, as she heard U.S. officials insinuate that Dorothy was a subversive and as the Reagan administration proved less than enthusiastic in uncovering the truth regarding her friend's murder.

Being a friend of Dorothy often had its unexpected side. Barb Sever, Dorothy's long-time crony from her days as a high school teacher, would rush to meet Dorothy at the Cleveland airport whenever Dorothy came back to the States for a visit:

> She would get off the plane from El Salvador and have in tow a bewildered and lost-looking Colombian or somebody else from Latin America who was coming to Cleveland for medical treatment. Of course, she would have already offered my services to him on the plane, to help him get settled in his hotel room and such. But first, naturally, he was to get a grand tour of Cleveland. So off I'd go with him in my car, trying to point out the sights of interest in English, while he would just nod and smile, since of course he only spoke Spanish.[52]

But Dorothy's vivacious, fun-loving personality had a deeper spiritual dimension as well. "She read the scriptures every day," says Martha, "because she felt that one should always be open to the movement of the Spirit. She also had the custom of giving up little pleasures—a favorite food or beverage—as a sacrifice for individuals she knew were suffering emotionally or physically." The last of Dorothy's sacrifices, Martha recalls, was to swear off chocolate candy for the sake of the suffering people of El Salvador. There was also a certain vulnerability about Dorothy that practical jokes and personal charm could never conceal. "She had no defenses whatever," Martha remembers, "she was very open. She would cry when she was hurt. But even when hurt or depressed, she would still be looking toward the future, ready for the next challenge to come along."[53]

Dorothy's outlook on life was essentially cheerful. As Paul Schindler later commented:

> The whole team drew much from Dorothy's optimism. . . . She was basically a healer, a communicator. We relied on her to patch up little differences on the team. But every once in a while she would show anger at a team meeting, and it seemed so out of character that we at first might laugh and not believe what we were hearing. So she would say, "Look, *I am serious*; this problem has got to be taken care of!"[54]

In 1979, the time came to rotate members of the mission team. Dorothy and Martha had both been in El Salvador for five years, but it was decided that one would stay on for awhile to train a replacement. Who should stay? The two friends spent much time praying over this decision, Paul remembers. Since Cindy Drennan, who had worked the same area of La Libertad as Dorothy and Paul, had returned to the United States the year before, the decision was finally made that Martha should leave and Dorothy would stay, so that Paul would not be left without an experienced missioner.

Although Martha was now gone, Dorothy had a new companion—a young woman who had recently joined the Cleveland team. Fortified with enthusiasm, a sense of adventure, and a desire to help, Jean Donovan appeared on the scene in La Libertad.

•

Jean was only twenty-six when she arrived in El Salvador. Some of her friends had been astounded to learn of her decision to become a missionary. They thought they knew Jean well: she enjoyed the limelight at parties, rode noisy motorcycles, was generous with money, visited bars with her friends, and liked nothing better than a good laugh. There seemed to be something incongruous between her carefree lifestyle and her apparently sudden decision to join the missionary ranks of the Catholic church.

In fact, her early years hardly seem to have been a dress rehearsal for the role she would one day play in poor and violent El Salvador. Born on April 10, 1953, Jean had grown up in an environment of upper-middle-class comfort. John Murphy, her maternal grandfather, a first generation Irish-American Catholic, had climbed up the ladder of success, beginning as a salesman and after much hard work ending as president of Christian Dior Hosiery Company. A staunch political conservative, he had become along the way very wealthy and influential in Republican circles. At a New England ski resort in 1947, John and his wife Marie's only daughter, Patricia, met Raymond Donovan, a promising young engineer from Cleveland. They married six months later and in 1951 had their first child, Michael Raymond; two years later Jean Marie, their second and last child, was born.

Like his father-in-law, Ray Donovan moved ahead rapidly in the corporate world, attaining the position of executive engineer and eventually chief of

Jean Donovan

design for the Sikorsky Aircraft Division of United Technologies in Connecticut. By 1963, the family was able to move into a spacious home on an acre and a
half of land in Westport.[55] Following in the Murphy family tradition, the
Donovans were all stalwart Republicans, especially Pat, who from her college
years on was a regular volunteer at party headquarters during election time.[56]

Thus Jean was raised in an atmosphere of financial security, success, and
conservative politics. But these were only the most obvious forces shaping her
life. The Donovans not only raised their children to strive for success and
material well-being, but also, as Ray Donovan remembers, to have a healthy
sense of "moral judgment."[57] Before the children were born, the Donovans had
lived in Dallas, and Pat had worked with various Catholic social agencies there.
Later, she would tell Michael and Jean, without attaching a particularly
religious connotation to it, about her work with poor Southern children who
had been orphaned or abandoned. Jeannie, an active, rather boisterous youngster, who was endowed with a healthy independent streak, was absorbing much
more than her mother realized at the time. Indeed, for the rest of her life, Jean
would struggle to reconcile the tension created in her when the quest for success
and her politically conservative upbringing would clash with her deep sense of
compassion and generosity and with the "moral judgment" her parents had
fostered.

Michael and Jeannie were both excellent students and had athletic ability.
Mike ran track, while his sister was passionately devoted to equestrian sport.
When Jean first showed interest in horses, she was allowed to enroll in the fine
riding school at Fiddle Horse Farm. From then on horses occupied nearly all
her after-school time until she graduated from Staples High School in 1971.
Jean's competitive spirit and skill in riding helped develop her into a champion;
the countless trophies and ribbons she won testify to her ability.

Throughout high school, Jean never languished on the sidelines but managed to juggle studies, after-school jobs, and good times remarkably well. To
earn spending money, Jeannie groomed horses, gave riding lessons, and
worked in a discount store. Outgoing, adventurous, and intelligent, she earned
very good grades and was president of the junior class and co-president of the
senior class. As a junior, she was one of only a couple of dozen students in the
state to win a trip to the Yale Science Symposium.[58]

Nevertheless, Jean also participated in her share of pranks. Although for
years she willingly attended religion classes at her parish church for students
like herself who went to public school, as a teenager Jean suddenly decided she
had better things to do with her time. Knowing her parents would in no way
countenance her truancy, Jean would arrive for the class, but would then
immediately escape through the hall and out the back door unnoticed. Unfortunately, it was a plan with one formidable hitch: the only route of escape
involved a rapid climb over the rectory fence and a speedy getaway across the
pastor's yard. The inevitable finally occurred, as Jeannie one day found herself
face to face with the pastor in the very act of flight. As she nervously waited for
the axe to fall, the priest instead invited her into the rectory, sat her down, and

asked her to tell him why she wanted so much to cut her religion class. They chatted awhile; then Jean left, impressed with—not to mention relieved by— her pastor's tactful way of handling his rebellious young parishioner.[59]

By the time Jean graduated from high school in 1971, her political attitudes were well forged—or at least they seemed to be. Her father's position as executive engineer at the Sikorsky plant drew him into the design and production of helicopters for use in the Vietnam War. The Murphy and Donovan families, not surprisingly, supported the war, and Jean, who loved nothing better than a heated discussion, did not hesitate to outline for her friends the many objections she had to the very idea of marching or demonstrating against the increasingly unpopular war.[60] The Donovans, at that time, did not question what the U.S. government was telling the American public about its military efforts in faraway Asia: as Ray concedes today: "I was busy with my job, and as soon as anything happened in the world, our State Department would immediately put labels like 'Left' and 'Right' on it. I knew that 'Right' was where I was. They were the good guys, and 'Left' was the bad guys."[61]

Jean left home for the first time in 1971 when she entered Mary Washington College in Fredericksburg, Virginia, where she majored in accounting. Prior to beginning college, Jean had had few major problems; during her freshman year, however, this changed. She was devastated to find out that her brother had been diagnosed as having Hodgkin's disease, which is often fatal. The compassionate and selfless side of Jean immediately came forth, as her brother's suffering tapped Jean's deepest reserves of energy and generosity. Michael, at this time a senior at the University of Pennsylvania in Philadelphia, was forced to undergo painful chemotherapy treatments, and Jean gave up much of her free time to travel to Philadelphia every other weekend to be at his side. Such an experience had a profound effect on her. "It made me realize," she wrote at the time, "how precious life is."[62] Michael eventually conquered the disease, and the bond between him and his sister became closer than ever.

With this family crisis over, Jean, like many adventurous North American students who can afford it, decided to spend her junior year of college in Europe as an exchange student. Perhaps because of her ethnic background, she chose University College Cork in Ireland. College officials had arranged for the American exchange students to reside with lower-middle-class families in small, newly constructed homes situated on the periphery of the city. There the students could experience firsthand the way a typical Irish family lived, while the rent money paid to the homeowners would make their struggle to provide for their families a bit easier. Such an arrangement seemed sensible, but in Jean's case it did not work out well. The room she shared with two roommates was overcrowded, damp, and chilly, and the house itself was quite a distance from the college; but Jean, who was used to all the conveniences of life in the United States, adapted surprisingly well to these discomforts. Nevertheless, other problems arose. When the three boarders realized that the family they lived with could not afford to put a well-balanced meal on the table, they decided to contribute extra money to the family for food, hoping that their hosts as well as they themselves would benefit from a healthier diet. Unfortunately, the meals did not improve at all, and after a few months, the young women asked their parents' permission to look for other quarters. Leaving their host-family with a vacant room and a whole year's worth of rent, they set up housekeeping for themselves in a small house they rented nearer the campus.[63] This too was damp and chilly, the house being heated by only a peat fire, but Jean had already realized that many of the conveniences she had accepted as necessities in America were actually irrelevancies. She was growing to respect and appreciate the simpler and more challenging lifestyle of the Irish.

Their new dwelling had no refrigerator, and in a land where diet foods were hard to come by, Jean wrote home at first in dismay. What was she to do? Diet foods were simply not available in all of Ireland, yet she was a girl who was forced to count calories! Jean soon found a simple solution—a bicycle which she pedaled to and from school and social engagements to burn off those heavy Irish meals. Commenting much later on her year as an exchange student, she noted that living in Ireland without many of the things North Americans hold so dear had opened her eyes to the fundamental irrelevancy of these conveniences.[64] In another letter she remarked that an enduring legacy of her experiences abroad was a sense of global consciousness.[65]

Jean's gregariousness and sense of humor were appealing to the Irish, and consequently she made friends easily with the native students. One day a new companion, Maura Corkery, asked her to come along to a meeting of the Legion of Mary. This invitation was to have momentous repercussions on Jean's future, for at this gathering she met Father Michael Crowley, a dynamic priest who was able to challenge Jean as no one had before.

Crowley, the college chaplain, had organized the local Legion, which consisted of students who volunteered several hours of their time each week in service to the needy. Each Monday night the group would hold a combination meeting and party at his small home near the university. About thirty to forty students would attend, and Irish music and conversation would flow as freely as the tea that was served. The talk often dealt with Latin American poverty and international relations, for Crowley had only recently returned from a ten-year mission commitment in the barrios of Trujillo, Peru. The priest was also quite familiar with both the poverty and affluence of the First World, for prior to his tenure in South America he had worked in a Hispanic slum in East Harlem.

In an interview with Ana Carrigan, Crowley shared his initial impressions of Jean:

> When I first met Jean, she was like a cross section of American young people . . . confused, searching for a meaning to her life. She was a conventional Catholic, if you will, but took it . . . tongue-in-cheek, in the same way as so many Christians around the world. She practiced . . . but she really didn't have personalized a meaning for her own life.
> I often had bull sessions . . . at the house, where we discussed the

world's problems and challenged these young people that when you come out now, with a nice degree and a nice job, don't become a nice comfy capitalist. Feel it as your Christian duty to change the wrong structures around you. Try and improve the world.[66]

Indeed, Father Crowley gave the students much food for thought with his stories of oppression and misery in Peru, and Jean was one of his most attentive listeners. Constantly expressing his conviction that the rich nations have a duty to share their wealth with their poor neighbors, he told them that Christians of the First World must especially cease from viewing the cry of the Third World's poor for human dignity as part of a sinister international communist plot. If the First World genuinely committed itself to ending world poverty, he believed, communism would die on the vine. On a smaller scale, Crowley challenged the students not to ignore the plight of the poor on their very doorsteps. Jean took his plea to heart and soon began working with "Meals on Wheels," bringing food to the homes of the elderly. She also visited patients in hospitals and mental institutions.

Jean was receptive to Crowley not only because he was persuasive and charismatic, but because he touched the chord of compassion and generosity within her. As a youngster, she had often been responsive to the appeals of her pastor to aid the poor in her community.[67] Later, as a young woman, she had confronted her brother's illness with tireless efforts to ease his emotional and physical suffering. Now, while her experiences in Ireland were challenging her to live a simpler life, Crowley was challenging her for the first time to confront suffering and poverty in their international dimensions as well as on the personal and community levels. Long talks with the former missionary about his experiences in Peru even led Jean to wonder if she herself might have a calling to missionary life.[68]

In the summer of 1974, after completing her second semester at Cork, Jean returned to the United States. Just a few weeks later, she made an appointment with Father Lawrence McMahon at her parish in Westport, Connecticut, to ask him for information on religious orders. As McMahon remembers it, Jean was not clear as to whether or not she was interested in actually joining an order or becoming a lay associate, but she was quite insistent that her interests were in missionary work and not in nursing or teaching. She also asked him to keep her visit confidential because she had not yet made a decision.[69] Although her year abroad had changed much in Jean, it had not changed her conservative political outlook. Soon after her return from Ireland Richard Nixon resigned from the presidency, and Pat Donovan, describing her daughter as a "rock-solid Republican" then, recalls that Jean tenaciously defended Nixon even well after his resignation.[70]

In September 1974 Jean began her senior year at Mary Washington College. Graduating the following spring in accounting, she could look back with pride at her scholastic achievements: she had earned the National Economics Medal, an alumnae scholarship, and a scholarship to work on an M.B.A. at Case

Western Reserve in Cleveland, Ohio. A year later, with her M.B.A. in hand, she was hired by the Cleveland branch of Arthur Andersen and Son, the largest accounting firm in the United States. Her starting salary was impressive for the time, and soon Jean had adopted a free-wheeling, free-spending lifestyle. She and her cousin Colleen Kelly rented an apartment on the exclusive "Gold Coast" of Lake Erie; she bought a large, noisy Harley Davidson motorcycle as well as a new automobile, and she, Colleen, and Debbie Miller, her former roommate at Case Western, proceeded to work by day and party and "bar-hop" by night.

But Jean was not the carefree person she appeared to be. True, her career was off to a promising start, and she was able to revel in the monetary rewards that accompanied her success; yet for Jean this was not enough. The challenging discussions she had had with Crowley in Ireland often preoccupied her thoughts and she wondered at times: Was she turning into the "nice, comfy capitalist" Crowley had warned so often against?

At her office's Christmas party in 1976, only a few months after she began working at Arthur Andersen, Jean won two tickets to Spain. She promptly exchanged them for a round-trip ticket to Ireland to visit her old friend. Perhaps this visit with Crowley inspired Jean to work out a new agenda for her life or perhaps it only confirmed her in the direction she had already chosen; but soon after her return to Cleveland in January 1977, Jean began to make some serious readjustments. She introduced herself to Father Ralph Wiatowski, who agreed to meet weekly with her for religious counsel; she also began doing volunteer work with inner-city youngsters through the Cleveland diocese's youth ministry program. Before long she had gravitated into the diocese's "Kaleidoscope Project," a program designed for young adults who sought opportunities to give service to the church. It was there that she met two young women, Rita Mikolajczyk and Mary Fran Ehlinger, who would soon become her close friends. She helped them organize retreats and stage youth rallies for high school students.

Rita vividly remembers that her first encounter with Jean was not a positive experience: Jean suddenly appeared in the diocesan office where Rita worked and explained that she was arranging for a religious retreat for a group she belonged to and that she needed a priest to give talks and conduct the liturgy. She wanted to see Father Wally Hyclak. Somewhat annoyed that Jean had not called to make an appointment, Rita explained that Father Hyclak was quite busy and would be unable to see her at that time. Undaunted, Jean replied that she would take a seat and wait. Later, when Hyclak entered the room, Jean sprung to her feet and, ignoring Rita, immediately accosted him: "I'm Jean Donovan. I'm organizing a retreat and need a priest, and I want you." Rita later mused at the memory, "It took me a long time to like Jean."

Jean's aggressiveness and tendency to dominate were kept in check, however, by her deep love for others. "There was no pettiness in Jean," says Mikolajc-zyk. "She wanted to do things her way, but if you stood up to her, she backed off. She loved her friends too much to intentionally hurt their feelings."[71] Later, when Rita felt comfortable enough with Jean to tell her this, Jean readily agreed, remarking that her mother had told her the same thing years earlier:

Once, when my brother had introduced me to his new girlfriend, I suggested that the three of us go out together. This was o.k. with him, but not with the girl. She didn't want me tagging along. I thought my brother should have insisted that I go with them, but he didn't. When they left, I was furious and said I would never forgive my brother. But my mother knew me better. "Jeannie," she said, "you're incapable of holding a grudge; you love people too much for that."[72]

Mary Fran Ehlinger's impressions of Jean were similar to Rita's:

Jean was very competitive, in sports, in everything. I think she felt called to do something significant with her life, not necessarily on a religious level, but in whatever she attempted. She was a go-getter who loved to be in charge. But she wasn't the slightest bit "snooty." She was concerned with her own spiritual formation but also that of others. I remember she would take it upon herself to organize retreats; she'd get the priest, set up committees, and then give everybody a particular job to do.[73]

Mary Fran was particularly impressed with how Jean related to those who expressed interest in doing voluntary work in the Kaleidoscope Program but backed off out of shyness or because they found it difficult to find a niche for themselves in one of the ministries. "She always worked to get them involved and was often able to bring out the best in them."[74]

Eventually Jean decided to devote additional energy to other areas of social work, so she asked Wiatowski for information on the diocese's other programs. Included in the brochures was one on the Cleveland diocesan mission in El Salvador. Jean felt strongly that this was exactly what she had been seeking; and before long she found herself applying for a three-year commitment. She was accepted and in late 1977 told her parents of her decision. Not surprisingly, they were baffled and troubled by their unpredictable daughter. But Jean tried hard to reassure them. Pat Donovan recalls, "When she told us, she said . . . , 'You know, I'm following in your footsteps,' " alluding to Pat's work with orphaned and abandoned children in the Dallas area years before. "I'm going to be doing the same thing, only in another country," Jean explained to her parents.[75] Although understandably uneasy about Jean's plans, Pat and Ray had always encouraged their children to make mature and independent decisions and felt they could not stand in Jean's way now. Nevertheless, over time they grew more aware of the political climate in El Salvador, and Jean's decision would sometimes become a rather heated topic of discussion when she visited them. In the Donovan household, as in many Irish-American families, everyone held strong opinions on politics and religion and no one was too timid to express them.[76] Jean's brother Michael was opposed to her plans right from the start and told her so without hesitation. He had looked into El Salvador's recent history and immediately feared for his sister's safety. But Jean's mind was made up, and his countless entreaties that she reconsider were to no avail.

Jean's decision to spend several months at Maryknoll, New York, in training and then two years in Central America was made more complicated because a new man had entered her life in the summer on 1977, and they were developing a close relationship. Doug Cable, a young medical school graduate, recalls with amusement his first meeting with her. He was moving into an apartment complex in the same building where Debbie Miller lived. It was an extremely humid summer day. He had just finished carting several boxes of heavy books and was resting to catch his breath, when someone knocked on the door. There stood Jean with a bottle of whiskey. "Hi, thought you might need a drink," she said with a smile.[77] From that day on they had become good friends and gradually had grown more serious. Although Doug knew he would miss her, he supported Jean as she made plans to work in El Salvador. He felt that she had made a rational decision: she would help out in any way she could, avoid violent areas, and hop on the next plane if the situation grew life-threatening. Or so Jean said at the time.[78]

Jean was not unaware that danger lurked ahead; in fact, she often acknowledged the possibility of death with a certain "dark humor," as one friend puts it. Rita Mikolajczyk can still see Jean at her farewell party, in the center of attention where she liked to be, laughing, drinking, and chatting with all her Cleveland friends. An enormous incongruity suddenly struck one of Jean's girlfriends—this same young woman now basking noisily and happily in the party limelight would soon be a missionary in Central America. The friend began to kid Jean good-naturedly: "What are you going to El Salvador for anyway, Jean? So you can be known as 'St. Jean the Playful'?" Jean was thoroughly amused by this remark, and from then on would tell those who asked her why in heaven's name she was going to dangerous El Salvador: "Look, it's a can't lose situation for me! Either I will get three years of great experiences out of it or I will die—and then *you'll* have to pray to St. Jean the Playful for the rest of your life!"[79]

Jean began her missionary training at Maryknoll, New York, in the fall of 1978. Two of her teachers, Josie and Frank Cuda, a married couple who had previously served as lay missionaries, remember her well. As Josie recalls,

> I must confess that at first I did not think Jean was all that serious. She spent a lot of time at Izzy's lounge in [nearby] Ossining drinking with the seminarians. She saw Frank and me as authority figures, and she and her group were sort of rebellious in an adolescent way. But I saw another side of Jean on the day of the final mission-sending ceremony. I was late for the event, so I took a short cut through the crypt to the chapel and there was Jean, obviously wrestling with some kind of a problem. She had on some very expensive jewelry, which she explained had special significance to her family; but it bothered her to be wearing this jewelry to an event

that marked the beginning of her missionary work in a poverty-stricken country. And this struggle over the jewelry was making her conscious of all the things she would be leaving behind her. She was really struggling with what she was doing with her life.[80]

With her Maryknoll training period over, Jean looked forward to the final phase of her transition from accountant to lay missionary: she would spend three months—from early May to August 9, 1979—at a language school in Huehuetenango, Guatemala, before heading for La Libertad and a new career among the Salvadoran people.

The year 1979 had begun ominously for the people of El Salvador. In January, a priest, Octavio Ortiz, and four youths were gunned down by National Guardsmen at a church complex outside of the capital, where these five and others had gathered for a weekend retreat. The next morning in his Sunday sermon, Archbishop Romero spoke of the tragedy, read an eyewitness report of what had occurred and denied the Guardia version which depicted the young men as engaged in a shootout. President Carlos Humberto Romero (no relation to the archbishop) had recently denounced the archbishop as "political" and had claimed there was no persecution of churchpeople in El Salvador; but, the archbishop said, the five bodies proved "how great a liar he is."[81] Confrontations between church and state were obviously escalating.

Guerrilla groups too were adding to the tension; a Salvadoran landowner, two Englishmen, and a Japanese had been kidnapped. Archbishop Romero likewise spoke out against these tactics of the left wing: "Keep it in mind, you who are violent with kidnappings. Kidnapping is not civilized, any more than making people disappear. . . . It is savagery, that's all."[82]

By the end of her Maryknoll training, Jean, of course, was aware of the ever-increasing violence in El Salvador. Her parents, though, had no knowledge of it, and this was the way she wanted it. Unfortunately for her, this changed dramatically in early May, when, prior to her flight to Huehuetenango, she spent a week with them in Sarasota, Florida, where they were then living. When five leaders of the BPR (Bloque Popular Revolucionario) were arrested and the police claimed no knowledge of their whereabouts, demonstrators occupied the French, Venezuelan, and Costa Rican embassies, as well as the San Salvador cathedral and several other churches. James Brockman relates what happened next:

> On May 8, while Romero was in Rome, a small demonstration stopped in front of the cathedral. . . . Suddenly the police opened fire, as foreign journalists watched and television crews filmed. As bullets struck the crowd and glanced off the cathedral steps, people desperately tried to reach the doors. Bullets struck many in the back as they tried to reach the safety of the cathedral. For a time the police kept the Red Cross and other medical help from the cathedral, as the wounded lay bleeding inside. The

total was twenty-five dead and seventy wounded in the action. Millions around the world later watched the scene on their television screens.[83]

A CBS cameraman had been one of those who filmed the episode, and consequently some North Americans, including Ray and Pat Donovan, saw for the first time government-sponsored brutality in El Salvador. They were understandably upset; Jean later described their reaction to a friend at Mary-knoll:

> My parents don't seem to be aware that there's any problem in Central America at all. They're very surprised that any of this is happening, and their solution to the problem is that the revolutionaries should stop; that there shouldn't be any violence, and they don't understand the kind of governments . . . that are there. When I wanted to talk to them about it, they weren't interested. They just didn't want me to go.[84]

Ray and Pat Donovan also remember the above incident. When Jean had first told them of her plans to be a missionary in El Salvador, they had not even known where the country was located.[85] By the time she left, however, they had indeed become distraught:

> We knew there was violence in El Salvador; we read very graphic reports in the *Miami Herald*, and we tried desperately to talk Jean out of going to El Salvador and do her work in a less volatile atmosphere. But she felt very strongly that she "belonged" in El Salvador.[86]

While Jean studied Spanish in Guatemala, violence in El Salvador escalated even more, so much so that she feared she would not be permitted to join the Cleveland team. In June she took a short break from her studies to meet the people she would be working with in La Libertad. When she arrived she found that Father Rafael Palacios, a priest from Santa Tecla, a town forty miles north of the mission, had just been murdered. Palacios, who had been active in forming base communities, had received a written death threat from a death squad, the White Warriors' Union, on June 14. Six days later he was dead.[87]

With all the heightening tension, however, the work of the mission team in La Libertad was not drastically affected at this point. A cassette tape made by Dorothy Kazel and Paul Schindler on August 9, 1979, for Martha Owen, now back in Cleveland, told of an enthusiastic turnout of catechists for a meeting, of confirmation plans, of talks on nutrition—all customary activities of the Cleveland missionaries. But Dorothy and Paul were not deceived as to the reality of recent events in El Salvador; as they commented to Martha: "We don't want you to think we're over-optimistic—because we're not." They then related the murder a few days before of the sixth priest to die in El Salvador in a little over two years, Alirio Napoleón Macías. Macías was killed in the sacristy of his church; he had been approached by three men while cleaning up and had warned his sacristan, "Look out! These guys are police." The sacristan escaped, but Macías did not. On the tape Paul then described a grisly chore that had befallen him recently. In a rocky seaside area nearby, a total of eleven corpses had been dumped on two occasions. Although at first the team expected authorities to remove them, they had just remained there rotting and attacked by vultures until Paul himself had gotten permission from a local judge and the church to burn them. Dorothy and Paul told Martha that the Salvadoran government showed "no signs of change," but they were encouraged that the U.S. ambassador, Frank Devine, had strongly condemned the assassination of Macías.

Not wanting to dwell excessively on unpleasant topics, Paul then changed the subject, mentioning a plan he had come up with to get Jean to take over the mission's account books when she arrived. Dorothy was a bit skeptical, especially when Paul said maybe Jean would want to set up a "whole new accounting system." Dorothy asked, "Does Jean know about that?"

Paul admitted, "No. But I figure . . . she'll look at [the books] and say, 'Oh, you did this wrong and that wrong,' and I'll say, 'Gee, if you can do better, Jeannie, why don't you just take them over?' "

The small talk continued, with Paul looking forward to the day when Ken Myers would return from a trip to the United States: "With Ken away, I've been doing all the masses—I'm *so* tired of my preaching." "And so am I!" added Dorothy.[88]

The day after Dorothy and Paul made the tape, Jean arrived from language school in Guatemala to begin her full-time missionary work in La Libertad. Paul's little scheme worked and Jean took over the mission's account books. She also assisted Dorothy with her work in the Caritas food and hygiene programs. Each Cleveland team member had been assigned primary responsibility for a particular zone. With Martha Owen's return to the United States, however, all of the missionaries had had to assume a larger work load. This was especially true with Dorothy. But Jean was quick to learn, and as she became more familiar with mission life, she gradually took on a more independent role, relieving the others of some of their extra duties while becoming responsible for the mission's work in several *cantones*.

Jean's tendency to jump in and take charge, however, caused her some problems initially. As Sister Cris Rody remembers:

> Jean was a gifted, confident young woman who had always been a success in what she did. But her perception of herself was sometimes bigger than reality. She was unequal to the other team members because she lacked their missionary experience. This was hard for her to accept, but in El Salvador she met her match.

When Jean's "take-charge" tendency got out of hand, Dorothy or another team member would not hesitate to tell her so, but always in a considerate way. To Jean's credit, recalls Cris, she was always able to accept this constructive criticism. "She was never confrontational, never held a grudge, but was always able to handle it."[89]

Whenever the need arose, Jean found a sympathetic shoulder to cry on in Dorothy Kazel; the Ursuline nun was perfect for Jean. She not only took it upon herself to introduce her to the people and ways of El Salvador, but she was patient and understanding with the young North American who was struggling to adjust to the dangers of Salvadoran life and to grow emotionally and spiritually. Indeed, as Martha Owen later commented, "Dorothy had an innate ability to accept others as they were, an ability that was enhanced by her training in counseling. She believed that people were where they were at a given time in their lives because they had to be at that stage in order to survive. She never tried to push them too far or too fast and she always respected them."[90] Thus, Dorothy accepted it if Jean slept too late or partied a bit. And Jean, too, had her youthful energy and lively sense of humor to offer her new companions. Paul remembers, "The women would have days of recollection down at the beach or in the mountains every so often, and Jean would always join the nuns. She fit in very well with them." The fourteen-year age difference was not a barrier between Jean and Dorothy. "They kidded around with each other like a couple of teenagers," Paul says, and adds, "It was always a treat to pay a visit to their house; if you needed a boost they really provided a pick-me-up."[91]

The physical discomfort and inconveniences, which missionaries must adjust to in a Third World country like El Salvador, never bothered Jean. "She took it as an adventure," notes Cris Rody. "It was no big deal to her."[92] Soon Jean had formed a choir for teenagers and was helping the cotton laborers and their families in the town of Santa Cruz to conduct evening Bible study meetings. On Sundays, during the Celebration of the Word, she served as a *delegado* (catechist) for this impoverished community.

By October, about two months after Jean had arrived in La Libertad, murders and disappearances had become even more widespread. It was obvious to all that El Salvador was on the verge of civil war. For this reason Bishop James Hickey of Cleveland decided to send Father Alfred Winters, his diocesan mission director, to La Libertad to determine whether or not the project should be abandoned and the missioners withdrawn. A meeting was called and the entire team discussed the seriousness of their situation with Winters. All decided that they should stay. As a result of the meeting Dorothy wrote the following very personal letter to Martha:

We had a good meeting today followed by a swim and a beautiful Liturgy. . . .
    Before I have to give this to Al, I do want to say something to you—I think you will understand. We talked quite a bit today about what happens *IF* something begins. And most of us feel we would want to stay here. Now this depends on *WHAT* happens—if there is a way we can help—like run a Refugee Center or something. We wouldn't want to just run out on the people. Anyway, Al thinks people we love should under-

stand how we feel—in case something happens—so he and the Bishop don't have to yank us out of here unnecessarily. Anyway—I thought I should say this to you—I don't want to say it to anyone else—because I don't think they would understand. Anyway, my beloved friend, just know how I feel and "treasure it in your heart." If a day comes when others will have to understand, please explain it for me—thanks. Love ya lots, D.[93]

Jean likewise expressed her concern in a letter to Gwen Vendley:

I have tried to write this letter three times but it just doesn't seem to come out right. I am writing today because Al Winters is here on a visit from the States and he can mail it in the U.S. I want to write about what's happening here but it's so hard to put into words. . . . All I can say is that things are really heating up and the tension is unbelievable . . . .

I am working with a really great lady who is an Ursuline nun. We also see two Maryknoll nuns [Terry Alexander and Madeline Dorsey] that are really neat women. One of them . . . is giving Dotty and me ideas on how to run refugee camps. If war does break out I have tentatively decided to try and set up a center in Zaragoza or La Libertad. Who knows? It's strange—probably when my spiritual life is at an all-time low I know that I need more help from God than I ever had before.[94]

On October 15, 1979, soon after Dorothy and Jean had made their individual decisions to stay on in El Salvador, a coup occurred in which a reformist junta of junior military and civilian moderate leftists overthrew the government of President Romero. This junta outlined a program it hoped would save El Salvador from sharing the same fate Nicaragua had endured—a bloody civil war culminated by a victory for the popular revolutionary forces. The program called for agrarian reform and the cessation of right-wing terrorism, among other things. The left and the popular forces in El Salvador never held any hope for the junta, but Archbishop Romero and moderate leftists initially supported it. Within weeks, however, it became evident that attempts at reform were doomed. For one thing, repression by security forces actually increased in the first three weeks under the junta. Even more ominous was the fact that a conservative officer of the junta, Colonel Jaime Abdul Gutiérrez, appointed another rightist, Colonel José Guillermo García, as defense minister without consulting the members of the junta. After this power play, the efforts of the junta's moderates to check right-wing violence were nullified, for the armed forces would respond only to the new defense minister. When liberal members of the junta and cabinet resigned in early January 1980 in protest, members of the Christian Democratic party then made a pact with the military and formed a new government. Although the pact stipulated that repression would cease, it did not. One of the new junta members therefore resigned and was replaced by another Christian Democrat—José Napoleón Duarte. This new junta was in reality a right-wing military regime with a civilian veneer, and its strategy became "reform combined with repression." An outstanding example of its cruel tactics was the regime's attempt at agrarian reform which combined limited distribution of land in the countryside with widespread terror. Local peasant leaders were singled out by members of ORDEN (Organización Democrática Nacionalista—a paramilitary organization) for belonging to grassroots movements or to the guerrillas; many were tortured and killed.[95]

The atmosphere of escalating tension was alleviated for Dorothy and Jean during the Christmas season of 1979, when Jean's parents and Ursuline sister Sheila Marie Tobbe came for a visit. On December 26, Ray and Pat Donovan, Sister Sheila, and Dorothy and Jean all piled into the white microbus for a short trip to Guatemala. They spent a pleasant day shopping and sightseeing in Guatemala City and Antigua and after dinner headed for a tiny village in Quiché, where Jean had arranged for them all to spend the night with an Irish priest she knew. Unfortunately for the little group of tourists, they got lost. As they drove over a seemingly endless succession of twisting, narrow, mountainous roads that all looked remarkably alike in the dark, they began to think ominously that they would never reach their destination. Jean remained buoyant, however, promising every now and then that they were only "one or two villages away." In hindsight, it was all highly amusing to Dorothy; as she told Martha, "I was driving. We were all *so* tired and her father and mother were fit to be tied." They were all growing a bit skeptical at Jean's vague promises that the journey would soon be over, when all at once Pat Donovan asked her daughter anxiously, "Jean, *now tell me the truth*. How many more villages *is* it?" Pat's remark broke the tension as everyone began to joke about their predicament, but it was not until 4:30 A.M. that the weary band of travelers finally pulled into the sleeping village. In spite of such an awkward prelude, their stay turned out to be most pleasant.[96]

In fact, the entire visit with their daughter that holiday season—the last Christmas for Dorothy and Jean—was memorable for the Donovans and represented a turning point for them. They had tried in the past, without real success, to understand their daughter's desire to live and work in El Salvador. Now, seeing the meaning and satisfaction Jean was finding in her work, Pat began to grasp what Jean had been pointing out to her—that this experience for her daughter was similar to her own experience as a young woman with the tragic results of poverty in the United States. Ray also was moved. He had never been convinced by his daughter's contention that poverty and injustice, not Cuba or the Soviet Union, were at the root of the political and social turmoil in El Salvador; but now his perspective began to change. He simply could not shake the haunting sight of desperation he had witnessed on this trip:

One of the things I'll never forget is the sight of corn growing on a 45-degree slope. It was growing on land the oligarchs didn't want, and, at great risk to life and limb, a *campesino* must have tied a rope, lowered himself down there, and planted some corn on that little 10-by-15 patch of earth to try to get something for his family to eat.[97]

The Donovans also saw that their daughter was surrounded by the warmth and laughter of the other missionaries; like Dorothy's parents a few years earlier, they too saw the beauty of the land and the people and for the first time felt a sense of relief about Jean's decision.

For Sister Sheila Tobbe the visit was also unforgettable:

> Jean and Dorothy lived under rather primitive conditions—no hot water, not even indoor plumbing. . . . Their main source of entertainment—to replace TV—were the antics of their three cats whose job it was to keep the cockroach and lizard population under control. Dorothy and Jean were a fun-loving pair, always teasing each other. They enjoyed life and people and made others feel comfortable and happy to be with them.
>
> . . . Despite all the dangers that they daily faced, they considered themselves very ordinary. They told me repeatedly that they weren't doing anything that everyone else wouldn't do under the circumstances.
>
> . . . Everywhere I went with Dorothy and Jean we were enthusiastically welcomed. It was so obvious to me that they were well loved by the people that they served.[98]

Nevertheless, none of the visitors was reassured by the ubiquitous presence of armed soldiers. After her parents' return to Sarasota, Jean would often have to calm their fears for her safety. Pat comments, "Jeannie used to say, 'Well last night we had this many people killed in the capital. How many people were killed in New York City?' And of course it was 3 or 4 times more. So we were shielded from the worst."[99]

The year 1980 had begun on a note of pleasure and adventure for Jean and Dorothy, with visitors from the United States and plans being made for a short trip to Nicaragua. But it seems that Dorothy was becoming inexplicably uneasy about the future. In a tape to Martha that she began in December 1979 and finished January 10, 1980, Dorothy spoke of her plans for the future, for in the spring her assignment in El Salvador would be over (or so she thought). After mentioning a myriad of possibilities, including a retreat in New Mexico, a trip to Bolivia or Brazil, and course work at Maryknoll, she commented that she really did not know what kind of niche she would fill after leaving Salvador. Would she work with Hispanics in the United States? Maybe. Or with blacks in Cleveland? Possibly. Finally Dorothy admitted with considerable frustration:

> I really don't know what I want to do, Martha. . . . I just don't know what my problem is. I just don't know. I have *no* inclination to any special area. . . . Isn't that terrible? I've been like this for so long and I keep praying about it, but I just don't know what the Lord has planned. . . . To know what will really happen! . . .[100]

Dorothy habitually used the phrase "to know" (or in Spanish *saber*) to indicate uncertainty in the future. Sometimes this was done lightly or in jest, but in her last year the expression seems to have acquired a deeper meaning at times. Martha, after reading some short notes Dorothy made on a retreat in mid-1980, was struck by her friend's inability to get a grasp on her future—the scribblings were filled with questions marks.[101] For a woman who had always been able to ascertain which path to take when confronted with a dilemma, such a murky future was obviously disturbing. She was searching, praying, reaching out for something tangible to hold onto. But there were no answers—only more question marks.

On January 20, 1980, four women from the Cleveland team—Dorothy, Jean, Cris Rody, and Elizabeth Kochik—set off for what was supposed to be a four-day visit to Nicaragua. It had been six months since the dictator Somoza had been overthrown; with the civil war now over it was considered a relatively safe trip, by Central American standards. To save on expenses, the women decided to take the ferry from La Unión; this way they could bring along their Toyota microbus to use once they arrived in Nicaragua. The trip was a memorable experience for Dorothy and Jean, but it was not necessarily what they had expected. Dorothy was so amused by their adventure that she sent a long letter to many of her friends in the United States describing it:

> "We left on the ferry at 1:00 a.m. Monday. The ride was beautiful—the heavens were full of stars and the milky way was close and heavy. The southern cross rose over us. Cris and I slept on the outside benches. . . . "

For four days the women toured areas that had been torn by civil strife and devastated by earthquake, took short excursions to scenic volcanoes and to refugee centers, and visited with friends in Chinandega, León, and Managua. Dorothy continues:

> On Friday . . . [we left] for Potosi to catch the ferry [back to El Salvador]. . . . About 8:30 a.m. we learned that the ferry would NOT be going for a few days. What to do! Well, we decided to send Cris and Elizabeth in a dug-out canoe with a motor . . . over to La Unión . . . about a 5-1/2 hour trip. . . . After we sent them, we were worried, as neither of them swim—and being in one of these canoes on the open ocean does leave something to be desired. . . . However, they got safely home by the next day.
>
> Meanwhile Jean and I stayed with the Micro—it became our "mobile home." . . . In Potosi there is no drinking water or lavatories. Also the one water spigot they had . . . did not work after Friday. There were only two comedors—and one was a greasier spoon than the other. This of course forced us to a 3 times a day potty schedule. We would get up at 4:30 a.m. while it was still dark; at noon we visited a friend's outhouse;

then again before we went to sleep we hit the beach. We would eat in the comedor once a day—and try to share a meal. However the truck drivers thought we didn't have enough money, so they would offer to buy us our meals. In the mornings we usually waited to hear . . . news about the ferry. Then we would go down to the beach for our dip in the ocean and then go to the fresh water river to wash up. This is also where the people wash their clothes, their kids and themselves—along with the cows and horses. Usually in the late afternoon we would go back down to the ocean and sit on the rocks and read or write or whatever. It was good getting to know the people there—there was hardly a person you talked with that had not lost a loved one in the war. . . . The truck drivers were . . . an interesting group—when they know you're a religious they all want to talk about God—so that we did. . . . Most of them were Salvadorans who drove the huge cargo trailers. They were dependent on the ferry also because they had Salvadoran license plates—and with those you cannot cross through Honduras because we [El Salvador] are still at "war" with them (since 1969!). Now Sunday we thought would be our last day there because they kept telling us it would leave that evening. So Jean and I took our last river bath (in which we used her $20 bar of Estee Lauder soap!) and put on our clean clothes. Well, Sunday night came and went—and they were promising Monday. . . . [Finally] we decided to chance going through Honduras. . . . We passed through the Nicaraguan frontera without any trouble. As I pulled in to the Honduran frontera and got out of the car to go to Immigration with our passports, the man said he could do nothing for us because of the Salvadoran plates. So I talked to the jefe there who told me I had to go to Choluteca to get permission from the Comandante to pass through. I asked if he could be called— they said they had no means of communication. I asked if they were sure he would be there—they said yes. . . . I finally got a man in a pickup truck to take me in for $10. . . . [When I got to Choluteca] they told me the man I needed to see went to Tegucigalpa and NOBODY else could help me. . . .

After major confusion and much running around, a captain finally took Dorothy to the head of Tránsito. Dorothy describes what then happened:

This man was bien amable [very kind]. When I walked in he said, "What can I do for you?" I said, "Help me! I've got to get back home" and I told him my plight. He kept holding his head and assuring me that he would think of something. So he says, "I can't help you but I know who can." Then he sent me . . . BACK to the place where I had been originally. . . . [Finally] a soldier . . . tells me to go inside to talk to the Comandante (Head of the Army in Choluteca). Well, it was like a movie. I walk into this warehouse-sized office room with air-conditioning. There was a huge desk in the middle [and behind it was this] enormous gentleman with cigarette holder and cigarette. Behind him was this very red drape. To his left was a huge map of Central America. To his right was a drawing board. To the right center was his television. I could hardly believe it. He too was bien amable. . . . I said, "I've GOT to get home! My problem is that I have a car with Salvadoran license plates." Well he then reiterated all the laws that tell I can't pass through Honduras. . . . Then I told him . . . how the ferry wasn't working and we didn't have water, etc. . . . Well, he finally got me cleared through and gave me a note to take to some Colonel. Before leaving he said, "Do come back again—but when you don't have such problems." He was really dear. . . .

Meanwhile Jean had been babysitting the Micro. Neither of us had been signed into the country—but here we were. . . . The next morning we had to take the front plate off—and because we couldn't get the back one off they just covered it with paper and tape. Then we had to have a soldier go with us to the other border. Two others came along to get dropped off at other places. At the other Honduran border they were waiting for us and processed us through as quickly as possible. Then we had to put on the front plate and uncover the back plate and pass into the Salvadoran frontera. This was quite a treat for [the Salvadoran border guards] because cars with Salvadoran plates NEVER pass through Honduras. So they asked, "How did you do it?" I said, "With GREAT difficulty!" . . . Our four day trip to Nicaragua cost us six days to get home![102]

On returning from Nicaragua, Jean began to look forward with great excitement to a two-week visit in early February from Doug Cable, who was by now assistant director of the department of communicable diseases at Los Angeles County Hospital. When Doug arrived in La Libertad, Paul lent them the mission jeep, and the young couple took advantage of this opportunity to visit some of the most scenic and romantic vacation spots in El Salvador. With the heightening political tensions, most of these mountain and seaside resorts were all but deserted, and Doug and Jean both later realized what a chance this had been for their relationship to grow. Doug felt he had finally seen the "real Jean," who was more reserved and vulnerable than the one most people saw tackling life and full of "bravado." After Doug left, Jean wrote to a friend in Cleveland:

Well, Doug came to visit. . . . Built my ego like crazy that he came all the way from Los Angeles to Salvador on his only vacation just to visit me— must be true love! But it was hard on me too. As a matter of fact it was harder on me than I expected it would be. I went into a little bit of depression since he left. I mean the day after he left, I was just on the floor. . . . I was so deeply depressed.

But both Doug and Jean had plans and obligations, and Jean was not quite ready to make a commitment to Doug as yet; nor did Doug ask her to. For the moment they simply decided to see each other when they could; Jean was already planning a trip to Ireland in September and Doug would arrange to be with her there.[103]

About a month after Doug's visit, El Salvador was rocked by the assassination of Archbishop Oscar Romero. Even at the risk of his own life, Romero had been speaking out tirelessly against all violence, but particularly against the spiral of right-wing repression in El Salvador. To say that Romero had gained the respect and love of his countrypeople in his three years as archbishop is an understatement. Martha and Dorothy had once been in Tamonique when he came to visit during fiesta time. The whole town and countryside had turned out for the event; the people had lined the streets with palm branches and had strewn beautiful, fresh, large purple flowers in his path as they welcomed their archbishop to the fiesta.[104]

In his long Sunday sermons, as repression grew, he condemned the brutal injustices inflicted on the Salvadoran people; he would recount the people's sorrow in his weekly litany of particular cases of the jailed, the murdered, and the disappeared. The people hung on his every word, and the ones who could not attend mass in the capital would listen to his sermon on the radio; the homilies of the archbishop became the most popular radio show in El Salvador.[105] By February 1980, Romero had lost hope that the October junta was capable of social and economic reform. In his February 17 sermon, he called upon President Carter to cease military aid to the Salvadoran regime and pleaded with him not to exert pressure to "try to determine the destiny of the Salvadoran nation":

> At this time we are living through a grave economic-political crisis in our country. However, without question, moment by moment our nation is being conscienticized and organized. Through this process, our people have begun to make themselves capable of managing and taking responsibility for El Salvador's future. They are the only ones capable of overcoming this crisis.
>
> It would be a deplorable injustice if, through the introduction of foreign weapons and force, the development of the Salvadoran nation was frustrated. . . .[106]

Not surprisingly, these words attracted both national and international attention. A few weeks later, Romero's fate was sealed when he spoke out against the vicious repression that was taking place in the countryside as the junta's agrarian reform was carried out; to the National Guard, the police, and the military, the archbishop pleaded:

> Brothers, you . . . kill your own *campesino* brothers and sisters. And before an order to kill that a man may give, the law of God must prevail

that says: Thou shalt not kill! . . . We want the government to take seriously that reforms are worth nothing when they come about stained with so much blood. In the name of God, and in the name of this suffering people whose laments rise to heaven each day more tumultuous, I beg you, I ask you, I order you in the name of God: Stop the repression![107]

The next day, March 24, 1980, Romero was gunned down while saying mass.

Two days after his death, a procession of five thousand people, including Dorothy, Jean, and Cris Rody, accompanied his coffin through the streets of San Salvador to the cathedral. Cris remembers this journey: "We were leading the casket. . . . First the nuns, then the priests, then Romero, and finally the [auxiliary] bishop. It was one of those times that Jean claimed to be a nun so she could be right up front with the rest of us. . . ."[108] For four days, Salvadorans filed by the body in the cathedral. During that time Dorothy, Jean, Cris, and Elizabeth, as well as many others, took turns guarding the coffin. Dorothy sent a newspaper photograph of the scene to Martha; the photo shows the coffin and the backs of several gringa heads in the honor guard. "How many heads do you recognize?" Dorothy wrote under the picture. The funeral was held on March 30, Palm Sunday, and it was a sad commentary on events that even the funeral could not take place in peace. Shooting erupted and a bomb went off—a delegation of foreign visitors later issued a statement claiming that witnesses had seen the gunfire come from the National Palace itself. This contradicted the government version which blamed leftist elements. Forty people died, most of whom were trampled to death in the panic and stampede that resulted.[109]

Bishop Hickey of Cleveland had traveled to Salvador for Romero's funeral; and while visiting the team a mutual decision was reached that Dorothy would stay on in El Salvador. Dorothy, because she had been in Salvador for six years, felt that the people needed and trusted her at this critical time. She therefore called her superior in Cleveland a few days after Romero's death and asked that her time be extended. Unknown to Dorothy, Hickey had also contacted the Ursulines, requesting an extension of Dorothy's commitment. As Martha later commented: "She was supposed to come home in June 1980, but because of Romero's death she decided to stay on longer. This turned out to be about six months too long."[110]

By the time of Romero's death Jean's political perspective had changed significantly. Five months earlier, when the ill-fated October coup had taken place, she had been filled with hope and spoke disparagingly about leftist groups which might have to miss out on their "glorious revolution." And even as recently as their visit to Nicaragua, Jean had revealed her conservative skepticism when she made a disparaging comment to a friend about the "twerps that run Nicaragua."[111] But by February 1980, she had agreed totally with Romero's plea to Carter not to aid the remnants of the October regime she had once stalwartly defended. One reason for Jean's growth was undoubtedly Romero himself. Before his death, Jean wrote a friend:

> I work in the La Libertad Parish in the Archdiocese mostly because I wanted to work in the diocese of Archbishop Romero. He is a great guy. He is the leader of Liberation Theology in practice. . . . It is so inspiring when you see and hear a man like Archbishop Romero. He doesn't back down for nothing. He really is the voice of the people. The way they respond to him is great. It is like the Pope when he enters church. They stand on the pews and clap for him. They clap his sermons, and at the recessional, everyone tries to shake his hand. And I think he does manage to shake most people's hands. At the same time he is a very humble person. He has been nominated for the Nobel Peace Prize.[112]

Jean, although a late sleeper, would rise early on Sunday mornings to listen to Romero's 8:00 A.M. mass over the radio with Dorothy and Cris. But Romero alone did not change Jean's views. In her work, she saw the people's fear of government and paramilitary forces; she saw catechists that the Cleveland team had trained being singled out by death squads; she saw the humiliating poverty of people she knew to be intelligent, idealistic, and courageous.[113] Jean was in El Salvador only about eight months when Romero was killed, but in that short time she had learned volumes.

Soon after the death of Romero, in April 1980, a broad coalition of opposition political and popular groups combined into a united front called the Frente Democrático Revolucionario (FDR). The opposition became even more unified by mid-summer as the guerrilla movements coalesced under a single command in the Frente Farabundo Martí de Liberación Nacional (FMLN), named after the leader of the 1932 uprising. Right-wing repression continued unabated and civil war lurked just around the corner.

In La Libertad itself death squad violence was increasing in the port as well as in the little surrounding villages that the team served. In April, Santa Cruz, where Jean had worked since her arrival, was visited by a death squad—armed civilians riding in military trucks. A twenty-four-year-old catechist was decapitated, and six other young men and women were mutilated in various ways, two of them beyond recognition. Cris Rody remembers how this tragic event affected Jean:

> She insisted on going to Santa Cruz to participate in the next Celebration of the Word. She realized the danger, but felt her presence would give the people courage. She thought her example might help to convince the villagers not to give up, but to go on with their lives. Jean had a passionate concern for people.[114]

A few weeks later the area was struck again and three were tortured and killed. Jean had worked with two of the young catechists and was heartbroken.

By the summer of 1980 Jean, Dorothy, and Paul were being called upon more and more to bless and bury the twisted bodies that were turning up in ditches around La Libertad and in the surrounding towns. Moreover, on several occasions Paul had gone to the headquarters of the security forces and demanded that they hand over someone he knew had disappeared. If this aggressive tactic did not work, he would call the U.S. embassy, which would contact a high-level Salvadoran commander and often the *desaparecido's* release would be obtained.[115] Salvadoran security and military forces were surely aware of the North Americans' efforts to aid the living and bury the dead. And perhaps it is no coincidence that on July 6 tragedy struck the team even closer to home and to their hearts.

There were at least a couple of hundred people on the streets of La Libertad that Sunday night, says Paul. Carlos Jérez González, Paul's twenty-year-old unofficial foster son, had been playing the lottery. Armando Arévalo, about twenty-four, had been talking with Jean and Dorothy in Jean's little apartment above the parochial school in the plaza. (Dorothy still shared a house in Zaragoza with the other nuns, but almost as often as not stayed with Jean in La Libertad.) Around 10:00 P.M. Carlos met Armando and the two headed over to the church to lock it up for the night. Suddenly, a few feet from Jean's door, three armed men grabbed Armando and Carlos and tried to drag them off into a waiting car. But the young men struggled desperately with the thugs, knowing that to go off with them was to join the ranks of the hundreds of *desaparecidos* who had faced clandestine torture and execution. The struggle did not last long. Both were shot; Armando died immediately, and Carlos, still breathing but unconscious, was left to die nearby. As if on cue, no sooner had the assassins left when two police jeeps drove up to the scene, took note of the two young men lying in the street, and quickly drove off. No one who witnessed this seriously thought that the police had come to offer aid or gather evidence to solve this crime, since hundreds of victims died similar deaths in El Salvador every month, and no murderer was ever brought to justice. Dorothy and Jean, having heard the shots, were huddled together upstairs, too fearful at first to venture out. Someone on the street called for an ambulance, and someone else ran to get Paul, who was in his house not far away. But Carlos died on the way to the hospital.[116]

Carlos and Armando had shared hard work, tears, and laughter with the Cleveland team and they all grieved over this loss. Armando, an engaging young man, was the parish sacristan and had worked with the church's youth group; as Paul says, he could have been pegged by authorities for his leadership role with youngsters and for speaking out in the group against repression. At one time Armando had applied for the seminary, but because he had a girlfriend and two children he had eventually withdrawn his application. He was three years younger than Jean, but the two had hit it off and become good friends. They loved to clown around, but Paul remembers many a night when the "kids"—Jean, Armando, and Carlos—would stay up till the wee hours of the morning, thrashing out theological mysteries that have baffled the human race for millennia. If God was good, if indeed God existed, why was there so much evil in the world? Why, in particular, were the people of El Salvador suffering so much? Why did God permit so much sorrow? Why . . . ? On and on it went. Often Dorothy and Paul joined these discussions, offering consolation and drawing on the experiences, perspective, and mature religious faith of their longer lives.[117]

Paul was particularly devastated by the death of Carlos. Carlos had been orphaned as a boy, and an old woman had taken him in; he did odd jobs for her and she gave him shelter and food. After her death he had bounced around the port town, calling no place his home; he had befriended the surfer crowd and become involved in drugs. "He was a holy terror," Paul says affectionately:

When he started hanging around the church, even the nuns could not tolerate him—he was such a terrible thief. So eventually I inherited him; he moved in with me and became known as "the padre's kid." He lived with me for seven years, and believe it or not, he was beginning to shape up. I used bribery and everything else to keep him off drugs and away from the surfers. I even promised to bring him to Disney World. And he did stay off drugs, so sure enough he got his trip to Disney World. He had met a girl—Sarah—who had such a good influence on him. She and her family had had to leave El Salvador and were living in the States, and I had promised Carlos if he finished the eighth grade, I'd find a way to get him into the States, where he could see Sarah again and go to school. He was doing so well with this goal in mind—he really responded to my bribery! He would have graduated in November. But Carlos was a tough kid, a street kid, and he had spoken out many times against the government. He knew there was a chance he'd be killed; he often told me they would never take him alive. . . . [118]

Not long after this blow, Dorothy went to the United States for a well-deserved visit with family and friends. While there, Dorothy revealed on a couple of occasions the intensity of her life in El Salvador. In a conversation with her superior, she admitted, "When you sit in the house in Zaragoza and somebody's car backfires, you want to jump under the table." And on a long car trip with her family to Florida—a memorable time for all the Kazels, for it was filled with laughter, stories, and song—the conversation at one point turned to the subject of death. Dorothy grew quite serious then and thoughtfully told her family. "I am prepared and ready to die."[119]

While Dorothy was away still another tragedy struck the North American community in El Salvador. During the past few years the Cleveland team had become quite close to the various Maryknoll nuns serving in El Salvador—Sister Madeline Dorsey, who worked in Santa Ana, and Sisters Teresa Alexander and Joan Petrik, who lived in La Libertad and often collaborated with the Cleveland team. In April 1980, there were two new Maryknoll arrivals, Ita Ford and Carla Piette, who had chosen to serve in Chalatenango, a northern province that was already racked by civil war. They had seen the need in that province for persons willing to transport refugees to safer areas near the capital and to bring food, medicine, and clothing to those who had been forced to flee their villages by army sweeps. Carla and Ita's work with refugees began to draw in members of the Cleveland team. Their assistance at first was rather sporadic; then, while Dorothy was in the United States, Jean and Cris began to work with the Maryknollers on a more regular basis, often arranging for or providing the necessary transportation for the refugees and attempting to reunite family members who had become separated in the chaos. Realizing that Salvadorans' lives were at stake, Jean threw herself into this work with special intensity, recalls Cris.

In late August, just after they had dropped off a refugee in Chalatenango, Carla and Ita's jeep overturned in a stream swollen by a flash flood. Carla managed to push Ita out of the window to safety, but she herself drowned. Carla's sudden death, coming as it did so soon after the murder of Carlos and Armando and in the midst of escalating violence all over El Salvador, was not only a personal loss for the Maryknollers and for the Cleveland team but also a graphic reminder that life was all too precarious in El Salvador. But paradoxically the death of this outgoing, generous woman was also an inspiration, and seemed to confirm several of the missionaries in their resolve to remain in El Salvador. Sister Terry Alexander recalls that Jean had spoken on several occasions about leaving El Salvador, but that Carla's death convinced her to stay to help continue the refugee work Carla had initiated.[120] Dorothy, too, wrote to Mercy sister Theresa Kane in the United States about Carla's death, calling it a "resurrection experience."[121] Of course, Ita, who had been Carla's best friend and companion for seven years, was grief-stricken and seriously depressed afterwards. In spite of this, no amount of persuasion could change Ita's mind about continuing their work in Chalatenango. And Maryknoll sister Maura Clarke, who had come to El Salvador only three weeks before to take Joan Petrik's place, was moved, by Carla's death and Ita's commitment, to volunteer to help Ita continue the work she and Carla had barely begun.[122]

The deaths of the archbishop, the Santa Cruz catechists, Carlos and Armando, and Carla were all woven into the macabre tapestry of death and violence that seemed to have no end. The scent of death was becoming ubiquitous as more of Dorothy and Jean's friends were terrorized or slain by the death squads. Soon after Dorothy's return to El Salvador she wrote Martha:

> Other sad news is that on Friday I went out on my moto [motorcycle] to advise our catechists about Confirmation charlas. Just past Cangrejera . . . —by Hacienda Santa Lucía—there were 3 cadavers. I didn't stop cuz people were there—I thought I'd go to Valle Nuevo first—and stop on the way back. Well, as I pulled into Valle Nuevo—where the health clinic is—there were lots of people—and I saw the candles and *caja* [coffin]. Here they also shot and killed the father of Margot (the girl catechist there who helps us). He was the *cuidandero* [caretaker] of the

Center. It seems a group of masked men came in around midnight and shot him. A 17 year old son and 8 year old boy were there but they hid in a bathroom that doesn't work and luckily weren't found as these guys hung around till 4:30 A.M. There was one other killed from Valle Nuevo, one from Cangrejera, and one from Los Planos. . . .

Jean just came back from Zaragoza—the Escuadron de Muerte [death squad] is running around up there—tried to get a man out of [the sacristan's] house—but the daughter intervened. Also, supposedly the "boys" (Julio, etc.) are all on their list—so they're all in Ken's house. . . . The E.M. went into the Clinic and seems to be still there.

It's now Monday. Zaragoza calmed down after the E.M. left—they seemed not to have killed anyone—thank God. . . .

. . . Hope this gives you some idea of what's happening. . . .

Love ya—
D.[123]—

The work of the Cleveland team from its inception had been a response to the needs of the people. Over the years, team members had trained hundreds of catechists, distributed tons of food from Caritas, and spoken to multitudes of Salvadorans about the gospel, family life, first aid, and the sacraments. With thousands of civilians losing their lives to death squads and soldiers, with villages under siege and families uprooted, with civil war fast approaching, the needs of the Salvadoran people were rapidly changing. As these needs changed, so did the response of the Cleveland team to the challenge. The training of catechists and visits to outlying villages were cut back sharply when the team became aware that *campesinos* were often harassed by the Guardia after the team left the area: "They want to know what the padre said," Paul explained in an interview with the *National Catholic Reporter* in September 1980; and Jean commented, "We're keeping a very low profile at this point."[124] The team became housebound after 7:00 P.M. every evening because the streets were dangerous. In late summer team members decided to re-evaluate their pastoral work and determine what they could best offer the Salvadoran people in their hour of need.

It was apparent that the most pronounced need was now in refugee work. Dorothy, Jean, and Cris had earlier begun to help Carla and Ita transfer refugees, and Carla had gotten Cris involved in managing a refugee center, San Roque, in San Salvador. Father Ken Myers now decided to turn a church building into an "Hogar del Niños," a home for lost and orphaned refugee children. And what about Dorothy and Jean? The answer was obvious. "It seems like Jean and I will be helping Ita and Maura out in Chalatenango when needed," wrote Dorothy to Martha.[125] From this time on, the efforts of Dorothy, Jean, Maura, and Ita would have a single focus—to transport to safety the victims of civil war, usually women and children, and to provide food, shelter, clothing, and medicine for them.

Dorothy and Jean thus became accustomed to being called upon at a moment's notice to drive the white Toyota microbus into zones that had recently seen bitter fighting. Sometimes it was Ita and Maura who asked them for help; sometimes it was archdiocesan refugee committees or Vicar General Ricardo Urioste who requested their aid. They never asked those they helped if they were supporters of the guerrillas or the government.[126] Furthermore, their work was no secret; in fact, they would inform the police or other governmental authorities each time they went out into the countryside. And they were much in demand, for their blonde hair and blue eyes eased them and their passengers through roadblocks and checkpoints guarded by armed men. Monsignor Urioste often said that "nobody in the country was safer than Dorothy and Jean."[127]

In early September, it was Jean's turn to take some time off. For some months Jean had been planning an elaborate six-week trip to the United States and Europe. She and Doug had spoken about it when he had visited in February and since then her plans had coalesced into a definite itinerary. She would fly from San Salvador to Miami for a visit with her parents, then on to England to meet Doug and sight-see in London. From there they would go to Ireland for two weeks, in time for the wedding of one of Jean's friends. Finally, Jean and Doug would part; and Jean would head for New York, Maryknoll, and Connecticut, finishing up with a visit to friends and relatives in Cleveland and a few days with her parents in Sarasota, Florida.

Filled with parties, camaraderie, and reminiscences of old times, the trip to Ireland was a welcome respite from the violence of Central America. At the wedding, it seemed to everyone that Doug and Jean would be the next couple to be married. But Jean was hesitant about marrying a doctor, whose job might demand long hours away from home, and she was determined to return to turbulent El Salvador to complete her commitment. So Doug and Jean put off making a decision on marriage and agreed to decide this question in Costa Rica where they planned to meet in January 1981—a date that Jean would not live to keep.[128]

Jean also used this opportunity to talk freely about El Salvador—she felt the story needed to be told, that not many on the outside were aware of the truth behind the escalating violence in that bitter country. On one such occasion, she spoke to a youth group and the unburdening seemed to be a kind of catharsis for her.[129]

Nevertheless, there were also many difficult moments for Jean. Because she feared that her letters from El Salvador were censored, she had not been able to relate to her friends the level of terror that life in Salvador had reached. The openness with which she now spoke about some of the gruesome sights she had seen and about some of the friends and acquaintances she had lost in the repression horrified Doug and Father Crowley, as well as others, who all tried to dissuade her from returning to El Salvador. Crowley, the man who had first opened Jean's heart to the suffering of the Third World and had encouraged her so in the past, was adamant that she should not return to El Salvador:

"I did my damnedest to dissuade her from going back. . . . In my judgment her life was at risk and I told her that in very, very clear terms. I said, 'You're going to get it. You'll be picked, lifted, and tortured and killed. It's going to happen.' "[130]

But Jean responded to their concern with flippant remarks. Although she often brushed off the pleading of friends with one-liners like "They don't shoot blond, blue-eyed North Americans," in reality their warnings deeply affected her. On the plane back to New York she wrote an eight-page letter to Father Crowley trying to justify her decision. When she arrived at Maryknoll in early October she was a "basket case," according to one nun. A friend and teacher of hers at Maryknoll, Gwen Vendley, recalled that Jean was "almost shell-shocked" on her last visit; however, it was not death she feared, but torture.[131]

Jean also sought out Josie and Frank Cuda and paid them a surprise visit. Josie could see that Jean had changed dramatically in the past year and a half. Before, many, including Josie and Frank, had wondered if the rather rebellious and outspoken missionary recruit was serious about the step she was taking. Now, Josie found a mature young woman, who had learned a great deal about herself:

I feel that perhaps this was Jean's way of making peace with us. We had never been particularly close and it was a little trouble for her even to find us, since we had moved. But there she was in our house, sharing her experiences of Salvador and her fears of the future with us. I found her more open and honest. She was fearful about going back and she told us, "I don't want to go and get killed." And she said because of the danger she may not return to Salvador after Christmas.[132]

It is obvious that all the discussions in Ireland concerning her safety had been painful for Jean. She was now facing the facts at Maryknoll, and the facts troubled her deeply. Whether her bluster and bravado in Ireland had been a front to avoid discussing the dangers with people she thought might not understand her motivation or whether she simply had not faced reality at that time is not certain. But Jean somehow made peace with herself at Maryknoll. When she got to Cleveland, she spoke candidly with her friends about her "dark night of the soul." "We talked a lot about her dying," recalls Rita Mikolajczyk. "She said she spent much time in the chapel [at Maryknoll] coming to grips with the possibility of dying. She told me she yelled at God and he yelled at her. She was trying to work out her going back to El Salvador—and she did."[133]

Mary Fran Ehlinger's last conversation with Jean was especially emotional:

I told her, "I love you, Jeannie, and I want you to come home alive." She answered, "I love you too, Mary Fran, but I can't make you that promise." She had worked out her fears before she returned to El Salvador for the last time. She had put it all together before she died.[134]

By the time she arrived in Sarasota, Florida, she had cast aside the "shell-shocked" Jean. Her mother is convinced that she never could have merely acted the part of the "old Jeannie" on her last visit, joking and carefree; she must have in some way "reconciled herself to what was happening and what she was to do, and . . . made her peace with whatever frightening thoughts that she had."[135] While in Florida, Jean seized the opportunity to talk with her parents about politics. It was the fall of 1980, an election year, and Jean's parents were firmly behind Republican candidate Ronald Reagan because of his emphasis on fiscal responsibility. Jean, however, felt that Reagan's lack of concern for the human rights abuses that were rampant in El Salvador would be perceived as a green light for their escalation if he was elected. She tried to convince her parents that a Reagan presidency would bring about a "blood-bath" in El Salvador, but at the time they did not fully understand her point of view and a few weeks later cast their votes for Reagan, a decision they grew to regret.[136]

Only a few days after her return to Salvador, Jean was confronted with a scene that was a chilling reminder to put behind her any thoughts of security and complacency that she may have carried with her from Ireland and the United States. She was riding her bike and passed a man and a woman huddled on the side of the road. Realizing they were hurt, she turned around and went back to them. Seeing that she was a North American, the man, who had been shot in the stomach and whose entrails were exposed, asked if she worked for the Catholic church; when Jean answered yes, he proceeded to pour out his last confession to her. The woman had only a wound in the leg and might survive, so Jean left them to go for help. When she did so, she passed a truck full of soldiers heading in the direction of the wounded couple. Returning to the spot where she had left them, Jean was shocked to find that they had simply disappeared. Did the soldiers pick them up? Did they finish them off and throw them somewhere? Jean was angry, because the woman would surely have survived. Feeling bewildered, helpless, and furious, Jean hurried back to the house to find Dorothy. "I can't believe this has happened," she told her. Dorothy later related the story to Martha: "It was spooky," she said, "they were there, and then they were—gone. Those are the kind of things that are going on. People are being killed all over."[137]

On this same tape, Dorothy told Martha about a recent trip she had made to pick up refugees. Dorothy had been asked by a refugee committee to travel up to Metapán in northern El Salvador near the Honduran border. During recent heavy fighting, all the houses in the area had been burned down, and forty-five children and ten women remained in the debris that had once been their village. At first Dorothy had some misgivings when Monsignor Urioste and Ita asked her to go on this errand of mercy. How would she get all those people out of there? she asked. They promised her a large truck and a driver. In the tape to

Martha, Dorothy made light of the journey, which was to take place the next day. But beneath the surface one can detect a current of apprehension: "It's always good to have a gringa face there in case something happens," she told Martha; ". . . It seems to be about a three and a half hour trip, so—to know! I just don't know where I'm going or exactly what is going to happen."

The rescue mission actually went fairly smoothly. It was a nice day and the trip into the mountains over winding roads offered a beautiful view. As Dorothy later commented to Martha, they kept driving farther and farther into unfamiliar territory: "You know how it is—you never know *where* you're going, or *what* you're getting into; it's just a riot." When they finally arrived at their destination, they found that eight days before the Guardia had come into the village, opened fire on the people, and burned their houses. Fifty-five women and children remained in the rubble. There were also two "muchachos" trying to protect the people with "overgrown b.b. guns." They were organized into some group, maybe the FPL (Fuerzas Populares de Liberación), Dorothy said, but to her the whole scene was disheartening: "Martha, honestly, they're like Daniel Boone; this is worse than rinky-tink cowboys and Indians; it's like Indians against the U.S. marines of today. Really, I don't know how these guys are ever going to win this war. . . . You just wonder *how* this is all going to turn out." As usual, Dorothy was touched by the "dear" people who had lost all their possessions. There was a tiny newborn fellow, six days old, "just an itty-bitty skinny little thing—was he ever undernourished"—but "so cute":

> My heart just aches for these people, when I see what they've got to work with. And they're really hoping to win. I just don't know how in God's name they're going to do it. . . . We [the U.S.] give money for communication equipment and huge trucks and such so the military can get up there easier to kill them. . . . It just makes me ill when I see us doing this kind of garbage.[138]

On this same tape, the last one that Dorothy would send Martha, she tried to convey to her friend something of the reality of El Salvador. Sometimes in a low voice, almost incredulous, and sometimes more passionately, Dorothy said:

> People are being killed all over. . . . You know, they massacred all these people up at Santa María en Palomar. . . . They killed ten men there— well not even all men—one old man who was walking down the road with three cows, and one young girl, twelve years old, who was singing or had the words of a song in her hands; so they decided she was a "guerrillera" and killed her. I was so depressed with that because I went up there . . . and saw all these cadavers and all these weeping people. . . .[139]

This experience compelled Dorothy to write a letter to President Carter to protest how she saw U.S. aid being used against the people of El Salvador:

Dear Mr. President:

My name is Sister Dorothy Kazel, and I am a North American missionary working in the Central American country of El Salvador. I have been
here for six years, and I have seen the oppression of the people grow
worse each year.

My reason for writing this letter comes from an experience I had
yesterday afternoon. I realize my experience is a very COMMON happening here, but it's one that truly makes a person sick. And it makes a
North American even sicker because of the help our country has given to
the Government here—as it was stated—for "vehicles and communication."

Early Monday morning (September 22, 1980), the Army soldiers of El
Salvador [made] house searches in San José Villa Nueva. This in itself is a
terrorizing tactic when at one o'clock in the morning, when everyone is
sleeping, soldiers with rifles and equipment come pounding at your door.
Of course, if you do not open the door, they will knock it down. You then
have to present your papers proving who you are, etc.

It seems that this group (of soldiers) kept going further up the isolated
road to the cantones above in their HIGH POWERED TRUCKS with
their COMMUNICATION equipment.

About 6–6:30 in the morning, they killed 10 or more people in one
cantone and then went farther up (the road) and killed another 10 or
more people. One old man was coming down the road with three cows—
he got killed. One young man was going to wash down by the well—he
got killed. One young girl about 12 years old had in her hands the words
of a song which had been written in honor of one of the priests who had
been martyred. They (the soldiers) claimed she was a subversive and
killed her.

There were three masked men with the soldiers pointing out the houses
to them and naming the people in them. When taking a man from his
house, the soldiers never asked him if he was the "name" they were
looking for. When a wife asked, "Where are you taking him?" or "Why
are you taking them?" there was no answer. No words of explanation
were ever given.

Now I realize these soldiers are looking for "subversives" and they
may have a right to do that—but do they have a right to do it in this
manner? Do they realize how many really INNOCENT people they kill
because they have received wrong information? Do they investigate the
information they receive before they come and kill people?

And the most appalling thing to me is that I am a North American and
MY government gave them money for the "durable equipment" they
have so that it's relatively easy to get into the worst [most isolated]
cantones without much trouble and kill innocent people because of the
wrong information they have received.

I really would like to know what you think of this situation, Mr. President, and whether you really realize how many innocent people we are helping to kill. How do you reconcile all of this?

Sincerely,
Sister Dorothy Kazel[140]

The letter Dorothy received in response from the U.S. State Department, dated November 7, 1980, neatly circumvents the issues Dorothy had raised. It dwells on the left's refusal of amnesty and mediation, but fails to mention that those refusals must be seen in the context of the right's brutal repression of anyone it deemed "subversive." Moreover, it ignores, except for a reference to "violence . . . carried out by both extremes," the indiscriminate slaughter by right-wing and government forces, the bloody results of which Dorothy herself had witnessed:

Dear Sister Kazel:

I am responding to your letter of September 23 to President Carter concerning our policy in El Salvador.

We deplore the violence in El Salvador which is continuing at a high level. We have made clear to the Salvadoran Government our hope and expectation that it bring the violence under control from whatever source, right or left, official or unofficial. As you undoubtedly know, it is being carried out by both extremes.

However, the leftist opposition has refused both the government's offer of amnesty announced October 15 and the Conference of Bishops' offer to mediate announced October 18. The FMLN has announced what it terms as the "final offensive." In such situations involving widespread violence from a variety of sources it is tragic that innocent people become the victims. Nevertheless, the government's plans for elections and reforms are moving forward and may succeed in alleviating some of the conditions which have spawned the violence.

Sincerely,
John D. Blacken, Director,
Office of Central American Affairs
Department of State[141]

Knowing as she did that some of the government's "reforms" alluded to by Blacken had already been carried out in the countryside, accompanied by violent repression, surely Dorothy was not deluded, as the U.S. State Department apparently was, that such reforms would "succeed in alleviating some of the conditions which have spawned the violence." Indeed, Blacken's letter overlooks the fact that the real power behind the junta at the time was Defense Minister García, who had for months been maneuvering his hardliners into key posts in the military and transferring out more moderate elements. By early September 1980 there simply were no so-called "reform-minded" officers with power; but as Phillip Berryman comments, "United States government spokespersons downplayed the significance out of either ignorance or lack of real concern for reform."[142]

In their work transporting refugees, Dorothy and Jean certainly had a glimpse of reality that most Washington analysts could not claim. On each trip, they came into contact with victims who had suffered terribly, indescribably really, in the bloody war. In August 1980, Mercy Sister Betty Campbell visited San Roque in San Salvador, the refugee center run by Cris Rody, where Dorothy and Jean often dropped off refugees from war-torn regions. Betty found two hundred refugees crowded into a basement under the church, sleeping on bits of paper, plastic, or clothing and sharing one faucet and one bathroom. Many of the children were sick with diarrhea, coughs, fevers, malnutrition, and running sores. Yet seldom did a nurse or doctor visit them, because throughout 1980 many who had offered their services had been murdered or threatened for treating "subversives." Betty, like Jean and Dorothy, heard the refugees relate their stories; a woman eight months pregnant told Betty:

> My home is in the countryside. For many months my husband along with men in the area had been sleeping further up in the hills because the army would come looking for men and boys to kill them. Recently, the army said that the next time they would kill women and children, too. So I started to sleep in the hills with my three children. Late one afternoon as we were preparing to close the house and head up the hill, the soldiers came. Many of them came. They told us all to walk to the edge of the [village]. Under the eyes of the soldiers, I hurried along with my husband and children. There were several families hurrying with us.
>
> As we gathered together near a large open field, the soldiers started to shoot at us with machine guns. People were screaming and moving about. One soldier near me said, "Fall over the others and play dead." I fell over bodies and tried not to move. Soon I heard one soldier as if in charge, coming near and saying, "Let's make sure they are all dead!" My back was cut with a machete as you can see. It sounded like other people were being cut, too. Then the soldiers left. I got up and looked for my children, my husband. They were dead. Only five of us survived. I found something to cover up my back and we left through the hills.
>
> Late evening we came to the town and sought refuge at the parish. The priests and sisters gave us help. They had no medicine but boiled a sewing needle and thread to close the wound in my back. After futile attempts they covered it with something clean. The next day a nurse took care of me. I thank God!

And another woman, also pregnant, related:

> Many people in our [basic] Christian communities have been killed. We are here because the National Guard killed our neighbors. One afternoon I saw the National Guard and the ORDEN [a paramilitary group] men coming toward my home. The ORDEN men are from our own areas, but they are against us. They watch us all the time. They put our names on lists that they give to the army, police, and National Guard.
>
> That afternoon when I saw these men I prayed God would help me to say the right thing to them. Thirty National Guard surrounded my home and six ORDEN men entered. They asked, "What kind of meetings do you hold here? Who comes to them? What is in that loft? Where do you have the arms? Where is your husband?" After what seemed a long time, eight National Guard came in and started to question in the same manner. They pushed me with their guns. I thought they were going to kill me, they were so angry. I feared for the children. Some of them were hanging on to me and were very frightened and crying.
>
> Finally, the National Guard and the ORDEN men left. I waited. I could see from the window that there were soldiers around other homes, going in and out. Sometimes I heard screams. After what seemed a couple of hours I went to my neighbor to see how she was. I found her stuffed into a small well. Her stomach was cut open and her baby taken out. I went to another neighbor and she was dead. Her eyes were pulled out and her breast cut off.

The woman could not go on. Finally, she concluded:

> Terror had come to our area. Those of us who survived gathered up our children and some few belongings and made our way to people who could get us here to the capital. Some of our husbands were working that day and when they returned home late they found that terrible situation. Only days later did they find us here.[143]

Aside from the tales of terror they heard from refugees, Dorothy and Jean also experienced a couple of incidents that they found rather disconcerting. The first concerned a boy scout canteen that Jean had brought back with her from Ireland. Claiming it was "military equipment," Salvadoran customs officials had confiscated it at the airport. Aggravated by this overreaction to a harmless canteen, Jean characteristically decided to pursue the matter up the chain of command. Sometimes in Dorothy's company and sometimes on her own, Jean made several trips to customs, then to a lieutenant's office, then to the plush office of a colonel in a military school. Finally, this colonel, who thought Jean was a tourist, told her to come back for the canteen another day. When Jean returned, she was taken aback to see a high-ranking colonel from the U.S. embassy poring over what seemed to be data on U.S. military aid. The colonel looked over at Jean, apparently surprised by the presence of another North American. Jean left without the canteen.[144]

A couple of weeks later, while rescuing a family on a hill in the countryside, Jean was tracked by a helicopter; those in the helicopter spotted her and a companion on the hillside and began to circle overhead. Although frightened, Jean managed to get a good look at the helicopter and was convinced it was a U.S. Huey. Since her father had worked in the design department of another U.S. helicopter plant, Jean called her mother and asked her if she could mail her a picture of a Huey. When the picture arrived, Jean recognized it as the same type of aircraft that had followed her; and she became incensed that U.S. aircraft were being used to track civilians and refugees. On the day before she was killed she told Betty Campbell she intended to bring up the issue at Ambassador Robert White's dinner party that night.[145]

In the fall of 1980, the civil war was gaining momentum. In September, Colonel García, the defense minister, had clearly shown who controlled the government when he reshuffled the military, replacing the supporters of Colonel Majano, the junta's moderate military representative, with his own uncompromising followers. In October, María Magdalena Henríquez, publicity secretary of the Salvadoran Human Rights office, was picked up by ten men, including two policemen; her corpse was found four days later. There were invasions and bombardments of the province of Morazán, accompanied by heavy casualties in the countryside. In all of 1980, at least ten thousand Salvadorans were killed. And throughout 1980, thousands of refugees had crossed over into Honduras. When questioned by journalists or churchpeople as to why they had fled El Salvador, they invariably claimed they were fleeing Salvadoran military forces who had burned their villages and killed their friends and relatives. The government's strategy in these campaigns was to destroy the infrastructure of support for the guerrillas. The fact that this strategy terrorized civilians, completely alienated the countryside from the government, and thus provided future human resources for the insurgency was apparently considered a risk worth taking.[146]

Although it was often difficult to get word out to friends in the United States, Dorothy had tried in late October 1980 to convey some of the frightful reality. In what turned out to be her final tape to Martha, she concluded this part of her narration:

> There's just been so many stories. . . . Up in San Antonio de los Ranchos they chopped up women, you know, cutting off their breasts, and spearing the kid in their wombs. . . . I mean sick, sick stuff. Oh . . . it just makes you ill. . . . You wonder—it's just so diabolical, it makes you want to weep.[147]

Both Dorothy and Jean had seen more than enough to make them weep in the last few months of 1980. Yet they continued their refugee work and did not succumb to exhaustion and despair. Why did they choose to stay?

Clearly, one reason for Dorothy's ability to persevere was her deeply in-grained, cheerful attitude toward life. In her tapes to Martha, Dorothy would avoid concluding them on a note of bloody mayhem or sorrow but would invariably add humorous little stories from daily life, like one about finding a bat in her bedroom: "I thought it was a little bird; but when it hung from the ceiling, I knew it was a bat! . . . You just never know what you're going to find in your house these days!"[148] In the antics of her cats, Dorothy found a limitless source of comic relief. She marveled over the birth to one amorous feline of her twenty-first, twenty-second, and twenty-third kittens and could not resist describing the births in detail to Martha. "Can you *believe* her?" Dorothy asked in amused admiration.[149] Shopping expeditions with Jean or Cris for clothing for the refugees and light-hearted get-togethers in their apartment with friends were also opportunities for fun. In October 1980, in the midst of rising fear and violence, the Maryknollers and Franciscans joined the Cleve-land team members for a "dress up" Halloween party. "It's our escape from reality!" Dorothy commented.[150]

If one were to choose a single word that best describes Dorothy, it would perhaps be "optimistic." "Even towards the end, with all the repression and terror, she did not lose hope," says Paul Schindler; "We all, everyone, drew from Dorothy's optimism."[151] Yet despite her joking reference to an "escape from reality," Dorothy was actually not one either to distort or to avoid reality. To her El Salvador was "a country that is writhing in pain." Her optimism sprang not from a shallow perception of the world around her but from a deep spirituality:

> The steadfast faith and courage our leaders have to continue preaching the Word of the Lord even though it may mean "laying down your life" in the very REAL sense is always a point of admiration and a vivid realiza-tion that JESUS is HERE with us. Yes, we have a sense of waiting, hoping, and yearning for a complete realization of the Kingdom, and yet we know it will come because we can celebrate Him here right now.[152]

Dorothy also found tremendous hope for the future in the conscious choice being made by some in the church to serve the poor. In September 1980 she read excerpts of Sister of Mercy Theresa Kane's address to the Leadership Confer-ence of Women Religious (LCWR), and was particularly moved by the follow-ing:

> The intention of our predecessors was not to erect buildings solely, but to do whatever was essential for the missionary service. . . . Today, when two-thirds of the world's population live below subsistence level, women are again being challenged by the overwhelming needs of the poor and the oppressed to respond anew. Today we who are women religious

need to de-institutionalize ourselves and become missionaries once again. . . .

The concentration of women religious in the United States, and especially on the East Coast, is not a witness to a global consciousness; it is not a witness to the overwhelming needs of the poor and the oppressed in the Third and Fourth Worlds. There needs to be a redistribution of woman power if we are to be in solidarity with the poor and the marginated of our society. This call may even cause many to step outside of the established systems, to eventually withdraw from traditional-based ministries such as Catholic schools and health systems.[153]

Inspired by these words, Dorothy wrote to Theresa Kane:

Dear Sister,

I am an Ursuline Sister from Cleveland, Ohio, working in the Central American country of El Salvador. . . . [Your address to the LCWR] truly was impressive—and hopeful—as well as challenging. I was especially impressed with what you had to say about the "middle-class nature of U.S. nuns' work"—and how important it is to serve the poor and oppressed. I believe that wholeheartedly—that's why I'm here in El Salvador. I should be coming back to the states next year—it will be then that I face a greater challenge. I hope to continue working with the poor and oppressed. Just *HOW*—is where the challenge will come in.

Actually my real reason for writing to you was to share a "resurrection" experience. A very good friend of mine—a Maryknoll Sister—Carla Piette—was drowned while crossing a river after taking a political prisoner home. I think her beliefs, her life, her whole being go along with what you are saying. . . . She, too, was a great woman.

Within this past year I had been fortunate to meet women theologians like Barbara Doherty and Sandra Schneider. They—along with the little I've actually read about you—do give me the hope that the reign of God is making headway—and for this I am grateful. Do continue to be Spirit-filled and challenging. Please keep the people of Salvador before the Lord as we are literally living in times of persecution. We need His strength.

Thank you for being freed up enough to speak the truth so clearly and publicly.

God Love You—
Sister Dorothy Kazel[154]

A stubborn, spiritual streak of hope that would not die fortified Dorothy in her last months in El Salvador. But it was clear to those who knew her that those months had taken their toll. "Normally Dorothy was of light spirit but not those days," commented one co-worker who saw Dorothy at the chancery on November 28, four days before she died. At the time Dorothy was desperately seeking medical aid for a critically ill refugee woman with several children.[155] And just three days before her death, Martha called Dorothy to wish her a happy Thanksgiving. "She sounded so tired," her friend remembers.[156]

Dorothy's perseverance was also a response to the needs of the people of El Salvador. She never dwelled on her spiritual motivations or tried to explain her actions with elaborate rationales. And Dorothy certainly was not one to consider herself indispensable. Yet four days before her death, she did indicate in her last letter to Sister Martha that if necessary she would extend her time even further:

> You asked about summer—one thing I am doing is making that Ursuline Institute in July. I hope to be home by May 18 the latest—my sister-in-law is graduating from Ursuline [College] then. Right now I'm thinking about leaving here mid-March but nothing is positive. I hope to travel around and make a QUIET retreat before coming back—so we shall see. I *may* stay till Easter—depending on need—saber! . . .
>
> Take care—My love
> —D[157]

Easter 1981 would have been nearly two years past the date that had once been scheduled for Dorothy's departure. But, as Dorothy had learned in the past year and always stressed when she spoke of the future, nothing was certain.

Jean too was driven by the desperate situation of the Salvadoran people. The young North American who had once examined her promising career and her affluent lifestyle with a critical eye and found them lacking in some intangible way had grown in selflessness and spiritual maturity in El Salvador. Having overcome her most nerve-racking fears of torture and death while she was at Maryknoll in October, she was able to work quite effectively upon her return. Early on in her stay in El Salvador she had commented to friends on how much the poor were teaching her about spirituality, but she felt she was still learning; after her final trip home, she wrote her old friend and spiritual counselor, Ralph Wiatowski:

> . . . We are still plugging along. Sister Christine is running a center, and Dorothy and I are doing anything needed. Mostly driving and watching out for funds we receive.
>
> Life continues on with many interruptions. I don't know how the poor survive. People in our positions really have to die unto ourselves and our wealth to gain the spirituality of the poor and oppressed. I have a long way to go on that score. They can teach you so much with their patience

and their wanting eyes. We are all so inadequate in our help. I am trying now more and more to deal with the social sin of the first world. It's not an easy question. Well, take care, Ralph.

Love, Jean[158]

Her thoughts of Doug and their plans to meet in Costa Rica in January often occupied her spare moments. It seems that Jean had become more comfortable with the thought of marriage, for Paul remembers that she frequently spoke of making wedding arrangements: "She looked forward to it when her commitment in El Salvador was over; she talked about where and when it would take place, who would be there, whether we would all be able to come."[159] With thoughts of the future to sustain her, perhaps the present reality was made more bearable. No matter how much evil she had seen or would see, no matter how many times she was tempted to pack her bags and walk out, she simply could not back out on the people. About two weeks before her death she said in a letter to a friend:

> . . . and so the Peace Corps left today, and my heart sank low. The danger is extreme and they are right to leave, but it seems that the more help is needed, the less help is available. Now I must assess my own position, because I am not up for suicide. Several times I have decided to leave—I almost could except for the children, the poor bruised victims of adult lunacy. Who would care for them? Whose heart would be so staunch as to favor the reasonable thing in a sea of their tears and loneliness? Not mine, dear friend, not mine.[160]

Many, like Gwen Vendley, Jean's teacher at Maryknoll, have been drawn by this deep sense of loyalty and commitment in Jean: "She would fight for a person; that was probably what was most lovable about Jeannie. She really loved others and would go out on a limb for them."[161] The hungry and terrorized children of El Salvador were no exception.

Thus Dorothy and Jean stayed. When asked what kept them—and the rest of the team—from leaving as fear and bloodshed mounted all around them, Paul Schindler answered: "Of course, we often discussed the big question, 'What if. . . .' But," he added, "they just could not abandon the people."[162] And so Dorothy and Jean offered what relief and consolation they could to the victims of war in El Salvador, until they too became victims on the night of December 2, 1980.

9

Ita Ford and Maura Clarke

Maryknoll Missionaries

Most Americans have probably forgotten a minor protest that occurred at Smith College in the spring of 1983—if they were ever aware of it at all. Jeane Kirkpatrick, ambassador to the United Nations, had been asked to speak at the upcoming graduation and to accept an honorary degree. However, a debate was stirred up in the college paper and around the campus, and on an uncomfortably cold and windy day, a teach-in on the issue attracted 250 students. Why was there such a hostile reaction to the choice of Kirkpatrick for an honorary degree that spring? A glance at the roster of graduating seniors that year would answer the question. Miriam Ita Ford, twenty-one-year-old niece of the slain Maryknoll missionary, would also be at the graduation ceremony, and Miriam had not forgotten Kirkpatrick's callous rationale for the murder of her aunt and three other women in El Salvador. They were "political activists," the future ambassador had said, "we ought to be a little more clear on this than we actually are."

As Miriam explained to writer Michael Gallagher:

I was shocked when I heard about her getting an honorary degree. I felt it as a personal insult. Here it would be graduation, the last event of my life as a student at Smith, and this woman would be getting honored. It seemed to mock everything that my family and I stood for. . . .

The question we put to the trustees was where does morality come into politics. For it wasn't just what Mrs. Kirkpatrick said about my aunt and the other women but her whole outlook toward the rest of the world.

We felt that it was up to us who represented the future to stand up and say: "No, we don't want a person like this to be honored at a time when we're being honored."

Nevertheless, Kirkpatrick was awarded the degree *in absentia*, a trifling consolation for Ita's niece.[1]

Ita Ford

Ita, for whom Miriam had been named, was born on April 23, 1940, the second of three children of Mildred and William Ford. The family lived in a red-brick row house in Bay Ridge, Brooklyn, where, as her brother Bill described it, "most of the people were not very rich and not very poor."[2]

Not one to be tied to mother's apron strings for long, at the age of three, Ita ventured out alone—unknown to her mother—onto the busy streets of Brooklyn to "go to school" like older brother Billy. She wended her way down three city blocks, crossing two busy streets before she eventually approached a woman and asked her hopefully, "Is this school?" The woman reported the lost child to the police station, where Mildred Ford finally located Ita after searching the neighborhood for her little girl.[3]

As a youngster, Ita displayed considerable scholastic ability. She was a serious student but not one to become totally immersed in academic pursuits; in fact, when she graduated from Visitation Academy in Brooklyn in eighth grade, her well-rounded interests earned her the General Excellence Medal.[4] Ita went on to high school at Fontbonne Hall, a Catholic school in Brooklyn. It was at this time that her father, an insurance man, suffered a relapse of tuberculosis and had to retire. It was also during her high school years that Ita confided in a close friend her incipient dream of one day entering the Maryknoll order.[5] The Catholic Foreign Mission Society, popularly called Maryknoll, was well known to the Ford family, for William Ford's cousin, Maryknoll bishop Francis X. Ford, had died in a Chinese prison camp when Ita was twelve.[6]

After high school, Ita went on to Marymount Manhattan, a Catholic women's college that primarily served liberal arts students who commuted from the New York metropolitan area. There, Ita studied literature. Two of her close friends at Marymount were Kate Monahan and Ana May. Ita's biographer, Sister Judith Noone, describes the antics of these three classmates:

> In a cramped Volkswagen "bug," they ate hamburgers and french fries and laughed all the way across North America and down into Mexico. While staying at the least expensive and most interesting places along the way, they never hesitated to use the next door pool. Ita's "Peter Pan" shape and size and haircut puzzled the ticket seller at Disneyland, who admitted her as Ana May's son.[7]

In her senior year at Marymount, Ita acted on her early dreams of Maryknoll and finally sent in her application. Before her entrance into the order, however, an event occurred that confirmed Ita in this decision—a trip, along with other Marymount students, to the communist countries of Russia and Poland. She was touched by the depth of religious belief in some of the people she met and was profoundly disturbed that such sincerity of faith, which she had not witnessed in the United States and was not aware of even in herself, was stifled by those authoritarian East European societies. Ita wrote to her friend Jean Reardon:

For the first time in my life I am sure about what I want to do. You can't imagine what it was like being in Russia and feeling so impotent when people needed your help. A man next to me during a Russian Orthodox service cried during the whole Credo which the congregation chants. Religious barriers made no difference then—it no longer matters to whom one pledges allegiance, to the pope or patriarch—it was the idea that these people—the only ones I saw who really believed in God—not lip service offering as my own is—but a soul-wrenching belief—the ones who really deserved freedom of religion—they were the ones denied it. It was pathetic and nauseating at the same time. I wanted so much to do something and couldn't. It was this—more than anything else in my life—which has made me aware now, that I really have to go to Maryknoll. I couldn't ever stay away after being in Russia.[8]

In September 1961, Ita entered the Maryknoll Sisters' Motherhouse in Ossining, New York, located near the Hudson River about thirty miles north of the heart of Manhattan. Ita's first three years in the order were fraught with unexpected difficulties, and the fact that she persevered as a postulant and novice reveals the young woman's inner determination. At the time that Ita entered Maryknoll, close friendships with other aspiring nuns were discouraged as a hindrance to spiritual growth. Therefore, although her class of sixty shared the same life and the same rigid schedule day in and day out, Ita experienced an uncomfortable loneliness. But as she would often do in the future, Ita found an outlet for her thoughts in long letters. A literature major in college, Ita not only had an appreciation for creative writing, she also had the ability to express herself on paper honestly and descriptively—often with considerable humor. Moreover, her knack of creativity seemed to serve a two-fold purpose; besides offering a source of insight and entertainment to the reader, Ita often was able to work through some of her innermost thoughts and even some serious dilemmas by means of unburdening herself in letters. In a letter to her friend Jean, Ita touched on several of the nuisances—loneliness, boredom, and lack of challenge—she was encountering during her first weeks at Maryknoll:

As for the group around me, there are fifty-nine very different people. I know them all and not at all. For the next three years it's not allowed to recreate in two's and it's impossible to communicate mob-style. The ages range from eighteen to thirty-two; no one is very offensive and there are many affable ones . . . It's lonely. Not in the sense of being alone in a crowd but in an emotional way. No one knows you well enough to be able to say the right thing when you need it and as yet no one cares enough. I miss many people, some much more than others. This is sheer institution, because of the large group, and I hate this phase of it, to the point that when I thought I'd climb a wall I expected to see everyone else there too.

. . . My whole problem, one that's plagued me my whole life, is impatience. I expect to conquer everything in one try and with one look. You don't do that with a new life.

. . . School-wise the only thing new is Gregorian chant. I get very bored because most of the classes seem repetitious and ridiculous.

. . . Thursday night is confession night and every week I resist the impulse to go in and say, "Bless me, Father, I'm a saint." But tonight, as I was gabbing away, the priest said I could have the *New Yorker* after I've digested all of St. Paul's epistles to the point of application![9]

But later letters would reveal not that Ita had finally adapted to the "restrictions" of religious life, but instead that she had had a "dizzying"peek into the spiritual dimension that made the initial annoyances insignificant:

I'm not a fan of much of the symbolism attached to religious life. But there is a definite relationship to be established with God, and maybe with less sentiment it could be clearer. It's joy, it's peace. It's wonderful to be called. It's dizzying to know you're loved so. Just to have the knowledge of the love that exists, and the reality of the relationship you can have with God—something I am at a complete loss as to how to explain . . . to anyone who thinks this is a waste of time.

I guess I finally committed myself. I sort of realize I can only be myself by doing it. Even if it means being a mediocre clod, I've got to be one now, here. It's a little like the "Hound of Heaven"—you run right smack into God. And in the beginning it's elation. Then you realize what it means. It's good I don't know it all now, but only a little because it would be crushing—especially because I can no longer chuck it.[10]

By this time Ita and her classmates had moved to Maryknoll's East Coast Novitiate in Topsfield, Massachusetts, several miles north of Boston and not far from the Atlantic Ocean. Only a few months before the novices were to make their first vows, however, Ita began to experience frequent nausea and other stomach problems, which, in collaboration with another novice, she managed to conceal from her superiors for a while. When her illness was discovered, however, Ita's doctor and the Mother General concurred that she should not be "under the pressure of taking vows," as Ita put it, with the rest of her class.[11] Ita's former "elation" regarding her calling and spiritual growth was dashed. Almost three years of hope and perseverance seemed to end in a huge question mark. As Judith Noone describes Ita's reaction to this serious setback:

The next few months were difficult. Ita could not understand what happened or why. . . . She spent long hours listening to . . . piano recordings and talked as if puzzled about what had happened. But she was never bitter, only baffled and wounded.[12]

Ita did not nurse her wounds for long. Almost immediately she landed a job as an editor in the religion department of Sadlier Publishing Company, and embarked on a new, active, and productive phase of her life. For the next seven years the young woman edited English and religion textbooks. Her experiences at this time broadened her outlook considerably and immersed her in two of the major controversies of the turbulent sixties: the civil-rights issue and the Vietnam War. Along with many of her Catholic co-workers at Sadlier's, Ita would join in protests against the war and travel to Washington, D.C., to demonstrate for the civil rights of American blacks.[13]

Living and working in New York City, Ita was not far from the homes of her brother Bill and sister René, who were busy raising their young families, and thus she was able to form long-lasting, warm relationships with her little nieces and nephews. As Bill's daughter, Miriam Ita Ford, would later recall:

We were very close. . . . Before she became a nun, she was working for Sadlier as an editor of children books and she had this apartment in the Village. In some of the books she worked on, there're pictures of my brothers and sisters and me and my cousins.

I was tall for my age and she was small, and she could wear my clothes. I'd give her things. In some of those pictures in El Salvador she's wearing a shirt or something else of mine.[14]

Miriam's memories and those of other friends reveal another aspect of Ita's years as an unmarried career woman—simplicity. To Ita, friends and family were to be cherished, but not expensive clothes or furniture; Ita would have found today's yuppie lifestyle meaningless and boring. Although, according to Noone, "as an editor, Ita was highly respected and depended upon for her compassionate and critical mind," her need for authentic substance in her life caused her to look for it in directions beyond her career. The editor took courses in education at Hunter College in Manhattan, taught catechism to Puerto Rican junior high school students, and offered her time to read for the blind. Her social life was far from extravagant; she would meet friends for dinner, walk and chat with them in the Village, and once in a while purchase the cheapest tickets available for the opera or theater.[15]

Ita never totally relinquished her dreams of Maryknoll during her seven years in the professional world. She kept in touch with the friends she had made in the order, friends who had been allowed to make their vows when she had not. They wrote to her from Maryknoll missions halfway around the world and when they were in the United States would visit with Ita and stay at her apartment in the Village. A relationship also developed during this time between Ita and a Japanese-American lawyer and the two talked of marriage and a family. But even the unfortunate conclusion of those first three years as a Maryknoll novice was not painful enough to defeat a woman of Ita's determination, and she decided to try again.[16]

In 1971, ten years after she first entered the order as a postulant, Ita again began religious life with Maryknoll. This time, however, she found herself in a large family-style residence in St. Louis, Missouri, and there were many other changes as well. Now Ita's "class" consisted of two other career women and herself, and the post-Vatican II years permitted more flexibility in the women's schedule. Moreover, she found her courses at St. Louis University challenging, perhaps a bit more so than she had expected. As usual, she shared these thoughts with her old friend Jean:

> Sorry it has taken me so long to answer your notes, sabbatical year is a little busier than I had anticipated. Between Scripture courses at the divinity school and theology here at the house, work has been piling up. I'm at a slight disadvantage not knowing Greek, German, Hebrew, but I admire it on the pages. Greek is especially graceful!
>
> . . . After a month I can say I'm glad I'm here. It's strange to realize that I'm back again going toward what I want. And I may have a case of arrested development, but sometimes I feel as if I've been through it before. In a sense I feel like I'm back home. Of course it's different and I am too, and I expected that, but sometimes when praying or free-associating, I have the feeling that my heart is moving or being moved as it may have eight years ago. Either I'm very consistent or I'm still in the same place I was then.[17]

Because of her prior years in the Maryknoll novitiate at Topsfield, Ita was rather suddenly confronted with a decision, after only a few months in St. Louis, whether or not to make a "promise of fidelity" (similar to the old vows). She did not hesitate long before deciding to go through with it, and by August 1972 was on her way to language school in Cochabamba, Bolivia, in preparation for her first mission assignment in Chile. Five hours a day for six months, Ita studied conversational Spanish.[18] As talented as she was with the written word, Ita was not the most gifted speaker, debater, or storyteller. In fact, although she loved a lively discussion, she often seemed to "grope" for the perfect word, particularly if the topic at hand was an important one.[19] Learning to understand and be understood in a foreign language must have been rather difficult for her, but her desire to succeed and her sense of humor helped her through. As she wrote Jean: "I'm looking forward to the time when I get out of the one-word-at-a-time-with-a-big-pause-in-between-phase. At this stage, if the person listening to me hasn't forgotten what I started to say, I probably have."[20]

Six months of language school in Bolivia not only prepared Ita linguistically but also culturally and emotionally for some of the difficult moments that would be part of her experience in other Third World countries. She wrote home about some of Bolivia's problems—martial law, curfews, devaluation of currency, and suspension of civil rights—and she expressed surprise that when two unions in La Paz called a strike "out rolled the tanks."[21]

In March 1973, Ita, almost thirty-three years old, headed for Santiago,

Chile, and what she termed "a big leap into the unknown."[22] As it happened, she was about to witness one of the most significant political events in the history of that South American nation which, unknown to Ita, was on the brink of political upheaval.

For well over a century, Chile had avoided the domestic unrest which had so often plagued its neighboring countries—so much so that Marxist Salvador Allende Gossens was able to win the presidency in 1970. A mere three years later, however, his democratically elected government was overthrown by the military, Allende was murdered, and a rightist dictatorship came to power. How could Chilean democracy be toppled so easily? Historians Keen and Wasserman explain:

> In retrospect, the bounds of Chilean democracy were narrowly drawn; the elite never allowed political freedom and the practice of politics to endanger its basic interests. Instead of seeking to solve the nation's desperate economic and social problems, successive governments merely evaded them.

When the Allende government inaugurated structural reforms which seriously threatened the privileged position of the elite, evasion was no longer possible. The elite saw no acceptable alternative. It called on the army to destroy democratic government and replace it with a brutal dictatorship, one that would retain the status quo.[23]

What were some of Chile's unsolved economic problems? A major hindrance to progress was the fact that copper, Chile's primary export after World War I, was mined virtually exclusively by large North American corporations. Although Chile benefited from taxes on the copper industry, the lucrative profits went to the United States-based enterprises, and the copper industry itself offered little stimulus to the overall Chilean economy.

The foreign-owned copper industry also contributed indirectly to the inefficiency of Chilean agriculture. Because of the taxes it received from the mining of copper, the government managed to steer clear of taxation on large estates. Large tracts of land thus went unfarmed and a nation that could have fed its own population had to import food, which further contributed to the outflow of money from Chile.[24] Chilean agriculture remained backward and land remained concentrated in the hands of a few.

> By the 1960s, the 77 percent of Chilean farmers, who owned less than a hundred acres, held only 10.6 percent of the land, while the majority of the rural work force, over 700,000 people, were totally landless. Moreover, the average annual income of small farmers and farmhands was only $100.[25]

These then were the severe problems in Chile's economy and society that had fermented over the decades and remained unresolved in 1957 when the reform-minded Christian Democratic party was formed. Led by Eduardo Frei, this party attempted to follow a path between capitalism and socialism. In the election of 1958, the Conservative party candidate, Jorge Alessandri, won, but the Christian Democrats, and, surprisingly, a coalition of the left, headed by Salvador Allende, a socialist, emerged as important contenders. Alessandri, like his predecessors, was not able to make headway against Chile's overwhelming economic problems. It was during his presidency that the United States, alarmed by Castro's success in Cuba, began to support moderate reform candidates in Latin America in hopes of preventing revolution. With U. S. backing and with the support of conservatives who feared Allende and the socialists, Frei won the election of 1964.

Frei's attempts at reform solved few of Chile's problems: His plan to nationalize the copper industry benefited the foreign companies more than it did Chile. His agrarian program was hampered by inflation and by his own reluctance to implement fundamental land reform. Moreover, labor became increasingly disillusioned with Frei, and workers turned more and more to socialists and communists for leadership. By the 1970 presidential election, Frei's Christian Democratic party had fragmented. The vote was split between Allende (36 percent), rightist candidate Jorge Alessandri (35 percent), and Radomiro Tomic, the leader of the left wing of the Christian Democratic party (28 percent);[26] a total of 64 percent of the popular vote thus went to leftist candidates. The Chilean Congress named Allende as the winner and he became the first Marxist president ever constitutionally elected in the Western Hemisphere.[27]

Initially, Allende's programs were both successful and popular: worker income rose significantly; there was a marked decline in inflation; unemployment dropped; and advances were made in housing, education, sanitation, and health. By April 1971, Allende's Popular Unity party was able to claim almost 50 percent of the vote in local elections. But the triumph was short-lived. Copper prices declined; inflation became rampant; there were severe shortages of consumer goods. Allende's expropriation of large companies (both Chilean and foreign) made it impossible for Chile to obtain U.S. investment capital or loans from international banks under pressure from the United States. Allende's experiment with socialism did not benefit the majority of laborers who worked for small or medium-sized businesses, and they began, on their own, to seize factories and farms that the Allende government had left untouched. Such actions, combined with a worsening economy, frightened the middle class, who had initially cooperated with Allende, and turned it against his government.

By late 1972, chaos threatened Chile, but this crisis can by no means be blamed entirely on the shortcomings of Allende. Undoubtedly it was generated in part by Chilean capitalists working in unison with their North Amercan associates. Indeed, according to CIA Director William Colby, who testified before a U. S. Senate subcommittee, between 1962 and 1970 the CIA spent $11 million to undermine Allende's election bid. Moreover, after Allende became president, Secretary of State Henry Kissinger further authorized the CIA to spend $8 million to "destabilize" the Chilean economy.[28]

Allende's problems began in earnest in October 1972, when a truckers' strike, partially financed by the CIA, mushroomed into general sabotage of Chile's economy with the closing of most factories and shops. The strike finally ended when Allende agreed that generals would be included in his cabinet to maintain law and order. Congressional elections were scheduled for March 1973, the same month that Ita Ford arrived in Santiago, the capital city, to begin her missionary work. Although Allende's party received a relatively large share of the vote (44 percent), this did not enable him to control Congress; and he continued to face an opposition that was growing more threatening and more militant.

While Ita was trying to find her niche as a missionary in Chile, she was witnessing the disintegration of Allende's government. There was an attempted coup in June 1973, which was put down by troops loyal to Allende. But more and more of the military were turning against the president. Soldiers began a campaign to disarm factory workers with leftist sympathies, but made no attempt to control extremists on the right who were not only armed but organized into paramilitary squads.[29] A coup was imminent.

As she tried to fathom the problems of Chile and how she could be of service to the Chilean poor, Ita felt "confused and tired." She wrote a friend: "Some people say I couldn't have come at a more exciting time, while others say this is a terrible introduction. I guess that's indicative of what's going on."[30] After two months of "roaming," as Ita called it, she spent several weeks in Población Manuel Rodríguez, one of the numerous neighborhoods made up of squatters that surrounded the capital city; there she began to feel that work among the urban poor would be most satisfying to her. In late July 1973, Ita finally did settle down in a *población* outside of Santiago, called La Bandera. Ita moved in with three other Maryknoll sisters—Mary Tracy from Illinois, Connie Pospisil of New York City, and Carla Piette from Wisconsin.

She was only there a few weeks and had barely become acquainted with her colleagues and with her work when she received word that her father had died. Coincidentally, the phone call from Ita's brother Bill bearing the news of their father's death came only a day before the coup began in which Chile lost its democratically elected government and President Allende lost his life. On September 10, when Carla and an American missionary priest, totally unaware that a coup had begun, drove from La Bandera into Santiago to book a flight to New York for Ita, they were surprised and frightened to see tanks in the streets and fighter planes flying low overhead, and as quickly as possible they returned to La Bandera without Ita's plane ticket.[31]

For ten days after the overthrow of Allende, the four-man rightist junta led by General Augusto Pinochet tightened its grip on Chile by means of martial law, early curfews, and raids on the *poblaciones*. Undetermined thousands of professionals and laborers alike were arrested arbitrarily and thrown into detention camps; many were tortured and many simply disappeared, never to be seen by their families again. For Ita, the sight of the bombed- out presidential palace, the tanks, and the soldiers everywhere armed with machine guns was an intense strain. When civilians were finally allowed by the new regime to leave Chile, she was on board the first flight out on September 21; however, Ita was too late for her father's funeral.[32]

In spite of the turmoil she had seen in Chile, Ita returned to La Bandera after several weeks in New York to continue the work she had barely begun. In the years to come, Ita would see first-hand the effects of an unjust society on the poor. The terror that raged through Chile under Pinochet has been compared to that spawned in Nazi Germany: interrogation and torture by means of electric shock, solitary confinement, arbitrary arrests and military trials, neighborhood spy networks, censorship of the press and publications, and rigid control of dissent.[33] Yet, in spite of the suffering Ita witnessed, her own spirituality deepened and matured. She wondered if she was humble enough to learn from the "poor ones":

> Am I willing to suffer with the people here, the suffering of the powerless, the feeling impotent. Can I say to my neighbors—I have no solutions to this situation. I don't know the answers, but I will walk with you, search with you, be with you. Can I let myself be evangelized by this opportunity? Can I look at and accept my own poorness as I learn it from other poor ones?[34]

Her years in Chile were not spent on the verge of despair; rather her vision of Christian commitment to the poor expanded. In 1978, after over four years of life under the oppressive Pinochet regime, Ita tried to put these thoughts into words, while explaining why she had remained and would remain in Chile as long as she sensed it was "the right place to be":

> What is important to me is creating or building the kingdom [of God], trying to understand just what the future might be if there really were bread for all the people, if there really were justice. . . . It really seems more urgent in some parts of the world than in others. The kingdom is there and not there at the same time because in the middle of the oppression or the sinful structure, the reaction to that is the beginning of the kingdom. . . . There are a lot of things that are very uncomfortable about being there, but it is the right place to be. . . . I can't say it's my place for ever and ever. . . . It's not the most comfortable place in the world.[35]

Life among the poor in La Bandera, difficult enough before the coup, was even more challenging after the fall of Allende. It was not easy to become accustomed to the sound of gunshots reverberating in the streets once the

6 P.M. curfew began. And the sight of their neighbors being rounded up at dawn by soldiers with machine guns was a nightmare. While the Maryknoll nuns watched helplessly, men and teenage boys of La Bandera were forced into a field where troops detained anyone suspected of "subversion" against the regime; grounds for arrest in these round-ups included traffic violations or other minor offenses recorded within the past ten years. After these "fishing expeditions," as Ita called them, some of the detainees were eventually released, but many were not, and Ita and the other sisters grieved with the families of the jailed and missing. They struggled to find some meaning in the madness they witnessed. In a report sent to the Maryknoll sisters back in the United States, Ita tried to explain this apparent paradox:

> Until you experience it, or somehow make someone else's experience your own, it never is truly real. The only way you and your neighbors could face up to and overcome arbitrary "fishing expeditions" and organized terror is by being very concerned for each other and by having a deep faith—not in the judicial process or human justice—but in a God who cares for his people. Of course, experiences like this among the poor and the powerless run through the Old Testament and up to today's headlines. We are privileged to have shared this, to know and feel a little of the suffering of the powerless, of those without voice.[36]

For Ita, the hardship of life in Chile was eased by the close friendship that developed between her and another Maryknoll sister, Carla Piette, who was also a newcomer to La Bandera:

> Ita's passion for a clear and many-sided view of things left her open to receive and fairly evaluate a wide variety of opinions and attitudes—even Carla's abrasive ones which often irritated others. Carla's tendency to react impulsively was held in check by Ita's need to analyze, just as Ita's hesitancy to act until everything was clear was pushed along by Carla's need to move. . . . They both devoured books and loved discussing them, often long into the night when they were at their best and everyone else had gone to bed. . . . They were opposite and alike: Carla, outgoing, boisterous, argumentative, large in size and presence; Ita, retiring, unimposing, listening, petite—they made an incongruous pair. But what they shared most deeply was a seriousness about life which touched humor and felt pain, and was impatient with anything less than the truth or contrary to the kingdom of God. In common, too, was a love for the people of La Bandera.[37]

Sometimes militaristic terror came quite close to home for Carla and Ita; the house of the Maryknoll missionaries themselves was rudely and thoroughly searched at least three times by the army, the air force, and the security police.

But it was the third time that was the most frightening for the women, for hidden away on a closet shelf were some textbooks on Marxism. The books had followed a rather circuitous route to the nuns' closet: They had originally belonged to a priest in the neighborhood who was teaching a political science course on Marxism at the Catholic University when the coup occurred. Not knowing what else to do with the texts, he had buried them in his yard before he was forced to leave Chile. The people who moved into the house eventually became fearful that the books would be discovered and asked the sisters for advice. The Maryknoll nuns took the texts; but instead of destroying the expensive books, they decided to hide them in a suitcase, a decision which Sister Connie Pospisil later acknowledged was "crazy," since to possess reading material on Marxism was considered a crime against the state.

When six plainclothes detectives barged in one day, three of them forced the missionaries who were present—Ita, Carla, and Mary Tracy—up against the wall and held them at gunpoint, while the others proceeded to conduct a disorderly search of the premises. When the policemen found a book they thought looked suspicious (not one of the hidden textbooks), Ita answered— truthfully—that it was a work written by a Catholic theologian outlining the inherent evil of Marxism. "My mother sent it to us," she explained in a shaky voice, a comment which for some reason perversely amused Carla. As the panic-stricken women watched, the policemen got dangerously close to the "subversive" textbooks, even emptying out a suitcase full of clothes that was directly in front of the one that contained the texts. The six men finally left, taking the book—Mrs. Ford's gift—with them.[38]

Although they had been spared, it should not therefore be assumed that the nuns were immune to arrest or torture simply because they were religious or because they were foreigners. A priest in their neighborhood was arrested in 1974; Ita describes the incident in a letter to her old friend Jean Reardon Baumann and her husband John:

Last week arms were planted in the tabernacle in a small chapel in the same section of Santiago as we are. The priest was taken on the charge of aiding the extremists. So it continues, but the Church is taking a stand. Within a day and a half a [bishop's] pastoral letter was sent out, denouncing the whole incident as a put-up.

The tension between Church and State helps keep us all honest. You have to make decisions, even though they won't be popular and can easily be twisted. . . . [39]

An even more brutal incident, one which became internationally known, was the ordeal of a young British citizen, a medical doctor named Sheila Cassidy. In 1975, while working in a clinic in the city of Santiago, Dr. Cassidy met and befriended Carla and Ita. Every week for six months the three women would gather together for an afternoon of prayer and reflection either at

Sheila's house or the sisters' home in La Bandera. But the sequence of peaceful afternoons was shattered abruptly when Sheila was arrested on October 29, 1976, by the Chilean secret police. Because she had given medical treatment to an opponent of Pinochet's regime, Dr. Cassidy was stripped, questioned, tortured, and held incommunicado for several days. International pressure, however, forced authorities to reveal her whereabouts. Eventually, Ita and Carla were allowed to visit their friend in a detention camp where she was being held along with hundreds of other political prisoners.* The two sisters brought her books and some treats, and also smuggled in the Eucharist for her.[40]

The repression of Chilean society was so pervasive after the overthrow of Allende that the Catholic church became virtually the only outspoken critic of the authoritarian junta.[41] Not long after the September 1973 coup, the ecumenical Committee of Cooperation for Peace was founded by Protestant, Jewish, and Catholic leaders. Its daring goal was to locate and defend the thousands of political prisoners who were either in detention camps or had disappeared. The Pinochet government soon dissolved this committee, however, expelling its Lutheran co-chairman, Bishop Helmut Frenz, from Chile.[42] Cardinal Raul Silva of Santiago then founded another one under the protective auspices of the Catholic church. This "Vicariate of Solidarity" continued aiding prisoners and their families and also began a comprehensive nutrition program. The food program was initiated to help the 60 percent of Santiago's children who were severely malnourished, but when adults and teenagers, faint with hunger, showed up with the children, the program was expanded to include them. The distribution of free lunches was a criticism in itself of Pinochet's economic policies, which had driven unemployment up drastically and had "pushed large numbers of Chileans to or over the edge of starvation."[43] Consequently, the storekeepers and housewives involved in the food distribution were harassed and threatened by police inspectors. Carla and Ita, who lived in one of the many slums that ringed Santiago, quite naturally became involved in the church's lunch program, and every week they sought donations for the five free lunch centers in their locality.[44]

Before a Maryknoll nun can make her final vows, she must leave her mission post to observe a "reflection year." Ita was to depart for Maryknoll, New York, in late 1977, but managed to have her year of reflection postponed. Her decision to wait a year certainly was not the result of inner turmoil over her vocation; on the contrary, as she mentioned in a letter to her friend Jean, a year seemed "a very long time to reflect about something I am already convinced of."[45] Actually, her desire to stay in La Bandera grew from her commitment to the poor of Chile for whom study and meditation was an unheard-of luxury; moreover, Ita worried that her friend Carla—always impulsive and

---

*Dr. Sheila Cassidy was later released from prison in Chile due to the international attention her case drew and has since written an account of her spiritual commitment, *Audacity to Believe* (Cleveland: Collins/World, 1978).

outspoken—might get into trouble with authorities without Ita there to keep her in check.

By the time Ita did return to Maryknoll the next year, however, she was clearly in need of a lengthy respite from the hardship of life among the Chilean poor. She herself may not have been aware of this; but friends, family, and her spiritual adviser detected the symptoms of a vague malaise almost immediately. This "gentle and vivacious" woman, as her brother Bill described her,[46] returned to New York critical, angry, and physically and emotionally exhausted after five years in a Third World slum.

Her mother Mildred, in a letter to Judith Noone, relates some of the difficulties of Ita's reunion with her family:

> We all went to meet her at the airport and I had lots of food that she especially liked. We all talked and ate but Ita didn't talk all that much and ate only bread. I'm sure the variety and quantity seemed extravagant. For some weeks she was depressed and we all were questioned as to why we discarded bottles and wasted food.[47]

Ita's behavior was not unusual at all for a missionary returning from a poor country to one of the richest nations on earth. Father Guadalupe Carney, before age tempered his tongue a bit, managed to offend nearly his entire family on his visits from Honduras; even jovial Brother James Miller could not restrain himself from lecturing his high school students on their laziness in learning and lack of gratitude for educational opportunity. Indeed, for a missionary *not* to react with a certain righteous indignation at real or perceived waste and luxury would have been unusual.

At first, during her year of reflection at Maryknoll, Ita found prayer virtually impossible; her spiritual frustration was complicated by her intense desire to hop on a plane for Santiago to escape the United States, where so many seemed totally unconcerned about the misery in Chile that Ita could not forget. Eventually, however, she asked Fr. John Patrick Meehan for spiritual counseling. As Meehan recalls:

> From the first she was very open and honest about herself. . . . She found prayer cold, empty, dark and useless but kept trying. In what proved to be a short time the Spirit began to touch her in many evident ways . . . ; she was suddenly flooded with the kind of joy and love that can only be a gift. From that point on she began to experience true contemplative prayer and the peace, love and joy that accompany it.[48]

Ita by then was a far cry from the "seething volcano"[49]—to use the words of her friend Sister Rachel Lauze—who had arrived at Maryknoll haunted by the ignorance she perceived in her own country toward the needs of the Third World poor.

Her reflection year over, Ita spent some time during May 1979 making a retreat in Watch Hill on the Rhode Island shore and from there headed for Massachusetts with three friends for a short vacation before returning to Chile. On the highway just outside of Watch Hill, a freakish hit-and-run accident occurred in which Ita alone was injured. It was nighttime, and none of the four saw exactly what happened, but they believe that the car which hit theirs had been traveling toward them when it inexplicably swerved sharply and rammed the left rear door where Ita was sitting. So instead of departing for Chile, Ita found herself recovering in a Rhode Island hospital from a broken pelvis and torn knee.

Ita's attitude during the long weeks of convalescence in the hospital and at the Watch Hill retreat house surprised many—particularly her spiritual adviser Father Meehan, who fully expected that the accident would cause a relapse of depression. Instead Ita was cheerful and exercised persistently to hurry along the day when she would be able to return to her work and friends in Chile.[50]

While Ita was recuperating during the summer of 1979, the explosive events occurring in Central America began to capture her thoughts. She had been aware of the struggle in Nicaragua against the repression of Somoza and his National Guard, and when the conflict heightened in the late spring of 1979, Ita and others worried about the safety of the Maryknoll sisters who were running a refugee center in León, a town in the midst of the fighting. They were relieved in July 1979 when the war ended as the dictator Somoza fled the country. Ita admired the nuns who remained there to help the people while civil war raged around them; one of those sisters, Julie Miller, had been a close friend of Ita's for eighteen years. The tiny country of El Salvador was also increasingly in the news; and one voice was consistently heard beyond its borders speaking out for the poor in a way that Ita, already deeply affected by her years of work in Chile, found irresistible. The man with the charismatic words was, of course, Oscar Romero, the archbishop of San Salvador, and he was appealing to religious personnel in North America to come help his people. Ita began to consider working in El Salvador as a possible future for herself.

But Ita kept her thoughts to herself as she prepared to return to Chile in the fall of 1979. She decided she would stop off on the way in Nicaragua to visit her friend Julie and the other Maryknoll nuns there. By November, Ita's doctor pronounced her healthy and fit—she was walking without even a trace of a limp, but he jokingly advised her "to avoid countries where she might have to run."[51] Before she left the United States, Ita finally mentioned to Julie by telephone that she was thinking about volunteering for El Salvador; Julie reacted with dismay: "No, not you, Ita. Not El Salvador after the Chile coup and now this accident."[52]

After discussing El Salvador at length with Julie while in Nicaragua and with every Maryknoll nun she knew in Chile, and after scrupulously examining her own motives for wanting to work in that Central American country, Ita finally made her decision. From Chile, she attempted to break the news gently to her mother in a letter:

The last week or two have been spent mostly letting the El Salvador possibility roll around inside me. I went to the new house of prayer and what I came to and feel good with is the decision to go. I realize this isn't the greatest news I've ever given you and, in fact, one of the cons was that the family would not be overjoyed, but I think it's a good decision.

And to ease the blow, Ita cheerfully observed, "I'll also be a continent nearer!"[53]

It is impossible to know exactly why Ita was drawn to El Salvador, a sorrowful country whose people were victimized by land shortage, hunger, and political injustice and who were terrorized by the National Guard, the Treasury Police, the army, and paramilitary death squads. Obviously, her five years in Chile had not been a romantic or transitory interlude in her life, but had strengthened Ita's character and commitment. There she had grown in determination and in the knowledge that she herself could eliminate some of the misery, if only on a small scale. The courage of Romero and the example of the Maryknoll sisters who had stayed in Nicaragua despite real physical danger to themselves during the recent civil war were inspirational, but Ita's spirit had already been prepared for the challenge.

While Ita was agonizing over her decision, her friend Carla was acting with typical impulsiveness. She had left Chile for Nicaragua to help the people rebuild after the civil war, and while there made a trip to look over the situation in El Salvador. Almost immediately she decided that El Salvador would be her new home:

I like this place with its spunky people. If this country had had the democratic government that Chile had for so long, El Salvador would be the most developed country in the world. I've never seen such an energetic crowd. Even road gangs really work. I call them little ants, always on the run, selling things or fixing their houses or cleaning. I can't keep up with them. But given their history and the people who have had the power, they just make ends meet and now the top is about to blow off—and with reason.[54]

So it happened that Carla and Ita would be working together again in "this concentrated little bouillon cube of a country," as Carla dubbed the densely populated tropical land.[55]

Carla arrived in El Salvador first in March 1980 while Ita was still in Chile. It was an ominous introduction for her to the violence that would now be an inescapable aspect of her life: on the evening of March 24, a few minutes after Carla descended the bus from Nicaragua, Oscar Romero was gunned down in San Salvador. Carla and Maryknoll sisters Madeline Dorsey and Joan Petrik heard the news a couple of hours later when they arrived at Madeline's clinic in a barrio outside of Santa Ana. For the next week Carla found herself standing "unworthily," as she put it, in the honor guard, watching the people file by the casket of their beloved archbishop in the cathedral.[56] Then, at Romero's funeral on March 30, Carla was one of thousands of terrified spectators, including international dignitaries, to witness the panic that broke out when bombs and gunfire erupted in the plaza outside the cathedral.

By this time Ita was in Nicaragua waiting to leave for El Salvador. With the death of Romero, what excitement she might have felt about her future work there deteriorated into "free-floating anxiety," as she admitted in a letter to a friend, but, she continued, " . . . with fear and faith we'll get on the bus tomorrow for El Salvador."[57] With her mother Ita was honest, though she did not dwell on her apprehension:

> I don't even know how to begin this letter, how to react to the last week and a half. The Archbishop's death started a continental examination of conscience about how each local Church was or wasn't being faithful to the Gospel. . . .
>
> For myself, I have all sorts of reactions—from feeling robbed of not having had the opportunity to know Monseñor Romero to horror at the paranoia and fear of the right and their brutality, to wonder at the Gospel message and the impact for acceptance or rejection that it has on people, to feeling with the poor of Salvador and their loss of someone who they knew cared for them. But we believe that his death will bear fruit and it's part of the Christian mystery we celebrate this week [Holy Week], and in that same Christian tradition, we'll go to El Salvador.[58]

In El Salvador, after several weeks of getting acquainted with the Salvadoran countryside and people, Carla and Ita finally decided to work in the northern department of Chalatenango. It was not a decision they made lightly: Chalatenango, with a population of about 200,000, was a province of landless or nearly landless *campesinos*. Landlessness had increased dramatically throughout El Salvador—12 percent of rural families had no land in 1961 compared to 29 percent in 1971 and 41 percent in 1975. As successive Salvadoran regimes and the oligarchy dragged the tiny country closer to chaos by refusing to alleviate the desperate need of their people for agrarian reform, guerrilla organizations won the support of many peasants; a bitter commentary on their hopeless situation was a popular saying of the rural poor, "Better to die of a bullet than die of hunger."[59] By early 1980, the popularity of guerrilla groups in troubled Chalatenango had drawn the attention of the Salvadoran military to this province. In May of that year, while Ita and Carla were considering the possibility of offering their services to the people there, the Salvadoran high command declared Chalatenango a "military emergency zone." The province thus became the object of military "clean-up" sweeps that terrorized peasants in the villages and countryside while trying to root out the guerrillas. Anyone, including women, children, infants, and elderly men, was a potential target in these operations. Those who were sought out in particular were leaders of cooperatives, teachers, and catechists who were active in the Christian base communities. The army was aided in these expeditions by the Guardia Nacional and by members of ORDEN, a paramilitary organization and rural spy network. Headed by former army officers, ORDEN's ranks included many peasants who collaborated with those in power for various reasons—to obtain a job, to plunder the homes of other peasants, or simply for personal security in a violent country. Members of ORDEN were not paid salaries, but of course were allowed to carry weapons.[60]

Perhaps a brief description of one particular event that occurred on the Chalatenango-Honduras border will clarify the degree of human misery caused by military sweeps through the countryside. In August 1980, Sister of Mercy Betty Campbell and Carmelite priest Peter Hinde interviewed several of the survivors of the "Río Sumpul Massacre," which had taken place in May:

> The story had begun for some in January when they were chased from Las Flores and other towns and villages of Chalatenango. . . . Combined units of army, police, National Guard, and paramilitary swept towns and villages, at times making selective captures and executions, at times wiping out entire villages, burning homes, robbing or destroying stores of grain, clothing and animals. People trying to flee through fields, that had been set on fire were shot down. In Las Flores four girls were burned alive in their home.
>
> . . . They joined up with some five hundred other displaced persons, settled on the narrow flats of Las Aradas, and immediately proceeded to start a new life building shelters and planting crops. All went well until the morning of May 14, when a combined force of Salvadoran soldiers, National Guard and paramilitary herded an additional four hundred people into the area, then took up positions to keep all of them trapped at the river bank.
>
> About ten in the morning, the troops on the ground and helicopters overhead began to shoot. People ran desperately in all directions as they saw friends and family members collapse under the hail of bullets. . . . Some tried to escape upstream, others plunged into the river where the rushing waters carried off the wounded or the smaller people. Honduran soldiers waiting on the other bank, obviously summoned there by prearrangement, drove back those who succeeded in crossing.
>
> Some two hundred people . . . got ashore on the Honduran side at points not guarded by the Honduran military. . . . [These survivors told Betty and Peter] "We thought we saw cattle lined up at one point, until we saw them fall over and heard the gunfire. Then we realized they were women bent over, some of them women bent over their children."
>
> . . . The Salvadoran soldiers shouted to [those who escaped] to come back, then began to threaten, and finally they grabbed young children and tossed them in the water. The violence rapidly escalated with its obscene logic, so that soldiers actually threw infants into the air to impale

them on machetes or shoot them as for target practice. . . .

It was August when we took these testimonies, two and a half months after the massacre, and as yet not a single United States reporter had come to verify the facts, said the refugee workers.[61]

Clergy of the diocese of Santa Rosa de Copán in Honduras visited the site of the massacre the next day, and estimated there were at least six hundred corpses on the river banks and in the nearby fields.[62]

This hideous event occurred in May, the same month that Carla and Ita made up their minds to work in that troubled province. Whether or not they knew of the massacre at that time, they did realize that their work in Chalatenango would indeed be a challenge. Religious workers there were honest with the two newcomers, telling them that they would primarily be aiding refugees—Salvadorans who had fled from the villages to the hills in the wake of army sweeps. These refugees needed food and medicine, which Carla and Ita would try to provide. But to aid such refugees was considered "subversive" by the governing regime. In fact, traveling through the province of Chalatenango itself was dangerous; on their return from one of their first visits there, Carla and Ita were stopped by soldiers with machine guns at a roadblock and were "really treated rough in words and deeds," as Carla described it to a friend.[63]

An initial frustration for Carla and Ita was trying to obtain the necessary food and medicine from relief agencies that would not or could not send humanitarian aid because the Salvadoran civil war was undeclared. Ita wrote to her sister René:

There are a lot of bizarre things that go on in this country including "help" from Uncle Sam. It's pathetic that there's millions for army equipment but nothing for humanitarian help until war is declared. Carla keeps asking, "How many dead make a war? What's the magic number?"[64]

But Carla and Ita were not only aiding the victims of army and right-wing repression. They were also available to help a second type of rural refugee—the *campesino* who was fleeing the guerrilla groups. On one occasion, Ita explicitly wrote of the suffering, fear, and distrust experienced by those who had had to flee either the right-wing security forces of the government or the left-wing popular forces.[65] At another time, she listed the responsibilities that she and Carla had undertaken; item number three indicates that they were driving food supplies to refugees hiding from both government and guerrilla forces.[66]

It should be mentioned here, however, that various groups which monitor human rights in El Salvador determined that most murders (well over 80 percent) were committed by right-wing forces. On this subject, Berryman writes: "In . . . El Salvador . . . the official troops as de facto policy have engaged in massive kidnapping, torture, rape, murder, and mutilation of individuals, and indiscriminate large-scale military attacks on whole towns and villages."[67] Carla and Ita's work, then, generally did entail obtaining food, medicine, transportation and shelter for *campesinos* fleeing government forces, for the obvious reason that there were far more of them than there were victims of the guerrillas.

The letters and reports written by Carla and Ita during June and July 1980, the first two months of their new ministry in Chalatenango, are a mixture of matter-of-fact observations, poignant pleas for understanding and support, and expressions of horror at the suffering of the people they helped. In this respect, their correspondence would be similar to that of any compassionate eyewitness, for instance, a nurse or a journalist. But there is an additional element in the letters of those two friends which reveals their source of hope and perseverance. To analyze their work in El Salvador as an heroic political commitment is to overlook the significance of the spiritual dimension in their lives. A few excerpts from their correspondence during the violent summer of 1980 reveal the depth of a faith that went beyond a reliance on human law and justice. Carla wrote a friend:

> . . . As the repression and genocide continue, it becomes harder and harder to do pastoral work. So what do I do? I drive people places—like other Sisters who are more and more afraid to stay in the isolated parts of the country areas—I drive *Caritas* food to refugees of which there are 2000 families in the Department of Chalatenango. . . . I have come to appreciate what Jesus means when he says, "I am the Way." The way here is daily changing as one tries to respond to this genocidal situation. In one parish where there are no longer any priests or Sisters because of the situation, there were forty-two adult catechists—all forty-two have been brutally murdered. No one wants to be a catechist anymore since it usually means your life and yet we try to attend to these remote parts of the country. . . . It's so hard to see the suffering—and harder yet to know that what you do helps so little. I believe in the Lord of the impossible.[68]

And Ita metaphorically described her work with refugees:

> I don't know if it is in spite of or because of the horror, terror, evil, confusion, lawlessness—but I do know that it is right to be here. To believe that we are gifted in and for Salvador now, that the answers to the questions will come when they are needed, to walk in faith, one day at a time, with the Salvadorans along a road filled with obstacles, detours, and sometimes washouts.[69]

In a joint letter to several Maryknoll sisters, Carla and Ita wrote:

> We have learned a total dependence and trust in God, a deepening of our commitment and availability . . . ; [the Salvadoran experience] had been

an opportunity to know the situation of repression and all its consequences; an exercise in humility and faith . . . ; an awareness of ability to
adapt to incredible situations.[70]

Her faith revealed to Ita some of the secrets of the "deep meaning" of life,
insights that she shared in a birthday letter to her teenaged niece Jennifer:

> I want to say something to you, and I wish I were there to talk to you
> because sometimes letters don't get across all the meaning and feeling.
> But I'll give it a try anyway.
>
> First of all, I love you and care about you and how you are. I'm sure
> you know that. And that holds if you're an angel or a goof-off, a genius
> or a jerk. A lot of that is up to you and what you decide to do with your
> life.
>
> What I want to say, some of it isn't too jolly birthday talk, but it's real.
> Yesterday I stood looking down at a sixteen-year-old who had been killed
> a few hours earlier. I know a lot of kids even younger who are dead. This
> is a terrible time in El Salvador for youth. A lot of idealism and commit-
> ment are getting snuffed out here now.
>
> The reasons why so many people are being killed are quite compli-
> cated, yet there are some clear, simple strands. One is that many people
> have found a meaning to live, to sacrifice, to struggle and even die. And
> whether their life spans sixteen years, sixty or ninety, for them their life
> has had a purpose. In many ways, they are fortunate people.
>
> Brooklyn is not passing through the drama of El Salvador, but some
> things hold true wherever one is, and at whatever age. What I'm saying is
> that I hope you can come to find that which gives life a deep meaning for
> you, something that energizes you, enthuses you, enables you to keep
> moving ahead.
>
> I can't tell you what it might be. That's for you to find, to choose, to
> love. I can just encourage you to start looking and support you in the
> search.
>
> Maybe this sounds weird and off the wall, and maybe no one else will
> talk to you like this, but then, too, I'm seeing and living things that others
> around you aren't. I hope this doesn't sound like some kind of a sermon
> because I don't mean it that way. Rather, it's something that you learn
> here and I want to share it with you. In fact, it's my birthday present to
> you. If it doesn't make sense right at this moment, keep this and read it
> some time from now. Maybe it will be clearer. Or ask me about it, OK?[71]

The team of Carla and Ita only worked together in Chalatenango for three
short months before they themselves were hit directly by a tragedy which,
ironically, took the form of a "washout."

As has been mentioned previously, one of their tasks in Chalatenango was to
transport refugees to places of safety and bring them food. On the evening of

August 23, Ita and Carla found themselves faced with an urgent problem: a prisoner had just been released to Ita by the colonel in the town of Chalatenango, and when she brought him to a temporary refugee shelter in the town, the other refugees there whispered to Ita that they did not trust the man because he had betrayed some of their neighbors. The Maryknoll sisters decided that he must be moved to his own home immediately for everyone's safety. Although it was a dark, menacing evening and Carla and Ita knew they would have to cross the meandering El Zapote River five times, they ventured out in their jeep with the refugee and two seminarians. Soon a heavy rain began and the river started to swell. After crossing it four times safely, Carla, who was driving, became fearful and refused to go on; Ita told the refugee he would have to walk the rest of the way. Carla turned the jeep around and started back to Chalatenango but in the five minutes that had elapsed, El Zapote had become a dangerous torrent. When they tried to cross it, the jeep was swept out of Carla's control. The seminarians managed to escape and tried to help Ita and Carla get out, but the rushing water turned the jeep on its side with the two women trapped in the front seat. As the jeep filled with water, Carla pushed Ita through the open window. Ita was swept downstream; her lungs filled with water and she was cut and battered by rocks. As she later told her mother in a tape, she at first resigned herself to death, but then was driven to save herself by an inner voice that urged her on: "The Lord has saved you to continue serving the poor and you've got to get out of this river." Suddenly, Ita saw some tree roots and grabbed hold of them; an hour or so later, exhausted, she managed to pull herself onto the river bank, where she was found the next morning by a search party. It was not until much later that day that Ita learned Carla's body had been found, washed up on a sand bar.[72] When death seemed imminent for both of them, Carla kept a promise she had made somewhat humorously to Mrs. Ford just two weeks before:

> I admit I do try to protect Ita although she doesn't like that. As far as risk goes, I never invite her to accompany me in a risky thing. In this insane situation who's to know what is risky and actually all we're doing is very humanitarian.
>
> There is a certain amount of freedom for me since contact with my family is so minimal. I always say to Ita that if anything happens to me, she has only to advise Maryknoll, but should she be harmed, I dread having to advise the Ford Foundation.[73]

After Carla's death, Ita suffered "the guilt of the survivor,"[74] as her brother Bill put it; in fact, her despondency over her friend's death would last right up until a day or two before she herself was murdered. It was only then that Ita's "elfin grin and buoyant personality" would return.

In the meantime, though, Ita not only insisted upon remaining in El Salvador but in Chalatenango. When asked whether she was fearful of another accident, or of the possibility of being captured and tortured, she answered,

"But the agony ends. It is over for Carla and we must keep working."[75]

When it became obvious to everyone that Ita simply would not give up the refugee work she had begun with Carla, another Maryknoll nun—who had been in El Salvador only one month—volunteered to help Ita in Chalatenango. Her name was Sister Maura Clarke.

•

Maura Clarke was born in New York City on January 13, 1931, the first child of John and Mary McCloskey Clarke. Although she was baptized Mary Elizabeth, her Irish-born parents Gaelicized her name and affectionately called her Maura. The Clarkes had two more children, Bud and Judy, and the close-knit family moved from Brooklyn to Rockaway Beach in Queens when the children were still young. Because Rockaway is a popular summer resort area for the urban dwellers of New York, rents began to rise more and more each year with the approach of hot weather. The Clarke family could not afford the escalating prices, so they would often move away in the summer, only to return in the fall when the rent was again more reasonable.[76]

Like most Irish immigrants in New York City, the Clarkes were willing to struggle and sacrificed many luxuries so they could give their children a Catholic education. Maura attended Saint Francis de Sales Elementary and Stella Maris High School, where she applied herself diligently to her studies and received good grades. She made friends easily and in high school participated in several extracurricular activities including the yearbook, Sodality, Glee Club, and Mission Circle.[77]

Maura entered Saint Joseph College for Women, a small liberal arts college in Brooklyn conducted by the Sisters of Saint Joseph, where she majored in elementary education. During her freshman year, she began to think about becoming a nun. She talked it over with her mother and decided on Maryknoll. After receiving her acceptance, she left Saint Joseph College and took a job at Saks Fifth Avenue, hoping to earn enough to pay her own way at Maryknoll. "Typically, though," comments Sister Judith Noone, she did not save a dime but took her salary home in the form of presents for her parents and Judy and Bud."[78] This reckless, Saint Francis-like generosity was a trait that would always remain an endearing quality of Maura's. As Sister Margarita Jamias, who worked with her in both Nicaragua and the United States, notes:

> She was outstanding in her generosity. She would give whatever she had to the poor. She was accustomed to living in poverty. We were laughing the other day remembering how in Nicaragua she was always drawing advances on her monthly allowance (about $15), because as soon as she got it, she gave it away.[79]

Kay Kelly, who was working at the time in the countryside outside of Siuna, Nicaragua, but would return to the town at the end of each week for a few days, remembers once confronting Maura with being an easy mark:

Maura Clarke

Maura could never say NO to anyone so there was a constant line at the door asking her for money. She would give her whole allowance. One day . . . our cook told me that those who came would tell their friends that Maura was a soft touch. I remember telling Maura this and her being so angry with me because, as she said, "You're not here every day and don't have to answer the door and tell the people 'I don't have money' when you know we have it."[80]

In one of her last letters to her parents from El Salvador she asked for a pair of shoes—the one pair she had owned she had given away to a poor peasant woman. Sister Peggy Healy, the Maryknoller who delivered the new shoes from Mr. and Mrs. Clarke when she went to El Salvador after a visit to the United States commented after Maura's death: "I don't think Maura knew how to say no. She just didn't know how to keep people waiting."[81]

In September 1950 Maura entered the Maryknoll novitiate near Ossining, New York. Her parents, both in their mid-eighties when she died, told journalist Jimmy Breslin, on the day of her funeral that they could still remember the time she left for the convent as if it were yesterday. It was a beautiful, sunny day and Maura, true to her Irish heritage, was dressed in a pretty green suit. Her parents drove her up the Hudson River to Maryknoll, accompanied by several cars filled with her friends. Mrs. Clarke recalls telling Maura "that if she couldn't last it out and become a nun, she shouldn't be discouraged. She should come right back to me and become a teacher."[82]

Maura, of course, did "last it out" and in the spring of 1954 received her bachelor's degree from Maryknoll Teachers' College. She hoped to be assigned to the African missions, but was only slightly disappointed when she was sent to teach first grade at Saint Anthony of Padua School in the Bronx. Although the Bronx lacked the romance of far-away places, its impoverished black and Puerto Rican students could certainly use her teaching skills; besides, her new assignment was not far from Rockaway Beach, so Maura would be able to see her parents, brother, and sister often. Teaching first graders at Saint Anthony's was no "soft job." The school, located in a ghetto with one of the highest unemployment and crime rates in all of New York City, provided a beacon of hope for its students. It also served to acquaint Maura with the dismal results of poverty. As Judy Noone depicts the harsh environment:

Beyond the red brick walls, drugs, prostitution, related crimes and the accompanying violence—though camouflaged by day—raged undisguised at night.

The sounds of shattering glass, screeching tires, drunken cries, a shot in the night were so common that a certain insensitivity towards tragedy seemed to hang in the air. Maura never grew accustomed to hearing the children's stories about theirs mothers being beaten, their fathers slashed, their brothers shot, their sisters raped. At first she was incredulous and then saddened when she realized how many women had children by several men, and saw how many children were apparently deprived of the love with which she had been lavished.

"Sista," a surprisingly obstinate little boy called out in class one day, "if God's a father, Sista, I don't want nothing to do with Him and I sure don't want Him messing around with me!"[83]

In late 1959, after five years at Saint Anthony's, Maura received a new assignment—her first foreign one; she was to teach grade school in Siuna, Nicaragua, a small gold-mining town near the east coast. Another Maryknoll sister, Kay Kelly from Chicago, was also assigned to Siuna; before long the two would become best friends and would remain so for life.[84]

At that time, however, like most U.S. residents, neither of the nuns was even capable of pointing Nicaragua out on a map.[85] Nevertheless, on October 9, the two enthusiastic—if somewhat nervous—young women bid farewell to Maura's parents at the airport. Kay remembers that while they waited for the arrival of their plane, an airline pilot, recognizing their religious habit, introduced himself as the father of a Maryknoll nun they both knew. As they prepared to board, the pilot turned to Mr. and Mrs. Clarke and said: "Thank you for giving your daughter to Maryknoll." These words came back to haunt Kay after Maura's murder: "Little did we realize the extent of the 'giving'," she later thought to herself.[86]

The two nuns were quite apprehensive about their lack of language skills. Maura had had one semester of college Spanish and Kay only two years in high school—but over ten years earlier. Since Maura's limited knowledge did include the Lord's Prayer and Hail Mary, she spent considerable time on the plane ride teaching them to Kay. Both women were relieved to find out upon reaching Nicaragua that after a month or two in Siuna they would be sent to language school in Guatemala for a few months.

Upon arriving at their mission home the two newcomers were delighted to be greeted not only by all the Maryknollers but by the school's fife and drum marching band as well. Indeed, the welcome made it a day to remember for Sister Kay and Sister Maura. Siuna was a small town of about five thousand inhabitants near a similar pueblo, La Luz, where a Canadian multinational company operated a gold mine. Both places provided laborers for the mines. Siuna was situated in a depression surrounded by mountainous jungle thick with green vegetation; to Maura and Kay, both from large urban areas, it was a wondrous and beautiful sight. Kay once mentioned this to a student only to be startled and enlightened by her very different view: "We're trapped in a hole and there's no way out."[87] In fact, for most of the poor this was certainly true, for there were no roads to Siuna; the town was only accessible by plane or by a long, arduous horseback ride through the jungle. The plane trip took about forty-five minutes from Managua and Kay recalls that at times that flight could be terrifying:

When the plane hit air pockets, it was really scary. I remember us going over on one occasion, when it was really turbulent. Maura and I were hanging on to each other and praying like mad. Meanwhile we tried to reassure the passengers as they looked to us for protection. They always felt safe somehow when a priest or sister accompanied them. But they didn't know we were as petrified as they were. I remember on one trip I threw up a couple of times. I just mention this because it will explain another cross Maura had when she was named Superior. This meant that she had to fly to different meetings and she hated flying. One time I remember she was coming from Managua and the weather was bad and they couldn't land in Siuna, so they went to Bluefields and back to Managua before finally arriving in Siuna. Poor Maura was really grey when she got off the plane. I guess God was preparing her for so many other things. Also, I remember on that first trip [Sister] Marie Lamond pointing out a wreckage of a plane that crashed on the mountain on the takeoff from Siuna. That was really encouraging news![88]

The two new missionaries arrived in Siuna in time to help prepare for a going-away party for Sister Rose Anna Tobin, one of the nuns they were replacing. It was decided that Maura and Kay should teach a few dances to the young students; in this way they could contribute to the festivities while getting acquainted with the children. Maura threw herself into the project with gusto. With her natural artistic ability, she made costumes for the students for a dance in which each child was imaginatively dressed as a different type of clock. "It was really something trying to get across in Spanish what we wanted the children to do," recalls Kay. "We showed them most of the time, pushing the poor kids here and there. But God takes care of the foolish. It really turned out well."[89]

As the above episode makes clear, Maura and Kay needed to learn how to speak Spanish quickly if they were going to be of much benefit to their students. So they were soon sent to the Colegio Monte María in Guatemala City for language studies. They remained there for six months, but they did not attend formal classes. Instead, a few of the lay teachers were assigned to them and two other nuns on a daily tutorial basis. The arrangement, however, did not turn out as planned. Two of the nuns on permanent assignment with the Colegio community contracted hepatitis. Short-handed, the other sisters called on Maura and Kay to fill in for them during their convalescence. This soon proved quite frustrating, however, because the two were forced to spend so much time doing necessary communal tasks that they were unable to concentrate on their studies. "We could see [their] needs," Kay later noted, "but also the urgency for us to learn the language since we had to go immediately to the classroom after language study."[90] They debated whether or not they should bring up their dilemma to the convent superiors, but Maura was too timid to do so. They "let the matter ride," with Maura promising Kay that "God would provide." The two felt their progress in Spanish was so inadequate that when Holy Week approached, they made excuses to remain in Guatemala City rather than return to the Siuna community where their ignorance would be transparent to those who were counting on them to be sufficiently prepared for the next school term. In the long run, Maura and Kay did become proficient enough in Spanish to perform very effectively as grade school teachers.[91]

The Siuna that the two Irish-American nuns returned to in mid-1960 was, like many towns in the Central American landscape, a social tragedy. The miners toiled long hours for extremely low wages in the Canadian-operated mine; most of the workers would eventually develop a lung disease and would then be left to fend for themselves, without any form of worker's compensation, disability, or health insurance. The miners and their families lived in long rows of dilapidated, unpainted, company houses; they had no running water and sanitary conditions were appalling. The shanties were infested with mosquitoes, vermin, and rats, and the children all suffered continually from parasitic infections. Mortality rates, especially for infants and young children, were quite high.[92] One of Maura's most touching letters to her parents treats this dire fact of life.

> One dear little farm boy, Natividad, came the other day for his religion class; he stood there all ragged but happily smiling with his gift of a little bag of bread that he had bought in the pueblo for the Madres [nuns]. Today he came with big tears to ask for a coffin and clothes for his baby brother who had died this morning. When I told him that he now has a little saint in heaven, he answered, "I have four."[93]

Above the "hole," high on the mountain was "the Zone," the exclusive area where the Canadian company officials and their families lived in large North American, suburban-like homes with beautifully landscaped flower gardens and green lawns. "The Zone" had its own golf course and private club, complete with a swimming pool, a cruel contrast to the poverty down below where the Nicaraguan miners lived. No one was permitted to enter "the Zone" except the Canadians, their guests, and of course their servants—the hired help from Siuna and La Luz. Armed Nicaraguan soldiers guarded this private domain from any potential interlopers.[94]

The wife of the director of "the Zone" was always very kind to the Maryknollers; sometimes she helped out at the clinic run by the sisters and on occasion even gave small sums of money and material goods to some of the townspeople who were especially impoverished.

She and her husband once invited Maura and the other sisters to "the Zone" for Christmas dinner. Kay Kelly relates the considerable agitation churned up by this visit:

> When we entered their house, I felt like I was back in the States again. Surrounded by beautiful, rolling green lawns, one house was more

beautiful than the other with lots of space. The Zone was located up on a hilly area so that you looked down upon the village below. We gazed out the window and felt as if we were in another world (we were !!!). . . . We nearly gagged on the *filet mignon* that was served by one of our villagers, who worked as the maid for the . . . family. [The director's wife] offered us one of the empty houses in the Zone if we wanted to get away for a day. I think we used it once or twice for a community meeting. Somehow we felt it a betrayal to our friends in the village to spend time in the Zone.[95]

In the 1950s, the miners of Siuna and La Luz tried to better their dismal condition by organizing a union, but the National Guard murdered or kid-napped the union leaders and the terrified miners quickly withdrew from the movement.

Maryknoll nuns had first arrived in Siuna in 1944; upon news of their coming the people of the pueblo built a school-convent complex for the *madres*. By 1959, when Maura joined the community, a clinic had been added which treated an average of one thousand people per month. Although the convent was modest by U.S. standards, it was a palace in comparison to the hovels of the people.[96] Each nun had her own small room, with a bed and desk, although at times two nuns would have to share quarters.

Since the residents of Siuna had little to do for recreation, aside from frequenting the bars, Father Roderick Brennan, the Capuchin pastor of the parish, decided to have movies flown in from Managua to be shown each weekend in the parish auditorium-theater. Although most of the films were quite dated, they nevertheless proved a hit, especially with the young people. Moreover, the weekend movies often provided humorous if slightly embarrass-ing moments for the sisters. Every time they would enter the show, someone would call out in a loud voice, *"Alabado sea Jesús Cristo!"* (Praised be Jesus Christ!), and all would come to attention (this was the way the children greeted the nuns as the latter entered the classroom at school). Only when the sisters answered *"Por los siglos de los siglos"* (forever and ever) did the audience again relax. To be the object of such reverent esteem was always a bit disconcerting to the sisters on social occasions but never more so than one evening when the nuns happened to enter the darkened theater late. Since all the ground floor seats were then taken they went up to the balcony which to their embarrassment was filled with teenage couples hugging and kissing. "It was a riot," recalls one of the nuns. "Someone called out in a high voice *'Alabado sea Jesús Cristo'* and all the young fellows who had been hugging their girls separated and came to attention."[97] At another time, the movie had a romantic scene which Maura felt was slightly risqué; she insisted that the nuns all get up together and immediately leave the auditorium, less they give bad example to the people. Some of the other sisters tried to tell her she was being too prudish, but she insisted. So in the middle of the movie they all rose in unison, dressed in their habits, and deliberately walked out.[98]

Since Siuna was so isolated, the community of sisters had to create their own entertainment. Often they put on little skits, perhaps take-offs of movies they had seen, and Maura enjoyed this immensely. The nuns also had "simplicity nights." Maura, who loved to dance, would contribute her version of an Irish step dance.[99] One of the major highlights in Siuna was the annual school play. Maura was always in charge of the scenery since she was so creative; the plays may have been "schmaltzey" and sentimental, says Kay Kelly, but the scenery was truly a sight to behold.[100]

Although she loved to paint, because of her heavy workload Maura had little time for artistic creation. She would usually find a few moments, however, to paint a religious message on a rock or small piece of wood and give it to one of the nuns on her birthday. On one occasion, a few of the sisters went to Poneloya on the Pacific coast for a few days of rest and recreation. Maura walked along the beach busily collecting seashells. Later she glued them in the shape of a cross to a wooden board and printed in beautiful lettering: "There is no greater love than this: to lay down one's life for one's friends." She gave her creation to Kay, who she knew was upset over the recent murder of *campesino* union organizer, Félix Pádro González. Little did she realize that years later Kay would treasure the plaque as a testimonial of Maura's own "no greater love" for the Central American poor.[101]

In 1962, Maura received news from Maryknoll headquarters in New York which surprised and disturbed her but which also provided a new avenue of growth both in the religious life and in her commitment to the poor. She had been appointed school principal and superior of the community of nuns at Siuna. Maura, one of the youngest nuns at the convent and with less foreign mission experience than most of the community, never saw herself as leadership material. She could not understand why she was chosen and was reluctant to accept the positions. Finally, she resigned herself to her new role but only after telling the rest of the sisters that since her gifts certainly did not include analysis and decision-making, everyone would have to make special efforts to help her.[102]

Maura remained superior and principal for six years. During this time, due to the influence of the Second Vatican Council, the community, as well as the Maryknoll congregation as a whole, began to examine its entire way of life and decide if changes should be made. Some nuns felt that the community must strive for a closer identification with the poor they had come to serve. They argued that their house, with its plumbing, phonograph, furnishings, and stockpile of tasty foods from the U.S. only served to brand them as outsiders and distance them from the *campesinos*. They felt that their material well-being caused the poor to identify them with the ruling class and that their relationship with the peasants was not one of equality; on the contrary, it resembled one of paternalism. Maura, the "soft touch," had always given money and goods to needy families, but these sisters contended that such charity only served to maintain the unjust status quo. The missionaries would do better, they concluded, by addressing the causes of the people's misery and that meant a more active involvement in efforts to terminate institutionalized injustice. Some of the nuns even questioned whether they should continue to run their school; could others not be found to replace them as teachers, leaving them to pursue a more active ministry? A few asked to be relieved of their teaching duties and sought permission to go out to the remote villages where they could share directly in the people's way of life, where they could make a "preferential option for the poor."

Other, more conservative nuns as well as the bishop of the diocese felt such views were too radical. They believed the sisters should continue to live as they had always done; they were not overly concerned about the comforts from home they enjoyed, and they felt that the rigors of traveling on foot and by horseback to remote villages were certainly unacceptable for females, to say nothing of their sharing in the impoverished lifestyle of *campesinos*.

Maura agonized over these alternatives. As community superior, she, more than the other nuns, had to decide on which course to follow. She suffered intensely but at the same time grew spiritually. Finally, she committed herself and steered the community toward the more activist position. Two of the nuns were released from their teaching duties and allowed to accompany Father Gregory Smutko on his mission to the small villages between Siuna and Managua; at the same time, the community searched for a congregation of native Nicaraguan nuns to take over the school. The Divina Pastora sisters, consisting of Nicaraguans and Spaniards, consented to replace them,[103] so in December 1968 the Maryknoll women left Siuna permanently, some of them to pursue a more personal apostolate among the poor in the barrios of Managua.[104]

Maura, however, returned to the Unites States where she made a retreat at Maryknoll and then visited her family. When her mother took sick, she received permission to extend her visit since the elderly Mrs. Clarke needed her help. Altogether, she spent about a year in New York before returning to Nicaragua. As her sister Judy later noted, during this time the family detected a distinct change in Maura. She had come to believe that the "Band-Aid" approach to mission work—that is treating the wounds that festered from injustice and poverty without attempting to change the structures which caused those wounds—was no longer enough. Missionaries must toil alongside the oppressed to eradicate oppression. To do otherwise was little more than meaningless in the long run.[105]

Once her mother had fully recovered, Sister Maura again returned to her mission work, but this time she joined Sisters Bea Zaragoza and Rita Owczarek in the barrio of Miralagos on Lake Managua. The three nuns had taught together at Siuna; now they would work with the poor, forming small basic Christian communities in hopes of strengthening the religious faith of the people and helping them to better their material situation.

The Miralagos barrio comprised thousands of poor families who had been displaced from their rural homes by rich landowners expanding their agro-export businesses. With no fields to plant, these *campesinos* came to the city in hopes of finding employment so they could feed their families. Few would be successful, those that were, were forced to work for extremely low pay; if they objected, they could easily be replaced by others from the unending stream of unemployed.

Shortly after her arrival, Maura explained the rationale of her new apostolate to her family:

> The area where we live is filled with poor people living in tents and shacks and just waiting for the government to give them the land they promised. Some live in one-room hovels, very dark and miserable. Many of the little children run around dirty and naked while their mothers try to sell some fruit or baked goods in the market. I am trying to get to know them and after a while we hope to begin having meetings with them to form the "Family of God" which is a way of trying to unite them to solve their own problems and to be formed in their faith through discussions at night.[106]

In October 1970 Maura, her two co-workers, and about three hundred residents of the barrio were forced to relocate when an exceptionally rainy season caused the waters of Lake Managua to flood their homes. They were sent to an area about seven and a half miles from Managua called OPEN (Operación Permanente de Emergencia Nacional). There, 2,400 lots had been set aside for landless families with promises that eventually they would be granted ownership titles. Once the 2400 lots were occupied, new families simply moved in along the periphery of the project, expanding the shantytown for several miles and increasing its population by the thousands. Maura still worked in Miralagos and was now forced to spend three hours traveling to and from OPEN to her job each day. She was therefore doubly thrilled to receive word that her old friend Kay Kelly was returning to Nicaragua to join the staff of the Instituto Promoción Humana, a lay organization in Managua. This meant not only that Maura would again enjoy the companionship of her close friend, but also that she could leave Bea and Rose at the distant OPEN community, and rent a small shack in a barrio in the capital city with Kay and a third nun, Melba Bantay.[107] After about a year, the three were offered the third floor of a newly constructed parish center; they were reluctant to accept, since the residence was large and comfortable and therefore superior to the houses of the barrio. After much prayer and discussion, however, they decided to make the move, since the parish center would be rent-free and they could use the money they saved on much-needed projects.

Shortly after midnight, on the morning of December 23, 1972, the three nuns were awakened by the tremors of a devastating earthquake, only to find themselves trapped within their home. A few days later Maura wrote to her parents describing the chilling event:

> I thought that was our end. We were frightened when with all the efforts of the priests we couldn't get out of any door of the house. Another tremor came and we feared the house would crush us. Finally, we climbed

out the window of the second floor after breaking the glass. We had to tie sheets together to slide down and with the help of the priests and a small ladder we got down to the ground. Our whole city came down in a few seconds. Many, many people were crushed to death. Everyone ran all over trying to rescue people from below the cement walls crushing them.[108]

Kay Kelly takes the story further:

Maura's first concern was for all the people she knew in the parish. We heard that Carolina and her husband [Sergio, two friends who lived in the barrio] were trapped under the rubble about a couple blocks from where we lived. When we arrived at the site, Maura immediately jumped on top of the rubble to where someone said they had talked to Sergio trapped beneath. She began to pray in English with him (in her excitement) until he said to her "Please pray in Spanish, I don't understand English." The men were able to free both of them finally but their baby girl died. Melba and I returned to OPEN to sleep the next night but Maura said she couldn't leave the people. The tremors continued for two or three days. When I returned the next day to Managua, there was Maura walking down the street with [Father] Marciano, S.J., who was distributing communion to the people housed on the sidewalks in front of their belongings. Melba and Maura lived in Tent City with the people who were relocated there from Managua, which is another story of Maura's total identification with the poor.[109]

The tent city mentioned by Kay was called Campamento Esperanza (Camp Hope); it was one of several temporary camps built by the U.S. Army Corps of Engineers. Two priests also lived there and together with Maura and Melba, they tried to alleviate the suffering of the homeless thousands, a task made especially difficult by the Nicaraguan military, who forbade religious personnel there to assist in the relief effort or to form prayer and discussion groups for the displaced.[110] As has been stated in a previous chapter, the dictator was pocketing the relief money sent from around the world. Evidently he feared that religious workers would refuse to "look the other way," and hoped that such restrictions on their activities would diminish criticism of his chicanery.

Just a few months after they were settled in Camp Hope, the problems of the homeless were further compounded. As Maura explains in a letter to her brother:

We just received word that the people have to be out of their tents and moved to another temporary housing project within twenty-four hours. . . . The reason for the hurry in getting them out is that the American Embassy is building on the neighboring property and they don't want these people next door. This is very unjust but there is little we can do here in Nicaragua except, God willing, to help the poor to gain confidence in themselves and to unite in a peaceful but strong protest.[111]

Evidently the protest was to no avail, for the people of Camp Hope were moved to another camp near Lake Managua. Maura and Melba did not accompany them, however. Instead, they returned to the community at OPEN, where Maura would serve for the next three years. She had plenty to do; so many of the homeless had relocated in OPEN that the barrio now held 25,000 people.[112]

During this period of her apostolate, tensions mounted as opposition to Somoza and his National Guard increased. Towards the end of her last year in Nicaragua an incident occurred which raised the usually diffident Maura to new heights of courage. The water company, in which the Somoza family held much interest, decided to hike up the cost of water in the barrio to twice that for Managua. The people held emergency meetings, resolving not to pay the unfair increase. A committee of leaders was formed, leaflets were circulated throughout the barrio, and peaceful marches were held. Increased pressure, including violence, was brought to bear on the barrio people, but the protest went on for four months. At one point, the Guardia Nacional broke up a demonstration and attempted to arrest some of the protesters. Seeing what was happening, Maura stepped in front of one of the military vehicles and began smashing her fist on the hood, demanding that the soldiers release their prisoners. Not used to such aggressive behavior, especially from a woman, and afraid to antagonize a North American, they released the demonstrators. Maura's action may have saved their lives or at least prevented their torture.[113]

In the fall of 1976, Maura received word that she was reassigned to the United States, where she was to work for the next three years. She had known for some time that such an assignment was coming and attempted to prepare herself for it. Nevertheless, as often happens to missionaries returning to the comfortable society of the industrialized world, she was thrust into deep depression soon after her arrival:

> I entered into a time of sadness and deep loneliness and wept over my separation from the people I love, the Sisters, Fathers, all. I saw the tortured people who fight for justice today in the place of Christ, and I pictured the rulers and the military as the high priests. I envisioned the poor . . . as the tortured Jesus.[114]

Maura knew all too well, however, that justice for Central America must be won, in part, in the United States. The North American people must be made aware of the sufferings of their southern brothers and sisters so that they would demand that their politicians alter U.S. policy to be more supportive of the poor against dictatorial military governments. Consequently, she shook off her depression; for the next three years she dedicated herself to the *concientización* of North Americans by presenting workshops on the problems of the Third

World, called "World Awareness Programs," to church and school audiences throughout the Boston archdiocese.

Maura, though far from Central America, never ceased to follow closely the struggle of the Nicaraguan people against Somoza and lend moral support whenever possible. Although she found it extremely difficult to speak in public, she forced herself to do so in September 1978 at a protest against U.S. aid to Nicaragua. She told of the poverty and injustice she had witnessed during her missionary tenure, concluding with an eloquent appeal to President Carter and the Congress to terminate U.S. support for the oppressive dictator.[115]

Like most North Americans, she was horrified when on June 20, 1979, Somoza's soldiers, unaware that they were being filmed by a television news team, were shown on U.S. national news dragging ABC correspondent Bill Stewart from his automobile, forcing him to kneel in the street, and executing him with a bullet through the head.[116] Unlike most of her fellow citizens, however, she expressed her indignation with action. On July 15 she joined several other Christians at Riverside Church in New York City in a prayer vigil and fast expressing solidarity with the Nicaraguan people.[117] Two days later, Somoza fled Nicaragua in defeat. Finally, on July 17, 1979, Maura was able to join her impoverished friends in Siuna and the barrios of Managua—if only in spirit—in celebrating their liberation from the Somoza family after forty-five years of U.S.-supported dictatorship.

Maura's three years of mission awareness work in the United States were rapidly coming to an end, and for a long time she had anxiously awaited the day she would be able to return to Nicaragua. Shortly before the overthrow of Somoza, however, she had received a message from her Maryknoll congregation in response to the plea of Archbishop Romero calling for volunteers to serve in El Salvador. As soon as Maura got it, she began to think that perhaps this, rather than Nicaragua was where God wanted her to work; and as Mrs. Clarke watched her daughter ponder this message, she suddenly foresaw that El Salvador would be Maura's new mission home.[118]

Maura herself was still unsure, however, and in a letter to Sister Jennie Burke she tells of her feelings:

Since El Salvador has been made a priority for Sisters with some Latin American experience I may be going there. This I must pray about and discern so that I will not be naive and go on superficial motivation, but by what the Lord wishes only.[119]

The assassination of Archbishop Romero on March 24, 1980, far from discouraging her, only strengthened her belief that this violence-ridden country was where she was meant to be, but her parents, not unexpectedly, were skeptical and begged her to return instead to Nicaragua. Perhaps it was in deference to their wishes that she resolved to visit her friends in Nicaragua before coming to any final decision. She did this in July 1980, and at the end of the month, she wrote to her mother and father in words that clearly show her almost childlike faith:

> My dearest ones, I would really love to stay here in Nicaragua where there is so much to do, but I know I must go to El Salvador to see if it is right for me to be there as one of our Sisters there has been alone for some time. . . . Don't worry about me. The Lord takes care of us all. If I see that it isn't the place for me I'll return to work in Nicaragua very soon. . . . We must not be afraid. No matter what happens we are one with God and with one another.[120]

Maura arrived in El Salvador on August 5, 1980. She spent her first few days at the port town of La Libertad where she met Jean Donovan, Paul Schindler, and Ken Myers. Dorothy Kazel was out of the country at this time, visiting her family in Ohio. Teresa Alexander, a Maryknoller who worked with a catechist program in Tamonique, was also on hand to greet her. The next day Ita and Carla came from Chalatenango and Madeline Dorsey from Santa Ana to welcome her. Madeline ran a clinic single-handedly for about 4,000 residents of Colonia Lamatapec and it seemed that Maura would join her there after getting acquainted with the overall work of the various missionary teams.

The four Maryknoll nuns came to La Libertad not only to greet Maura but also for a more serious reason. They, and Maura as well, were to confer with Sister Ellen McDonald, who had been sent by the Maryknoll governing board in New York. The board, shocked by the incredibly high rate of murders in El Salvador, was concerned about the danger faced by the Maryknoll Sisters in that country. Ellen was to inform the community that they had full approval to leave if they thought it necessary. This meeting, along with the sight of mangled bodies of murdered *campesinos* sprawled about the countryside, brought home to Maura the fact that the violence in El Salvador exceeded anything she had witnessed in Nicaragua. She relates her first impressions in a letter to a friend:

> We had a community meeting all day Thursday. The point kept coming up—you don't have to stay, you should feel free to go. The answers from the four who have been here a little while—one five years and the others only three or four months—was that they believe deeply that God wants them to be here and they don't want to be anywhere else, although why God wants them here is what they are searching out.
>
> The above strangely reflects where I am, I believe. The deep pain or fear hasn't really touched me yet. I hear about it and have witnessed it somewhat as we saw five dead men thrown by the roadside on Saturday and one in the town where we went for Mass yesterday.[121]

After a short time in La Libertad, Maura went with Teresa Alexander to observe her work with a basic Christian community. She then traveled with

Madeline Dorsey to Santa Ana where she familiarized herself with the clinic. Her comments in a letter to her friend Mary Manning concerning the catechists she had met through Teresa betray the fact that Maura was rapidly being drawn to the poor of El Salvador.

> These are the most rugged, browned, simple and faith-filled men and women who are religious leaders of their various pueblos. It takes courage for them to continue any celebration of the Word or meetings because anyone suspected of being in an organization or attached to the Church is in serious danger. I was so impressed by this little group. . . . The poor really strip you, pull you, challenge you, evangelize you, show you God.[122]

Only three weeks after Maura came to El Salvador, Carla Piette drowned and Maura volunteered to become Ita Ford's new partner in strife-ridden Chalatenango. Even in her grief at the loss of Carla, Ita perceived that the refugee work in Chalatenango would be enhanced by Maura's presence. Maura's years of experience in Nicaragua, her warmth and her openness were invaluable assets; and Ita saw her as "God's gift" to the traumatized people.[123] Some wondered if Maura would be able to hold up under the demanding physical requirements of her new work, for she was somewhat frail. "As the months passed . . . and the pressures grew from daily involvement in the terror in people's lives," remarked Betty Campbell and Peter Hinde, who worked in El Salvador at this time, "she began to lose weight, and shadows frequently crossed her usually smiling face."[124] Nevertheless, she performed her tasks untiringly and complemented Ita well. As Betty and Peter observed:

> Ita and Carla made an excellent team, and they in turn dynamized the pastoral team of that area. Ita did not drive a car and sometimes gave the impression of simply being a companion to Carla. "Carla y Ita" glides into the Spanish diminutive "Carlita" and it was like Ita was but the diminutive part of the team.
> Ita was not a replica of Carla but she was of the same fire and spirit . . . apparent to even the casual observer. Ita grew to a fuller potential when teamed with Maura. Maura was a person builder. And for all that it cost Maura . . . to step into Carla's shoes, the end result was a beautiful team. "Ita and Maura" people would say as though to respect the seniority of Ita in the work and the charism of Maura in the team.[125]

It would not be long before Maura became as immersed in the refugee work as Carla had been. Shortly after her arrival in Chalatenango, the two Mary-knollers were called upon to aid sixty refugees who had fled Aldeita and were staying in the house of a local priest. They brought the *campesinos* powdered milk and sacks of corn; the people even gathered up the few kernels that had fallen out of the bags into the bed of the pickup.

The North Americans then listened to the story of these twelve women, four older men and forty or so children: For eight months they had been sleeping in the hills in the cold and rain to avoid nighttime raids by death squads and early morning sweeps by the army. They would return by day to their village, post a lookout, and try to tend their fields. Some of their houses had been burned; the ones that remained had been stripped of all possessions, for the soldiers and particularly their collaborators in ORDEN had thoroughly plundered their homes. The villagers had finally fled Aldeita just after midnight one morning because the soldiers had threatened that the next time they came through they would "finish off the women and children." After a five-hour trek, the *campesinos* had arrived at the priest's house, where one woman almost immediately gave birth to twins. Ita promised to make arrangements for safe transport of the group to San Salvador the next day, and the North Americans then returned to Chalatenango.[126]

Also around this same time, another town in the area, Reubicación, was targeted for attack by a death squad. The assault on at least one family there was apparently linked to its active association with the church. Two of the women belonged to an order of nuns whose convent and high school had recently been machine-gunned by security forces, probably because their school's curriculum had been revised to include social justice courses inspired by the teachings of the slain Archbishop Oscar Romero. The family itself was involved in parish bible study groups and had aided refugees from other areas who were fleeing army invasions. One evening in late summer, nine members of this family (not including the two nuns who lived elsewhere) were all sleeping together in one room for safety, because in the village death threats had been circulating and there were rumors that spies were turning in names to the security forces. At midnight the death squad forced its way into the house, quickly found the sleeping family, and opened fire with machine guns, splattering the walls with blood and human flesh. Only two survived to tell this story—an old lady, who passed out from fright and was taken for dead, and a little ten-year-old girl, who slipped unnoticed under a bed. Maura visited this town often in her pastoral work and was shocked not only by this tale of terror but also by similar ones told by the refugee families who had fled to Reubicación from isolated areas.[127]

The activities of the death squads never ceased to horrify those who had to confront the consequences of their bloody handiwork. A small newspaper, *El Independiente*, managed to publish accounts of the atrocities perpetrated by government security forces and death squads, despite the fact that its offices had been bombed and machine-gunned. In late 1980, *El Independiente* reported:

In Apopa . . . very many dead bodies have appeared over the past months. Hundreds of relatives of disappeared are coming daily to look for their beloved. Seventeen corpses appeared there on a single day after government forces raided the area of Amatepeque taking 68 youth[s] captive, their bodies appearing in the by now favorite dropping places and many times with a notice and warning attached to the bodies or mounted on a nearby sign from the Death Squad. Often the bodies are most difficult, even impossible, to identify because of destroyed faces, tortured, mutilated, mangled and chopped up, skinned chests, abdomens and extremities.[128]

Not surprisingly, one result of such indiscriminate torture and murder was that the relatives of victims would often join the guerrillas as their last hope for survival in the cycle of violence from which there seemed to be no peaceful exit. Even youngsters, barely in their teens, were leaving their villages and heading for the hills. Betty Campbell, who had been going from village to village in the Chalatenango area giving first-aid talks to the peasants, told Maura and Ita about a girl she had met on one of these trips. An elderly woman had approached Betty while she was visiting the home of a sick peasant and begged her to speak with her granddaughter, Esperanza: "She says that she is joining the resistance in the hills tomorrow. She is only thirteen years old. My husband doesn't approve at all." Betty went with the old woman to meet her granddaughter and discovered that the girl's parents had both been killed by the National Guard. Esperanza was vivacious, bright, and talkative; when Betty asked her about joining the resistance, she answered: "I want to defend my grandparents, my village. Many people have been killed here and in the countryside. If we don't defend ourselves we will all be killed." Esperanza's grandfather was dismayed. "Doesn't it say in the bible, you shall not kill?" he asked. Betty repeated the question, and the girl answered, "I am not going to the camp because I want to kill. I am going because I want to defend my people . . . even if I have to give my life. It is not [even] safe for us to go to school. One of our teachers was killed last week. He was trying to improve our school and on the way home from a meeting he was killed."

Betty happened to meet Esperanza again a month later; the girl had come out of the hills to make sure her grandparents were all right, but planned to return shortly. "We live in community there," she told Betty enthusiastically. "The men and boys even wash their own clothes and help to make tortillas. . . . Some are young like me . . . but most are in their twenties, thirties, and forties, men and women. The commander of my column is a woman. We grow our food and take care of the people who live in the area. . . . " When Betty related this story to Ita and Maura, Maura particularly was touched by Esperanza's precocious commitment.[129]

There had been continual tension in Chalatenango between the members of the pastoral team and the local army commander, Colonel Ricardo Peña Arbaiza, since the spring of 1980. With the slaying of Archbishop Romero in March and the army sweeps of the province in May, Colonel Peña had adopted an openly hostile attitude toward the efforts of the parish team (which included Ita and Carla and later Maura) to aid the refugees. In the late summer and fall of that year, around the time of Maura's arrival, the tensions were mounting ominously.

In an attempt to keep ill-founded rumors about their activities from flourishing, Ita and Maura were always open about their work and quite visible on their missions. They would speak directly to local officials about the refugees in their areas who had come to them for help, outlining what transportation or relief the team intended to offer. At one point, frustrated by the unrelenting hostility of Colonel Peña, the Chalatenango team even went to his headquarters, which was across the street from the church, and asked him to pay a visit to the parish house. They hoped to let him see for himself the refugees, food, and supplies that were there, and in this way demonstrate that rumors of the church's "subversive" activities were simply lies. However, Colonel Peña did not respond to their request.[130]

The series of attacks on San Antonio de los Ranchos, a little town that Maura often visited in her pastoral work, illustrates the increasingly hostile atmosphere in which churchpeople had to operate. Many of the *campesinos* there had joined the Popular Revolutionary Bloc (BPR), a political organization composed of various labor and peasant groups that had united to exert pressure for land reform and other changes. In 1980, the army began its sweeps of the region to root out the guerrilla forces; and before long, claiming it was "defending" the people, the military sent in troops, supported by tanks, artillery, helicopters, and planes, which resulted in heavy civilian casualties in the surrounding area. At one point in the conflict, the army offered the populace of San Antonio de los Ranchos the services of a contingent of National Guardsmen, who would "protect" the town from the guerrillas if the people would provide room and board for them. In a town meeting, the people turned down the offer; this rejection infuriated Colonel Peña, who fumed to a reporter, "The priest of Los Ranchos has ruined the people of this town." Later on, he referred to this same priest, Father Salazar, as a "guerrilla commander," making a play on words since there indeed was a guerrilla leader in the region nicknamed "Cura [priest] de los Ranchos." Salazar was so dismayed by this slander that he went with a lawyer and another priest to speak with the colonel. But the rumors and innuendoes continued.

The first actual attack on Los Ranchos was launched on August 15, 1980. A helicopter circled over the fields, its guns mowing down three men and one woman. Two *campesinos* were taken prisoner and brought back to the Chalatenango garrison; but Father Salazar and another priest interceded for them, saying that they were "responsible catechists." The men were freed; one of them apparently had been on the brink of death just as the priests were speaking with the colonel about his release. This catechist later told the churchworkers in Chalatenango he had been kneeling in front of the troops, while one man, who seemed to be in charge of dispatching him, shouted to his men: "Who is this man?" "A communist son-of-a-bitch," they shouted back. "Shall we kill him?" asked the soldier in charge. "Yes, kill the communist son-of-a-bitch!" they answered. A moment or two later, the order came to return the prisoner to his cell. The would-be executioner became so frustrated at not being allowed to complete his grisly task that he began to roll his head from side to side, twisting his hair with his fingers, and whining, "No! We can't kill him?"

This incident and similar ones caused the army to cease bringing prisoners back to the garrison, for, as one soldier told Ita, "the priests or sisters free them and all our work is for nothing."

This attack was only the beginning for San Antonio de los Ranchos. In October, soldiers under Colonel Peña's command overran the town, shooting indiscriminately at the people. A tank bombarded the buildings, and soldiers plundered the homes. A convent and church were raided; consecrated hosts were profaned, and donations for the poor were seized. Two young mothers were dragged off behind their houses; soldiers cut off the breasts of one of the women and then decapitated them both. The next week, San Antonio de los Ranchos was again marauded. A pattern of attacks on the church was evolving in the area; this time the soldiers invaded the sacristy of the church and fouled the altar linens with their urine and excrement.[131]

Throughout the fall of 1980 rumors persisted and spread in the province of Chalatenango that the Catholic church was engaged in "subversive" activities. Nevertheless, Maura and Ita, as well as other members of the parish team, continued to aid the victims of civil war. At one point, Ita actually confronted National Guardsmen who had stopped a bus on which she was traveling for an identification check of the passengers. When the Guardia took a young man from Chalatenango off the bus and told the driver to go on, Ita stood up to the soldiers. "If you take him you take me," she said firmly. Her action may have saved the youth's life, for the Guardia decided to let him go.[132]

Their obviously effective work in the province did not endear Maura and Ita, or the other churchworkers in Chalatenango, to the suspicious Colonel Peña Arbaiza. He and his men continued spreading rumors that derided the activities of the Catholic church in the province. Moreover, the attacks on San Antonio de los Ranchos, conducted by troops under his command, were vicious and obscene assaults on Catholic sacraments and ritual. Around the time the series of invasions had begun, Colonel Peña questioned two young boys who claimed they had been shot by guerrillas. Peña, insisting that the boys had told him of contacts between churchworkers and guerrillas, then summoned individuals from the parish team to his office and harangued them about the church's alleged "subversive" activities. Colonel Peña Arbaiza was quite serious about these accusations; he even made several trips to San Salvador to relay his concerns to Salvadoran army officers. It was apparently due to his influence that a ten-year-old boy from Chalatenango—a rather dubious authority on the subject—testified to high government officials in the capital regarding church contacts with guerrilla groups. During this meeting Defense Minister García singled out churchworkers in Chalatenango for criticism in this regard.[133]

Thus the activities of Maura and Ita, as well as the other churchpeople of Chalatenango, were viewed at high levels as suspicious. Although they were undoubtedly upset about this antagonism, Ita and Maura had other pressing concerns, since both were trying to adjust to dramatic changes in their lives. Ita was wrestling with the loss of her old friend Carla. A trip to the American embassy to deliver Carla's death certificate embroiled Ita in so much red tape that she was reduced to tears. She revealed her struggle to deal with Carla's death in letters to friends and in a tape to her mother:

> This is kind of a heavy experience, but I guess it just says that God is extremely active in our lives and is certainly the Lord of life, the one who's in charge, the one who decides. I've come in contact with a lot of people who sleep outside at night. They say they sleep in the hills. These are the things that bind you to people. I'm sure that what all this means will come about and be clearer later on. Meanwhile, I must stand humbly before the wisdom and love of our God who chose to call Carla to Himself that night and not me. Our years together are a great gift and source of strength. I miss Carla very much, yet I also believe that we are still bound in a relationship whose depths I still must discover. I believe she is still fully alive and I rejoice with her. May she help us continue serving those whom the Lord puts in our lives.[134]

Knowing that Ita was going through a difficult period, Maura tried to relieve her of some of the more physically and emotionally taxing aspects of the refugee work. Ita kept busy, however, by taking care of the paper work, calling relief agencies, and handling the incoming calls for aid. She found the busy work therapeutic; as she told her mother, "Being busy is fine for me now—especially on some days when I just don't feel like myself. I guess it's the blahs that come after someone close to you dies. I presume it will pass with time, and in the meantime I'm running Maura ragged."[135] Occasionally, her old spirit and sense of humor returned, a sign to those who knew her that she would indeed make it through this personal crisis. Ita was somewhat amused by one of the tasks, purchasing large quantities of food for refugees, that fell her way at this time; she wrote a friend, "These days I feel like a Chicago merchant specializing in grain futures—or maybe Joseph in Egypt—storing grains against the coming shortage. There's nothing more absurd than two Brooklynites judging the quality of red beans and corn!"[136] But Ita still made regular trips into the countryside with Maura to deliver supplies or transport refugees, for both North Americans felt that their presence was helpful in ensuring that the *campesinos* and the supplies would reach their destinations safely. During these weeks, Maura and Ita saw a great deal of Dorothy Kazel and Jean Donovan, who were often called upon to transfer refugees from Chalatenango to camps in safer areas. As Ita observed, "Their biggest asset is being blonde, which makes roadblock passing easier. Carla kept threatening to bleach her hair when she saw how they got through."[137] Ita's comment would later prove to be more bitterly ironic than humorous.

Maura, too, was finding her new life in Chalatenango somewhat of an adjustment; as she wrote her old friend Kay Kelly:

I am beginning to see death in a new way, dearest Katie. We have been meditating a lot on death and the accepting of it, as in the Good Shepherd reading. There are so many deaths everywhere that it is incredible. It is an atmosphere of death. The work is really what Bishop Romero called "acompañamiento" [accompanying the people], as well as searching for ways to help. This seems what the Lord is asking of me, I think, at this moment. We are on the road continually, bringing women and children to refugee centers. Keep us in your heart and prayers, especially the poor forsaken people.[138]

And in a very open letter to her parents that Father Paul Schindler carried out of the country, Maura wrote of the violence and terror in El Salvador, which she found much more frightening even than her experiences in Somoza's Nicaragua:

My dearest ones, Father Paul is leaving for the States tomorrow and I will ask him to mail this letter when he gets there. I know that you would like to hear a little bit more of the reality here and what we are doing. Ordinarily, by mail or phone call, one cannot really say the truth because of the extreme vigilance. There is a great deal of tension and violence. The situation is very tragic. People are fleeing from their homes looking for some kind of safety as the so-called death squadron strikes anywhere and everywhere. The squad is made up of the military rightists who are the most ruthless. The cutting up of bodies by machete is one of the tactics to terrorize the organized groups from continuing their efforts. There are crimes on both sides, but the military and the rich oligarchy have committed extreme crimes, and many more.

The effort of the oligarchy is to wipe out the farmers and the workers who have organized for change, and they do this in the name of fighting communism. It is a much more vengeful, confusing and frightening case than that of Nicaragua. The other day, by way of example, a very Christian family in a nearby town was machine-gunned, killing seven members including a five-year- old. The organized groups do not trust or accept the present Revolutionary Junta as it continues to permit such outrageous slaughter of human lives, so they feel they must fight, even with their little, almost toy pistols.

Each day we trust the Lord to guide our ways as to what he wishes of us. Often there is a lot of frustration and pain involved as one cannot do enough; or anything, at times. At times one wonders if one should remain in such a crazy incredible mess. I only know that I am trying to follow where the Lord leads, and in spite of fear and uncertainty at times, I feel at peace and hopeful.

Perhaps I should [not] tell you all of this bad news, but often when I write I feel superficial as I cannot say the truth; and the truth is best.[139]

Maura had barely had time to become acquainted with her work when an ominous threat appeared on the door of the parish house in the town of Chalatenango. On the sign that was tacked to the entrance was drawn a knife and a head, dripping with blood. A verbal threat was also attached: "Everyone working here is a communist, and anyone entering here will be killed."[140] Around this same time, early November 1980, Colonel Peña told Ita personally that he believed the Catholic church was "indirectly subversive because it's on the side of the weak."[141] By late November, hostility toward the church had reached the point where uniformed soldiers came and went freely in the church buildings and had all but taken complete charge there. In order to ring the bells, churchworkers even had to have the permission of the army. The climate of fear was pervasive. Because their convent was next door to the National Guard building in Chalatenango and feeling that there was some safety in numbers, the three Assumption Sisters who lived across the street from the church began sleeping in the parish house with Maura and Ita.

It seemed that a pall of death and terror had settled over Chalatenango. Yet, like Dorothy and Jean in La Libertad, Ita and Maura persevered. Ita wrote to her friend Jean Reardon Baumann trying to explain this commitment: "We keep plugging along here, because life is threatened by other evils worse than death—hatred, manipulation, vengeance, selfishness."[142] And Maura wrote to friends:

> The way innocent people, families, children are cut up with machetes and blessed temples of the Lord thrown and left for the buzzards to feed on them seems unbelievable but it happens every day. . . . The other day passing a small lake in the jeep I saw a buzzard standing on top of a floating body. We did nothing but pray and feel. We don't know how long this can continue but the pain goes on and there are many hungry people hiding and struggling. Being here with Ita and working for the refugees has its sweetness, consolation, special grace and is certainly a gift. The courage and suffering of these people never ceases to call me. [143]

Outside of the provinces of Chalatenango and Morazán, much of the conflict at this time either centered on the church or was church-related. In mid-September, the FDR (Frente Democrático Revolucionario), which had been established in April 1980 and which united various political parties, unions, professionals, church sectors, the BPR, and other grassroots organizations, staged a joint occupation of several churches all over El Salvador to protest the rampant repression. In the following weeks, government security forces drawn from the National Guard, the army, and the police attacked many of the occupied churches and basilicas, killing at least fifteen on the spot and capturing scores of others, many of whose corpses were later found with notes attached that read, "Thus die subversives who go around occupying churches."[144] Also at this time, the seminary in San Salvador was bombed and burned, causing extensive damage to the building and adjoining archdiocesan offices.

The attacks on the FDR culminated in late November with a massacre that attracted international attention. Five leaders of the FDR had gathered in the Jesuit high school in San Salvador on November 27, when suddenly the building was surrounded by about two hundred soldiers and police. While most of the troops remained outside, twenty soldiers entered the building and captured the FDR leaders. By the next day, all five of their bodies had been recovered, bearing signs of torture. Two of them, Enrique Álvarez Córdova, an oligarchical dairy farmer who favored land reform, and Juan Chacón, a leader of the BPR, had been horribly mutilated. An "investigation" was launched by the Salvadoran government; but it was obviously designed to be a mere cover-up and the archdiocesan legal aid office denounced it as such.[145]

While El Salvador was suffering through this latest crisis, Maura and Ita, as well as Sisters Madeline Dorsey and Teresa Alexander, were attending the annual regional assembly of Maryknoll sisters in Managua. Sister Maria Rieckelman, a psychiatrist who had flown in for the week from the United States, observed the psychological state of both Maura and Ita at this time. Maria found Maura to be adjusting to and coping with her new life in Salvador surprisingly well, considering the terrible situation of violence to which she had been abruptly exposed:

> Maura had arrived in better shape than Ita, principally because she was not grieving as heavily for Carla, but also because—though she could not understand it herself—she was dealing with the horror quite well. She spoke of the mutilated bodies and the little children but it was as if she were walking through it with the sense that God was going to bring good out of that tremendous evil, and she was very conscious of her faith.[146]

Maura herself told her friends at the assembly that she felt strong "not in myself but in the sense that the Lord will be faithful to me and his great love will take care of it."[147] In Maura's last letter to her parents, which was mailed while she was en route to the meeting in Nicaragua, she expressed this inner peace and trust, but also hinted that she was aware of the uncertain direction her life was taking: "It was so good to get your letter, Pop, telling me about Mom resting on the couch after supper. I can see you so well with the eyes of my heart and have so many precious memories of you always. Here we are all well and trusting very much in the Lord's strength." Then, explaining that it had "a lot of meaning for me these days," Maura included this quote from Thomas Merton:

> My Lord God, I have no idea of where I am going. I do not see the road ahead of me. I cannot know for certain where it will end. . . . But I believe that the desire to please you does in fact please you. And I know that if I do this you will lead me by the right road though I may know nothing about it. Therefore will I trust you always. Though I may seem to

be lost, and in the shadow of death, I will not fear for you are ever with me, and you will never leave me to face my perils alone.[148]

Ita, however, was not faring so well. At the Thanksgiving dinner that began the sisters' assembly in Managua, Ita told Maria she really did not feel very thankful. She spoke of Carla and El Salvador, and related an episode that had occurred a few weeks earlier in Chalatenango, which she could not chase from her thoughts: While Maura had been out doing pastoral work and Maddie Dorsey, Terry Alexander and Jean Donovan were visiting Ita at the parish house, a woman had come to the door and asked Ita to accompany her to look for her son, who had disappeared and was feared dead. Ita and Jean went with her to a little farm outside of town, where a *campesino* had offered to uncover the grave of a boy he had found dead and had buried two days before. When the man pulled the handkerchief off the boy's face, the mother exclaimed, "That is my son; now I can rest for I know he is at peace and with God." Ita was still shaken by this memory and told Maria, "I could not do that again." Maria suggested to Ita that perhaps she should spend some time in Chile or in the United States, and Ita promised to think about it.[149]

But to everyone's delight, Ita seemed to recover from her depression as the meeting progressed. On the second day, after a healthy bout of tears, Ita regained some of her old cheer, became more relaxed, and was able to participate effectively in several of the sessions. It was partly due to her influence that the sisters agreed to compose a letter to encourage more Maryknoll personnel to come work in El Salvador. When the week-long series of meetings was over, Ita finally told Maria she did not want to go to Chile or the States but was ready to continue her work in El Salvador.[150] Toward the end of the assembly, Ita received news from home that a baby had been born to her brother Bill and his wife Mary Anne. Apparently the message had been garbled, for Ita wrote the following postcard to the Fords back home:

> *Felicidades* [congratulations], as they say here. With you I celebrate birth and new life—because at this point that's all I know. The message I received was that "a child has been born," and that's good enough for me! When I get near a phone that works, I'll get filled in on the particulars. Love to all, Ita.[151]

Ita never made that phone call; her cheerful postcard to the family was her last communication with them and was received after they had been notified of her abduction and execution.

The Maryknoll nuns at the assembly were all aware of the dangers to which their friends Maddie, Terry, Maura, and Ita were returning. To conclude their assembly they expressed their faith and their fears in prayer on the evening of December 1. Ironically, two of the prayers they chose for meditation were a presage for the deathly drama that would unfold upon Maura and Ita's return to El Salvador the next evening. Maddie read:

The waves of death rose about me, the torrents of destruction assailed me. The snares of the grave entangled me. The traps of death confronted me. For the poor who are oppressed and the needy who groan, I myself will arise, says the Lord.[152]

And Ita chose this passage from a sermon of Oscar Romero:

Christ invites us not to fear persecution because, believe me, brothers and sisters, one who is committed to the poor must risk the same fate as the poor. And in El Salvador we know what the fate of the poor signifies: to disappear, to be tortured, to be captive and to be found dead.[153]

But the assembly ended on a happy note; a little party was held during which Ita, almost her old self again, joined in one of the skits and amused everyone with her rendition of the "barnyard shuffle" as the group sang "Old Mac-Donald Had a Farm." And Maura, who could never resist an opportunity to dance and entertain, performed an Irish jig.

The next day, December 2, Maddie, Terry, Ita and Maura left Managua for San Salvador in two shifts, with Maddie and Terry on board the early afternoon LANICA flight and Maura and Ita waiting for the later COPA flight. Arrangements had already been made with Dorothy and Jean to pick them up at the San Salvador airport; Maura and Ita, since they would be arriving near dark, had decided to spend the night in La Libertad and return to Chalatenango the next day.

But these plans were never realized. Unknown to any of the women, the arrivals of first Maddie and Terry and then Maura and Ita at the airport were being closely monitored by the Guardia Nacional. It was apparently either Ita or Maura the Guardsmen wanted, for the white Toyota mini-van carrying Dorothy, Jean, Maddie, and Terry was allowed to leave the airport unmolested after the first flight arrived from Managua.

That same evening, in the town of Chalatenango, still another threat was added to the series of warnings directed against churchworkers. On a street in Chalatenango, the sacristan of the parish was approached by a stranger and shown a death list containing the names of nearly everyone on the parish staff, including Sisters Ita Ford and Maura Clarke. The stranger shook the list in the sacristan's face and said, "The killings will begin tonight."[154]

Was it only coincidence? Or was it a conspiracy emanating from high levels of authority? That night at a roadblock near the airport, Dorothy, Jean, Ita and Maura were halted by the Guardia Nacional and would never be seen alive again.

The Aftermath

The murders of Dorothy, Jean, Ita, and Maura were obviously a devastating shock to their families and friends. Nevertheless, knowing that violence was growing daily in El Salvador, they had all lived with the fear that some day their loved one might be killed. What none of them suspected, however, was that officials from the Reagan administration would insinuate that the church-women had been involved in subversive activities or that the U.S. government would collaborate with Salvadoran authorities in an attempt to protect those responsible for the crime.

Since the four women were unknown to officials in Washington before their deaths, Ita's brother Bill wondered why officials like Jeane Kirkpatrick, Alexander Haig, and Ernest Lefever would make irresponsible and derogatory remarks about them. Eventually he concluded: "It can only be that the work they were doing was seen by their client state of El Salvador as a threat—and consequently has been seen by the United States as a threat."[1] Joseph and Malvina Kazel were likewise troubled by the conduct of their government. In July 1981 they commented:

> Added to our pain and confusion is the unclear position the United States government has taken since this tragedy has happened. We have been hurt by the comments, indifference, and accusations of high members of our own government. We do not want revenge, but only that the truth be known and justice done.[2]

After experiencing countless frustrations at the hands of an uncooperative State Department, Ray Donovan told a reporter in early 1984: "I voted for Reagan, my wife voted for Reagan. And after three years I really have only one question: Why is President Reagan rewarding the murderers of our daughters?"[3]

Perhaps the most telling statement is that of former ambassador Robert White who, testifying on March 20, 1984, before the Senate Subcommittee on Western Hemisphere Affairs, said: "I regard the continuing cover up on this case as one of the most shameful chapters in the history of United States diplomacy."[4] Indeed, White's refusal to remain silent in the face of the State Department's behavior had cost him his job; on February 1, 1981, he had been recalled as ambassador to El Salvador by Secretary of State Alexander Haig. In his March 20, 1984, testimony, he relates the reason:

On January 22, 1981 . . . I received a telephone call from Acting Assistant Secretary [of State] John Bushnell. His statement shocked me to the point that I immediately dictated a memorandum of the conversation and sent a copy to the office of Central American Affairs, Bureau of Inter-American Affairs (ARA), Department of State. The memorandum reads. . . .

"John Bushnell called to tell me that ARA had finally succeeded in getting something which would pass for a policy statement on El Salvador from the people working with Secretary Haig. According to Bushnell, Haig stated that El Salvador was a government under stress and that he therefore was not going to be a party to any criticism of this government. This statement attributed to the Secretary was in response to ARA's concern about how it should handle the problem of how to characterize the Salvadoran government's investigation into the murders of the American churchwomen.

"Bushnell said that the Secretary's statement obviously created a problem for all of us.

"I responded that I could certainly see how it created a problem for ARA but that I did not believe that it created a problem for me at all. . . . I said . . . my assertion that no serious investigation was under way was in my opinion accurate and that I did not intend to change it.

"Bushnell stated that it could be a problem for me. . . . He went on to say that ARA had only said that there was 'progress in the investigation' and that this did not necessarily mean that there was a 'serious investigation.' In effect, he stated that both positions could be held, 1) that the investigation was on-going and 2) that it was not a serious investigation.

"I responded that to me this was playing with words and that either there was an investigation or there was not and if there was not, we should say so. . . ."

Three days later I received a call from the personnel officer of the ARA bureau in the Department of State who informed me that he was calling at the [insistence] of Acting Assistant Secretary John Bushnell to point out to me that now was a particularly advantageous time to retire from the foreign service.[5]

The cover-up actually began while Jimmy Carter was still president, but it would deepen significantly after the inauguration of Reagan. Three days after the December 2 murders, the Carter administration suspended $25 million in aid to El Salvador. Carter also commissioned a special fact-finding team to investigate the crime. After spending only three days in Salvador, the commission reported that there was "circumstantial" evidence that security forces may have been involved in the killing but there was "no direct evidence" linking high-ranking officials. Based on a Special Investigative Commission set up by the Salvadoran government, the U.S. team concluded, over the strong objections of Ambassador White, that "positive steps were being made by Salvadoran authorities in their attempt to solve the crime." On January 14, Carter announced the resumption of military aid, citing "progress" being made in the case.[6] In all, the suspension had lasted little more than a month.

While the investigation of the U.S. fact-finding team was taking place, another U.S. citizen was killed in El Salvador after claiming he had evidence linking the churchwomen's murders to the Salvadoran security forces. On December 11, Thomas Bracken went to the U.S. embassy in San Salvador offering to provide this proof if the embassy would arrange to have gun-running charges against him in the United States dropped. Unfortunately, Bracken was referred to FBI and U.S. military personnel rather than foreign service officials. After interrogating him, the officers concluded that he had nothing significant to offer and sent him away. On December 16, Bracken returned to the embassy and was again interviewed and dismissed as an opportunist desperate to have charges against him eradicated. On the following day, the 46-year-old North American was shot to death. According to a Salvadoran military press service (COPREFA) bulletin, Bracken had accompanied the National Police in a search for a kidnapped Salvadoran business-man. As they entered a house, a gunfight ensued and Bracken was shot and killed by a "wounded subversive."[7] Contacted later by a reporter, State Department spokesman John Caulfield commented that the department did not suspect foul play. "In times of military conflict, it is not unusual for someone to be caught in a crossfire," he said.[8] Therefore, the State Department saw no reason to investigate the killing. Only after Ambassador White reported the Bracken death to the House Subcommittee on Inter-American Affairs, did the U.S. government look into the matter. In an overall investigation of the churchwomen's murders commissioned two and a half years after the event by Secretary of State George Shultz, chief-investigator Harold R. Tyler stated:

On December 17, 1980, Thomas N. Bracken, a United States citizen, was killed in a shoot-out in the streets of San Salvador. Just one week prior, on December 11, 1980, Bracken had gone to the United States Embassy in San Salvador to offer information about the churchwomen murders. The proximity of the two events has caused some speculation as to whether Bracken's appearance at the Embassy and his subsequent murder were causally connected.

We have found no such connection. Bracken was interviewed at the Embassy prior to his death, and had no specific evidence concerning the crimes. He offered the theory that the murders had been committed by a right-wing splinter group, but had no evidence to support the charge. Bracken's stated purpose in coming forward was to trade his vague rumors for dismissal of a criminal warrant outstanding against him in El Paso, Texas. It seems to us clear that his offer of information was merely the act of a desperate man trying to find a way to return to the United States.

An inventory of Bracken's quarters, after his death, revealed twenty-five molotov cocktails, wiretapping equipment, handguns, ammunition and military manuals. He had told the Embassy that he was employed as an instructor for the Salvadoran National Police. It was in this capacity that he appears to have met his death. Bracken accompanied several National Police officers who were chasing armed suspects and, in the process of attempting to make the apprehension, was shot dead by one or more of the suspects. In turn, the National Police shot and killed two of the suspects. Based on these facts, we find no connection between Bracken's contact with the embassy and his death.[9]

Tyler, whose Report was issued on December 2, 1983, lists as his sources an FBI memorandum dated December 31, 1980, and cables from the U.S. embassy in San Salvador to the Secretary of State dated December 12 and December 23, 1980, and October 11, 1983. The above text of the Tyler Report on Bracken as well as the sparsity of sources cited indicate that the Tyler investigation of this murder went no deeper than a cursory review of the few statements released by officials at the U.S. embassy in San Salvador.

One source that Tyler was perhaps unaware of was an article by Pat Williams which appeared in the *National Catholic Reporter* on April 22, 1983. Williams looked into Bracken's past as well as into the events surrounding his murder, uncovering some rather disturbing information.

Bracken had worked for the North Las Vegas Police Department from 1962 to 1976, when he retired. In 1977 he and about ten other people from North Las Vegas, Nevada, formed Guardmaster Security Company, which was supposed to build armored cars and provide security for Salvadoran businesses. Bracken served as the company's agent in San Salvador. Even though Guardmaster Security never built a single armored car, he remained as its Salvadoran representative until its dissolution in 1979. In 1978 Bracken allegedly began running guns from the United States to El Salvador for the Salvadoran military; he also became a paid consultant for the National Police. In March 1980, he was arrested by police in Brownsville, Texas, for gun smuggling. According to his wife, states Williams, who attempted to interview her, "he escaped." A warrant for his arrest was then issued by the U.S. Justice Department. Yet former North Las Vegas mayor and police officer, Ray Daines, told Williams that between this time and his death, he made frequent visits to his home town to visit family and friends and from his open behavior gave no indication he was hiding from law enforcement authorities.

Although Bracken's family refused to talk to Williams about his death, the *National Catholic Reporter* correspondent was able to find that the remains of the deceased were never shipped to the United States since the family could not raise the money which the U.S. government demanded, in full, to cover the cost of transportation. Investigating further, Williams found that there is no record, either U.S. or Salvadoran, of where or when he was buried. In short, his body seems to have disappeared. Although the unusual circumstances of Bracken's death and the disappearance of his body do not seem to trouble the

State Department, they did, indeed, bother the families of the four churchwomen. Consequently, their lawyers petitioned the State Department, FBI, and Defense Intelligence Agency for access to the specific details of Bracken's two meetings with U.S. officials in San Salvador. All three agencies refused to release the information, leading the families to wonder what the U.S. government felt the need to hide.[10]

Bracken was only one of four U.S. citizens to be murdered in El Salvador within a few weeks of the slaying of the four churchwomen. On December 28, John Sullivan, a 26-year-old reporter, disappeared after registering at the Sheraton Hotel in San Salvador. Sullivan, who had previously covered the Nicaraguan revolution for ABC radio, was hired by Flint Publications to write an article on violence in El Salvador. When his mutilated body was finally recovered more than two years after he had been killed, his family spoke bitterly about the lack of U.S. initiative in pursuing the case. "Washington saw us as a thorn in their side," said his sister Debbie Indrieri.[11] His mother, who along with her husband had voted for Reagan in 1980, was even more cynical, revealing that the search for her son "cost them $20,000 and their confidence in the U.S. government."[12] A personal visit to the State Department had little effect, she further explained, and even letters from the family to Mr. and Mrs. Reagan went unanswered.[13] Asked its side of the story, administration spokesperson Susan Pittman replied: "The State Department does not have any investigative authority in any country anywhere. It is the responsibility of the host country to conduct its own investigation."[14] But like the families of Dorothy, Jean, Maura, and Ita, the Sullivans knew that a government which provided El Salvador with millions of dollars in aid could pressure Salvadoran officials into undertaking a serious investigation. The truth, they felt, was that the State Department did not want to uncover any evidence that might jeopardize its "anti-communist" policy in El Salvador by causing Congress to waver in sending military aid there.

Realizing that if they were to discover John's fate they would have to do the groundwork themselves, the Sullivans placed advertisements every week for fifteen months in Salvadoran newspapers offering a reward for information on his whereabouts.[15] In early 1982 they received an anonymous letter asserting that the victim had been mistaken for an activist Belgian priest by the National Police and had been tortured and executed. The writer, who claimed to have been a member of the death squad that killed Sullivan, agreed to come forward in exchange for a promise of asylum in the United States. The Sullivans' hopes were quickly dashed, however, as the new U.S ambassador in El Salvador, Deane Hinton, refused to take the letter seriously, referring to its author as an obvious extortionist. A second letter was received in July 1982, also unsigned, stating that Sullivan's remains were buried near the village of Nuevo Cuscatlán, twelve miles south of San Salvador. A crude map was included pinpointing the exact location. The State Department finally took action. Embassy officials went to the gravesite and pressured a reluctant Salvadoran government to exhume the body. Salvadoran forensic experts then examined the remains, concluding that they could not be Sullivan's since the body was too short and appeared to be that of a male about twenty years older than the U.S. reporter. When the Sullivans requested that the cadaver be transported to the U.S. for further examination by American doctors, the Central American government refused. After initial hesitation, it did permit x-rays to be taken for comparison with those of Sullivan's in New Jersey. When both sets proved identical, including even a deformity of the right knee, El Salvador still refused the family's request for the body, citing a law prohibiting the transfer of unidentified remains.[16] The situation remained unchanged for the next six months. Finally, Democratic Congressman Robert Torricelli, a newly appointed member of the House Foreign Affairs Committee, which oversees aid to El Salvador, flew personally to that country where he was able to coerce the government into relinquishing the body.[17]

The corpse arrived in the United States on February 19, 1983, and was examined at family expense by Dr. Frederick Zugible, chief medical examiner of Rockland County, New York. He concluded that it was definitely that of John Sullivan and that he appeared to have been murdered. The head and hands had been ripped from the torso and were missing.[18]

The family was also able to find from Salvadoran death records that the body had actually been located the day after Sullivan disappeared, but Salvadoran officials had "concluded" it was not him and therefore said nothing to U.S. authorities.[19] At a funeral service held March 12 at Saint Joseph Church in Bogota, New Jersey, John's sister Donna Igoe told reporters that the case "still has to be pursued. We have to find out why Johnny was murdered, and by whom."[20] To this day, the killing remains unsolved.

Sullivan's disappearance was followed by the slaying of two more U.S. citizens on January 4, 1981. Michael Hammer and Mark Pearlman, AIFLD (American Institute for Free Labor Development) labor union advisers, and José Rodolfo Viera, director of Salvador's Agrarian Transformation Institute, were dining in the coffee shop of the Sheraton. According to witnesses, Lieutenant Rodolfo López Sibrían, Captain Eduardo Alfonso Avila, Major Denís Morán, and conservative businessmen Hans Christ and Ricardo Sol Meza were also eating there. When these five had finished their meal, López Sibrían, Avila, and Christ went to the parking lot, where they ordered Corporal José Demas Valle and Corporal Santiago Gómez González to kill the two U.S. advisers and Viera. Since the two National Guard triggermen did not know their intended victims, Christ led them to the coffee shop, pointed out the table where the three labor officials sat, and watched the gunmen murder them. The three then casually left the hotel.[21]

In April 1981, Christ, who was then in Miami, and Sol Meza were arrested, only to be released about five months later. A year and a half after the murders, the two National Guard corporals were taken into custody. In sworn statements they confessed to the crime, claiming that they had been ordered by López Sibrían and Avila to do it. Investigations by the U.S. and Salvadoran authorities corroborated their claim.

With such overwhelming evidence, the Reagan administration decided to turn this into a showcase to prove that death squad members, even officers, were being brought to justice and therefore that aid to El Salvador should continue. Brimming with confidence, U.S. Assistant Secretary of State Elliott Abrams called the supposedly upcoming trial "a test of American influence." He further predicted that: "Convictions [of the officers] in this case would symbolize a fundamental change in El Salvador, to where members of the elite and officers' corps can be brought to justice and subjected to the rule of law."[22] An unnamed lawyer who had served as an aid for the slain Viera made a different prediction. "This case," he said, "will demonstrate that justice doesn't function here. They can kill when they want, even gringos, with or without permission."[23] Abrams proved wrong and the Salvadoran lawyer right. No trial would take place until nearly five years after the crime, and then only the two corporals would be found guilty and both would be released from jail less than two years later. The Supreme Court would order all charges against Lieutenant López Sibrían dismissed in November 1984 and drop those against Captain Avila in July 1985. Prior to this, Avila's uncle, a Supreme Court justice, would take charge of the case. As Clifford Krauss of *The Wall Street Journal* tells it:

The uncle used his judicial position to assign to the Sheraton case judges clearly sympathetic to the officers. One such judge, for instance, allowed Lt. López Sibrían to dye his hair black (from red) and to shave off his mustache prior to appearing in a lineup before a crucial witness. The witness then didn't recognize the lieutenant.[24]

Although such judicial conduct caused a frustrated Salvadoran lawyer to affirm that López Sibrían and Avila "will never be touched," Abrams was not so easily dissuaded. Again he predicted that eventually higher-ups in this case would be convicted. President José Napoleón Duarte, for his part, made the most of the situation. He ordered López Sibrían dismissed from the military without benefit of pension. The U.S. news media, in turn, responded with high praise for this "courageous" act. One man, however, saw the move differently. In an "op-ed" column in the *New York Times*, Frank Hammer, Michael's brother, sarcastically wrote:

It gets hard to believe some of the stuff you read in the papers.

I'm talking about the American editorial response to the recent decision by President José Napoleón Duarte of El Salvador to dismiss and sever the pension of Lieut. López Sibrían. . . .

Under the circumstances, the congratulatory chorus that has greeted Mr. Duarte's decision seems just slightly out of place. Since when is losing your job and pension considered the appropriate punishment for a triple murder?

In fact, in the rush to embrace the Duarte Government, many Americans have chosen to ignore some of the more unpleasant truths about El

Salvador. The State Department is embarrassed by the nearly four-year failure to pursue the murders of my brother and his colleagues, and so it seizes on any action by the Salvadoran Government that reduces that embarrassment. But let us tell the truth. Let us acknowledge that the decision to fire this lieutenant has more to do with public relations than with justice. . . .

The point is . . . the State Department can't call for justice on one hand and then indirectly support the death squads with the other. . . .

Our taxes are buying lots of bullets for the Salvadoran Army these days. One of them killed my brother. It's time that we made use of our power to end the killing in El Salvador.[25]

The Sheraton murder case and that of the four U.S. churchwomen have much in common. Both crimes were perpetrated by Salvadoran security forces; also—unlike the tens of thousands of other right-wing sponsored murders in El Salvador—both received extensive coverage in the U.S. media and became a rallying point for Congresspersons who opposed the Reagan administration's policy toward Central America. Nevertheless, in one respect they were quite different. The Pearlman, Hammer, Viera case is the single Salvadoran murder case in which, even though it failed, the Reagan administration pressured its ally to convict higher-ups responsible for the crime. With regard to the churchwomen's deaths, the same cannot be said. Here, to its discredit, the administration did all it could to protect higher authorities who might have been involved in the crime or its cover-up. In 1983, commenting on the conduct of White House officials, Mildred Ford, Ita's mother, put it neatly: "I think the State Department would like to see it all go away so they could go on with their business."[26]

Indeed, it seems that the lame-duck Carter administration's strategy was to "make no waves" and pass on the Salvadoran problem to the Republicans. In the weeks following the killings, Ambassador White sent several cables to the State Department showing that the investigation of the Salvadoran government was a sham. Included were ballistics tests, fingerprints on the van, and other evidence linking the Salvadoran National Guard to the murders. The Carter administration, however, refused to make this information public. Moreover, although the families of the women were promised that the State Department would relate to them all pertinent data it received concerning the case, when Carter left office the families had learned nothing.

On January 20, 1981, Ronald Reagan began his presidency. The next day Ambassador White relayed his views to the new administration in a cable to the State Department:

In my opinion, on the basis of the evidence available to me, there is no serious investigation being undertaken by the government of El Salvador into the deaths of the American churchwomen.[27]

On the same day, he decided to go public, reporting to the *New York Times* that the Salvadoran government had failed to conduct a serious investigation and that he had strongly protested to the State Department when it reported that authorities of that government had taken "positive steps." He concluded with the startling words, "I am not going to be involved in a cover-up."[28]

As has been noted above, a few days later, on February 1, White was removed as ambassador to El Salvador. Taking this perhaps as a sign that the Reagan administration was "in its corner," the Salvadoran Special Investigative Commission was terminated by the junta on February 27 without filing a report.[29] Shortly after, on March 2, White House officials announced their decision to send an additional $25 million in military aid to El Salvador, along with twenty new military advisers who were to set up a training program for the Salvadoran armed forces. When the Senate Foreign Relations Committee questioned this action, the administration noted that it had no intention of linking aid to human rights improvement.[30] Around this time the State Department also announced that a six-man U.S. Navy training team had been assigned to El Salvador to help maintain patrol craft equipment.[31] Highly disturbed by such actions, Senators Edward Kennedy and Paul Tsongas told reporters that they intended to present legislation to the Senate calling for the termination of all military aid to El Salvador until a thorough investigation of the churchwomen's murders was completed.[32] Jeane Kirkpatrick, however, immediately spoke in defense of the Salvadoran government, calling it, in a debate with Robert White, "the best Government available for El Salvador."[33] Then, on March 14, the *New York Times* reported that the White House now planned to send fifty-four military advisers to El Salvador and to ask Congress for approval of an additional $60 million in military aid.[34]

Realizing that Congress might be reluctant to sanction such an escalation of involvement in El Salvador just after the recent murders of U.S. citizens there, the Reagan administration felt it essential to do whatever was necessary to convince not only the legislators but also the American people that the process of justice was moving forward in that tiny country. And since the public was particularly disturbed by the rape and murder of three nuns and a lay missionary, the State Department was willing to go so far as to lie to Congress in this case. An incident related by former Ambassador White illustrates this point:

On March 18, 1981, before the Senate Committee on Foreign Relations, Mr. Francis M. Muller, Executive Assistant Director of Investigations, Federal Bureau of Investigations, volunteered the information that the legal attache in El Salvador believes "a conscientious effort is being made to solve this crime" [the murders of the churchwomen].

Yet on January 20, 1981 the legal attache in San Salvador [had] submitted a report to Washington which made clear that the ongoing investigation was a hoax.[35]

Such inconsistencies did little, of course, to stem the growing opposition to increased involvement in El Salvador. Grass-roots reactions began all over the country. On March 24, 1981, demonstrations, vigils, and hunger strikes took place in most major cities.[36] Bumper stickers appeared on automobiles saying "U.S. out of El Salvador" and "El Salvador is Spanish for Vietnam." At the end of March, the American Lutheran Church issued a statement opposing U.S. policy toward that country. This was followed by similar statements from leaders of a dozen major Protestant denominations, as well as from Catholic and Episcopalian bishops. Even the bishop of San Salvador, Arturo Rivera y Damas, risked his life by saying publicly that U.S. military aid to his country was resulting in even more repression and helping to expand violence.[37] Indeed, in April, after President Duarte and all opposition groups agreed to allow Rivera y Damas to mediate the Salvadoran conflict, the Reagan administration refused to grant its approval. Without U.S. support the proposal for negotiations had to be dropped.[38]

The Reagan policy soon received a powerful blow. At the end of April, the House Foreign Affairs Committee voted 26 to 7 to require the president to provide assurance every six months that "indiscriminate torture and murder" by security forces were being brought under control; if he could not do so, aid should then be terminated.[39] The House was not through yet; on May 1 eleven House Democrats filed suit in U.S. District Court to force the administration to end military aid to El Salvador and withdraw all U.S. military advisers on the grounds that the White House had violated the Constitution and the War Powers Act.[40] Finally, the administration was forced to bear newspaper editorials throughout the country asking similar questions to that of the *New York Times* on May 3: "Why," the editorial staff asked, "are there no Administration voices demanding an end to the torture and murder by El Salvador's 'security forces'?"[41]

In face of such mounting criticism, it became apparent, even to the Salvadoran generals, that some dramatic gesture was necessary to prevent an eventual cut-off of aid. Thus, on May 9, 1981, Defense Minister García announced at a press conference that six members of the National Guard had been arrested for the murders of the churchwomen.[42] That this was merely an attempt to sway U.S. public opinion is shown by the fact that the guardsmen would not even be handed over to the civilian courts to decide if they should be tried until February 1982. Furthermore, on March 11, 1983, the Salvadoran Appeals Court would rule that there was "insufficient evidence" to try them, in spite of the fact that in February 1982 one of the accused actually confessed to the murders and implicated four of the other guardsmen. The State Department issued an enthusiastic statement soon after the arrests, commenting that "this action demonstrates that the investigation is making progress and shows the firm determination of the Government of El Salvador to act against wanton violence whatever its source."[43]

Unfortunately for the Reagan administration, the arrests did not weaken congressional opposition to continued Salvadoran military aid. A few days after the guardsmen were taken into custody, the Senate Foreign Relations Committee passed an amendment similar to that approved earlier by the House Foreign Affairs Committee. But this time the vote was even more lopsided. Eleven of twelve members voted to require Reagan to certify that "substantial progress" was being made by the Salvadoran government in implementing human rights. Even though junta leader Duarte angrily accused the Senate of interfering in "an internal political problem" of El Salvador and Secretary of State Haig and other State Department officials cried that such measures only served to encourage the leftist guerrillas,[44] the full Senate approved the amendment on September 23. Henceforth, Reagan would have to certify every six months that "significant progress" was being made in ending human rights abuses. If he could not do so, aid would be suspended. Furthermore, the amendment stipulated specifically that progress in the investigations of the four churchwomen and the two U.S. labor advisers had to be demonstrated.

It soon became clear, though, that the congressional decree would prove no obstacle to the Reagan administration. Despite the obvious evidence over the next few years that no serious effort was being made in El Salvador to curb abuses, President Reagan simply certified semiannually that "significant progress" was taking place, and this in spite of the fact that killings were escalating daily. As Robert White remarked before a Senate subcommittee, Reagan's conduct sent a message to the Salvadoran military: "These officers believe the Reagan administration is protecting them from the insistence of Congress that justice be done."[45]

Reagan's policy suffered further embarrassment in November 1981 when El Salvador announced that there was insufficient evidence to charge anyone with the women's murders. A report of the investigation was given by Defense Minister García to Representative Mary Rose Oakar, in whose district Jean and Dorothy had lived; three days later, after reading it, she angrily told the news media that it was "a slap in the face to the families and friends who believed that the Salvadoran government was intent and sincere upon seeing justice carried forward."[46] Moreover, the United Nations had issued a report earlier that month which estimated that 9,250 political murders had been committed in tiny El Salvador in the first six months of 1981; this was followed a few days later by a governmental statement that the United States had doubled its economic aid to El Salvador over the last two years.[47] It seemed clear to many congresspersons that increased aid paralleled increased violence. This was obvious also to many Americans and they expressed their feelings on December 2, 1981, the first anniversary of the deaths of Ita, Maura, Dorothy and Jean. On that day candlelight vigils and memorial services were held across the nation; in town squares, streets, and churches—both Catholic and Protestant—speaker after speaker eulogized the four women and denounced the Salvadoran policy of the White House as morally bankrupt.

On January 28, 1982, Reagan was required to certify that progress was being made in ending human rights abuses in Salvador and in solving the murders there of U.S. citizens. A dramatic gesture was necessary, or his "certification" would undoubtedly be followed by demonstrations against his policy in city after city. Thus, on January 26, Defense Minister García, now a general, announced that his government was ready to bring the six previously arrested National Guardsmen to trial "within a very few days."[48] This enabled Reagan, in spite of the ever-increasing number of political murders in Salvador, to say that progress in ending human rights abuses in that country was being made. With Reagan's certification in hand, Congress released $135 million in military and economic aid. Shortly thereafter, in early February, the White House announced that it would ask Congress to increase military and economic aid to El Salvador from $135 to $235 million for fiscal year 1982 and, moreover, that the president planned to sign an executive order releasing $55 million in Defense Department funds for emergency aid to its Central American ally.[49]

If the White House and Congress sighed in relief when, on February 10, the military finally turned the six guardsmen over to the civilian courts, their satisfaction was short-lived, for a day or two later five U.S. military advisers were filmed carrying M-16 rifles in what seemed to be a combat zone in El Salvador. This violation of U.S. law, witnessed by millions as they watched the evening news on television, further brought home to many the parallels between current U.S. involvement in El Salvador and past involvement in Vietnam. The announcement by Ambassador Hinton that Lieutenant Colonel Harry Melander had been ordered to leave El Salvador because he was responsible for this violation, did not stifle public disapproval: On February 20 about four thousand people in New York City demonstrated against U.S. aid to El Salvador; this was the same day that the National Conference of Catholic Bishops issued its strongest statement yet against such aid.

Meanwhile, on February 14 Salvadoran authorities announced that one of the detained guardsmen had confessed to the murder of the four women and implicated four low-ranking associates. There followed a television appearance by Duarte in which he noted that lie detector tests taken by the five accused plus a guardsman who was released satisfied him that no higher authorities had been involved in the crime.[50] Others were not so sure. In his Sunday homily Archbishop Rivera y Damas told his Salvadoran congregation: "But there is one thing that worries me. And that is how a sergeant could give orders unless beforehand, at least in a general form, someone has not opened the way for decisions of this nature to be taken."[51] Earlier, on July 23, 1981, Ambassador White had expressed similar doubts to a House Subcommittee on International Development. He also testified that two guardsmen who might have been able to connect high-ranking officers to the murders were assassinated by a military death squad. One was then officially listed as killed in action and the other as missing in action.[52]

A week later, Bill Ford told a House Inter-American Committee hearing that he was far from satisfied with the direction of the case, and felt important questions were being ignored. He noted that a document shown to the four families indicated that after the murder some of the guardsmen had thousands of dollars in U.S. currency in their possession. Yet it seemed no attempt was being made to find out where the money had come from. Likewise, no investigation of any Salvadoran holding a position higher than subsergeant was taking place. Yet of the three judges assigned to the case, two had resigned, supposedly out of fear for their lives.[53] If only five low-level soldiers were involved in the murders, Ford continued, then why should the judges be so fearful?[54]

In mid-March, Reagan's pro-Salvadoran policy was dealt a further blow when it was learned that a four-man Dutch television crew had been ambushed and murdered by soldiers in Chalatenango.[55] As demonstrations took place in Holland, many Dutch people asked how the United States could arm and support such a country. Similar demonstrations were held throughout the world, including one in Washington, D.C., in which, according to estimates, at least 23,000 and as many as 50,000 people took part. Finally, newspapers throughout the country reported on June 30, 1982, that the families of the churchwomen had found it necessary to file a suit against the U.S. government, charging that the State Department had violated the Freedom of Information Act by refusing to give them access to files on the case.[56] Such a revelation apparently did not embarrass the president, for on July 28 he boldly certified to Congress that "significant progress" was being made both in the case of the churchwomen and in ending human rights abuses. To back his assertion, he noted that Salvadoran Criminal Court Judge Bernardo Rauda Murcia claimed "sufficient evidence now exists to order the case to trial, and that he will set a trial date in the near future."[57] Furthermore, Reagan again asked that military aid be increased for the following fiscal year. But a month later, his policy suffered another setback when Catholic church officials in San Salvador publicly noted that following his certification, political murders had sharply increased. Surprisingly, the U.S. embassy in San Salvador concurred.[58] Two months later, on October 29, the embassy actually went a step further when Ambassador Hinton, addressing the local Chamber of Commerce, called the Salvadoran legal system "rotten" and threatened to end U.S. aid if the security forces continued to murder civilians. When similar statements followed from the ambassador, including one in which he acknowledged that as many as thirty thousand people had been murdered in El Salvador in the last three years, Reagan officials ordered him to refrain from further public criticism of human rights abuses by security forces.[59] But the damage was already done; it was obvious to Congress, the media, and the American people that Hinton had differences with the administration and could no longer be part of Reagan's political team. In May of the following year, the State Department announced that Thomas Pickering would be the new U.S. ambassador to El Salvador and that Hinton was being removed because he had not effectively carried out administration policy.[60]

But Hinton was not alone. Assistant Secretary of State for Inter-American Affairs, Thomas Enders, was likewise becoming disillusioned, especially concerning the unwillingness of the administration to push for negotiations between the Salvadoran government and the popular forces. After the president again certified on January 21, 1983, that progress was being made in El Salvador, Enders conceded to the press that U.S. policy was "confused" and obviously projected "mixed signals" to Salvadoran authorities. Like Hinton, he would also have to be removed, and in May 1983 White House officials announced that Enders was being replaced by Langhorne Motley, since the former had advocated an overly conciliatory policy toward leftists.[61]

The peak of frustration reached by Hinton and Enders is understandable in light of the ever worsening situation in El Salvador between October 1982 and their dismissal in May 1983. In October, another U.S. citizen, Michael Kline, was murdered by Salvadoran soldiers. The aftermath of his death, not surprisingly, followed a similar scenario to that of other North American victims. Kline had been removed from a bus by the military and "shot while attempting to escape," according to Salvadoran officials. When the State Department refused to return his body unless his mother immediately paid $3,500 for expenses, actor Jack Lemmon—star of the movie "Missing," the story of a U.S. citizen murdered in Chile during the overthrow of Allende—offered to pay the bill. An autopsy later showed that Kline was shot at very close range and that he had first been tortured. His mother charged the U.S. embassy in San Salvador with ignoring the obvious discrepancies in the official military report of his death. Finally, when Salvadoran authorities were asked by embarrassed embassy officials to investigate the killing, they reported that Kline was a "mercenary" working for leftist guerrillas. This charge was not supported by any evidence.[62] In March 1983, three enlisted men were arrested for Kline's murder, but as of the present writing they have never been tried.[63]

The Kline murder was only one of many discomfiting incidents for the Reagan administration. In January 1983, John McAward, head of the Unitarian church's Universalists Service Committee, claimed that gunmen had kidnapped two teenaged boys who worked for him. When the boys were found in police custody, Salvadoran authorities remarked that they had been arrested because they were messengers for the guerrillas.[64]

On February 2, 1983, a most serious revelation greatly disturbed Congress. U. S. Staff Sergeant Thomas Stanley was wounded when his helicopter was hit by guerrilla ground-fire. The aircraft had clearly been operating in a battle zone in violation of U.S. guidelines for military advisers in El Salvador.[65]

On March 13, Marianella García Villas, president of El Salvador's Human Rights Commission, was murdered; the army reported that she was killed while fighting along with guerrillas. Her colleagues at the Human Rights Commission denied the charge.[66] A few days later, after Archbishop Rivera y Damas criticized the Salvadoran government's refusal to set a specific date for the trial of the murderers of Ita, Maura, Dorothy, and Jean, Republican senator Nancy Kassebaum joined Democrats Christopher Dodd and Daniel Inouye in calling for sharp reductions in the administration's latest request for Salvadoran military aid. White House policy was clearly in jeopardy and the promotion to Minister of Defense of General Vides Casanova, who had been director of the National Guard when all nine U.S. citizens had been murdered, did not help matters any. Finally, when it was disclosed in May that charges had been dismissed against the killers of the three labor union advisers and that Hinton and Enders had been fired, and when at the end of the month Lieutenant Commander Albert Schaufelberger became the first U.S. military casualty in El Salvador when he was gunned down by leftists, it was evident that dramatic gestures were needed to salvage Reagan's aid program. Thus, in July 1983 the administration announced the formation of a commission headed by former judge Harold Tyler which was to investigate the churchwomen's case thoroughly and report its findings to the State Department; it was also at this time that Reagan officials gave their fourth certification on human rights improvement in El Salvador and on progress in the investigations of U.S. citizens murdered there.

Much more would be needed, however, to stifle growing congressional frustration and anger over El Salvador's human-rights failure. Although subject to intense pressure from Deputy Secretary of State Kenneth Dam who tried to dissuade him, Republican Senator Arlen Specter spearheaded a move by the Senate Appropriations Committee to hold back 30 percent of its Salvadoran military aid package until a satisfactory verdict was reached in the churchwomen's case. A week later, on October 6, the House Appropriations Subcommittee on Government Operations adopted a similar proposal.[67] In November both houses approved the measure; Reagan's request for $86.3 million was cut to $64.8 million, and $19 million of that was to be, as stated above, conditioned on a verdict in the trial of the killers of Ita, Maura, Dorothy, and Jean. Although Under Secretary of Defense Fred Iklé accused Congress of irresponsibility, there was little that the Reagan administration or the Salvadoran government could do. Moreover, a signal had been given: if a trial was not held and completed soon, Congress could be expected to take even sterner measures for the following fiscal year.

Reagan's problems would soon intensify, for on December 2, 1983—the third anniversary of the deaths of the churchwomen—Judge Tyler submitted his report to Secretary of State George Shultz. Far from lending support to the U.S. Salvadoran policy, its contents proved devastating—so much so that the State Department immediately classified the report "Secret," even though Tyler himself had told several people that he had deliberately withheld from it anything that could not be made public.[68] The administration's tactic actually backfired, for the essential thrust of the report was quickly leaked to journalists who not only made it public, but accused White House officials of attempting to cover up the circumvention of justice by Salvadoran military officers. Indeed, Anthony Lewis of the *New York Times* expressed the thoughts of many in his profession when he asked in his column: "Is there no decency in the Reagan administration?"[69]

Months later, on May 24, 1984, when the public had already been informed of its contents through leaks, Assistant Secretary of State Langhorne Motley finally sent a copy of the Tyler Report to Mother Bartholomew,

Dorothy Kazel's superior in the Ursuline order. In a cover letter he explained that the report previously had to be classified "Secret" because "official release . . . just as the trial [of the five guardsmen] was entering its final stage would have been perceived by some, and would certainly have been so portrayed, as foreign intervention in the Salvadoran judicial process."[70] This statement is an exaggeration; the guardsmen's trial was certainly not in "its final stage" when the administration decided to withhold the document from the public. The trial did not even begin until five months later and then only lasted one day. Motley's letter is insensitive and inaccurate on another count: Motley alludes to all four of the churchwomen as Ursuline nuns when only Dorothy was a member of this order and Jean was not a nun at all.[71]

What was so devastating in the Tyler Report to cause the Reagan administration to withhold it from the public? Tyler's revelation that "the evidence . . . shows irrefutably that the five defendants . . . raped and murdered the women,"[72] was not enough to warrant its classification as "secret." His comments that Salvador is "a society that seems to have lost its will to bring to justice those who commit serious crimes against it" and that its "criminal justice system . . . is in a state of disrepair"[73] would perhaps have brought the State Department a bit of discomfort, but certainly not enough to cause it to withhold the document. It was probably Tyler's conclusion that high-ranking Salvadoran officials could well have been involved in a cover-up of the crime that caused the administration to fear the report might provide Congress with a "smoking gun," which could justify a repudiation of current U.S.-Salvadoran policy. Moreover, it was especially crucial that the White House keep the contents of the report secret at this time. It was in the final stages of preparing to submit legislation to Congress in February 1984 requesting a four-fold increase in Salvadoran military aid, while also asking that further aid no longer be conditional on certification of progress in ending human rights abuses. In fact, on November 30, 1983, Reagan had vetoed a bill that would have extended the requirement for certification.[74] Obviously, Congress would have been hard-pressed not to comply with Reagan's request if such remarks from the Tyler report as the following had become public knowledge:

The first reaction of the Salvadoran authorities to the murder was, tragically, to conceal the perpetrators from justice. Evidence available to the United States, including the special Embassy evidence, shows beyond question that Colindres Aleman confessed his involvement in the crime to ranking members of the National Guard within days of the murder. They responded by concealing this fact from the outside world, and ordering the transfer of the killers from their airport posts and the switching of their weapons to make detection more difficult.

At a minimum, then Major Lizandro Zepeda Velasco, the National Guard officer in charge of the Guard's internal investigation, was aware of the identity of the killers and participated in these acts. Sergeant Dagoberto Martinez, Colindres Aleman's immediate superior, has admitted that he also knew of Colindres Aleman's guilt. We believe it is probable that Colonel Roberto Monterrosa, head of the government's official investigation of the crime, was aware of the identity of the killers and, further, that he participated in the cover-up by purposely failing to provide Colindres Aleman's fingerprints to the United States for analysis. We believe as well that it is quite possible that Colonel Carlos Eugenio Vides Casanova, then head of the National Guard and now a General and Minister of Defense, was aware of, and for a time acquiesced in, the cover-up.[75]

On the question of Salvadoran officials being involved in the actual murders, Tyler's report was inconclusive:

The question whether Colindres Aleman was ordered to commit this crime by higher-ups is a troubling one. To the extent the Salvadoran authorities have investigated this matter, their inquiry is not nearly as complete as we would have liked. There is some evidence suggesting the involvement of higher-ups; most importantly, two low ranking guardsmen have testified that, in ordering them to participate, Colindres Aleman told them he was acting on higher orders.

On the other hand, there is evidence to the contrary. . . . Although it is unlikely that a dispositive answer will ever be known, we record here our best judgment: *on the basis of the evidence available to us*, we believe that Colindres Aleman acted on his own initiative.[76]

Had Tyler waited a few months longer before issuing his report, he would have been able to obtain important new evidence which might have changed some of his conclusions, for in March 1984 the news media revealed that a former high-ranking Salvadoran official had provided Senator Paul Tsongas and Representative James Shannon, and later the *New York Times* and Walter Cronkite of CBS News, with detailed information on the inner workings of Salvadoran death squads. Although the senator and congressman refused to name their source, it was later learned that he was Colonel Roberto Santivanez, former chief of the intelligence unit of the Salvadoran army.[77] Along with other important information, Santivanez revealed that the murder of the churchwomen was "an unusual case" outside of "the normal structure" for military-sanctioned murders. Whereas most death squad activities involved Roberto d'Aubuisson, General García and Colonel Nicolas Carranza, head of the Treasury Police, in this case Colonel Oscar Edgardo Casanova had ordered the women "eliminated." He had been in charge of the La Paz zone where the murders took place, but was later transferred to Santa Ana as part of a shake-up designed to protect him and the other involved guardsmen. Santivanez further stated that Oscar's cousin, National Guard head, later Defense Minister, Vides Casanova took charge of the cover-up of the slayings. In other words, the Minister of Defense, an official who has an important say in determining how U.S. military aid will be used, had played the major role in protecting the killers of the churchwomen. If such a disclosure placed Reagan's Salvadoran policy in jeopardy, it was dealt an additional blow three weeks later, when Walter Cronkite of CBS News and Philip Taubman of the *New York Times* revealed that Colonel Carranza—also implicated by Santivanez in death squad involvement—had been secretly receiving more than $90,000 annually for five or six years from the CIA.[78]

With prospects for continued congressional support for the administration's Salvadoran policy growing dimmer each day, the White House moved to a new tactic, one which would prove quite successful. Administration officials finally convinced the power structure in El Salvador that it would have to allow a presidential election to take place, for not to do so would undoubtedly mean that Congress would soon cut off aid. President Reagan and his officials then touted the upcoming election as a turning point in Salvadoran history, proof that that country was finally achieving reform. When leftist parties announced that they would boycott the election—an understandable decision since their candidates would have been sure targets for the death squads—the State Department accused them of refusing to participate because they had no popular support. When United States-backed José Napoleón Duarte led Roberto d'Aubuisson by a comfortable plurality and prepared for a run-off election, U.S. public opinion on Salvador began to shift back toward the Reagan position.

Even the shocking revelations of a May 1984 Amnesty International report on El Salvador had little effect on the U.S. populace. The report, along with accusing the Salvadoran government of culpability in most of the 40,000 civilian murders in that country since 1979, claimed that governmental authorities likewise impeded human rights groups from monitoring deaths and disappearances. More specifically, Amnesty indirectly implicated Duarte in one case, noting that in January 1981 a senior official of CDHES, a human rights group, disappeared shortly after Duarte publicly accused him of being antigovernment. The report was also critical of the U.S. embassy in San Salvador, chiding it for being "seriously deficient" in collecting information on death-squad atrocities.[79]

Following Duarte's presidential run-off victory in May, Salvadoran judicial officials announced that they had finally completed arrangements for the long awaited trial of the five National Guardsmen accused of murdering the U.S. churchwomen. By curious coincidence, the trial would begin on the day the U.S. House of Representatives was to vote on a request by the Reagan administration for an additional $62 million in emergency Salvadoran military aid.

Armed with news of the upcoming trial, Duarte journeyed to Washington, where in a dramatic speech he pleaded that Congress pass the emergency aid request. He had put his life on the line, he said, and now congressional help was needed if Salvador was finally to be saved. His speech, along with the news of the forthcoming trial, won the day. Former congressional opponents of continued military aid assured Duarte that he could now count on their support. Even liberal *New York Times* columnist Tom Wicker urged those on Capitol Hill to pass the aid package, but to make it clear that they were only doing so because of Duarte.[80]

On May 24, 1984, three and a half years after the slayings of Ita, Maura, Jean, and Dorothy, the trial of their murderers took place in the small town of Zacatecoluca. In keeping with Salvadoran judicial procedure, a narrative of the crime was presented and the testimony of the accused National Guardsmen and witnesses was read. Arguments by both prosecuting and defense lawyers were then made.

Madonna Kolbenschlag, a legislative assistant to Representative Oakar, was present at the trial. She later pointed out that the arguments of the prosecution attorneys seemed eloquent, dramatic, and persuasive, while those of the defense seemed "vague and generalized . . . [with] no close analysis of the evidence, no arguments on technicalities, no character defense, no alibis, [and] no surprise testimony."[81] How astute Kolbenschlag's observation was becomes clear when one realizes that defense lawyers used only half their allotted time to argue their clients' case and that all three of the guardsmen's attorneys had never met with their clients until the day of the trial.[82]

Not surprisingly, none of the lawyers—neither prosecuting nor defense—or the judge brought up the possibility that higher officials might have ordered the murders. A year after the trial, Salvador Antonio Ibarra shed some light on the probable reason they had not. Ibarra had been the original lawyer for Carlos Contreras Palacios, one of the accused guardsmen. On May 5, 1985, Ibarra, then living in Texas where he was applying for political asylum, told a *New York Times* reporter that in 1983 his client's common-law wife had come to see him. She said that Contreras and the other guardsmen had only been "carrying out orders from above, from El Salvador," when they perpetrated their crime. At first Ibarra refused to pursue this defense because he had been ordered not to do so by authorities. "I feared for my life," he said. Later, however, he became less cooperative. He was soon warned "not to pursue the case on his own." He was then kidnapped and taken to National Guard headquarters where he was tortured. Finally, through the intercession of the U.S. embassy and the International Red Cross, he was released. He immediately fled El Salvador and went to Texas. He concluded his story by telling the *Times* reporter that the Salvadoran government's claim—that a possible cover-up of high official involvement in the slayings had been thoroughly investigated—was "an outright lie."[83] It is obvious that after he was kidnapped, Ibarra had been replaced by a more malleable attorney.

After the prosecution and defense attorneys presented their arguments, the jury members left the room for their deliberation. Only fifty-five minutes later they returned with a verdict of guilty on all thirty counts. Members of the four churchwomen's families were pleased with the convictions but agreed with William Ford when he noted that several questions remained unsolved: "Who ordered, who directed, who covered up, [and] who paid for these crimes?"

Once the defendants were found guilty, the U. S. House of Representatives voted 267 to 154 in favor of Reagan's $61.75 million emergency military request. According to the *New York Times,* on the day of the verdict, the U.S. embassy gave Salvadoran officials a copy of the classified Tyler Report, with its conclusion that higher-ups were probably involved in a cover-up.[84] A few days later, however, President Duarte remarked that he would not actively investigate whether high-ranking military officials were implicated in the crime: "If there is a case that I know absolutely, it is the case of the nuns. I don't need to investigate anything. I know it all."[85] He added that he had taken it upon himself to investigate the crime personally and was thoroughly convinced that no officials were involved. He likewise denied reports that on his recent trip to Washington he had told several congresspersons that he believed the cousin of General Vides Casanova (Colonel Edgardo Casanova) had been involved in the killings.[86]

In June 1984 Judge Bernardo Rauda Murcia sentenced all five guardsmen to thirty years each in prison. A Maryknoll spokeswoman then read a statement to the press. "True justice in this case will not be attained until the intellectual authors of this crime and those involved in the cover-up have also been prosecuted."[87]

A few months after the sentencing of the guardsmen, all charges against Lieutenant López Sibrían for the murder of the labor advisers were dismissed, despite overwhelming evidence of his guilt. Just days later, on November 22, 1984, Ernesto Fernández Espino, head of the Lutheran church in El Salvador, was kidnapped, mutilated, and killed by security forces; his "crime" seems to have been that he provided the poor with food. On February 8, 1985, the Salvadoran human rights office of the Catholic church reported that after a lull of almost a year, death squad murders were again on the rise. On February 12 the U. S. embassy in San Salvador admitted it had about 120 soldiers in El Salvador, even though by law it was allowed no more than 55. It claimed, however, that the additional 65 were not acting as "military advisers." In July 1985, the Salvadoran Supreme Court dismissed the evidence of new witnesses against Captain Avila, the accomplice of Lieutenant López Sibrían, declaring it "insufficient." The following month Pedro Rene Yanes, head of a Salvadoran investigative commission on official corruption, was gunned down.

But none of this mattered anymore; Duarte had been elected president and the murderers of Dorothy, Jean, Ita, and Maura had been convicted. In January 1985 Congress overwhelmingly approved $326 million in economic and $128 million in military aid for El Salvador for fiscal year 1985, but the Reagan administration claimed that was not enough; $200 million was needed for the military and at least $426 million in economic aid!

A few months later, when leftist suspects were arrested for the June 19 murder of four U.S. Marines, President Reagan congratulated Salvadoran authorities for their "speed and professionalism" in apprehending the killers. He saw no reason to question why such "speed and professionalism" had been lacking in the case of the four churchwomen or in the forty to fifty thousand unsolved murders committed by the right. And the U.S. public no longer cared.

PART IV

POSTSCRIPT

After 1983

At the time of this writing, four years after the last of the eleven U.S. missionaries was killed in Central America, the gloom has not yet lifted from the region. Although the U.S. State Department asserts that democracy has been restored in El Salvador and that the Duarte-led nation represents the best possible model for change in Central America, the facts do not support the claim. Duarte's government has had some success in land reform and its most notable accomplishment has been a dramatic reduction in the overt violence of the right-wing death squads. According to the archdiocese of San Salvador's Human Rights Office, at least 225 people disappeared or were murdered by death squads in 1985,[1] a significant improvement over the past. In 1986, the statistics were even better; the number killed was reduced to forty-two.[2] Indeed, Duarte's success contrasted with the conduct of the rebel opposition, which in late 1986 and early 1987 increased its human-rights abuses significantly by machine-gunning civilian vehicles traveling the highways and executing several *campesinos* suspected of supporting the government. In December 1986, for instance, guerrilla gunmen murdered fourteen civilians in San Salvador while rightist forces were responsible for only eleven deaths.[3]

The government has been perpetrating another type of terror, however, which is not so visible to international news reporters since it has been carried out in the less accessible rural areas where guerrilla power is strongest. There the Salvadoran military, supplied with modern U.S. aircraft and advised by American personnel, has been involved in the heaviest air bombardment in the history of the Western Hemisphere. Although the Salvadoran power structure denies it, the air war has been aimed not only at the destruction of the guerrillas but at eliminating any support they might receive from the civilian population by forcing the local people to relocate in distant refugee camps or suffer death at the hands of the military. Thus, air attacks have often been followed by Salvadoran infantry ground sweeps. Americas Watch, in a 1984 report, verifies the tragic results of Salvadoran policy:

Thousands of noncombatants are being killed in indiscriminate attacks by bombardments in the air, shelling, and ground sweeps. Thousands more are being wounded. As best we can determine, the attacks on civilian noncombatants in the conflict zones are part of a deliberate policy.[4]

What is especially disturbing to the poor of El Salvador is that they have been forced to do the fighting for the Duarte government against the guerrillas. There is no draft in this small nation, but the army regularly sweeps through poor neighborhoods, rounds up young men and presses them into military service. No attempt has been made to recruit from affluent areas.[5] Such blatant injustice prompted the following words from Bishop Gregorio Rosa Chávez in a January 11, 1987, homily:

> I am sure that the rich who defend with so much vehemence the military solution to the war would think differently if their children, who are today taking it easy studying, working or wasting their youth, had to fight on the battlefields. . . . The poorest people of El Salvador understand what this is like, because their children, almost all of whom are *campesinos,* carry the entire weight of the war.[6]

Indeed, rich landowners and businessmen have contributed to the economic destruction of their country by placing their fortunes in Miami bank accounts. Such capital flight, at a time when El Salvador is suffering from a 40 percent inflation rate and 50 percent unemployment or underemployment, has been estimated at $1 billion.[7] Moreover, the $2.5 billion in U.S. aid which El Salvador received in the past several years basically has served to maintain the unjust status quo. Some of the aid is unaccounted for and seems to have been stolen. Much has been used by Duarte to create a political machine through patronage; governmental jobs have been allotted to those who showed the greatest loyalty to Duarte, not to those most qualified, said U.S. officials.[8] Still, in the words of *New York Times* correspondent James LeMoyne, the vast majority of economic aid has been "parceled out to sustain urban businesses owned by the middle class and upper middle class. . . . Little of the money . . . appears to reach the impoverished majority of Salvadorans who live in the urban slums and the countryside."[9]

Duarte's problems have been dramatically compounded by the earthquake of October 10, 1986, which left a third of the capital city in ruins and 250,000 homeless, and caused over $1 billion in damage. Five months after the quake virtually no official aid had gone to poor neighborhoods. The Duarte government has refused to allow the Catholic church to be part of its National Emergency Committee, set up to coordinate international aid to victims. And, although the archdiocese received permission to accept donations directly and distribute them independently to the needy, church officials have claimed that governmental authorities obstructed the arrival of aid sent to them by foreign religious and secular institutions, thereby negating their work.[10]

As this book goes to press, the Salvadoran National Assembly has issued a blanket amnesty for all those who in the past have committed politically motivated murders. The only exception applies to those involved in the assassination of Archbishop Romero. The amnesty will prohibit the arrest or prosecution of any military or death squad members who took part in the massacre of tens of thousands of civilians. Ironically, the Salvadoran government justifies its action by claiming it as a step towards complying with the new Central American peace plan proposed by President Oscar Arias Sánchez of Costa Rica.

•

By 1985, right-wing-sponsored violence in Guatemala had become so extreme that the country was shunned by most of the international community. Large-scale condominium projects on Lake Atitlán, for instance, had to be abandoned, since tourism had been reduced to a trickle. With the economy in ruins and daily growing worse, the generals and their civilian allies realized they had to present a facade of respectability to the world. Thus, they decided to follow the lead of El Salvador: a free presidential election would be allowed, one in which even civilians would be permitted to run. The popular Christian Democrat, Vinicio Cerezo, won, taking office in January 1986. Genuinely reform-minded, he had previously survived several assassination attempts by the power structure. He realized that he was in no position to offend the military and landowners, however, and consequently seems to have concluded that reform could only be carried out in moderation and at a snail's pace. He abolished the notorious Technical Investigations Department, a secret police unit, but has refused to investigate the thousands of unsolved murders and disappearances.[11] Such inactivity has been especially repulsive to the Mutual Support group for the Appearance Alive of Our Relatives, an organization of family members of the disappeared. Their vocal demands for justice have received international attention, demonstrating to the world that Guatemala is still not the democracy its power structure tries to display.

Although human rights abuses have decreased since Cerezo has taken office, they have far from vanished. In his first year as president, at least 325 political murders and 78 disappearances occurred.[12] Moreover, no attempt has been made by Cerezo to reduce the army's control over the so-called "model villages," where many Indians have been forced to live and are required to form civil patrols to "protect" the area against guerrilla insurgents.[13]

To counteract his glaring inaction in bringing the death squads to justice and in curtailing the power of the military, Cerezo announced in September 1986 a land redistribution program, thereby hoping to retain his popularity with the masses. Since he had promised suspicious property owners when he was running for the presidency that he would not undertake land reform, Cerezo was quick to note that only unproductive government-owned areas would be involved. Nevertheless, if the project is successfully carried out it will benefit over seventy thousand *campesinos*.[14] Although Cerezo's reform plan seems insignificant in a nation where 300,000 peasants are landless, 43 percent of the people are unemployed, and 90 percent of the farms are too small to feed a family,[15] it is a start. Based on past history, however, odds are that even this modest plan will never reach fruition, and land ownership in Guatemala will remain the most unequal in all of Latin America.[16]

The Catholic church's view of Guatemala's human rights situation since the election of Cerezo is certainly not optimistic. In fact, Archbishop Próspero Penados of Guatemala City terms it "very bad":

> Labor unions and cooperatives are heavily controlled by government authorities. There is no respect for human dignity. Disappearances continue. People are still persecuted for their ideas. If someone disappears or is kidnapped, there is nowhere to seek redress. No one in authority accepts responsibility.[17]

In December 1986, the bishops announced plans to open a human rights office in early 1987 to monitor human rights abuses.[18] If they are successful, then cases like that of Manuel de Jesús Tzalam Coj will more easily be brought to international attention. Tzalam, a catechist working with Maryknoll Father Joseph LaMar in rural northern Guatemala, was shot to death during a religious service. LaMar, a retired lieutenant colonel in the U.S. Air Force, reports that the catechist had complained to the government on behalf of his village when a local landowner attempted to force the *campesinos* off their land. Despite the fact that authorities refused to help him and even threatened him, he continued to pursue justice; this, says LaMar, is why he was murdered.[19] The similarity to past murders of catechists is conspicuous; the statistics of death may have improved in Guatemala, but the underlying issues remain.

•

The fear generated by the 1975 massacre at Los Horcones caused the Catholic church in Honduras to tread a very cautious path for several years. Nevertheless, pervasive political tensions and social strains demanded a response, and by the early 1980s, the church began to speak out again, albeit somewhat timidly. Perhaps the most outspoken statement came from the Jesuits on March 12, 1984, just a few months after their former colleague, Guadalupe Carney, disappeared. Excerpts from their pronouncement reveal not only that the perennial issue of land reform was far from being resolved, but also that repression in the countryside was being revived.

> We Jesuits of Honduras are witnesses of how the *campesinos* among whom we live are left progressively unattended in their need for land to work and for credit to help them cultivate the land. The paralysis of the timid land reform has frustrated the hopes of many Honduran *campesinos* and has increased the number of landless Honduran families. . . .
>
> We witness how the poor among whom we work are often treated as "communists" or "subversives" when they try to organize in order to demand their rights. They are imprisoned without reason. . . . The

threat of "informants" and growing police control produce insecurity
. . . in the judicial system. We are also witness of how campesino and
labor leaders disappear, some assassinated in cold blood, without the
guilty parties being found or justly punished. . . .[20]

Honduras had seen repression and tension over land reform in the past, but in
the 1980s a new international dimension promised to complicate old domestic
problems. With U.S. military aid escalating to a proposed $88 million in 1987
from about $9 million in 1981, with nonmilitary aid from 1982 to 1987 more than
doubling the total amount authorized between 1952 and 1981,[21] and with Honduras playing host to the world's largest delegation of Peace Corps volunteers,[22] it
was obvious that this poverty-ridden nation was fast becoming a focal point of
U.S. foreign policy. Bases and airfields peopled by U.S. and Honduran soldiers
sprang up around the country and there were joint military exercises. Convoys of
army trucks could be seen on country roads and city streets, and authorities
made no secret that young Honduran men were being forcibly recruited from
bars and buses into the armed forces. The presence of an estimated 14,000
Nicaraguan counter-revolutionaries, known as contras, was tolerated on Honduran soil.[23] All of this signaled that, although Honduras's overwhelming social
and economic problems were far from solved, the major preoccupation of the
Honduran government was not hunger, illiteracy, landlessness or sky-rocketing
unemployment, but preparation for war. In this atmosphere, mysterious deaths
and disappearances approached two hundred by 1984.[24]

Seen in this context, the much-touted "democratization" of Honduras
under the new Liberal president, José Azcona del Hoyo, elected in November
1985, appeared rather premature. And indeed, the most prominent human
rights activist in Honduras, Ramón Custodio López, saw little in his nation's
so-called democratic government to praise: There were reported death threats
directed against outspoken Honduran critics of government policy;[25] the army's Civil Defense Committees, which were condemned in 1982 by the Catholic hierarchy for their repressive potential, were reactivated in 1985; the
"Commandos of Death," a death squad, had made an ominous appearance on
the scene; and there were numerous arbitrary and unconstitutional acts by
security forces.[26] Moreover, lamented Custodio, in the south Hondurans were
subjected to the whims of ex-Somocista contras entrenched there; he estimated
that about 20,000 Hondurans had been displaced by "La Contra" and by a war
their country had never declared upon its neighbor, Nicaragua.[27]

The U.S. role in this state of affairs was obvious to many Hondurans;
Custodio writes: "All this is the result of the subjection of our foreign and
domestic policy to the strategic interests of the Reagan Administration. So
much so that each day we are impelled more toward open war with Nicaragua.
. . ."[28] And in September 1986 a Honduran congressman and member of the
Christian Democratic Party predicted the unhappy consequences: "Honduras
will be facing in the short run polarization and violence similar to that of other
Central American countries."[29] Thus it seemed that by 1987 whatever hopes

Honduras might have had for democratization had been sacrificed to the short-sighted goals of the Reagan years.

As this manuscript goes to press, new, startling information has come to light. In June 1987 the Inter-American Court of Human Rights, the judicial arm of the Organization of American States, decided to bring charges against Honduras for the disappearances of four civilians. It was the first time a government had been brought to trial by the court. In early testimony Florencio Caballero, a former sergeant in the Honduran army now living in Canada, stated that he was a member of the 316 Battalion, an intelligence unit formed by the CIA, which ran several death squads. The unit, he claimed, interrogated and executed about 140 suspected "subversives" and the CIA was aware of their activities. After Caballero implicated former sergeant José Isaías Vilorio in the killings, the latter was assassinated just before he was to appear before the court. Later, another leading witness in the case, Miguel Angel Pavón, regional head of the Honduran Human Rights Commission, was likewise gunned down. In spite of these two assassinations there seemed to be considerable evidence against both the Honduran government and the CIA. As Aryeh Neier, vice chairman of a human rights organization, Americas Watch, noted in a press interview: "I have never seen a case in which the United States Government is so deeply linked to the human rights abuses of a Government as in Honduras." The court expected to reach a verdict in February 1988.[30]

•

With unjust structures still intact in El Salvador, Guatemala, and Honduras, the region remains potentially explosive, in spite of an improvement in human rights abuses and efforts toward "democratization" and reform. True democracy cannot be said to exist where vast segments of the population suffer from a severe maldistribution of wealth and have few political or judicial options to redress social and economic wrongs.

But it would be a discredit to these eleven missionaries to end the story of their lives on a note of despair. Not only did they offer much-needed hope during their lifetimes to thousands of victimized Central Americans, but this hope, like a relentless breeze, has crossed international borders and returned home to refresh North Americans as well. Thousands can trace their interest in the people and politics of Central America to the day they first questioned why a missionary had been shot to death and why the U.S. government was supporting the powers behind the execution. Thousands more have been heartened by the witness that these individual women and men have given to the vitality of Christianity in a tormented century when secular and religious institutions alike have often fomented or ignored injustice and enmity. And perhaps this volume has added another source of hope from which to draw: that commitment to the poor, like the gospel that inspires it, cuts across the political views, theologies, and ideologies imposed by human history. From Guadalupe Carney to Dorothy Kazel to John David Troyer, this is so.

Notes

All unpublished letters and reports cited in this book are in the authors' possession, in original or photocopy, unless otherwise indicated.

INTRODUCTION

1. Samuel Eliot Morison, *Christopher Columbus, Mariner* (New York and Scarborough, Ontario: Meridian Books, 1955), p.43.
2. Benjamin Keen and Mark Wasserman, *A Short History of Latin America*, 2nd ed. (Boston: Houghton Mifflin, 1984), p. 60.
3. Quoted in Hugo Latorre Cabal, *The Revolution of the Latin American Church*, trans. F. K. Hendricks and B. Berler (Norman, Oklahoma: University of Oklahoma Press, 1978), pp. 6–7.
4. Quoted in Enrique Dussel, *A History of the Church in Latin America: Colonialism to Liberation*, trans. and rev. A. Neely (Grand Rapids, Michigan: Eerdmans Publishing Co., 1981), p. 47.
5. Cabal, p. 7.
6. Dussel, *History of the Church in Latin America*, pp. 47–52; Dussel, *History and the Theology of Liberation* (Maryknoll, N.Y.: Orbis Books, 1976), pp. 83–84.
7. Dussel, *History of the Church in Latin America*, pp. 52–53.
8. Quoted in Anne Chapman, *Los Lencas de Honduras en el siglo XVI* (Tegucigalpa: Instituto Hondureño de Antropología e Historia, 1978), p. 3.
9. Quoted in Dussel, *History of the Church in Latin America*, p. 53.
10. Robert Chamberlain, *The Conquest and Colonization of Honduras, 1502-1550* (New York: Octagon Books, 1966), pp. 133, 239.
11. Dussel, *History of the Church in Latin America*, p. 55.
12. Stanley J. Stein and Barbara H. Stein, *The Colonial Heritage of Latin America: Essays on Economic Dependence in Perspective* (New York: Oxford University Press, 1970), p. 75.
13. Quoted in Keen and Wasserman, p. 74.
14. George Pendle, *A History of Latin America*, rev. ed. (Harmondsworth, England: Pelican Books, 1983), pp. 58–59.
15. Dussel, *History of the Church in Latin America*, p. 91.
16. Quoted in Longino Becerra, *Evolución histórica de Honduras* (Tegucigalpa: Baktun Editorial, 1983), p. 86.
17. José María Tojeira, *Los Hicaques de Yoro* (Tegucigalpa: Edición Guaymuras, 1982), pp. 22–28.
18. Ibid., pp. 30–31.
19. Ibid., p. 32.

20. Ibid., p. 34.
21. Ibid.
22. J. Guadalupe Carney, *To Be a Revolutionary* (San Francisco:Harper and Row, 1985), p. 280.
23. Chapman, p. 10.
24. Fernando Espino, *Relación verdadera de la reducción de los indios infieles de la provincia de la Taguisgalpa, llamados Xicaques*, prologue and notes by Jorge Eduardo Arellano (León, Nicaragua: 1968), pp. 28–29.
25. Ibid., p. 32.
26. John Coulson, ed., *The Saints: A Concise Biographical Dictionary* (New York: Guild Press, 1958), p. 614.
27. Quoted in Keen and Wasserman, p. 101.
28. Phillip Berryman, *Inside Central America: The Essential Facts Past and Present on El Salvador, Nicaragua, Honduras, Guatemala, and Costa Rica* (New York: Pantheon, 1985), p. 22.
29. Edward Cleary, *Crisis and Change: The Church in Latin America Today* (Maryknoll, N.Y.: Orbis Books, 1985), pp. 59–60.
30. Ibid., p. 61.
31. Ibid., pp. 60–61.
32. Ibid., p. 61.
33. Ibid., p. 42.
34. Ibid., p. 115.
35. Ibid., p. 50.
36. See Gerald M. Costello, *Mission to Latin America: The Successes and Failures of a Twentieth-Century Crusade* (Maryknoll, N.Y.: Orbis Books, 1979).

1. MICHAEL "CASIMIR" CYPHER

1. Ronald Olson, OFM, Conv., undated letter to the authors, 1984.
2. Anselm Romb, OFM, Conv., "How Long Is It Important To Live?" *Companion*, January 1983, p. 15.
3. Olson, letter to the authors.
4. Philip M. Wozniak, OFM, Conv., "A Special Supplement in Commemoration of Fr. Casimir's Death Two Years Ago: Reflections," no date.
5. Olson, letter to authors.
6. Kent Biergans, OFM, Conv., "Remembering Father Casimir," *Saint Anthony's Newsletter*, October 1975, p. 2.
7. Wozniak.
8. Olson, letter to the authors.
9. Leonard Wibberley, "He Gave Up Comfortable Hermosa Beach," *Los Angeles Times*, July 28, 1975, part 2, p. 7.
10. "AID Fiscal 1984 Congressional Presentation: Latin America and the Caribbean, 1983," cited in *Honduras: A Look at the Reality* (Hyattsville, Md.: Quixote Center, 1984), p. 12.
11. Ibid.
12. Tom Barry, Beth Wood, and Deb Preusch, *Dollars and Dictators* (Albuquerque: The Resource Center, 1982), p. 168.
13. Longino Becerra, *Evolución histórica de Honduras*, Colección Próceres, no. 2 (Tegucigalpa: Baktun Editorial, 1983), pp. 174–75; Walter LaFeber, *Inevitable Revolu-*

tions: The United States in Central America (New York: W. W. Norton and Co., 1984), pp. 178–79.

14. Mario Posas, *El movimiento campesino Hondureño* (Tegucigalpa: Editorial Guaymuras, 1981), pp. 10–11. For a detailed study of the 1954 strike, see Robert MacCameron, *Bananas, Labor, and Politics in Honduras: 1954–1963* (Syracuse, N.Y.: Maxwell School of Citizenship and Public Affairs, Syracuse University, 1983).

15. For an excellent study on the Catholic church's work with the *campesinos*, see Robert A. White, "Structural Factors in Rural Development: The Church and the Peasant in Honduras" (Ph.D. diss., Cornell University, 1977).

16. Nicholas D'Antonio, OFM, "How Personal Renewal Relates to Church Renewal," unpublished essay, no date, pp. 5–6.

17. Quoted in Bernardo Meza, OFM, *Padre Iván Betancur: Mártir de la Iglesia Latinoamericana* (Tegucigalpa: Editora Cultural, 1982), pp. 34–35.

18. D'Antonio, p. 4.

19. LaFeber, p. 182; D'Antonio, p. 5.

20. D'Antonio, pp. 15–16; Meza, p. 22.

21. D'Antonio, pp. 6–8.

22. Meza, p. 27.

23. D'Antonio, p. 16.

24. Ibid., pp. 8–9.

25. Dale Francis, "The Unlikely Martyr of Juticalpa," *Our Sunday Visitor*, August 31, 1975, p. 3.

26. Roberto Brauning, " 'I got to get it through my head that he is gone,' the mother says," *Our Sunday Visitor*, August 10, 1975.

27. Sister Mary García, notes to the authors, September 3, 1985.

28. Juanita Klapheke, "For Casimir on the Anniversary of His Death," unpublished poem, June 1976.

29. Michael Gable, interview with the authors, December 22, 1984.

30. Ibid.

31. Klapheke.

32. Wibberley.

33. Olson, letter to the authors.

34. Wozniak.

35. Romb, p. 16.

36. Francis.

37. Steven Volk, "Honduras: On the Border of War," *NACLA: Report on the Americas* 15, no. 6 (November–December 1981), p. 19; Becerra, p. 201.

38. Becerra, p. 204.

39. Volk, p. 19; Becerra, pp. 201, 203.

40. Quoted in Volk, pp. 20–21.

41. Becerra, p. 207.

42. D'Antonio, p. 17; Meza, p. 39.

43. Becerra, p. 207.

44. Penny Lernoux, *Cry of the People: The Struggle for Human Rights in Latin America—The Catholic Church in Conflict with U.S. Policy* (New York: Penguin Books, 1982), p. 109; Becerra, p. 207.

45. Meza, p. 38; D'Antonio, p. 15.

46. Quoted in Meza, p. 39.

47. Meza, p. 40.

48. Sister Mary García, interview with the authors, March 14, 1984.

49. Becerra, p. 207; Anne Street and Nancy Peckenham, "Translated Unpublished Transcript of an Interview with Bishop Luis Santos," July 30, 1984, p. 5; anonymous eyewitness, quoted in Sister Mary García, unpublished account of events in Olancho, July 1, 1975, pp. 1–2.

50. García, unpublished account of events in Olancho, p. 2; Meza, p. 41.

51. Street and Peckenham, p. 5.

52. García, unpublished account of events in Olancho, p. 3.

53. Meza, p. 41; J. Guadalupe Carney, *To Be a Revolutionary: An Autobiography* (San Francisco: Harper and Row, 1985), p. 344.

54. Lernoux, pp. 112–114; Meza, p. 42.

55. *Gaceta Judicial, Publicación de la Corte Suprema de Justicia de Honduras*, no. 1265, April–June 1980, p. 88.

56. D'Antonio, pp. 14, 18; García, unpublished account of events in Olancho, pp. 5–6; Lernoux, p. 112; "Bring Me the Head of Bishop D'Antonio," Editorial Comment, *The Christian Century*, September 17, 1975, p. 780.

57. García, notes to the authors; Meza, p. 44; Harry Maurer, "The Priests of Honduras," *The Nation*, March 6, 1976, p. 268.

58. Meza, p. 43.

59. Casimir Cypher, "Next of Kin" form, September 1974.

60. Quoted in Brauning.

61. Quoted in Meza, p. 46.

62. Alan Riding, "In Honduras the Land Issue Is Creating a Dangerous Class Feud," *New York Times*, July 26, 1975, p. 9.

63. "Informe de la Comisión Investigadora, Nombrada por el Consejo Superior de las Fuerzas Armadas de Honduras," July 23, 1975, as reported in Meza, pp. 83–85.

64. Lernoux, pp. 113–114; Maurer, p. 268; García, unpublished account of events in Olancho, pp. 5–7; letter from Father Emil Cook, OFM, Conv., to "Fr. Clement and All the Province," July 21, 1975.

65. Paul H. Wackerbarth (Officer in Charge, Honduran Affairs, U.S. Department of State), letter to Mr. and Mrs. Michael Gable, September 25, 1975.

66. D'Antonio, p. 19.

67. Letter from Father Lawrence Mattingly, OFM, Conv., to President Gerald R. Ford, August 5, 1975.

68. Lernoux, p. 114; García, interview with the authors, March 14, 1984; Janet Melvin, letter to the authors, December 28, 1984.

69. Street and Peckenham, p. 4.

70. "Informe de la Comisión . . .," in Meza, pp. 83–84.

71. Becerra, p. 208; Meza, p. 47.

72. Telegram dated August 2, 1975.

73. Letter dated August 7, 1975.

74. García, notes to the authors.

2. JAMES "GUADALUPE" CARNEY

1. J. Guadalupe Carney, *To Be a Revolutionary: An Autobiography* (San Francisco: Harper and Row, 1985), p. 441.

2. Carney, "A Challenge to American Consciences (Selected Excerpts from the Writings of Father James Guadalupe Carney)," no date, p. 1.

3. John Patrick ("Pat") Carney, "Memories of My Brother, Jim," unpublished essay, December 29, 1984, p. 2.

4. Carney, *To Be a Revolutionary*, p. 92.

5. The account of the summer's events that follows is condensed from "Memories of My Brother, Jim," pp. 2-4. There are some differences between Pat's recollections and Jim's, as recounted in *To Be a Revolutionary*, pp. 50-54.

6. Pat Carney, "Memories," p. 6.

7. Carney, *To Be a Revolutionary*, pp. 64-65.

8. Ibid., p. 68.

9. Pat Carney, "Memories," p. 6.

10. Carney, *To Be a Revolutionary*, pp. 81-82.

11. Walter LaFeber, *Inevitable Revolutions: The United States in Central America* (New York: W. W. Norton and Co., 1984), p. 177.

12. Carney, *To Be a Revolutionary*, p. 127.

13. LaFeber, p. 182.

14. Ibid., pp. 180, 184. LaFeber's work provides an excellent analysis of the effects of the Alliance for Progress on the countries of Central America.

15. Carney, *To Be a Revolutionary*, pp. 145-48; Longino Becerra, *Evolución histórica de Honduras*, Colección Próceres no. 2 (Tegucigalpa: Baktun Editorial, 1983), p. 175.

16. James Guadalupe Carney, "El precio más grande que puedo recibir es el martirio," *Diálogo Social* 16, no. 162 (November-December 1983), p. 48.

17. Carney, *To Be a Revolutionary*, pp. 181-83.

18. Carney, "A Challenge to American Consciences," p. 1.

19. Ibid., p. 2.

20. George Black and Anne Nelson, "Mysterious Death of Fr. Carney," *The Nation*, August 4-11, 1984, p. 81.

21. Carney, *To Be a Revolutionary*, pp. 164-65.

22. Ibid., pp. 193, 206-11; Mario Posas, *El movimiento campesino hondureño* (Tegucigalpa: Editorial Guaymuras, 1981), p. 25.

23. Quoted in José María Tojeira, S.J., "A Life of Service to Honduras," *Honduras Update*, November-December 1983, p. 9. Although Tojeira indicates that the date of the newspaper article was June 24, 1964, a comparison with Carney's recollection of the same events seems to place the incident in June 1966; see Carney, *To Be a Revolutionary* pp. 206-10.

24. Ibid.

25. Carney, "El precio más grande," p. 49; see also Carney, *To Be a Revolutionary*, pp. 212-13.

26. Letter of Fernando Bandeira, S.J., to Carney family, undated.

27. Steven Volk, "Honduras: On the Border of War," *NACLA: Report on the Americas*, no. 6 (November-December 1981), p. 10; Douglas Kincaid, " 'We Are the Agrarian Reform': Rural Politics and Agrarian Reform," in *Honduras: Portrait of a Captive Nation*, ed. Nancy Peckenham and Annie Street (New York: Praeger Publishers, 1985), pp. 138-40; Carney, *To Be a Revolutionary*, pp. 233-34.

28. Michael J. Farrell, "The Carneys: One More Family Lives 'Missing' Trauma,"*National Catholic Reporter*, February 24, 1984, p. 1; Virginia Smith, letter to the authors, February 19, 1985; see also Carney, *To Be a Revolutionary*, pp. 213-222.

29. Carney, *To Be a Revolutionary*, pp. 213-14.

30. Ibid., pp. 220-21.

31. Ibid., p. 225.

32. Pat Carney, "Memories," p. 6.

33. Virginia Smith, letter to the authors, January 4, 1985.

34. LaFeber, pp. 181–83.

35. Carney, *To Be a Revolutionary*, pp. 244–246; see also Becerra, pp. 180-81.

36. Quoted in "Datos Biográficos del P. Guadalupe Carney," undated biography put out by Jesuits in Honduras after Carney's death, p. 2.

37. Carney, *To Be a Revolutionary*, pp. 263–66.

38. "Datos Biográficos del P. Guadalupe Carney," p. 2; see also Becerra, pp. 182–94, for a detailed account of the 1969 war between El Salvador and Honduras.

39. Carney, *To Be a Revolutionary*, pp. 273–83.

40. Carney, "A Challenge to American Consciences," p. 1; Carney, *To Be a Revolutionary*, pp. 93–94.

41. Carney, "A Challenge to American Consciences," p. 1.

42. Carney, *To Be a Revolutionary*, pp. xvi–xvii.

43. Ibid., pp. 317–19.

44. Ibid., p. 118.

45. Ibid., p. 131.

46. Ibid., pp. 131, 144.

47. Ibid., pp. 176–77.

48. Ibid., pp. 266–67.

49. Ibid., p. 376.

50. Ibid., pp. 289–90.

51. Ibid., pp. 309–10.

52. Ibid., p. 310.

53. Ibid., pp. 408–409.

54. Ibid., pp. 291–93.

55. Ibid., pp. 313–14.

56. Ibid., pp. 390–91; see also Tojeira, "A Life of Service to Honduras," p. 10.

57. Philip Agee, *Inside the Company: CIA Diary* (New York: Stonehill, 1975), pp. 599, 601; see also Penny Lernoux, *Cry of the People: The Struggle for Human Rights in Latin America—The Catholic Church in Conflict with U. S. Policy* (New York: Penguin Books, 1982), pp. 211–13; Harry Maurer, "The Priests of Honduras," *The Nation* (March 6, 1976), p. 268; Volk, p. 10.

58. Tojeira, "A Life of Service to Honduras," p. 10.

59. Ibid., pp. 10–11.

60. Ibid., p. 11; Carney, *To Be a Revolutionary*, pp. 423–24.

61. Carney, *To Be a Revolutionary*, p. 421.

62. Ibid.

63. Robert L. Koenig, "Faith Led 'Padre Guadalupe' to Honduras," *St. Louis Post-Dispatch*, September 25, 1983, Section F, pp. 1, 14.

64. "Boletín IISE," Instituto de Investigaciones Socio-Económicas (Honduras), año 1, no. 7 (October 1979), p. 7.

65. Ramón Custodio López, "An Unjust System," Acceptance Speech for 1984 Letelier-Moffitt Human Rights Award, September 21, 1984, p. 2.

66. Carney, "A Challenge to American Consciences," p. 4.

67. Quoted in Carney, *To Be a Revolutionary*, p. 422.

68. Bob Adams, "Villagers Pay Tribute to 'Father Guadalupe'," *St. Louis Post-Dispatch*, September 25, 1983, p. 5.

69. "Memorials from Nicaraguan Communities," received by Carney family, no date, p. 1.

70. Ibid., p. 3.

71. Adams, "Villagers."

72. James Carney, "Message to the People of Honduras," December 23, 1982, *Honduras Update,* November–December 1983, p. 11.

73. Leyda Barbieri, "The Militarization of Honduras and Its Impact on Honduran Society," statement prepared for the Subcommittee on Military Installations and Facilities of the Armed Services Committee, March 27, 1984, p. 7.

74. Carney, *To Be a Revolutionary,* p. 433.

75. "An Interview with Father Fausto Milla," *Honduras Update,* May 1984, pp.5–6.

76. Quoted in Bob Adams, " 'Father Guadalupe'—Reluctant Rebel," *St. Louis Post-Dispatch,* September 23, 1983, p. 11.

77. Carney, "A Challenge to American Consciences," p. 4.

78. Black and Nelson, p. 81.

79. Ibid.

80. Farrell, p. 26; Black and Nelson, pp. 81–84; Michael Kelley, "Questions Surround Death of Padre Guadalupe," *Honduras Update,* November–December 1983, p. 8.

81. Tojeira, "A Life of Service to Honduras," p. 11.

82. Black and Nelson, p. 81.

83. Ibid., p. 82; Kelley, p. 8.

84. Kelley, p. 8.

85. The case is too complex to be detailed in this short biography, but the interested reader may refer to Black and Nelson, pp. 81–84.

86. James LeMoyne, "Honduras's Army Tied to 200 Deaths," *New York Times,* May 2, 1987, pp. 1, 8.

87. Joseph Connolly, interview with the authors, January 27, 1988; Virginia Smith, letter to the authors, May 23, 1987; Pat Carney, interview with the authors, January 24, 1988; George Black, "The Many Killers of Father Carney," *The Nation,* January 23, 1988, pp. 84–86.

88. Transcript of Father Joe Mulligan's interview with a Honduran Jesuit, February 12, 1987. The Honduran Jesuit is named in the tape, which was made for the private use of the Carney family. He is not identified in this book since such identification could cause him problems when he travels to Honduras.

3. WILLIAM WOODS

1. Moises Sandoval's interview with Bishop John E. McCarthy, 1984. A condensed version of the interview was published; see John E. McCarthy, "A Cowboy for Jesus," *Maryknoll* 78, no. 11 (November 1984), pp. 58–62.

2. Letter from Reverend A. E. Smith to the authors, January 4, 1985.

3. Sandoval-McCarthy interview.

4. Reverend William McIntire, "Memo to the Maryknoll General Council on the Death of Fr. William Woods and Others," (December 14, 1976), p. 4, in William Woods file, Maryknoll Archives, Maryknoll, N.Y.

5. Ron Chernow, "The Strange Death of Bill Woods: Did He Fly Too Far in the Zone of the Generals?" *Mother Jones,* May 1979, p. 35.

6. Sandoval-McCarthy interview.

7. Letter from Smith to the authors, January 4, 1985.

8. Undated essay by William Woods, Woods file, Maryknoll Archives.

9. Sandoval-McCarthy interview.

10. Father Rafael Dávila, telephone interview with the authors, January 12, 1985.

11. Ibid.

12. Ibid.

13. Walter LaFeber, *Inevitable Revolutions: The United States in Central America* (New York: W.W. Norton, 1984), p. 8.

14. Chernow, p. 35.

15. The above description is taken in part from the authors' "A Teacher and a Martyr in Guatemala," *America*, October 30, 1982, p. 253.

16. Phillip Berryman, *The Religious Roots of Rebellion: Christians in Central American Revolutions* (Maryknoll, N.Y.: Orbis Books, 1984), pp. 35-36.

17. Ibid., pp. 163-64.

18. Stephen Schlesinger and Stephen Kinzer, *Bitter Fruit: The Untold Story of the American Coup in Guatemala* (New York: Anchor Books, 1983); Berryman, pp. 35-39, 163-67.

19. Schlesinger and Kinzer, pp. 106-107.

20. Berryman, p. 169.

21. Ibid., pp. 170-73; Benjamin Keen and Mark Wasserman, *A Short History of Latin America*, 2nd ed. (Boston: Houghton Mifflin, 1984), pp. 441-42.

22. Quoted in Chernow, p. 34.

23. Sandoval-McCarthy interview.

24. Ibid.

25. Ibid; also, telephone conversation between McCarthy and authors, December 5, 1985.

26. Ibid.

27. Ibid.

28. Letter from William Woods, May 27, 1968.

29. Telephone interview between Father Rafael Dávila and the authors, January 12, 1985; letter from Dávila to the authors, February 27, 1985.

30. Sandoval-McCarthy interview.

31. Letter from Callan Graham to Father John McCormack, October 19, 1967, Woods file, Maryknoll Archives.

32. Quoted in Chernow, p. 37.

33. Woods, "Accomplishments of the Proyecto Ixcán," appended to a letter from Father Woods to President Laugerud García of Guatemala, May 17, 1976.

34. Chernow, p. 37.

35. Woods, "Report of Army Interference in Ixcán," January 14, 1976, p. 1, Woods file, Maryknoll Archives.

36. Ibid., pp. 1-2.

37. Sandoval-McCarthy interview; note from Ronald Hennessey to the authors, December 26, 1985.

38. Ronald W. Hennessey, "Report on the Plane Crash of Father William H. Woods on November 20, 1976, by Father Ronald W. Hennessey, Regional Superior of the Maryknoll Fathers, to Father Raymond A. Hill, Superior General," Woods file, Maryknoll Archives.

39. Ibid.

40. Letter from Father Woods to President Laugerud, May 17, 1976, Woods file, Maryknoll Archives.

41. Hennessey, "Report," pp. 7-8.

42. McIntire, p. 1.

43. Sandoval-McCarthy interview.

44. McIntire, pp. 1–3.

45. Hennessey, "Report," p. 1.

46. Ibid., p. 4; see also Chernow, p. 32.

47. Hennessey, "Report," p. 6.

48. Ibid., p. 2.

49. Ibid., p. 8.

50. McIntire, p. 3; see also Hennessey, p. 2.

51. McIntire, p. 3.

52. Hennessey, "Report," pp. 5–6.

53. Ibid., p. 7.

54. Chernow, p. 41.

55. Hennessey, "Report," p. 6; note from Hennessey to the authors, December 26, 1985.

56. Chernow, p. 41.

57. McIntire, p. 4.

58. Ibid., pp. 4–6.

59. Chernow, p. 36.

60. Ibid.

61. Letter written at the request of the authors from a source who wishes to remain anonymous and signs his name "a person who was there." The letter is undated but was received in May 1985.

62. Ibid.

63. Chernow, p. 32.

64. This priest wishes to remain anonymous. Three other Maryknoll priests have confirmed his story in interviews or written correspondence with the authors. They are Fathers Jim Curtin, Emmet Farrell, and Ron Michels.

65. Sandoval-McCarthy interview.

4. STANLEY ROTHER

1. Stanley Rother, *The Shepherd Cannot Run: Letters of Stanley Rother, Missionary and Martyr*, ed. David Monahan (Oklahoma City: Archdiocese of Oklahoma City, 1984), p. 31. For a short but good sketch of Rother's life see: Henri J.M. Nouwen, *Love in a Fearful Land: A Guatemalan Story* (Notre Dame, Indiana: Ave Maria Press, 1985).

2. Ibid., p. 39.

3. Bob Rivard and Tanya Barrientos, "Murdered Priest's Family Prays for Justice," *The Plain Dealer*, August 8, 1982, p. 3-AA.

4. David Monahan, "Afterword," in S. Rother, *Shepherd*, p. 91.

5. Monahan, "Foreword," in Rother, *Shepherd*, pp. 4–5.

6. Monahan, "Rotherville: A Place of Pioneers and Strong Faith," *The Sooner Catholic*, August 16, 1981, p. 5.

7. Ibid.

8. "Yearbook: 'Noise is Not His Specialty. Cooperation Marks his Personality,' " *The Sooner Catholic*, August 16, 1981, p. 4.

9. Rother, *Shepherd*, p. 81.

10. Martha Mary McGaw, C.S.J. "Father Stanley Rother: 'My People Need Me,' " *The Sooner Catholic*, August 16, 1981, p. 21.

11. Marita Rother, A.S.C., letter to the authors, November 25, 1984.

12. Father Marvin Leven, cassette tape to the authors, July 27, 1985.

13. McGaw, "Father Stanley Rother," p. 21; Leven, cassette tape to authors.

14. Father Harry J. Flynn, "I Remember Stanley Rother," *The Sooner Catholic*, January 3, 1982, p. 6.

15. McGaw, "Father Stanley Rother," p. 20.

16. *National Catholic Reporter*, November 19, 1982, p. 8.

17. Martha Mary McGaw, C.S.J., "Memories, Happy Laughter, Old Clothes, and Night Watches," *The Sooner Catholic*, August 16, 1981, p. 6.

18. Leven, cassette tape to authors.

19. Gerald M. Costello, *Mission to Latin America* (Maryknoll, N.Y.: Orbis Books, 1979), p. 44.

20. David Monahan, "Santiago Atitlan Was a Place Only for the Patient," *The Sooner Catholic,* August 16, 1981, p. 13.

21. The description that follows, unless otherwise noted, is condensed from a cassette tape made by Frankie Williams for the Religious Task Force, Washington, D.C., June 1982, a copy of which Mrs. Williams sent to the authors.

22. Monahan, "Foreword," in Rother, *Shepherd*, p. 2.

23. Ibid., p. 3.

24. Ibid., pp. 3, 6.

25. "Yearbook," p. 4.

26. Bishop Angelico Melotto, homily given at memorial mass for Rother on September 3, 1981, quoted in appendix to Rother, *Shepherd*, p. 102.

27. Rother, *Shepherd*, p. 15; Marita Rother, letter to the authors, April 6, 1985; Leven, cassette tape to authors.

28. Rother, *Shepherd*, p. 28.

29. Ibid., p. 55.

30. Rother, cited in Monahan, "Foreword," p. 8.

31. McGaw, "Father Stanley Rother," p. 21.

32. Rother, *Shepherd*, p. 39.

33. The descriptions that follow are condensed from Frankie Williams's cassette tape and phone interview with the authors, May 9, 1985.

34. Penny Lernoux, *Cry of the People: The Struggle for Human Rights in Latin America—The Catholic Church in Conflict with U.S. Policy* (New York: Penguin Books, 1982), pp. 375–77.

35. Williams, cassette tape.

36. Rother, letter to Marita Rother, Christmas 1979; Leven, cassette tape to authors.

37. Leven, cassette tape.

38. Williams, cassette tape.

39. Rother, letter to Marita Rother.

40. Williams, cassette tape.

41. Rother, *Shepherd*, p. 15.

42. McGaw, "Memories," p. 6.

43. Leven, cassette tape.

44. Rother, letter to Marita Rother; Monahan, "Foreword," to Rother, *Shepherd*, p. 9.

45. Rother, *Shepherd*, p. 18.

46. Williams, cassette tape.

47. Rother, *Shepherd*, pp. 87–89.

48. Rother, *Shepherd*, p. 66; Leven, cassette tape.

49. Williams, cassette tape, postscript to the authors, March 1985; interview with the authors, May 9, 1985.

50. Jude Pansini, quoted in McGaw, "Father Stanley Rother," p. 21.

51. Jon D. Cozean, *Latin America 1982* (Washington, D.C.: Stryker-Post, 1982), p. 64; Walter LaFeber, *Inevitable Revolutions: The United States in Central America* (New York: W.W. Norton and Co., 1984), p. 257; Phillip Berryman, *Religious Roots of Rebellion* (Maryknoll, N.Y.: Orbis Books, 1984), p. 173.

52. Berryman, p. 173.

53. Cozean, p. 64.

54. Ibid.

55. Berryman, pp. 190–91.

56. Cozean, p. 64.

57. Berryman, pp. 189–93, 196–200; Thomas P. Anderson, *Politics in Central America* (New York: Praeger, 1982), p. 42.

58. Berryman, pp. 200–205.

59. Cozean, p. 65.

60. Rother, *Shepherd*, p. 10.

61. Ronald Burke, "Cry from Guatemala: 'They killed Stan,' " *Maryknoll*, January 1982, p. 51.

62. Rother, *Shepherd*, p. 25.

63. Ibid., pp. 29–30.

64. Ibid., pp. 30–31.

65. Ibid., pp. 34, 77.

66. Berryman, p. 206.

67. Rother, *Shepherd*, pp. 54–55.

68. Ibid., p. 64.

69. Burke, p. 52.

70. Christopher P. Winner, "Guatemala Aid Issue Debated in Congress," *National Catholic Reporter*, August 14, 1981, p. 6.

71. Monahan, "Notes and Identifications," in Rother, *Shepherd*, p. 80.

72. Rother, *Shepherd*, pp. 61–62; Williams, phone conversation with the authors.

73. After Rother's death, the entire letter was printed on the editorial page of the *New York Times*. See "Cry from Guatemala," *New York Times*, August 15, 1981, p. 23.

74. Rother, *Shepherd*, pp. 61–64.

75. Williams, cassette tape.

76. Winner, p. 6.

77. Phillip Wearne, "Guatemala," *Central America's Indians*, Minority Rights Group Report No. 62 (London: 1984), p. 11.

78. Patricia Scharber Lefevre, "Pax Christi Study: Guatemalan Genocide," *National Catholic Reporter*, February 26, 1982, p. 20.

79. Monahan, "Notes," in Rother, *Shepherd*, p. 65.

80. Patty Edmonds, "Oklahoma Priest Murdered in Guatemala," *National Catholic Reporter*, August 14, 1981, p. 7.

81. Monahan, "Notes," in Rother, *Shepherd*, p. 69; Leven, cassette to authors. The copy that was sent to the archbishop is no longer extant.

82. Burke, pp. 51–52.

83. Rother, *Shepherd*, pp. 69–70; Leven, cassette to authors.

84. Rother, *Shepherd*, p. 70.

85. Ibid., pp. 76–78.

86. Amnesty International, "Guatemala: A Government Program of Political Murder" (London: 1981), p. 3; Berryman, pp. 208-10.

87. Rother, letter to Don McCarthy, June 1, 1981.

88. Dial Torgerson, "U.S. Priest Reportedly Killed by Guatemalan Kidnappers, Not Thieves," *Los Angeles Times*, August 25, 1981, Pt. I, p. 15.

89. Williams, phone conversation with authors; Leven, cassette tape.

90. Williams, cassette tape.

91. Ibid.; Monahan, "Afterword," in Rother, *Shepherd*, p. 91; Torgerson, p. 15.

92. Martha Mary McGaw, "His Indian Friends Kept His Heart in Guatemala," *The Sooner Catholic*, August 16, 1981, p. 3; Williams, interview with authors.

93. Edmonds, p. 8.

94. Torgerson, p. 15.

95. Rivard and Barrientos, p. 3-AA.

96. Leven, cassette tape to authors.

97. Edmonds, p. 8.

5. JOHN DAVID TROYER

1. "Guatemala: Religious Only a Fraction of Thousands Slain There," *National Catholic Reporter*, March 5, 1982, pp. 22-23.

2. Phillip Berryman, *Religious Roots of Rebellion* (Maryknoll, N.Y.: Orbis Books, 1984), p. 180.

3. Dallas Witmer, *The Guatemalan Cry: A History of the Mission Work of the Conservative Mennonite Fellowship Missions in Guatemala, Central America* (Seymour, Missouri: Edgewood Press, 1974), p. 127.

4. Ibid., p. 65.

5. John C. Wenger, *Who Are the Mennonites?* (Scottdale, Pa.: Herald Press Tracts, no. date), p. 6.

6. Ibid., pp. 8-9.

7. Ibid., p. 6.

8. Ibid., p. 3.

9. Witmer, p. 15.

10. Ibid., p. 109.

11. Ibid., p. 28.

12. Ibid., p. 86; see also pp. 89, 129.

13. "Mission Directors Revisit Guatemala Churches," *The Harvest Call* 13, no. 11. (November 1981), p. 4.

14. Letter from Gary Miller to the authors, September 17, 1984.

15. Confirmed by telephone call to Harry Hertzler, May 15, 1985.

16. "Reflections," *The Harvest Call* 13, no. 9 (September 1981), p. 5.

17. Letter from Alvin and Luellen Troyer to the authors, December 20, 1984.

18. Ibid.

19. Ibid.

20. Ibid.

21. Ibid.

22. Witmer, p. 108.

23. Ibid., p. 74.

24. Ibid., p. 116.

25. Ibid., pp. 116-17.

26. Ibid., p. 117.

27. "John Troyer's Obituary," *The Harvest Call* 13, no. 9 (September 1981), p. 4.

28. Letter from Gary Miller to the authors, February 20, 1985.

29. Ibid.

30. Marion Good, "Communion Service in Guatemala," *The Harvest Call* 13, no. 6. (June 1981), p. 8.

31. Witmer, p. 107.

32. Domingo Tubac, "Palamá Christian School," *The Harvest Call* 13, no. 10 (October 1981), p. 5.

33. Witmer, pp. 89, 106.

34. Ibid., pp. 35, 57, 62, 88, 91, 117; Harry Hertzler, telephone conversation with the authors, May 15, 1985.

35. Dale Miller, "My Stay in Guatemala," *The Harvest Call* 13, no. 10 (October 1981), p. 8.

36. Ibid.

37. "Guatemala News," *The Harvest Call* 13, no. 2 (February 1981), p. 4.

38. Miller, "My Stay," pp. 7–9.

39. Gary Miller, "Facing Death at Palamá," *The Harvest Call* 13, no. 11 (November 1981), pp. 5–8; no. 12 (December 1981), pp. 5–8.

40. "Reflections," pp. 4–5.

41. "Church News," *The Harvest Call* (October 1981), p. 12.

42. "Further Developments," *The Harvest Call* 13, no. 10 (October 1981), p. 4; "Mission Directors Revisit Guatemalan Churches," *Harvest Call* 13, no. 11 (November 1981), p. 4.

43. "Mission Directors Revisit," p. 4.

44. Witmer, p. 129.

45. Letter from Gary Miller to the authors, February 20, 1985.

46. Letter from Alvin and Luellen Troyer to the authors, February 15, 1985.

47. Telephone conversation with Harry Hertzler, May 15, 1985.

48. "Guatemala: Religious Only a Fraction," p. 23.

49. Letter from Delton Franz to the authors, April 8, 1985.

50. Letter from Rich Sider to the authors, April 12, 1985.

51. John Hammond, O.S.B., "Genocide in Guatemala," *Sojourners*, December 1983, p. 24.

52. David Stephen, Phillip Wearne, and Rodolfo Stavenhagen, *Central American Indians*, Minority Rights Group Report No. 62 (London: 1984), p. 16.

53. See Berryman, pp. 194–95.

54. Stephen, et al., p. 16.

55. Ibid., p. 17; Berryman, pp. 209–210; also see Amnesty International, "Guatemala: A Government Program of Political Murder" (London: 1981).

56. Witmer, pp. 30–31.

57. Stephen, et al., p. 17.

58. Quoted in Berryman, p. 209.

59. Jenny Pearce, *Under the Eagle: U.S. Intervention in Central America and the Caribbean* (London: Latin America Bureau, 1981), p. 176; Tom Barry, Beth Wood, Deb Preusch, *Dollars and Dictators: A Guide to Central America* (Albuquerque: Resource Center, 1982), p. 123.

60. Quoted in Berryman, p. 207.

61. Amnesty International, "Guatemala," p. 3.

6. JAMES MILLER

1. Some of the information in this chapter is taken verbatim from Edward Brett and Donna W. Brett, "A Teacher and a Martyr in Guatemala," *America*, October 30, 1982, pp. 253–55.

2. Brother Stephen Markham, F.S.C., "Brother James Miller, F.S.C., 1944–1982," *Memorial to James Alfred Miller, F.S.C., of the Winona Province* (Winona, Minn.: St. Mary's Press, no date), p. 1.

3. Ibid., p. 7.

4. Ibid., p. 2.

5. Ibid., pp. 1–2.

6. Ibid., pp. 1–2; Patty Edmonds, "Brother Slain in Guatemala 'Gave His Life for Students,' " *National Catholic Reporter*, February 26, 1982, p. 8.

7. Markham, p. 7.

8. Ibid.

9. Edmonds, p. 19.

10. Brother Gerard Pihaly, F.S.C., "Notes on Brother James Miller," written at request of authors, March 26, 1985.

11. Gregory Robertson, interview with the authors.

12. Mordecai Specktor, "Murder in Guatemala: The War Comes Home," *Twin Cities Reader*, February 25, 1982, p. 7.

13. Don Geng, "A Humble Servant: Brother James Murdered in Guatemala," *Cretin Quarterly Bulletin* (Spring 1982), p. 1.

14. Letter from Jane Campbell to Don Geng, March 8, 1982.

15. Geng, *Cretin Quarterly*, p. 1.

16. Markham, p. 7.

17. Walter LaFeber, *Inevitable Revolutions: The United States in Central America* (New York: W.W. Norton and Co., 1984), p. 30.

18. Benjamin Keen and Mark Wasserman, *A Short History of Latin America* (Boston: Houghton Mifflin, 1984), p. 443.

19. Ibid., p. 444.

20. LaFeber, p. 69.

21. Phillip Berryman, *Religious Roots of Rebellion* (Maryknoll, N.Y.: Orbis Books, 1984), p. 66.

22. Michael Dodson and Tommie Sue Montgomery, "The Churches in the Nicaraguan Revolution," in Thomas Walker, ed., *Nicaragua in Revolution* (New York: Praeger, 1982), p. 168.

23. Berryman, pp. 69–70.

24. Markham, p. 4.

25. Ibid., p. 2.

26. From a bulletin sent to the Christian Brothers of the Winona Province after Miller's death.

27. Edmonds, p. 19.

28. Letter from Markham to the authors, March 19, 1985.

29. Letter from Brother Nicholas Geimer to the authors, March 17, 1985.

30. Ibid.

31. Ibid.

32. Ibid.

33. Ibid.

34. Ibid.

35. Ibid.

36. Ibid.

37. Edmonds, p. 19.

38. Ibid.

39. See Donna and Edward Brett, "Letter From a Murdered Brother," *Santa Fe Reporter*, April 4, 1982, p. 19.

40. H. Lewis Twohig to the authors, no date, but received in March 1985.

41. Ibid.

42. Don Geng, "A Humble Servant" (see no. 15, above), unedited, unpublished draft, pp. 2-3.

43. Geng, *Cretin Quarterly*, p. 1.

44. Confidential source.

45. Berryman, p. 200.

46. Cited in Berryman, pp. 201–202.

47. Phillip Wearne, "Guatemala," in D. Stephen, P. Wearne, and R. Stavenhagen, *Central America's Indians*, Minority Rights Group, Report No. 62 (London: 1984), p. 12.

48. "Memorial Reflection: St. Mary's College, Winona, Minnesota, March 24, 1982," in Markham, pp. 15–16.

49. Wearne, p. 18; Victor Perera, "Pawns in the Political Game," *The Nation*, November 12, 1983, pp. 455–59.

50. Wearne, p. 18.

51. Ibid.

52. Markham, p. 4.

53. Ibid., p. 5; Edmonds, p. 19.

54. Pihaly, "Notes."

55. Joan Turner Beifuss, "Miller Eulogized," *National Catholic Reporter*, February 26, 1982, p. 19; letter from Brother H. Lewis Twohig to the authors.

56. Archbishop John Roach, "Pray that God Will Change Oppressors' Hearts," St. Paul, Minnesota, *Catholic Bulletin*, February 1982.

57. Geng, *Cretin Quarterly*, pp. 1, 5.

58. Edward Brett and Donna W. Brett, "A Teacher and a Martyr in Guatemala," p. 254.

59. Ibid., pp. 254–55.

7. FRANK XAVIER HOLDENRIED

1. Quoted in Nikki Ciardella White, "Kelseyville Folks Aid Kids in Guatemala," Santa Rosa *Press Democrat*, August 18, 1981, p. 3D.

2. Letter from Frank Holdenried to Richard Smith, December 8, 1978.

3. Unless otherwise noted, the following early biographical information is derived mainly from two letters written by Richard Smith to the authors in May 1984 and June 1985.

4. Letter from Richard Smith to the authors, June 1985.

5. Letter from Reverend David Leeper Moss to the authors, March 27, 1985.

6. Ibid.

7. Letter from Smith to the authors, June 1985.

8. Letter from Moss to the authors, March 27, 1985.

9. Kathleen Hendrix, "The Life and Death of a Good Samaritan," *Los Angeles Times*, May 4, 1983, Part V, pp. 1, 10–11.

10. Letter from Holdenried to Moss, May 27, 1978.

11. Hendrix, p. 10.

12. Ibid.

13. Letter from Smith to the authors, June 1985.

14. Mark R. Day, "American's Death Raises Questions at Home, Abroad," *National Catholic Reporter*, April 29, 1983, p. 6.

15. David Moss, although a Methodist, was for a time pastor of both the Presbyterian and Methodist churches in Kelseyville.

16. Letter from Moss to the authors, March 27, 1985.

17. Phone conversation, Reverend Gerry Phelps and authors, May 12, 1985.

18. Letter from Moss to the authors, March 27, 1985.

19. Phone conversation, Phelps and authors; also mentioned by Moss in a phone conversation with authors, December 30, 1985.

20. Phone conversation, Moss and authors, June 22, 1985.

21. Letter from Holdenried to Moss, October 24, 1980.

22. Frank X. Holdenried, "Terror in Guatemala," *America*, July 17, 1982, pp. 31–34.

23. Phone conversation, Moss and authors, June 22, 1985.

24. Letter from Moss to the authors, March 27, 1985; phone conversation, Moss and authors, June 22, 1985.

25. Phone conversation, Phelps and authors; Frank X. Holdenried, "El encontró la significación de la vida en la tierra donde murió," typed article prepared for *Hispanic Link*, April 17, 1982, pp. 2–3.

26. Phone conversation, Phelps and authors.

27. Letter from Holdenried to Moss, May 24, 1978.

28. Letter from Moss to the authors, March 27, 1985.

29. Letter from Holdenried to Moss, May 27, 1978.

30. Letter from Holdenried to Smith, December 29, 1976.

31. Letter from Holdenried to Moss, February 21, 1977.

32. Letter from Holdenried to Smith, May 8, 1979.

33. Letter from Holdenried to Smith, December 29, 1976.

34. Letter from Holdenried to Smith, May 8, 1979.

35. Ibid.

36. Letter from Holdenried to Smith, December 29, 1976.

37. Phone conversation, Phelps and authors.

38. Ibid.

39. Letter from Moss to the authors, March 27, 1985.

40. Ibid.

41. Ibid.

42. Letter from Holdenried to Smith, July 4, 1977.

43. Ibid.

44. Letter from Holdenried to Smith, May 8, 1979.

45. Ibid.

46. Holdenried, "Terror in Guatemala," pp. 31–32.

47. Ibid., p. 34.

48. Letter from Holdenried to Smith, March 14, 1980.

49. Ibid.

50. Letter from Holdenried to Matilda Smith, May 7, 1980.

51. Hendrix, p. 10.

52. Phone conversation, Phelps and authors.

53. Letter from Holdenried to Moss, October 24, 1980.

54. Day, p. 6.

55. Phillip Berryman, *Religious Roots of Rebellion* (Maryknoll, N.Y.: Orbis Books, 1984), pp. 216–17; Jon Cozean, *Latin America 1982* (Washington, D.C.: Stryker-Post, 1983), p. 65.

56. Hendrix, p. 10.

57. Letter from Holdenried to Ken Edwards, November 7, 1978.

58. Letter from Holdenried to Richard Smith, December 8, 1978.

59. Ibid.

60. Letter from Holdenried to Edwards, March 7, 1978.

61. Ibid.

62. Ibid.

63. Letter from Holdenried to Edwards, November 7, 1978.

64. Letter from Holdenried to Edwards, March 7, 1978.

65. Letter from Holdenried to Oscar Holdenried, August 21, 1980.

66. Letter from Holdenried to D. Moss and C. Moss, February 8, 1983; U.S. Representative Stephen Solarz' record of meeting with Holdenried in Guatemala on January 10, 1983—record dated January 15, 1983.

67. Letter from Holdenried to Smith, January 4, 1983.

68. Letter from Holdenried to Mosses, February 8, 1983.

69. Quoted in Day, p. 6.

70. Letter from Holdenried to Sister Betty Campbell, February 20, 1980 (this is a form letter which was probably sent to several people); Frank Holdenried, "Guatemala: A Proposal. U.S. Foreign Policy Goals and Options, 1981–82" (unpublished), January 9, 1981, p. 6.

71. Letter from Holdenried to Campbell.

72. Holdenried, Ayudantes de los Pobres form letter, February 14, 1979.

73. Holdenried, "Guatemala: A Proposal," p. 5.

74. Phone conversation, Phelps and the authors.

75. Phone conversation, Moss and the authors.

76. Letter from Holdenried to Smith, February 29, 1980.

77. Letter from Holdenried to Edwards, March 7, 1978.

78. Letter from Holdenried to Campbell.

79. Letter from Holdenried to Edwards, November 7, 1978.

80. Ibid.

81. Ibid.

82. Letter from Holdenried to Smith, December 8, 1978.

83. Holdenried, "Guatemala: A Proposal," pp. 14, 17.

84. Letter from Holdenried to Smith, May 27, 1978.

85. Letter from Holdenried to Campbell.

86. Frank Holdenried, quoted in White, "Kelseyville Folks Aid Kids in Guatemala," Santa Rosa *Press Democrat*, August 18, 1981, p. 3D.

87. Letter from Holdenried to Oscar Holdenried, November 1, 1982; letter from Holdenried to Smith, December 7, 1982.

88. Solarz' record of conversation with Holdenried.

89. Letter from Holdenried to Mosses, February 8, 1983.

90. For an excellent commentary on the brutality under Ríos Montt see "The Dirtiest War," editorial, *New York Times*, Sunday, October 17, 1982, p. 14E.

91. Letter from Holdenried to Smith, March 28, 1983.

92. This was later confirmed: "According to the police, the exact number of persons sleeping on the beach is not known, but there were probably several hundred." Letter from Paul D. Taylor, chargé d'affaires, American embassy, Guatemala, to Douglas H. Bosco, U.S. House of Representatives, California, July 1983.

93. Ibid.

94. The authors' report on Holdenried's death is a compilation of several sources: letter from Moss to author, March 27, 1985; phone conversation, Moss and authors, June 22, 1985; phone conversation, Phelps and authors, May 12, 1985; phone conversation, Father James Curtin and authors, June 20, 1985; letter from Moss to Friends of Ayudantes de los Pobres, April 20, 1983; newspaper articles from the *National Catholic Reporter*, April 29, 1983; Santa Rosa *Press Democrat*, April 5 and 6, 1983; the *Clear Lake Observer*, April 14, 1983; and the *Los Angeles Times*, May 4, 1983.

95. Letter from Moss to the authors, March 27, 1985.

96. "Holdenried Killed in Guatemala," *Clear Lake Observer*, April 14, 1983, p. 2.

97. Quoted in Hendrix, pp. 1, 10.

INTRODUCTION TO PART III

1. Ana Carrigan, *Salvador Witness: The Life and Calling of Jean Donovan* (New York: Simon and Schuster, 1984), pp. 240–41.

2. Ibid., p. 242.

3. T. D. Allman, "An American Tragedy," *Penthouse*, January 1984.

4. Lawyers Committee for International Human Rights, *Justice in El Salvador: A Case Study. A Report on the Investigation into the Killing of Four U. S. Churchwomen in El Salvador* (New York: February 1, 1983), pp. 22–23; see also Harold R. Tyler, Jr., *The Churchwomen Murders: A Report to the Secretary of State* (New York: December 2, 1983), pp. 55–56.

5. Betty Campbell, RSM, and Peter Hinde, O. Carm., *Following the Star*, ed. Gary MacEoin (Washington, D.C.: Religious Task Force, no date), p. 24.

6. June Carolyn Erlick, "Four U.S. Women Slain; Political Conflict Altered," *National Catholic Reporter*, December 12, 1980, p. 5.

7. Paul Schindler, interview with the authors, May 2, 1986.

8. Erlick, p. 5.

9. Carrigan, p. 244; Tyler, "The Churchwomen Murders," pp. 14–15.

10. Quoted in Judith Noone, MM, *The Same Fate As the Poor* (Maryknoll, N.Y.: Maryknoll Sisters Publication, 1984), p. 138; see also Tyler, p. 15.

11. Allman.

12. Tyler, pp. 17–21.

13. Ibid., p. 43.

14. Erlick, p. 5.

15. "U.S. Resumes Military Aid," *New York Times*, January 15, 1981, p. 9.

16. Quoted from a U.S. Embassy cable, San Salvador to U.S. State Department, January 21, 1981, in report of the Lawyers Committee for International Human Rights, p. 12.

17. Quoted in Stephanie Russell, "Nuns Hide Machine Guns?", *National Catholic Reporter*, March 13, 1981, p. 2; and Allman, "An American Tragedy."

18. Quoted in Russell, p. 2.

19. Anthony Lewis, "Showing His Colors," *New York Times*, March 29, 1981.

20. Carrigan, pp. 283–84.

21. Dorothy Kazel, cassette tape sent to Sister Martha Owen, Fall 1980.

22. Joseph Kazel, interview with the authors, August 23, 1985.

8. DOROTHY KAZEL AND JEAN DONOVAN

1. The biographical information that follows, unless otherwise noted, is derived from "Life of Love" [no author], a script and slide show prepared for viewing in the Cleveland area, 1983; from Joseph and Malvina Kazel, interview with the authors, August 23, 1985; and from Sister Martha Owen, OSU, interview with the authors, August 23, 1985.

2. Barbara Sever, interview with the authors, August 23, 1985.

3. Sheila Phelan, quoted in "Life of Love," p. 7.

4. See Walter LaFeber, *Inevitable Revolutions* (New York: Norton, 1984), pp. 9–10.

5. Ibid., pp. 70–71.

6. Ibid., pp. 71–72.

7. See Thomas P. Anderson, *Politics in Central America* (New York: Praeger, 1983), p. 64; and Phillip Berryman, *Religious Roots of Rebellion* (Maryknoll, N.Y.: Orbis Books, 1984), p. 93.

8. Anderson, p. 64; LaFeber, p. 74.

9. Anderson, p. 64.

10. Quoted in Berryman, p. 93.

11. See Thomas P. Anderson, *Matanza: El Salvador's Communist Revolt of 1932* (Lincoln: University of Nebraska Press, 1971) for the best work on this event.

12. Berryman, p. 95.

13. Ibid., p. 93.

14. Anderson, *Politics in Central America*, p. 65.

15. LaFeber, pp. 73–74.

16. Berryman, p. 98.

17. Ibid.

18. Ibid., p. 106. For Duarte's early career see Stephen Webre, *José Napoleón Duarte and the Christian Democratic Party in Salvadoran Politics* (Baton Rouge, La: Louisiana State University Press, 1979).

19. Berryman, pp. 106, 109–112.

20. Martha Owen, interview with authors.

21. Ibid.

22. Ibid.

23. Ibid.

24. Tom Barry, Beth Wood, and Deb Preusch, *Dollars & Dictators: A Guide to Central America* (Albuquerque, N.M.: Resource Center, 1982), p. 188.

25. Owen, interview with authors.

26. Ibid.

27. Ibid.

28. Ibid.

29. Ibid.

30. Ibid.

31. Ibid.

32. Berryman, p. 115.

33. Quoted in Berryman, p. 116.

34. Berryman, pp. 116–17.

35. LaFeber, p. 246.

36. Ibid.; James R. Brockman, *The Word Remains: A Life of Oscar Romero* (Maryknoll, N.Y.: Orbis Books, 1982), pp. 5–7.

37. Berryman, p. 117.

38. Ibid., pp. 106–109, 114.

39. Quoted in Berryman, p. 114.

40. Quoted in Berryman, pp. 120–21. For an excellent treatment of Rutilio Grande see William J. O'Malley, *The Voice of Blood: Five Christian Martyrs of Our Time* (Maryknoll, N.Y.: Orbis Books, 1980), pp. 1–63.

41. See Brockman.

42. Owen, interview with authors.

43. Ibid.

44. Father Paul Schindler, interview with authors, May 2, 1986; Owen, interview with authors.

45. Owen, interview with authors.

46. Ibid.

47. Ibid. These stories were originally told by Sister Regis, Vincentian Superior.

48. Owen, interview with authors.

49. Quoted in "Life of Love," p. 8.

50. Owen, interview with authors.

51. Quoted in T. D. Allman, "An American Tragedy," *Penthouse*, January 1984.

52. Sever, interview with authors.

53. Owen, interview with authors.

54. Schindler, interview with authors.

55. Raymond and Patricia Donovan, letter to authors, September 1987.

56. Joe Lynch, "Jean Donovan's Legacy to Her Parents," *Sojourners* (June 1987), pp. 21–22.

57. Ibid., p. 21.

58. Donovans' letter to authors.

59. Rita Mikolajczyk, telephone interview with authors, October 3, 1987.

60. Ana Carrigan, *Salvador Witness: The Life and Calling of Jean Donovan* (New York: Simon and Schuster, 1984), p. 43.

61. Quoted in Lynch, p. 21.

62. Quoted in (no author), "Way of the Cross in El Salvador," *Maryknoll* (March 1981), p. 24.

63. Donovans' letter to authors.

64. Carrigan, p. 53.

65. "Way of the Cross in El Salvador," p. 24.

66. Quoted in Carrigan, p. 52.

67. Donovans' letter to authors.

68. Carrigan, pp. 50–52, 55.

69. Father Lawrence McMahon, telephone interview with authors, September 26, 1987.

70. Lynch, p. 22.

71. Mikolajczyk, interview with authors.

72. Ibid.

73. Mary Frances Ehlinger, telephone interview with authors, September 19, 1987.

74. Ibid.

75. Quoted in Lynch, p. 22.

76. Donovans' letter to authors.

77. Carrigan, p. 72.

78. Ibid., p. 73.

79. Mikolajczyk, interview with authors.

80. Josie Cuda, telephone interview with authors, May 21, 1986.

81. Quoted in Berryman, *Religious Roots*, p. 137; see also José Marins, Teolide Trevisan, and Carolee Chanona, *Cry of the Church: Witness and Martyrdom in the Church of Latin America Today* (Quezon City, Philippines: Claretian Publications, 1983), pp. 131–35.

82. Quoted in Berryman, *Religious Roots*, p. 137.

83. Brockman, p. 156.

84. Quoted in Lynch, p. 22; see also Carrigan, p. 95.

85. Lynch, p. 22.

86. Donovans' letter to authors.

87. Brockman, p. 160; Marins, et al., pp. 135–36.

88. Dorothy Kazel and Paul Schindler, cassette tape to Martha Owen, August 9, 1979.

89. Sister Christine Rody, telephone interview with authors, September 23, 1987.

90. Owen, interview with authors.

91. Schindler, interview with authors.

92. Rody, interview with authors.

93. Dorothy Kazel, letter to Martha Owen, October 3, 1979.

94. Quoted in Carrigan, pp. 108–9.

95. Benjamin Keen and Mark Wasserman, *A Short History of Latin America* (Boston: Houghton Mifflin Co., 1984), pp. 463–64; Raymond Bonner, *Weakness and Deceit: U.S. Policy and El Salvador* (New York: Times Books, 1984), pp. 145–210.

96. Dorothy Kazel, cassette tape to Martha Owen, late December 1979–January 10, 1980; Donovans' letter to authors.

97. Quoted in Lynch, pp. 22–23.

98. Sister Sheila Tobbe, "Witness to Sister Dorothy and Jean Donovan," liturgical reflection delivered December 14, 1980.

99. Quoted in Lynch, p. 23.

100. Kazel, tape to Owen, December 1979–January 10, 1980.

101. Owen, interview with authors.

102. Kazel, letter to friends, January 1980, given by Sister Sheila Tobbe to the authors.

103. Carrigan, pp. 139–43.

104. Owen, interview with authors.

105. Brockman, p. 55; Edward and Donna Brett, "The Archbishop Could Not Keep Silent," *Santa Fe Reporter*, June 1, 1983.

106. Oscar Romero, *A Martyr's Message of Hope*, trans. Felipe Ortega, et al. (Kansas City, Mo.: Celebration Books, 1981), p. 105.

107. Quoted in Brockman, p. 217.

108. Quoted in Carrigan, pp. 159–60.

109. Brockman, p. 222.

110. Owen, comments on Dorothy's tapes, May 1984.

111. Carrigan, pp. 125 and 129.

112. Quoted in Carrigan, pp. 110-11.

113. Carrigan, pp. 136, 147–48; Rody, letter to authors, December 10, 1987.

114. Rody, interview with authors.

115. Carrigan, pp. 179–80, 184.

116. Schindler, interview with authors.

117. Ibid.

118. Ibid.

119. Quoted in Dorothy Chapon Kazel, *Alleluia Woman: Sister Dorothy Kazel, OSU* (Cleveland: Chapel Publications, 1987), pp. 35-36.

120. Carrigan, p. 200.

121. Kazel, letter to Sister Theresa Kane, October 6, 1980.

122. Judith M. Noone, M.M., *The Same Fate as the Poor* (Maryknoll, N.Y.: Maryknoll Sisters Publications, 1984), p. 127.

123. Kazel, letter to Owen, September 5, 1980.

124. June Carolyn Erlick, "Cleveland Team: 'We'll Stay,' " *National Catholic Reporter*, September 5, 1980, p. 28.

125. Kazel, letter to Owen, September 5, 1980.

126. Rody, interview with authors.

127. Quoted by Schindler, interview with authors.

128. Donovans' letter to authors, including comments from Doug Cable.

129. Carrigan, p. 215.

130. Quoted in Carrigan, pp. 214–15.

131. Carrigan, pp. 212–19.

132. Josie and Frank Cuda, interview with authors.

133. Mikolajczyk, interview with authors.

134. Ehlinger, interview with authors.

135. Quoted in Carrigan, p. 219.

136. Stephen T. DeMott, M.M., "Mission Inherited: 'Our Own Blood Spilled in El Salvador,' " *Maryknoll* (December 1983), pp. 53, 55.

137. Kazel, tape to Owen, October 21, 1980.

138. Ibid.

139. Ibid.

140. Quoted in Kazel, *Alleluia Woman*, pp. 37-38.

141. John D. Blacken, U.S. Department of State, letter to Sister Dorothy Kazel, November 7, 1980.

142. Berryman, *Religious Roots*, p. 157.

143. Betty Campbell, R.S.M., and Peter Hinde, O. Carm., *Following the Star: The Liberation Process of the People*, ed. Gary MacEoin (Washington, D.C.: Religious Task Force, no date), pp. 5–6.

144. Kazel, tape to Owen, October 1980; Campbell and Hinde, p. 24.

145. Campbell and Hinde, p. 8.

146. Anderson, *Politics in Central America*, pp. 90–91; Campbell and Hinde, pp. 22–23.

147. Kazel, tape to Owen, October 1980.

148. Kazel, tape to Owen, August 9, 1979.

149. Kazel, tape to Owen, October 1980.

150. Kazel, letter to Owen, November 5, 1980.

151. Schindler, interview with authors.

152. Kazel, letter to Ursuline community, November 1980.

153. Quoted in Mary Bader Papa, " 'Fight Sexism, Paternalism in Church'—Kane," *National Catholic Reporter*, September 5, 1980, p. 23.

154. Kazel to Kane, October 6, 1980.

155. Campbell and Hinde, p. 8.

156. Owen, interview with authors.

157. Kazel, letter to Owen, November 28, 1980.

158. Quoted in Carrigan, p. 227.

159. Schindler, interview with authors.

160. Quoted by Patricia Donovan, in "Families Respond to Murders and Disappearances," Campbell and Hinde, p. 27.

161. Quoted in Carrigan, p. 69.

162. Schindler, interview with authors.

9. ITA FORD AND MAURA CLARKE

1. Michael Gallagher, "Kirkpatrick's Views Invite College Protests," *National Catholic Reporter*, April 29, 1983, p. 15.

2. Quoted in Timothy M. Phelps, "For Two Nuns, Needs of Poor Hid the Danger," *New York Times*, December 7, 1980, p. 9.

3. Judith Noone, *The Same Fate As the Poor* (Maryknoll, N.Y: Maryknoll Sisters Publication, 1984), p. 19. Much of this chapter is based on this work.

4. Ibid., p. 20.

5. Ibid.

6. Erlick, "Four U.S. Women Slain: Political Conflict Altered," *National Catholic Reporter*, December 12, 1980, p. 4.

7. Noone, p. 20.

8. Ita Ford, letter to Jean Reardon, April 19, 1961, quoted in Noone, p. 21.

9. Ford, letter to Jean Reardon, November 8, 1961, quoted in Noone, p. 22.

10. Ford, letters to Jean Reardon, December 30, 1962, and August 18, 1963, quoted in Noone, p. 23.

11. Ford, letter to Jean Reardon, June 12, 1964, quoted in Noone, p. 24.

12. Noone, p. 24.

13. Ibid., p. 25.

14. Gallagher, p. 15.

15. Noone, p. 25.

16. Ibid., p. 26.

17. Ford, letter to Jean Reardon, October 6, 1971, quoted in Noone, pp. 27–28.

18. Noone, p. 28.

19. Ibid., p. 25.

20. Ford, letter to Jean Reardon, September 24, 1972, quoted in Noone, pp. 28–29.

21. Ford, letter to Jean Reardon, November 28, 1972, quoted in Noone, pp. 28–29.

22. Ford, letter to Jean Reardon, March 10, 1973, quoted in Noone, p. 29.

23. Benjamin Keen and Mark Wasserman, *A Short History of Latin America* (Boston: Houghton Mifflin, 1984), pp. 320–31.

24. Ibid., p. 322.

25. Ibid., p. 323.

26. Ibid., pp. 332–34.

27. George Pendle, *A History of Latin America*, rev. ed. (Harmondsworth, England: Penguin Books, 1983), p. 240.

28. Keen and Wasserman, p. 337.

29. Ibid, pp. 338–39.

30. Ita Ford, letter to Jean Reardon, May 23, 1973, quoted in Noone, p. 29.

31. Noone, p. 32.

32. Ibid., p. 33.

33. Jon Cozean, *Latin America 1982* (Washington, D.C.: Stryker-Post, 1982), p. 36.

34. Janice McLaughlin, "Four Heroic Lives End in Martyrdom: Ford," *National Catholic Reporter*, December 19, 1980, p. 27.

35. Ita Ford, interview with Maureen Flanagan, Maryknoll Sisters' Communications Office, 1978, quoted in Noone, pp. 38–39.

36. Noone, pp. 41–42; Ford (and Carla Piette?), report to Maryknoll Sisters, date uncertain, quoted in Noone, p. 42.

37. Noone, p. 35.

38. Ibid., pp. 40–41.

39. Ita Ford, letter to John Baumann and Jean Reardon Baumann, November 1974, quoted in Noone, pp. 39–40.

40. Edward L. Cleary, *Crisis and Change: The Church in Latin America Today* (Maryknoll: Orbis Books, 1985), p. 155; Noone, pp. 43–44.

41. Penny Lernoux, *Cry of the People* (New York: Penguin Books, 1982), p. 399; Keen and Wasserman, p. 339; Cozean, p. 36.

42. Lernoux, pp. 298–99.

43. Ibid., pp. 400–401; Keen and Wasserman, p. 339.

44. Lernoux, p. 401; Noone, pp. 37–38.

45. Ita Ford, letter to Jean Reardon Baumann, November 28, 1977, quoted in Noone, p. 45.

46. Quoted in Phelps.

47. Mildred Ford, letter to Judith Noone, January 28, 1982, quoted in Noone, p. 47.

48. John Patrick Meehan, letter to Judith Noone, May 1, 1981, quoted in Noone, p. 47.

49. Rachel Lauze, letter to Judith Noone, January 21, 1982, quoted in Noone, p. 46.

50. Noone, pp. 83–84.

51. Noone, pp. 86–87.

52. Julie Miller, letter to Judith Noone, February 14, 1982, quoted in Noone, p. 87.

53. Ita Ford, letter to Mildred Ford, March 2, 1980, quoted in Noone, pp. 92-93.

54. Carla Piette, letter to Cecelia Vandal, May 14, 1980, quoted in Noone, p. 92.

55. Ibid.

56. Carla Piette, letter to Rebecca Quinn, March 28, 1980, quoted in Noone, pp. 97–98.

57. Quoted in Noone, pp. 99–100.

58. Ita Ford, letter to Mildred Ford, April 2, 1980, quoted in Noone, p. 99.

59. Phillip Berryman, *Religious Roots of Rebellion* (Maryknoll, N.Y.: Orbis Books, 1984), p. 113.

60. Ibid., pp. 99, 113–114.

61. Betty Campbell and Peter Hinde, *Following the Star:The Liberation Process of the People*, ed. Gary MacEoin (Washington, D.C.: Religious Task Force, no date), pp. 3–4.

62. "Masacre de salvadoreños denuncia copaneca: pronunciamiento," in *Los refugiados salvadoreños en Honduras* (Tegucigalpa: Centro de Documentación de Honduras, no date), pp. 36–40.

63. Carla Piette, letter to Rebecca Quinn, May 17, 1980, quoted in Noone, p. 105.

64. Ita Ford, letter to her sister René Sullivan, May 29, 1980, quoted in Noone, p. 106.

65. Ana Carrigan, *Salvador Witness: The Life and Calling of Jean Donovan* (New York: Simon and Schuster, 1984), p. 191.

66. Ibid., pp. 191–92.

67. Berryman, p. 317.

68. Carla Piette, letter to Catherine Verbeten, July 16, 1980, quoted in Noone, p. 108.

69. McLaughlin, p. 27.

70. Carla Piette and Ita Ford, "Three Months Experience in El Salvador," quoted in Noone, p. 109.

71. Ita Ford, letter to Jennifer Sullivan, August 16, 1980, quoted in Noone, p. 118.

72. Campbell and Hinde, p. 10; Noone, pp. 121–22.

73. Carla Piette, letter to Mildred Ford, August 11, 1980, quoted in Noone, p. 119.

74. Quoted in Phelps.

75. Campbell and Hinde, p. 10.

76. Noone, pp. 49–50.

77. Ibid., p. 50.

78. Ibid., p. 51.

79. Moises Sandoval, "Four Heroic Lives End in Martyrdom: Clarke," *National Catholic Reporter*, December 19, 1980, p. 28.

80. Letter from Kay Kelly to Judy Noone, June 25, 1982; a copy of the letter was sent by Sister Kay Kelly to the authors.

81. Sandoval, p. 1.

82. Quoted in Sandoval, p. 1.

83. Noone, pp. 52–53.

84. Letter from Kay Kelly to the authors, April 21, 1984.

85. Noone, p. 54.

86. Letter from Kay Kelly to Judy Noone, June 25, 1982.

87. Ibid.

88. Ibid.

89. Ibid.

90. Ibid.

91. Ibid.

92. Noone, pp. 56–58.

93. Letter from Maura Clarke to her parents, December 25, 1963, quoted in Noone, p. 57.

94. Noone, p. 58.

95. Letter from Kelly to Noone, June 25, 1982.

96. Ibid.

97. Ibid.

98. Ibid.

99. Ibid.

100. Ibid.

101. Ibid.

102. Sandoval, p. 28.

103. Letter from Kelly to authors, April 21, 1984.

104. Noone, pp. 59–61.

105. Ibid., p. 65.

106. Letter from Maura Clarke to her parents, Palm Sunday 1970, quoted in Noone, pp. 65–66.

107. Noone, pp. 66–67; letter from Kelly to authors, April 21, 1984.

108. Letter from Maura Clarke to her parents, December 25, 1972, quoted in Noone, p. 68.

109. Letter from Kelly to Noone, June 25, 1982.

110. Noone, p. 69.

111. Letter from Maura Clarke to Bud Clarke, March 18, 1973, quoted in Noone, p. 70.

112. Noone, p. 70.

113. Ibid., pp. 74–75.

114. Notes written during an eight day retreat, quoted in Noone, p. 75.

115. Noone, pp. 77–78.

116. LaFeber, *Inevitable Revolutions: The United States in Central America* (New York: W.W. Norton, 1984), p. 235.

117. Noone, p. 85.

118. Carrigan, p. 201.

119. Letter from Maura Clarke to Jennie Burke, January 15, 1980, quoted in Noone, p. 93.

120. Maura Clarke, letter to her parents, July 28, 1980, Maryknoll Sisters' Archives, Maryknoll, New York.

121. Letter from Maura Clarke to Mary Manning, August 11, 1980, quoted in Noone, p. 115.

122. Ibid.

123. Quoted in Carrigan, p. 201.

124. Campbell and Hinde, p. 11.

125. Ibid.

126. Campbell and Hinde, p. 11.

127. Ibid., p. 12.

128. Quoted and translated in Campbell and Hinde, p. 20.

129. Campbell and Hinde, pp. 8–9.

130. Campbell and Hinde, p. 12; Schindler, interview with authors.

131. The series of army attacks on San Antonio de los Ranchos is described in Campbell and Hinde, pp. 12–13.

132. Ibid., p. 11.

133. Report of the Lawyers Committee for International Human Rights, *Justice in El Salvador: A Case Study. A Report on the Investigation into the Killing of Four U.S. Churchwomen in El Salvador* (New York: February 1, 1983), p. 22.

134. Ita Ford, tape to Mrs. Mildred Ford, September 6 (?), 1980, and Ita Ford, letter to Catherine Verbeten, O.P., September 12, 1980, quoted in Noone, p. 128.

135. Ita Ford, letter to Mrs. Mildred Ford, November 13, 1980, quoted in Noone, pp. 129–30.

136. Ita Ford, letter to Gertrude Vaccaro, M.M., November 25, 1980, quoted in Noone, p. 130.

137. Ita Ford, letter to Mrs. Mildred Ford, November 18, 1980, quoted in Noone, p. 130.

138. Maura Clarke, letter to Kay Kelly, October 21, 1980, Maryknoll Sisters' Archives, Maryknoll, New York.

139. Maura Clarke, letter to her parents, (early) October 1980, Maryknoll Sisters' Archives, Maryknoll, New York.

140. Report of the Lawyers Committee for Internation Human Rights, p. 23; Noone, p. 132.

141. Quoted in Report of the Lawyers Committee for International Human Rights, p. 23.

142. Ita Ford, letter to Jean Reardon Baumann, October 27, 1980, quoted in Noone, p. 132.

143. Maura Clarke, letter to Margaret Dillon, M.M., November 22, 1980, and letter to Patricia Haggerty, November 20, 1980, quoted in Noone, p. 131.

144. Campbell and Hinde, p. 21.

145. Berryman, pp. 133, 157–58; Campbell and Hinde, p. 24.

146. Maria Rieckelman, M.M., interview with Judy Noone, May 30, 1981, quoted in Noone, pp. 135–36.

147. Rieckelman, "Report to the Maryknoll Sisters' Community," December 5, 1980, quoted in Noone, p. 137.

148. Maura Clarke, letter to her parents, November 17, 1980, Maryknoll Sisters' Archives, Maryknoll, New York.

149. Rieckelman, interview with Noone, quoted in Noone, p. 131.

150. Noone, p. 136.

151. Quoted in DeMott, "Mission Inherited: 'Our Own Blood Spilled in El Salvador,' " *Maryknoll*, December 1983, p. 3.

152. Madeline Dorsey, interview with Judy Noone, July 1981, quoted in Noone, p. 137.

153. Oscar Romero, homily for February 17, 1980, quoted in Noone, p. 137.

154. Report of the Lawyers Committee for International Human Rights, p. 23.

THE AFTERMATH

1. Stephen T. DeMott, "Mission Inherited: 'Our Own Blood Spilled in El Salvador,' " *Maryknoll*, December 1983, pp. 45–46.

2. Betty Campbell and Peter Hinde, *Following the Star*, ed. Gary MacEoin (Washington, D.C.: Religious Task Force, no date), p. 27.

3. T. D. Allman, "An American Tragedy," *Penthouse*, January 1984.

4. "Oral Statement by Ambassador Robert White before the Senate Subcommittee on Western Hemisphere Affairs" (March 20, 1984), p. 8.

5. Ibid., pp. 6–7.

6. DeMott, p. 39; Allman; Religious Task Force on Central America, *Chronology of a Martyrdom—November 1980 to May 1984* (Washington, D.C.: 1984), p. 2; "U.S. Resumes Military Aid," *New York Times*, January 15, 1981, p. 9; Raymond Bonner, *Weakness and Deceit: U.S. Policy and El Salvador* (New York: Times Books, 1984), p. 224.

7. Pat Williams, "Did Salvador Killing Stifle Evidence on Slain Women?" *National Catholic Reporter*, April 22, 1983, pp. 1, 40; see also Allman; *New York Times*, December 18, 1980, p. 3, and December 19, 1980, p. 16.

8. P. Williams, p. 40.

9. Harold R. Tyler, Jr., "The Churchwomen Murders: A Report to the Secretary of State" (New York: December 2, 1983), pp. 65-66.

10. P. Williams, pp. 1, 40; Allman.

11. "In Jersey 400 Mourn a Reporter Slain in Salvador," *New York Times*, March 13, 1983, p. 14.

12. Ibid.

13. Campbell and Hinde, p. 28.

14. "In Jersey 400 Mourn," p. 14.

15. Jane Perlez, "Body from Salvador Thought to Be U.S. Writer's," *New York Times*, February 23, 1983, p. 10.

16. Albert J. Parisi, "Sullivan Family Asks, 'Why?' " *New York Times*, February 27, 1983, p. 10K.

17. "In Jersey 400 Mourn," p. 14.

18. Ibid.

19. Ibid.; Perlez, p. 10.

20. Parisi, p. 10.

21. Frank Hammer, "Not Really Big Deal Killing in Salvador," *New York Times*, December 11, 1984, p. 31; Bonner, pp. 44–47.

22. Clifford Krauss, "Justice Denied: Solving a Murder Case in El Salvador Is Hard if Suspects Are VIPs," *The Wall Street Journal*, December 10, 1984, p. 1.

23. Ibid.

24. Ibid., p. 10.

25. Hammer, p. 31.

26. DeMott, p. 41.

27. Quoted in Ana Carrigan, *Salvador Witness: The Life and Calling of Jean Donovan* (New York: Simon and Schuster, 1984), p. 279.

28. Juan de Onis, "Envoy Disputes U.S. on Salvador Deaths," *New York Times*, January 22, 1981, p. 14.

29. Lawyers Committee for International Human Rights, *Justice in El Salvador: A Case Study. A Report on the Investigation into the Killing of Four U.S. Churchwomen in El Salvador* (New York: February 1, 1983), p. 11.

30. Religious Task Force on Central America, *Chronology of a Martyrdom*, p. 2.

31. *New York Times*, February 28, 1981, p. 1 and March 1, 1981, p. 1.

32. Ibid., March 7, 1981, p. 1.

33. "Aims, Aid and Advisors: Debating the New Policy on El Salvador," *New York Times*, March 8, 1981, p. 20.

34. *New York Times*, March 14, 1981, p. 8.

35. "Oral Statement by Ambassador Robert White before the Senate Subcommittee on Western Hemisphere Affairs," p. 8.

36. *New York Times*, March 25, 1981, p. 3.

37. Ibid., March 25, 1981, p. 3; March 27, 1981, p. 5; April 5, 1981, p. 9; April 10, 1981, p. 3; April 18, 1981, p. 4; April 21, 1981, p. 5; April 23, 1981, p. 5; Bonner, pp. 230–31, 241.

38. Bonner, p. 285.

39. *New York Times*, April 30, 1981, p. 1.

40. Ibid., May 2, 1981, p. 5.

41. Ibid., May 3, 1981, p. 20D.

42. Ibid., May 10, 1981, p. 1.

43. Quoted in Carrigan, p. 291.

44. *New York Times*, May 13, 1981, p. 8; May 12, 1981, p. 10.

45. "Oral Statement by Ambassador Robert White before the Senate Subcommittee on Western Hemisphere Affairs," p. 9.

46. *New York Times*, November 17, 1981, p. 6.

47. Ibid., November 11, 1981, p. 4; November 22, 1981, p. 19.

48. Lawyers Committee for International Human Rights, p. 27.

49. *New York Times,* January 22, 1982, p. 6; January 29, 1982, p. 1; February 2, 1982, p. 1; February 11, 1982, p. 1.

50. Ibid., February 14, 1982, p. 18.

51. Ibid., February 15, 1982, p. 2.

52. Bonner, pp. 80, 374. For more extensive information on these two guardsmen see Carrigan, p. 308.

53. See *New York Times*, February 14, 1982, p. 18.

54. Carrigan, pp. 298–99.

55. *New York Times*, March 21, 1982, p. 22.

56. Ibid., June 30, 1982, p. 20.

57. Quoted in Lawyers Committee for International Human Rights, p. 27.

58. *New York Times*, August 29, 1982, p. 10.

59. Ibid., November 10, 1982, p. 1.

60. Ibid., May 30, 1983, p. 4.

61. Ibid., May 28, 1983, p. 1.

62. Ibid., November 30, 1982, p. 10; December 13, 1982, p. 13; December 16, 1982, p. 5; February 13, 1983, p. 12; March 9, 1983, p. 6; March 11, 1983, p. 1.

63. Ibid., March 12, 1983, p. 3.

64. Ibid., January 6, 1983, p. 8; January 7, 1983, p. 5.

65. Ibid., February 8, 1983, p. 20.

66. Ibid., March 19, 1983, p. 4.

67. Ibid., October 7, 1983, p. 6.

68. Anthony Lewis, "Is There No Decency?", *New York Times*, March 19, 1984.

69. Ibid.

70. Langhorne Motley, letter to Mother Bartholomew, May 24, 1984.

71. "As you know, on May 24, the jury in the case of the five ex-National Guardsmen charged with the murder of *your sisters*, Maura Clarke, Ita Ford, Dorothy Kazel and Jean Donovan were found guilty [sic]." Ibid.

72. Tyler, p. 7.

73. Ibid., p. 4.

74. *New York Times*, February 18, 1984; Bonner, p. xix.

75. Tyler, pp. 7–8.

76. Ibid., p. 10.

77. *Albuquerque Journal*, April 6, 1984, p. 3.

78. *New York Times*, March 22, 1984, p. 1.

79. *Albuquerque Journal*, May 21, 1984, p. B14.

80. *New York Times*, May 22, 1984, p. 27.

81. Religious Task Force on Central America, *The Road to Zacatecoluca: One North American's Journey* (Washington, D.C.: 1984), p. 1.

82. *New York Times*, May 25, 1984, p. 10.

83. *New York Times*, May 6, 1985, p. 1; *Pittsburgh Catholic*, May 24, 1985, p. 7.

84. *New York Times*, May 25, 1984, p. 10.

85. Lydia Chavez, "Duarte Is Not Planning Inquiry of Nuns," *New York Times*, June 4, 1984, p. 3.

86. Ibid.

87. *Albuquerque Journal*, June 20, 1984, p. D8.

AFTER 1983

1. Eric Arnesen, "El Salvador: Reminders of War," *Monthly Review,* October 1986, p. 22.

2. *Pittsburgh Catholic,* January 16, 1987, p. 6.

3. James LeMoyne, "After Parades and Promises, Duarte Flounders in Salvador," *New York Times,* February 16, 1987, p. 4.

4. Americas Watch, "Free Fire" (March 1984 report); cited in Arnesen, p. 21.

5. LeMoyne, p. 4.

6. Quoted in *Pittsburgh Catholic,* January 23, 1987, p. 6.

7. LeMoyne, p. 4.

8. Ibid.

9. Ibid.

10. *Latinamerica Press,* November 6, 1986, pp. 1–2; December 4, 1986, p. 6.

11. Stephen Kinzer, "Walking the Tightrope in Guatemala," *New York Times Magazine,* November 9, 1986, p. 37.

12. *Latinamerica Press,* December 25, 1986, p. 8.

13. *Latinamerica Press,* December 11, 1986, p. 7.

14. Kinzer, p. 34.

15. Ibid., p. 38; *Latinamerica Press,* October 16, 1986, p. 7.

16. Kinzer, p. 38.

17. Mike DeMott, "Interview/Archbishop Penados: The Gospel Liberates," *Maryknoll,* April 1986, p. 31.

18. *Latinamerica Press,* December 25, 1986, p. 7.

19. Stephen T. DeMott, "Murder in Guatemala," *Maryknoll,* February 1987, pp. 24–25.

20. "Public Communiqué of the Honduran Jesuits," in Nancy Peckenham and Annie Street, eds., *Honduras: Portrait of a Captive Nation* (New York: Praeger, 1985), p. 174.

21. Philip Bennett, "U.S. Aid for Contras Boon, Trouble for Honduras," *Boston Globe,* September 16, 1986.

22. Inter-Religious Task Force on Central America, *Update Central America* (February 1985), p. 6.

23. Philip Bennett, "Contra War Vaults Border to Displace Hondurans," *Boston Globe,* September 23, 1986, p. 14.

24. James LeMoyne, "C.I.A. Accused of Tolerating Killings in Honduras," *New York Times,* February 14, 1986, p. 1.

25. Bennett, "U.S. Aid for Contras."

26. Ramón Custodio López, "Más intervención, más represión," *CODEH* (June 1986), p. 1.

27. Ibid.

28. Ibid.

29. Quoted in Bennett, "U.S. Aid for Contras."

30. Phone conversation, Joseph Connolly and authors, January 27, 1988; James Le Moyne, "In Human Rights Court, Honduras Is First to Face Death Squad Trial," *New York Times,* January 19, 1988, pp. 1, 6; George Black, "The Many Killers of Father Carney," *The Nation,* January 23, 1988, pp. 84–86.

General Index